Christmas and
the British

Christmas and the British

A Modern History

MARTIN JOHNES

Bloomsbury Academic
An imprint of Bloomsbury Publishing Plc

BLOOMSBURY
LONDON · OXFORD · NEW YORK · NEW DELHI · SYDNEY

Bloomsbury Academic

An imprint of Bloomsbury Publishing Plc

50 Bedford Square	1385 Broadway
London	New York
WC1B 3DP	NY 10018
UK	USA

www.bloomsbury.com

BLOOMSBURY and the Diana logo are trademarks of Bloomsbury Publishing Plc

First published 2016
Reprinted 2016

British Library Cataloguing-in-Publication Data
A catalogue record for this book is available from the British Library.

ISBN: HB: 978-1-4742-5536-3
PB: 978-1-4742-5537-0
ePDF: 978-1-4742-5538-7
ePub: 978-1-4742-5539-4

Library of Congress Cataloging-in-Publication Data
Johnes, Martin.
Christmas and the British : a modern history / Martin Johnes.
New York : Bloomsbury Academic, An imprint of Bloomsbury Publishing Plc, 2016.
Includes bibliographical references and index.
LCCN 2016004384 (print) | LCCN 2016033219 (ebook) | ISBN 9781474255370 (Paperback) |
ISBN 9781474255363 (Hardback) | ISBN 9781474255387 (ePDF) | ISBN 9781474255394 (ePub) |
ISBN 9781474255387 (epdf) | ISBN 9781474255394 (epub)
Christmas–England–History–20th century.
LCC GT4987.44 .J65 2016 (print) | LCC GT4987.44 (ebook)
DDC 394.266309420904–dc23
LC record available at https://lccn.loc.gov/2016004384

Cover design: Sharon Mah
Cover image: *Be sure to post early this year* (Barbosa)/British Postal Museum and Archive, London, UK/© Royal Mail Group Ltd./Bridgeman Images

Typeset by Deanta Global Publishing Services, Chennai, India
Printed and bound in Great Britain

One just knew *that it was the nicest day of the year. Turkey and plum pudding in the middle of the day. Lounging over the fire in the afternoon, with books and nuts and piles of goodies. In the evening, games round the fire and a cold supper with everyone washing up afterwards, so that the maids had a clear kitchen when they came in.*

Woman's Own, *19 December 1936*

CONTENTS

ACKNOWLEDGEMENTS

No book is a solo effort. At some point in recent years, I have quizzed a great many people about what Christmas means to them and I have learnt a great deal from all their replies. I suspect the festive anecdotes I offered in return were not adequate compensation but thank you to them all anyway.

The following all suggested sources or offered feedback for which I am very grateful: Huw Bowen, Neil Carter, Matthew Cragoe, Dion Georgiou, Steven Gray, Leslie Hulonce, Richard Johnes, Christoph Laucht, Daryl Leeworthy, Katrina Legg, George McKechnie, Steph Mastoris, Gethin Matthews, Lucie Matthews-Jones, Louise Miskell, Dilwyn Porter, Noel Thompson, Matthew Stevens, Alwyn Turner, Chris Williams and all the students who have taken my HIH237 Practice of History seminar group on Christmas. Supervising the dissertations of Emma Garland, Clare Randle and Andrew Rowe also helped my thinking on Christmas and their shared enthusiasm for the festival's history was much appreciated. Neil Goodman and Gillian Moyes provided me with somewhere to sleep when I was on research trips to the British Library and the National Archives. The College of Arts and Humanities at Swansea University paid for me to get there. Material from Mass Observation is reproduced with the permission of Curtis Brown, London, on behalf of the Trustees of the Mass Observation Archive.

I tried to write some of the book while listening to festive songs. This research technique proved to be more irritating than enlightening, but I feel I owe Tracey Thorn's *Tinsel and Lights* some thanks for proving there is such a thing as a pleasant Christmas album.

My family have inevitably shaped my personal experience of Christmas and in recent years put up with my ponderings on customs. My parents ensured I did not grow up with bad memories of the festival (or much else). The Moyes clan showed me how other families do Christmas. My daughters, Bethan and Anwen, wandered the streets with me counting how many houses had decorations up, shared lots of Christmas movies, tolerated some of them being in black and white, and were important in reminding me of how exciting the festival can be. Heather Moyes was important in far too many ways to list.

This book was born, discussed and thought about on trains between Cardiff and Swansea. Richard Fry, Chris Millington, Andrew Neate, Sarah Rodgers and Steve Smith all allowed Christmas to infest their daily commute without complaining or taking the mickey too much. I can only apologize to them that there is not more about *Die Hard* in the book.

LIST OF ILLUSTRATIONS

INTRODUCTION

As darkness fell along the Western Front on Christmas Eve 1914, the atmosphere of war slowly faded. It began with soldiers ignoring signs of movement from the enemy trenches. Some Germans hoisted Christmas trees onto their parapets. Both sides listened to the other sing carols and then shouted greetings and suggestions of a ceasefire for the following day. In the morning, tentatively at first but growing in confidence and in number, some soldiers left their trenches and ventured into 'no man's land'. There they met the enemy, swapped cigarettes, food and drink and wished each other a merry Christmas. One Birmingham soldier wrote home: 'if you could only have seen this mob, you would have thought you were dreaming … it is an experience never to be forgotten.'[1]

The truce did not happen everywhere. In places it was simply an opportunity to bury the dead. Some soldiers took advantage of it to note the condition of the enemy's defences and others opened fire when they saw men leave the opposing trenches. The military authorities on both sides were not happy. But it was a remarkable occasion all the same. Indeed, the Christmas truce of 1914 has become one of the most powerful symbols of humanity amid the horrors of war. Yet what tends to get overlooked is how it had taken the festival of Christmas to bring out the front-line soldier's desire for a respite from fighting. As one soldier in the Queen's Westminsters put it, the events were 'a tribute to the spirit of Christmas'.[2]

The importance of Christmas in British culture was evident in the fact that Douglas Haig had already ordered that there were to be no reliefs carried out and that troops should be given 'as easy a time as possible'.[3] Back home, what had become established as the rituals of Christmas were being kept up. Pantomimes and charitable dinners and distributions to the poor, sick and elderly all took place. In Dundee, the local newspaper even thought that more effort than normal was going into giving children treats, perhaps, it speculated, because it was no longer permissible to show goodwill to all men. New recruits were told they would not have to report until after the holiday and were even given some advance pay to enjoy themselves first. Father Christmas could be found in department stores, and all manner of goods were being advertised as presents. War toys were popular gifts; appeals were made for troops to be remembered in Christmas prayers and for donations of mufflers, mittens, socks and shirts to be sent as presents to those in the forces.[4] There were other signs of the shadow of war. There was turkey and beef on sale for Christmas dinner, but prices were up.

Oranges, holly and mistletoe were all scarcer than normal. In Manchester, the Post Office estimated that it dealt with a third fewer Christmas cards than normal. In Burnley, a mill manager tried to stop the Christmas Eve tradition of stopping work for a while for 'a little jollification'. The result was that one of his workers punched him.[5]

Other officials also thought it wrong to celebrate at a time of war. Territorial soldiers complained that they were not getting Christmas leave and some local authorities turned down the many requests for extensions to licensing hours on Christmas Eve and Boxing Day. However, closer to popular opinion was the writer in *Nash's and Pall Mall Magazine* who maintained that the festival must be celebrated 'for the sake of the children if for no other reason'. Christmas, he argued, is for the 'Kiddies', and 'the dreadful shadow of war should not put a blot upon their beloved, happy Yuletide'. But he also saw something in it for the adults: 'we should be able to appreciate the charming flavour of the time-honoured Christmas legends and put a bit of it into our all too matter-of-fact and all too sternly real modern life.'[6]

Ultimately, Christmas carried on at both the front and at home because of the depth of its social and cultural functions. These extended far beyond a day to simply enjoy oneself in the depths of winter. It was a festival that celebrated the bedrocks of Victorian and Edwardian respectable society: religion, commerce and domesticity. Shopkeepers were often seen as the primary promoters of Christmas, but first and foremost, it was a religious celebration, not just of Christ but also of the values of charity and goodwill that were supposed to be integral to Christianity. One form that goodwill took was present-giving, and this freed the frenzy of Christmas shopping from the guilt or vulgarity that was associated with high levels of consumption and spending. The festival also brought families together and encouraged charity, soothing the consciences of those who shut their children away in nurseries and at boarding schools and who lived with plenty when there was poverty and misery all around them. Furthermore, Christmas celebrated tradition and the idea of a simple 'Merrie England' in a world of change and complexity.[7] One historian has argued that this helped make Christmas a symbol and expression of Englishness itself.[8] The idea of the Victorian and Edwardian Christmas as a national symbol is, however, undermined by the fact that material deprivations prevented many working-class families from enjoying the kind of festival that the middle classes knew. While the middle classes ate, drank and were merry, most workers were limited to a few simple presents for the children and a modest celebratory meal. A few could not celebrate at all. Christmas was thus as much an illustrator of social divides as something that crossed them.[9] Nor was the Victorian and Edwardian Christmas free from conflict and doubt. The middle classes worried about gluttony, drunkenness, begging and a lack of propriety and Christian feeling. Commercialization too was a matter of some concern, even though that was what had created much of Christmas culture in the first place.

But these concerns were clearly outweighed by the social good that was seen in Christmas. Middle-class charity meant those in institutions such as hospitals and workhouses had a pleasurable day too. Indeed, they probably enjoyed a more luxurious Christmas than the better off members of their class. Moreover, a Christmas of excess was something to aspire to for the workers, which meant Christmas was only ever going to get bigger. The general rising living standards of the interwar period and early post-war decades saw the working class embrace Christmas and its rituals, using them to brighten their lives and show off both their taste and affluence. In the process, they made the festival a more far-reaching part of national culture than it had been before the Great War. The hundred years that followed 1914 thus saw Christmas evolve, but there were also remarkable degrees of continuity. This was because Christmas was both a product of its time and an escape from it. The festival was changed by growing affluence, shifting family structures, greater expectations of happiness and material comfort, technological developments, a decline in religious belief and the fading of Scottish exceptionalism. It became a battleground for concerns over religious observance, holiday entitlements, social obligations, public behaviour and the influence of royalty and media. Thus, as one writer noted in 1931: 'the change in the celebration of Christmas is a measure of the change in the social life of England.'[10] But at its heart remained the same trinity of shopping, family and goodwill that had appealed so much to the Victorians. So, too, did the Victorian rituals of present-giving, dinner, trees, cards and Santa Claus and the fact that the majority of people appreciated the companionship and simple joys experienced on the day itself.

Understanding all history is about understanding continuity and change but this is especially true of Christmas because it was an event that encouraged reflection on the past. This did not just happen at a collective level but also at an individual level. To think about how Christmas had or had not changed was, for most people, to reminisce, to think about their own childhood and to contemplate the march of time since. People often did not have much choice in this: Christmas was inescapable. Grumpy old men, those alone, those of different religions and creeds all had Christmas thrown at them on the streets, on television, at work or school. It may only come once a year but it comes every year. It is an inescapable and permanent feature of Western culture. And this is not likely to ever change. Despite the cynicism and the nostalgia it could induce, Christmas was, above all, a happy time and for that reason it was, and continues to be, an integral feature of British culture.

Christmas's ubiquity has perhaps blinded us to the roles it plays both in our individual lives and in wider society. So, too, does its 'naffness'. Christmas is full of the kitsch, throwaway and the sentimental and such characteristics dominate many of the sources available to the historian of the festival. In 1978, the historian J. A. R. Pimlott claimed there was an 'aesthetic poverty' to the modern English Christmas. He argued there 'has probably been more bad writing, and particularly bad verse, about Christmas than about any other subject, and the relatively good has been painfully derivative'.[11] This was not entirely fair and perhaps owed something to Pimlott's generation not always seeing cinema and television as part of intellectual culture. Christmas has provided the setting for some classic films and programmes, but whatever the artistic quality of depictions of Christmas, they all tell us something about the 25th of December. Moreover, depictions of Christmas on screen and in the 'bad' writing of genres such as romantic fiction are more than just sources to tap into the practices of the past. They helped influence and shape that past too, creating a framework against which people judged their own celebrations. The Christmases of popular culture not only encouraged people to behave in certain ways but also allowed them to feel superior and sneer at the poor taste of others. Yet knowing what people thought of what they watched, read and received is very difficult and the historian of Christmas is faced with a situation where the volume of sources is overwhelming but their completeness is limited.

Nonetheless, through diaries, newspapers, social surveys, television, films, novels, advertising and a wealth of ephemera, the historian can begin to understand something of how people celebrated and thought about Christmas, from their philosophical and political musings to what they ate and did. These details matter. As Abrams and Brown argue: 'in the smallest aspect of daily life, in the smallest ritual or rite, is to be found an imprint of the whole of culture.' Moreover, they point out that 'Lives are shaped in the main by everyday practices rather than exceptional events'.[12] Christmas is both an everyday practice, in the sense that it happens every year, and an exceptional event, in that it involves behaviour very different to the rest of the year. Christmas says something about British culture, about how people live out and think about their lives, about their values, habits and tastes. But its details, its rituals and its rhetoric also all helped shape Britain and the British at both individual and collective levels.

This, then, is not a book about where Christmas practices and traditions came from, but about how these practices and traditions were lived out, adapted and thought about over the course of the century that followed the start of the Great War. It is about the social, cultural and economic functions of Christmas. It is about the ordinary and extraordinary things people did and continue to do on the 25th of December. It is about how Christmas is part of the fabric of society, and the complex web of beliefs, values and activities that unites people and turns them from individuals into a community. It is thus as much a book about Britain, its values, hopes and fears, its structures and its shape, as it is a book about the most unusual day of the year.

In 1957 C. S. Lewis wrote that there were three Christmases: the religious festival, a merry holiday and a 'commercial racket'.[13] Actually there were many more and this book looks at the different forms of the festival. It is organized around six themes that helped define twentieth-century Britain: consumerism, family, tradition and ritual, religion, local and national communities and government. Class and gender were also central currents within

British society and they too feature within the book, but cutting across all the chapters.

The first chapter examines the commercial and consumer Christmas. It explores the festival's economic role and the experience and nuances of Christmas shopping, focusing on what people bought as presents and why. The chapter argues that despite the complaints that Christmas was overly commercialized, gift-giving was actually something that brought great pleasure and reaffirmed social bonds. The chapter also investigates how the working class increasingly shared in the commercial Christmas, arguing that this was a time of year when the masses could signal their inclusion in a consumer society but when the poorest in society could feel most excluded.

The second chapter argues that the festival helped cement and celebrate the central place of family in British society. It looks at the different meanings of Christmas for men, women, children and the collective family unit. It shows how the festival could be a source of both considerable pride and stress for women, that men varied very significantly in their reactions to the festival and how the festival represented the increasing child-centred nature of society. However, while Christmas reinforced the family's place at the centre of society, it could also increase the isolation of the elderly and those alone.

The third chapter looks at the rituals that defined the festival, analysing the function and form of decorations, cards, Santa Claus and the Christmas dinner. It not only demonstrates the reverence for traditions that so often existed, but also shows that these traditions were malleable and subject to renegotiation and reinterpretation, something which was central to why Christmas was so ubiquitous.

The fourth chapter takes the spirit of Christmas as its theme, exploring the roles of religion, charity and individual and collective reflection as defining features of the festival. For poor and rich alike, Christmas was a contrast to the real world and everyday life and that lay at the heart of its spirit and the charity and happiness it could induce. Yet others took the festival as a sign of the times, and it also became a hook on which complaints about the nature of society were hung. One such common complaint was the secularization of society and Christmas itself; however, the chapter argues that the festival was actually central to upholding Christianity, particularly the values of Christianity, within Britain.

The fifth chapter looks at Christmas as communal culture, examining the shared aspects of the festival that became part of national and regional cultures. These varied from local customs, public decorations and carol singing that brought together and helped define local communities, to songs and films that nearly everyone knew and television programmes that were watched simultaneously in millions of different homes. Immigration did present new challenges to national unity, but as regional differences in the celebration of Christmas faded, most notably in Scotland, Christmas became, the chapter argues, a stronger part of the fabric of British culture, a shared story that helped unite people of different backgrounds.

The final chapter looks at government and other official interactions with the festival. These too were varied and ranged from regulation of rationing, holidays and public services to generosity towards those guilty of crimes. The chapter demonstrates how many wider public ideological battles were played out in microcosm through Christmas, but that ultimately the state's role in the most important day of the year tended to be reactive and self-serving.

With Christmas taking different forms and interacting with different trends, it is unsurprising that it generated different responses. As Pimlott points out, 'Devotion to the Holy Child may be juxtaposed with schoolboy greed and adult abandon, love of tradition and a strong sense of family with dislike of the Christmas chores and an aversion from particular customs.'[14] This was true of the nineteenth century too and Armstrong has argued that as 'an imagined ideal' in that century, 'Christmas attained the power to stimulate and intensify a range of emotions, including familial love, benevolence and anticipation, but also loneliness and disappointment.'[15] While that is true, we should be wary of exaggerating Christmas. Life for most people is not a matter of extremes. It is not about great happiness or sadness but more mundane feelings. The pleasures of life for most are simple – a drink or two, a good film or television programme, a conversation, a cuddle or a nice cup of tea. Christmas fits into that pattern. Some, especially children, derived huge pleasure from it. For those alone it was often a moment of despondency, but for many more it was a small moment of happiness shared with others, something generally nice, albeit accompanied by a number of irritations. It was not perfect, but nor was it usually tragic. It was part of the rituals of existence that made life not only tolerable but also enjoyable.

Thus, ultimately, the history of Christmas is a redemptive one. In a century beset by war and inequalities, there was still a basic decency in British society. Although few people, except in war, made significant sacrifices for strangers, Christmas showed that most people were committed to others and generally happy in themselves. If there is a big idea to this book, it is that Christmas, just as Dickens had tried to convince people, is a good thing. It may not be fashionable for historians to pass moral judgements on their subjects of study, but that does not mean it should not be done. In a century in which so many people felt so much was going wrong, Christmas was a force for the positive. It was a break from work for most. Its economic significance was huge. It could unite local communities and even the nation through shared traditions and a way of life. It also brought families together (and sometimes reminded them why they lived apart for the rest of the year). It put a smile on people's faces, especially children's. Of course, not everyone liked it. It made some angry or exasperated or sad. As Terry ranted in a 1974 episode of *The Likely Lads*: 'It's all got out of hand these days. It's just one big racket. ... People over eat, over spend and over sentimentalize.' But more in tune with public opinion was the reply of his friend Bob: 'I know, I know, I know and I love every minute of it.'[16]

CHAPTER ONE

The consumer Christmas

In 1931, the *Daily Worker* contrasted the lavish Christmas displays in West End department stores with the 'tawdry' cotton wool, paper festoons and tinsel in East End shop windows. Inside they were selling scrawny turkeys, Christmas packages that consisted of tea, sugar and a tin of milk, and pre-packed stockings containing vile sweets, paper toys and wooden whistles. The newspaper argued that capitalism was keeping Christmas gifts from children.[1] Both before and after the Second World War, Britain was a deeply unequal society but, unlike the *Daily Worker*, most people did not want to bring capitalism down, but simply share in its spoils. They wanted to consume and at Christmas the vast majority of people did.

The practice of buying and giving Christmas presents was well established by the Great War, at least among the middle classes. The late Victorian period had seen the emergence of a distinctive shopping culture based around the six weeks before Christmas. Its extension to the working class may have been limited, but among the middle classes Christmas gifts had become so established that even the Great War did not stop it. Of course, not everyone approved. Even in the Victorian era, there were those who saw the busy shops and extravagant displays as a sign that a religious festival was being tarnished by commercialism.[2] Such voices of disapproval grew in number and volume over the course of the twentieth century, as the festival grew more commercial and consumerism itself became more embedded in society. Whatever some critics thought, the cause of this was not the advertising of aggressive retailers. They were responding to demand rather than creating it. As society became more affluent, more and more people wanted to share in the festive indulgences that the Victorian middle class created. After 1914, all classes did some Christmas shopping, even if their budgets could not stretch beyond the cheap goods found in bazaars, backstreet shops and Woolworth's. Shopping became as integral to the festival as religion and one historian has called it the 'most visible and significant part of the English

Christmas'.[3] Indeed, so engrained was the culture of buying presents many people felt unable not to take part for fear of being seen as ungenerous. This does not change the fact that most people's Christmas spending was rooted in a generosity and a commitment to friends and family. The festival was thus not a monstrosity of commercialism but rather a sign of a deeper goodwill in society. Moreover, while Christmas may have been an extreme example of how integral consumerism was in British society, it was also a symbol of the pleasures and benefits consumerism could bring. People enjoyed spending. They enjoyed what they spent money on. However much the consumer society might be looked down upon, it helped bring a little colour and comfort to people's lives and this was never more true than at Christmas.

Going to the shops

By 1914, shopping itself had become a leisure pursuit for middle-class women, and a trip to the shops before Christmas was also never just about buying things: it was an experience in itself. The crowds, the elaborate shop displays and the public decorations were all spectacles to gaze at and enjoy. Influenced by trends in America, British department stores placed significant emphasis on making their interiors and window displays lavish. In larger stores, in the run-ups to interwar Christmases, this meant electric lights, and brightly coloured assemblages of moving mechanical toys and unusual gifts, arranged into seasonal scenes resembling theatrical sets. Smaller shops too tried to replicate this approach, although with their holly, cotton-wool snow and more commonplace toys, the result was far less spectacular. Spectacular, though, was what the larger stores offered. A visit to Santa was already well established in department stores by the Great War and in 1921 Whiteley's in London even had children climb aboard a submarine to visit him in Toyland. In the 1930s, Bentall's of Kingston had an in-store Christmas circus with elephants and a lion.[4] In the larger shopping districts, the cumulative effect of decorated shops was genuinely engaging. In 1933, a female correspondent in the *Daily Mail* wrote with delight: 'The shop windows are ablaze with tiny coloured lights; merchandise which would make our ancestors' eyes pop out of their heads is strewn in gorgeous profusion before us; jostling, chattering, laughing crowds, plentifully sprinkled with children, throng the pavements before the windows.'[5] Poet Vernon Scannell remembered of shopping in Aylesbury in 1932: 'The smell of excitement and extravagance was in the air.'[6]

The media was important in supporting and promoting such images and Christmas shopping in general. Children pressing their faces against department store windows to gaze at toy displays was a reoccurring image in interwar December newsreels. In the early 1920s, the *Evening News* even ran a competition for novel shop window displays. Local newspapers

PLATE 1 *Santa and his elf at the 'Land of Good Luck', Selfridges, London, 29 November 1928. Harold Clements/Getty.*

frequently ran features on the latest Christmas items in stores, providing readers with gift ideas and companies with free advertising. These were probably also intended to cement good relations with the shops, whose advertisements were an important source of revenue for the newspapers throughout the year. Advertisements enhanced the idea that shops were at the heart of Christmas and that a visit to them was more than a trip to buy things. A 1928 advertisement for Whiteley's claimed that 'we have a complete understanding and inside knowledge of the true meaning of Christmas, and we achieve this delightful atmosphere throughout the Store not only by beautiful decorations and merchandise, but by entering wholeheartedly into the true spirit of Christmas.'[7]

The spectacles were not limited to large towns and cities, although the scale and lavishness of Christmas shopping in small towns could not compete. In small country towns the Christmas market drew people from the surrounding villages and offered opportunities for men and women to socialize and drink, as well as shop. In 1938, the *Daily Mail* rather patronizingly remarked: 'Anyone travelling through rural England at this time may see in the small towns more than a little of the traditional spirit of Christmas among a people who are content with simple things and prize good will above all.'[8] But, as shopping trips to large towns became more common with rising living standards, and images of the more luxurious store displays appeared on the cinema screen, it was becoming difficult for the smaller shops and towns to impress. Indeed, the cinema itself was broadening horizons and imaginations. A 1920 story about a fancy goods shopkeeper bemoaned that children were no longer impressed with his Father Christmas display and even criticized the free entertainments, modern toys and 'real live Santa Clauses' of the big stores. The story concluded: 'Nowadays it seemed that children were less simple-minded.'[9]

The writer of this story was coming from and speaking to a middle-class audience. Interwar working-class children probably did not have the luxury of being so critical. Although shops were often unofficially demarcated by class, shopping districts were not and they included a variety of establishments serving different clientele. This meant that before the Second World War, the working class certainly witnessed the Christmas spectacles aimed at those with deeper pockets than themselves. Mass Observation, for example, noted groups of 'urchins' in a Bolton Woolworth's, looking at festive displays with no hope of getting anything.[10] It would be easy to interpret this as the inequalities of society being rubbed in the faces of the poor. We should not, however, assume that Christmas displays evoked envy. In the 1930s, a survey of York found that the working class enjoyed browsing in large stores without having to buy anything.[11] People were remarkably accepting of their situation in life and it was hardly just at Christmas that the inequalities

PLATE 2 *Toy shop window display, c. 1939. Daily Herald Archive/SSPL/Getty.*

of society were evident. Shortages and poor-quality clothing, housing and food were all regular reminders of how harsh it was to be poor. Perhaps the lavish Christmas shops were even a small distraction, affording a few moments of joy, even if the festivity could not be fully shared. Moreover, in the 1920s, some children discovered that if they visited toy shops in the run-up to Christmas and looked longingly enough at something, a well-off lady might actually buy it for them.[12]

Working-class adults enjoyed Christmas shopping too. Between the wars, most women did do at least a little festive shopping. Entries to a Mass Observation writing competition about Christmas shopping in Bolton noted the beauty of displays, the enjoyment to be derived from seeing so many happy faces among shoppers and shop assistants, and the whole act of choosing gifts and thinking about the delight the presents would give to the recipients. It was a chance to forget daily cares and one woman described Christmas shopping as a 'land of make believe'.[13] Yet entries also noted that the most enjoyable thing was having money to spend, something that was simply not a norm for the working classes. Shoppers thus enjoyed the freedom that savings gave them. They were able to browse and buy things normally out of their range. But limited budgets meant that not much of that shopping took place at department stores.[14] Instead, women shopped with the ingenuity that the working class relied on to turn life into something more than simply survival. Thus, for those who could not afford toy stores, hoops could be bought from blacksmiths and dolls' houses from carpenters.[15] The working classes scoured street markets, bazaars, Woolworth's and hawkers who laid out their novelties and cheap toys on pavements. A Woolworth's employee in Bolton told Mass Observation in 1938: 'People will buy any bloody thing put in front of them at this time of year.' In the three weeks before Christmas, his store's turnover and staff trebled. After toys, decorations and cards, its bestselling line was artificial flowers.[16] Such 'fancy goods' may have been easy to sneer at, but they were fancy for those without much and they gave a bit of colour to hard lives.

By the Second World War, the Christmas season was so well established that festive displays at department stores continued to be set up in November. But all wartime shops found sourcing goods difficult and in 1941 Christmas shopping was described as a 'strange ordeal'. The crowds were still there, although less numerous, but the counters were very austere, with limited choices. Metal toys were very scarce, wooden ones were common but expensive, many dolls were now in uniform and military toys had replaced racing cars. Yet there was still a determination to ensure children got presents and a reluctant willingness to pay inflated prices for the displayed items.[17] Nonetheless, giving second-hand toys became more common and there were official campaigns to salvage and restore old toys. The hike in prices did become a source of anger and in 1942 the government regulated the cost of toys to ensure Christmas prices were the same as in September.[18] Shortages and accompanying frustrations continued into the austerity of the late 1940s.

In 1946, *The Listener* argued that, compared with before the war, Christmas preparations now involved 'far greater' effort for 'reward infinitely less'. A 1947 writer noted the expense or unavailability of presents was causing 'tens of thousands of people' to wear 'themselves out thinking of presents they can't afford, to give to people they don't really want to give anything to'.[19] But people still took so much effort because even an austerity Christmas was a contrast to the greyness that then pervaded so much of everyday life.

In the early 1950s, the shops returned to their old brightness and variety. Indeed, Christmas became a marker, not just of the return of affluence but also of post-war economic progress and of the wider modernization of society. In the mid-1950s, some people were drawing contrasts between the array of toys on sale and the sweets, nuts and oranges that they had been so delighted to receive as children. It was not just the goods that marked a return to prosperity but the packaging too. By 1954, for example, crystallized fruit was available in wooden boxes, wicker baskets, brightly coloured pottery and plastic containers.[20] The development of cheap plastics in the 1950s not only improved food packaging, but also the toys, kitchen ware and decorations that were bought at Christmas. Electricity was another technological development whose impact on Christmas shopping gathered pace in the 1950s. In a 1961 novel about a small country town, an electricity showroom had a display of life-size wax figures sitting down to Christmas dinner, and hair dryers, torches, bed warmers and toasters labelled as 'Acceptable Xmas Gifts'.[21]

In a world where the prime minister could claim without ridicule that most people had 'never had it so good', such showrooms were as much aimed at the masses as the middle classes. The pleasures of Christmas shopping were democratized as affluence became more widespread. The working classes not only had more choice in what they could afford to buy but also in where they shopped. Major shopping centres grew more accessible as travel became more affordable; some small towns and villages even began organizing Christmas shopping coach trips. This was a chance for housewives to escape their own patch and head to the bigger shops of 'town'. Such was the sense of occasion that people dressed up for it.[22] London, in particular, drew people from all over the country. This had been true before the war, but then it was limited to the moneyed class 'up from the country'. Affluence changed that. In 1961, ITV found people shopping in London from as far as Dundee, Scarborough and Grimsby. They said they were drawn not only by the decorations, but also, more importantly, by the wide variety of items on offer. Some made a trip of it and stayed over.[23]

The allure of traditional shop displays thus continued well into the post-war years. However, the opulence they suggested and the wonder of their moving displays both lost power as the toys children actually owned became more sophisticated and as television raised the stakes on what looked wondrous.[24] The displays never disappeared but by the 1970s they were no longer spectacles of their own. By then, the spectacle had shifted to the electrical lights that adorned streets and public places rather than individual shops. In 1934 the local authority in Edinburgh decided to light the city's castle over Christmas and New Year after a trial the year before had helped bring in visitors.[25] External displays of electric Christmas lighting were also seen on interwar department stores, but it was in the 1950s that they became serious attractions across the country. The capital led the way here after the *Daily Telegraph* complained in 1954 that London looked 'drab'. This led Regent Street to begin an annual display of lights that quickly grew so elaborate that it caused traffic congestion, as people slowed down to look at it. London was not alone and the switching on of Hastings' Christmas lights in 1954, for example, was accompanied by Santa Claus driving through the streets, newsreel cameras and cheering crowds.[26] Usually paid for by shops and local authorities, such displays required cooperation between rivals, which was sometimes easier said than done. Oxford Street had followed Regent Street's lead in 1959, but cost meant it forewent the displays from 1967 to 1978.[27] The growth of competition from out of town retail parks in the last quarter of the century forced greater cooperation in the Christmas efforts of the traditional retail centres. Indeed, the importance of street lighting displays grew to the extent that costs were generally taken over by local authorities, although that did not stop shops from extending the provision at their own expense. By 2011, Manchester City Council was spending £336,700 on Christmas lighting.[28]

Lighting displays were important because they gave late twentieth-century Christmas shopping a sense of occasion that differentiated it from the

PLATE 3 *Christmas lights, Oxford Street, London, 1960. Fox Photos/Getty.*

wider shopping experience that had become so embedded in everyday life. Major shopping expeditions now took place all-year round and the experience of shopping itself changed as stores and local authorities placed a new emphasis on making it a pleasurable pastime. The growth of pedestrianized streets in the 1980s had given shoppers a safe distance from the noise and fumes of cars. Department stores had grown plusher and nearly every high-street outlet shifted to being a store where one could browse rather than depend on shop assistants. Moreover, the growth of chain stores imposed something of a uniformity on shopping across the UK. High streets still had their own character and the diversity of shops and quality of parking facilities often varied significantly, but inside the shops there was little to distinguish London from Loughborough. Christmas lighting was thus part of conscious attempts to imbue town centres with a sense of identity. This also extended to trying to create an imagined historic atmosphere through street markets, complete with stalls selling mistletoe, roasted chestnuts and other traditional foods. Whereas once it was modernity that gave Christmas shopping a sense of wonder, now it was tradition.

This imperative to enhance festive shopping trips gathered pace at the end of the 1990s as the internet emerged as a new threat to the retail hegemony that town and city centres had once enjoyed. By 1999 market research suggested that 3.6 million people were buying presents online in what was described as the UK's first cyber Christmas.[29] By December 2013 almost a fifth of all non-food purchases that month were made online.[30] Convenience and price were key to the growth but, for those on low incomes, online shopping was also attractive because it limited spending to what was needed and avoided additional expenses associated with a visit to a shopping centre, such as a cup of coffee.[31] But despite the growing volume of online Christmas shopping, neither the impact of nor the innovation in what was happening should be exaggerated. In some ways the internet was simply a development of mail order, something touted as a way of avoiding the Christmas crowds since at least the 1960s.[32] Moreover, the vast majority of Christmas shopping was still done in person. This was partly because people enjoyed the browsing and whole experience of visiting shopping centres. Research in America suggested that at Christmas people considered more possibilities, visited more shops and spent more time than when making normal purchases.[33] But the enduring appeal of Christmas trips to the shops also owed much to online shopping not actually always being as convenient as it first seemed. It created new headaches and anxieties – about delivery times, the need to be at home to receive large parcels, and even the fallout from being caught shopping online during work hours.[34]

The biggest change in post-war Christmas shopping took place not in present-buying but in grocery-shopping. Before the early 1950s, food shops were little changed from Victorian times, with most selling goods in whatever quantity customers wanted. Despite this personal service, food shopping was actually a precarious business. The difficulties of storing perishables at home meant people left festive food shopping until late and in 1934 the Early Closing Association argued that the bulk of festive trade was actually done two or three days before the festival.[35] With restrictions on opening hours generally lifted in the week before Christmas, some small shops even stayed open until 11.00 pm on Christmas Eve.[36] Although the 1950 Shops Act allowed retailers to deliver goods on a Sunday if Christmas was on a Monday, that falling of dates could create storage problems for customers unable to afford deliveries. They faced not being able to shop for food for three days. Meat prices could also change from day to day, depending on supply level and how fast stock sold. With butchers having limited facilities to cold-store meat, waiting until just before Christmas Day could either deliver a bargain or sometimes nothing at all. In 1956, there was no reportedly no turkeys left anywhere in Swansea on 23 December.[37] The growth of refrigerators and freezers in the 1950s, both in shops and at home, helped solve some of these issues. By 1969, 60 per cent of households

PLATE 4 *Turkeys, chickens and ducks on sale at Caledonian market, London, 17 December 1926. Kirby/Getty.*

had a fridge and this helped move households away from daily to weekly shopping. The range of produce on sale diversified too. 'We can give you beautiful green-tipped spears of Evesham Asparagus at Christmas, and they are as fresh as the morning they were cut' promised one 1937 advert.[38] But it was not until the 1970s that many people were able to take advantage of such possibilities. In 1973, just 9 per cent of homes had a deep freezer but five years later the figure had risen to 40 per cent.[39]

Even before most households started buying frozen foods, the supermarket had already revolutionized Christmas shopping. In 1957, there were only a little more than eighty supermarkets in Britain, but they offered people convenience and choice under one roof and took away the need to traipse up and down the high street. Their growth came in the 1960s, boosted by the development of own brands and the end of retail price maintenance on branded goods (where producers could dictate how much their products sold for), which enabled the supermarkets to undercut traditional shops. By 1970, there were 3,500 supermarkets, although they still only accounted for a quarter of grocery business.[40] Their advance however was unstoppable, especially as they branched out in the 1990s from groceries to almost every conceivable item a household might buy. Supermarkets also led a return to longer opening hours. Their December trials of 24-hour shopping in the mid-1990s were very successful and led supermarkets to normalize these opening hours throughout the year and to some toyshops following suit in the Christmas run-up.[41] The Christmas shop epitomized why supermarkets were so popular. A family could buy a large quantity of competitively priced food, presents and sundries in a single place that was easy to drive to, easy to park at, easy to get around and offered loyalty rewards for your custom.

Where and how people shopped may have changed, but there was far more continuity in who was doing it. Although men did take part, females continued to dominate shopping. This was true of both the middle and working classes, of the department store and the provincial and backstreet stores, and of Christmas shopping and other times of the year. In December 1926, one paper called the shopping area between Marble Arch and Oxford Street 'Ladies' Mile' and estimated there were 100 or more women to every man in the dense crowd.[42] This domination meant shopping was a sphere where women enjoyed some status even before their social and political emancipation became more complete. Department store shopping, in particular, gave women not just something that was fun to do but also choice and the power to consume.[43] Male storeowners had little option but to meet their demands if they wanted to be profitable. Yet, as the research of Hosgood has argued, in the Victorian and Edwardian periods, shopping had also left women vulnerable to accusations that they were overly concerned with trivial and petty vanities and this undermined its liberating effect. Christmas, however, was a time when they could reclaim shopping as a legitimate activity because it was being done for others and not themselves. Moreover, its necessity and their knowledge of it gave them some authority over their husbands, while its difficulties furthered the idea that women were enduring something for others rather than indulging themselves. Nonetheless, any power that women did gain was limited and temporary. In the Edwardian period, the excesses in behaviour and spending at the January sales soon brought back the image of the irrational female shopper.[44] Indeed, even at Christmas time it might not have completely disappeared. Some men were rather superior about their ability to shop quickly, while women were 'attacking every counter, buying heedlessly and frantically things they didn't in the least want', as one man put it in 1932.[45]

However limited and temporary it was, there is no reason not to think the empowerment Christmas shopping could bring was not also true of later periods. Victorian jokes about men having to pay for and then carry their wives' gifts carried on into the interwar period and beyond. In 1919, the *Daily Mirror*, pondering which sex was the fragile one, thought men lacked the patience and even the endurance needed for Christmas shopping.[46] Even at the end of the twentieth century, there was little doubt in most families about who was in charge of and doing most of the festive shopping. A 2007 survey suggested that women bought on average presents for 14.7 people, while men bought for 10.7; women spent £738 and men £588.[47] Three years earlier, another survey had suggested that 40 per cent of women spent twenty hours on Christmas shopping. In response to such levels of female activity, an Essex retail centre set up a crèche for men where they could play snooker, drink and watch football while their partners Christmas shopped. This female domination was partly because women gave more gifts, but also because they remained more motivated by domestic concerns than men.[48] That concern gave them control over many household issues but, like housework and childcare, Christmas shopping was not always an easy or pleasant responsibility. In families with low incomes, control over the household budget was a source of stress not power. It put women under pressure, making them worry and fret about making ends meet.[49] But what women's influence over family budgets and shopping does do is undermine any idea that society was a simple patriarchy.

Christmas was the one time when men could not escape shopping altogether, even before the Second World War. In the Edwardian and Victorian periods, Christmas shopping was often seen as emasculating and degrading for men, but it was also sometimes unavoidable.[50] The obligation upon males to buy some presents was not particularly popular, partly because of their general unfamiliarity with the whole experience of shopping. But a growing public pressure on them to get involved was undoubtedly there, at least among the middle class. In 1919 *The Times* claimed that 'A man worthy of his salt fares forth upon his adventure alone and unassisted'. It also noted though that most men enjoyed a trip to the toyshop and being taken back to their own childhoods. They thus happily spoilt their own children and realized from their shopping experiences that their wives had much to endure because this was 'her normal day'. By 1922, the same paper was noting the number of fathers in family shopping parties: 'He seems to recognize his Christmas duty better than he used to, perhaps from a noble change of spirit, perhaps under the modern wife's impressive compulsion.' This was not universal however and a 1935 *Times* editorial felt it had to urge men to do their duty and get involved.[51] Duty was a key word here and the involvement of men owed much to the growing mid-century expectation, in middle-class circles at least, that husbands and fathers could not simply abdicate all domestic responsibilities. That was clear in their growing involvement in shopping all-year round. Research in the late 1960s suggested that 35 per cent of husbands were regularly helping with the shopping.[52] Men may have been shopping more, but it nonetheless remained a predominantly female activity. Although men had a significant input in decisions over major purchases such as televisions, research in the early 1980s found that women were making or influencing over 80 per cent of all domestic purchases.[53] Christmas was no different.

Men's reluctance to Christmas shop was a source of recurring humour, but this also meant that if it was an activity that empowered women it was a power that many men were willing to concede. As one column in the *Spectator* joked at the end of the 1950s, to raise the question of present-buying two weeks before Christmas was 'at least thirteen days too soon for most men, who generally wake up to the problem some time around the afternoon of Christmas Eve'.[54] There seemed to be clear evidence to substantiate this. A 1973 survey found that by 20 December, only 52 per cent of men as against 85 per cent of women had bought presents. In 1970, a store assistant told *The Times* that on Christmas Eve her shop was full of men who had left their shopping until the last minute and were desperate for advice.[55] The difference in Christmas shopping habits extended beyond timing. At the end of the century, research found that whereas women started earlier, bought more presents and spent more time on the activity, men put in less effort, being more willing to seek advice from a salesperson or be guided by the implications and connotations of a particular brand or price.[56] By the twenty-first century, grumpy old men were even talking about how they had given up trying to find presents their wives liked and had resorted to letting them not just choose the present but buy it too.[57] This was at least an improvement on what happened in some families before the war. A 1937 response to Mass Observation recorded that the wife always gave a gift to her husband, but did not receive one in return. The logic was that it all came out of the same money and that she found amusement in choosing, whereas he found it hard work. The arrangement was his suggestion.[58]

Even for women, for all the spectacle and glamour of the shops, Christmas shopping presented a number of challenges. In a 2004 survey, 49 per cent said Christmas shopping was stressful, 6 percentage points higher than the proportion of respondents who said the same about going to the dentist.[59] A central cause of stress was the crowds, or what *The Times* in 1923 called 'the Black hole terrors of the real Christmas scramble'. In 1926, the *Daily Mail* said of London's Oxford Street: 'Such a dense crowd of shoppers thronged the pavements that many people found it difficult not to be pushed off the kerb, while at times shoppers could scarcely make any headway through the masses of people.'[60] Those who had to cope with this with excited children faced an even more challenging task; newspapers offered various pieces of advice such as wearing sensible shoes and not shopping for too many items at once. Some stores tried to help out and in 1964 Woolworth's in Dudley even opened for three hours after closing time to allow pensioners to do their Christmas shopping in peace and quiet. Shopping early in December or in the morning were two ways of avoiding the crowds, and shops were keen to encourage this, even sometimes suggesting that three times as much could be bought in one morning than in three crowded afternoons.[61] Before the Second World War, 'shop early' became something of a mantra that was exhorted on behalf of both shop workers and customers. In 1923 the *Daily Mirror* was calling early Christmas shopping a duty, like going to the dentist regularly and paying income tax.[62] Yet the mantra only existed because people did not follow it. In 1938 a sweetshop in Bolton noted that its working-class clientele liked to shop at the last minute; so it stayed open till 11.00 pm or midnight on Christmas Eve.[63] The problem did fade somewhat as opening hours extended, central shopping districts grew bigger and out of town retail parks drew away some of the crowds. But the congestion never went away, especially in the last day or two before Christmas and it was compounded by the fact that not all shoppers knew what to buy. In 1980 one commentator said, 'Christmas shopping combines the hopelessness of not being able to find anything with the terror of being swept away by the Gadarene stampede of those who enjoy shopping and know what they want.'[64] The size of these crowds was clear in Manchester where 1.168 million people visited the central shopping area in the week before Christmas 2011.[65]

After the war, such crowds generated significant congestion problems. By the late 1950s traffic was becoming a serious problem in Britain's towns and cities, and temporary car parks and extensions of parking restrictions had to be introduced to cope with the Christmas shoppers.[66] Cars did at least alleviate the problem of how to carry the purchases. In the 1920s car parking attendants were reporting that people might return to their cars twice to deposit parcels before heading back out to shop some more.[67] For those without cars there was little choice but to struggle with armfuls of parcels on public transport or to make several shopping trips. In response to this problem, the Central London Railway had introduced Christmas season tickets in 1912 to allow women unlimited travel after 10.00 am. The Great War led to a decline in shops offering staff who would carry parcels for people, and in 1918 *The Times* ran an article on 'The problem of the parcel', which argued that Christmas shopping required skills of 'elbowing, pushing, dominating, judging, and finally carrying … Brown paper has subjugated us all.'[68] This was perhaps most acute for those on middle incomes, able to buy presents in enough volume that they could not be carried, but not well off enough to pay for delivery. There was also a degree of humour in such complaints and surely a recognition that it was a fairly trivial matter compared to other social issues of the day. Indeed, the bustle of crowds, no matter how tiring and invasive, were all part of the spectacle and experience of Christmas shopping and helped make it an integral part of the season's festivities.

Gifts and giving

In 1919 *The Times* noted that 'anything and everything' from motor cars to hot water bottles were now being labelled as Christmas presents.[69] No matter how ingrained Christmas shopping was in the festival's culture, there was always the conundrum of what to buy people, and that added to the stress of the activity. Most people wanted to show that they had thought about what to give, but there was a risk of recipients not liking their gift or even being offended by it. Children, for example, could take umbrage at toys that were too young for them and women by clothes that were too large.[70] Throughout the period, the etiquette, nuances and problems of gift-giving thus led to long middle-class ruminations.[71] One 1962 example claimed that books might imply that there was an attempt to improve a woman's mind, while items from a sale might give the wrong impression if the recipient had seen the advertisement.[72] 'There is a definite art to giving Christmas presents and since there is no way you can get out of giving and getting them, you might as well master it,' concluded the future Conservative MP Gyles Brandreth.[73] Even magazines aimed at the intelligentsia ran articles giving suggestions about what presents to buy.[74] Females felt the pressure the most. In this they were encouraged by the claims of advertisers and women's magazines that presents should be things that people wanted and that the whole business had powerful emotional resonances. Typical was the 1923 advertisement for Selfridges' which claimed that Christmas shopping 'is altogether pleasing and unselfish. Every purchase made is a practical goodwill action, an expression of kindliness – a happy thought toward a friend or relative.'[75] In 1933, a columnist complained that her childhood stockings had contained oranges, notepaper and soap, all of which she could have got just by visiting another room in the house. Yet when her father bought her an unwrapped necklace – because he was too lazy to do a stocking – she was thrilled since it was the first piece of jewellery she had ever owned. Her message was that the idea that it was the thought that counted was trite; presents should be things that people wanted.[76] The standards women set themselves could also be very high. In a 2010 novel, a well-off middle-aged woman declared she wanted to give presents that led to a 'gasp of delight, the genuine grin of pleasure that makes you think the whole flipping Christmas faff is worth it'.[77]

Of course, there were always a few who were slightly more contrarian about the process, such as the 1934 female writer who declared she was going to give people what she thought they needed and not what they thought they needed.[78] By doing so she would be making a statement about her own taste. Social scientists have long argued that consumers' consumption habits defined them, and this became increasingly true as the traditional markers of class fell away and blurred amid the social mobility and economic change of the post-war period.[79] Gift-giving complicates that theory because it was often driven by social obligation and its motivations were not simply about oneself but others. Yet the choice of gift could still be as much a statement about the giver as it was about the receiver. Christmas was thus a time not just to spoil one's family but to show off your good taste while doing so; it involved a degree of exhibition of taste, aspiration and values. If people did not realize the link between the presents they gave and their values, there were often advertisements to tell them that. For example, in the mid-1950s Teasmades were specifically marketed as 'modern' gifts, with the implication being that it was the type of thing a forward-looking person would give. Others were less subtle: a 1960 advertisement for a London wine retailer declared: 'Wine is a gift of Character and a compliment to your good taste as well as to the recipient.'[80] It was not just advertisers and the fashion conscious that thought like this. In 1928 one pacifist magazine claimed, 'Something must be chosen which will interest and satisfy the recipient, but at the same time, something which shall not be alien to any principles you cherish for him.' Unsurprisingly, the writer did not approve of toy soldiers.[81] Even those who felt the tawdriness of Christmas gift-giving to be beneath them could show off their taste by not giving at all. By the 1970s a few were making charitable donations rather than giving presents.[82] This habit grew in subsequent decades as charities marketed what donations could buy so recipients could know, for example, that their present had been replaced by a goat for an African village.

Yet not everyone thought that their gifts were representative of their tastes. After all, most gifts were given to family members and relatives who either already had clear ideas about the giver's taste and status or were too close to either care or need impressing. Thus, people turned to more frivolous gifts. In 1957, C. S. Lewis complained that novelties and 'gaudy and useless gadgets' were often given as presents, things which 'no mortal ever bought for himself'.[83] Novelties were popular because they offered an opportunity to avoid being predictable or dull, but there were dangers in this and *The Times* remarked in 1937: '"Something different" too often in the cold light of the New Year turns out to be something freakish. Only at Christmas time would anyone seriously consider a cigarette ejector made in the image of a telephone – "Dial 0 and a cigarette shoots out at the side."'[84] Such gifts undermine the idea that consumption was simply a straightforward means of gaining social capital. The status such consumption signified could actually be a sense of humour rather than traditional social capital. This is clear in the emergence of presents that were deliberately ironical. One was the patterned jumper. Humour about receiving these dated back to the 1940s, but from the 1990s (particularly after being mocked in the 1996 novel and 2001 film *Bridget Jones' Diary*) they changed from something people dreaded getting to a joke where good taste was displayed by giving something that was clearly of bad taste.[85] This might show consumers were not slaves to the pretensions of taste but when people deliberately gave presents that the receiver would never actually wear then capitalism did not need to rely on aspirations and snobbery to ensure consumption flourished.

Novelty presents were the preserve of those with enough money not to worry about wasting it. Amid growing economic turmoil in the early 1920s, remarks on the growth of practical presents were common in middle-class publications. Certainly, many stores in the middle of the century emphasized that their gifts were actually useful. Of course, what defined useful was open to interpretation and in 1924 it was reported that shopkeepers were placing this label on pearl necklaces and cocktail shakers. But if these were things that people were going to use then they were useful, and definitions of utility were rightly very wide. Yet, however much stores and manufacturers tried to link their products to a Christmas market, they were actually operating against some powerful social norms on gifts: books and toys for children, luxury items for women and practical ones for men. These norms further blunted the use of Christmas to express one's own tastes. They were clear in interwar advertising for stores that sold a wide variety of products and thus had to highlight certain products. They were also reinforced by advice columns in newspapers and magazines.[86] Crucially, they were underpinned by people's general desire to buy things that people actually wanted.[87] Within this broad pattern there were, of course, variations. Books, for example, did not fit neatly into either male or female category but 6.1 million of them were sold in the UK in the run-up to Christmas 1999.[88]

The emphasis on luxury presents for women held good for the whole century. Christmas became a rare time when men were expected to acknowledge the domestic contributions of the women in their lives with some sort of material reward. This meant that women could expect to have more spent on them than men. Advertising played up this norm, reassuring men, for example, that expensive perfumes were a choice that they could not go wrong with.[89] The Great War had played a role too. In 1918, a shop assistant told the *Daily Mirror*: 'French girls have taught our English soldiers that every pretty woman powders her face. That is why nearly every fiancée, wife and mother will receive a powder puff and box and bottle of scent this Christmas.'[90] One result of the emphasis on luxury (which in clothing terms meant accessories rather than essentials) was that some middle-class interwar women ended up with too many handkerchiefs or gloves (and the latter sometimes too small because of people's politeness).[91] The neutrality of such presents also meant they were popular for less intimate relationships. In 1971 a writer claimed there was a feeling that 'a man should not dress a girl unless he undresses her'.[92] But even husbands struggled to know what to get their wives, especially if they were newly married and norms had not yet emerged in the relationship over what was appropriate. Longer-term marriages did not necessarily make things any easier. In a 1945 novel, a middle-aged man chooses a scarf for his wife more colourful than her usual attire. He frets over the choice and she reassures him but then relents after his insistence that the scarf could be changed. She asked if the shop sold woolly gloves instead.[93]

Of course, women did not just receive luxury items. Throughout the period, functional household items were also common presents in families on smaller incomes. The idea of practical gifts, such as kitchen gadgets or even washing machines, divided women. Some did not approve because they were associated with work and were not specifically for themselves, but others were well aware it was their only opportunity to get such objects. Men buying such gifts thus risked offending their partners. One response to this was a 1972 advertisement for Hoover domestic appliances aimed at women which encouraged them to ask for the items as gifts.[94]

Men, in contrast, expected practical things that they could use and their presents were far less varied in the first half of the period. Shaving equipment, ties and socks were always popular. Pipes, lighters or even just a packet of cigarettes were other popular choices, and manufacturers specifically advertised 'Cigarettes for Christmas'.[95] Their ubiquity as an everyday purchase could be overcome by simply increasing the volume, and boxes of fifty and a hundred could be bought, sometimes in special Christmas packaging. Cigarettes were especially popular for less intimate relations such as uncles and nephews who expected presents. People's tendency to resort to such presents led Embassy to run an advert in 1964 reminding people giving cigarettes that smokers normally had a favourite brand.[96] Functional choices dominated the presents given to men up till the 1970s. One young married man complained to his friend in a 1967 episode of Coronation Street that he took half a day off work to look for a decent present for his wife, but she seemed to get his present in a slot machine on Christmas Eve and it was the same every year – 'hankies, fags, socks and razorblades'.[97] No wonder then that an observer concluded in 1971 that she pitied men at Christmas, 'as they seem to be lumbered with receiving such awful things'.[98] Yet, as disposable incomes and living standards rose after the war, the necessity of giving practical items at Christmas fell away. Instead what constituted the practical began to evolve. The growth of hobbies such as golf, sailing and model-making all offered new ideas. More radically, the late 1950s and 1960s saw aftershave emerge as a popular gift for men. Many were often reluctant to embrace what could be seen as a feminine concern with how they smelt. However, Old Spice marketed itself as a very masculine product and, encouraged by a large number of bottles being given as Christmas presents, over half of adult males were regularly using aftershave by 1969.[99]

Aftershave was an example of how affluence had diversified what every class and gender bought, received and expected. Indeed, by the late twentieth century, both parents and children could often expect more than one present from their close family. Recorded music quickly established itself as a popular choice for all ages and was often given as an additional rather than main present. Christmas 1999, for example, saw 8.3 million CDs sold.[100] It was the development of such consumer technologies that most undermined the traditional gift patterns, especially since many were both luxuries and utility products. Indeed, Christmas played an important role in the spread of domestic electrical goods by giving people a focus for their wider aspirations. It allowed them to acquire such luxuries without the 'concomitant guilt of self-indulgence that might accrue from buying these same things'.[101] As early as Christmas 1919, the popularity of electric kettles, irons and toasters was being noted in London's West End.[102] Wireless sellers in 1930s Bolton were noting that while radio sets were not normally given as gifts, they were bought in time for Christmas.[103] By 1953, retailers were claiming that television parties were creating new levels of domestic pride, which in turn increased Christmas spending on furniture and electrical goods. In 1959, Selfridges' was telling reporters that take-up of hire purchase was up and that people were buying televisions and other electrical items as presents.[104] By 1970, 60 per cent of the annual sales of electric blankets, shavers, hair dryers, kettles, toasters and percolators were in the run-up to Christmas. As new technologies such as microwaves and mobile phones emerged, Christmas continued to give people an impetus to invest in them. In 1985, it was claimed that home computer companies did up to 70 per cent of their trade at Christmas. Christmas 1999, meanwhile, saw 4.1 million mobile phones sold in the UK.[105]

Despite the growing tendency to buy electrical goods that might be used by all the members of a family, it was children who were at the heart of the festival and they dominated the spending on presents. A 1973 survey suggested over half of Christmas presents were bought for children. This was nothing new. In 1914, a newspaper shopping feature was referring to Father Christmas giving 'in the usual bounteous manner'.[106] Brown has argued that children are the main beneficiaries of rising living standards and Christmas seems to affirm this point, as the volume of presents children received multiplied with post-war affluence.[107] In 1958 the *Children's Newspaper* was writing of stockings that bulged 'like a pumpkin' and Christmas trees doubled up 'under the weight of toys'.[108] Children's expectations were rising too. Some parents felt under pressure from children who expected more and bigger presents each year. The 1970s diaries of children and teenagers often recorded long lists of the annuals, games, toys, vouchers and money received.[109] Precisely what was in that haul of loot was subject to changing fashions. Even in the 1920s, there were presents, such as Hornby train sets, that were regarded as *the* presents to get.[110] In 1937, it was reported that aeroplanes were the most popular toys. Toy soldiers were always popular, although in the immediate wake of the Second World War red-coated soldiers were more popular than modern khaki ones.[111] Electronic toys rose to prominence in the 1970s, creating new family tensions when they did not work. On 29 December 1978, Michael Palin visited a toyshop over problems with his child's Scalextric controls, 'which have been such a headache over the last few days'. He recorded that the shop was largely full of parents returning malfunctioning toys: 'Kindly, middle-aged women with headscarves can be heard at the counter asking for advice ... "I pressed the auto-destruct and the bit came off ..." or "Every time it goes round a corner all the missiles fall out".'[112]

The popularity of such toys owed much to how central advertising had become in the Christmas toy market. Research into letters sent to Santa in 1971 highlighted the influence of television advertising, with some six-year-olds asking for pop records and 'sexy boots'.[113] American research on such letters also showed they were clearly influenced by advertising and television. In one 1990s study, 85 per cent of the sample mentioned at least one brand name.[114] Large companies such as Mattel and Fisher-Price had come to dominate the Christmas toy market in the 1970s, manufacturing cheaply in the Far East and exploiting not just television advertising but also tie-ins with popular programmes and films.[115] Their marketing and associated hype grew so effective that demand could outstrip supply, leading to 'the toy' of the season selling out. One such example was Teletubbies at Christmas 1997. There were claims that 3 million dolls were needed in the UK, but only 1 million were in circulation, leading some parents to queue all night outside shops with new stock.[116] Yet there were also suspicions raised that the shortages were deliberate, an illustration of how consumers sometimes felt they were being duped, even if that did not stop them buying.

For those who could not or did not want to choose gifts, there was always the option of giving money. Although it was regarded as an inappropriate present for older relatives, it was a common present for children and young people throughout the period. Sometimes it might even be given in advance of Christmas, so that the child could buy his or her own present.[117] During the Second World War, encouraged by a lack of wrapping paper and appeals not to send parcels, cash presents became particularly common. But giving certain types of money was already something of a tradition in itself. Banks between the wars reported significant demand for shiny pennies. Indeed, the Royal Mint was even known to darken new pennies so they would not be held back from circulation by people keeping them for presents. In 1937 *The Times* called the unusual 5s. piece 'a really dignified' present for nephews. These coins were last made in 1953 because there was no demand for them except at Christmas.[118] Money, however, was always liable to be misspent and thus tokens emerged as an alternative that allowed givers to say something about their tastes while still giving freedom to the receivers to make their own choices. Book tokens were launched in 1930 and quickly caught on, influencing Boots to launch their own vouchers in 1936. Gift tokens were given a boost by the war, which made the whole concept of coupons more respectable, as well as limiting the alternative options.[119] The government encouraged this by introducing National Savings Christmas Cards that could be given to people. After the war, tokens continued to grow in popularity because they avoided the difficulties of choosing, were easy and cheap to post and enabled people to receive what they actually wanted. Yet there were always those who saw cash or tokens as rather vulgar, while some advised against them on the simple grounds that they gave away how much you had spent and risked being upstaged by others.[120] Such people probably preferred gifts that were clearly educational and, as Chapter 2 discusses, Christmas consumption was not divorced from people's aspirations for their children. Indeed, the demand for this led some toyshops in the 1970s to reinvent themselves as 'early learning centres'.[121] Yet some parents had no such luxury, and throughout the century, in low-income families Christmas was an opportunity to get their children clothes, something that was more important than giving them toys.

The working-class Christmas

For the working class, meeting the expectations and obligations of gift-giving was not easy, especially between the wars. Poverty then was very real; there was not perhaps the near starvation of the Victorian era, but malnutrition, disease and terrible housing conditions were afflictions that, even if not actually experienced, were never far away, and this created a sense of insecurity. They were also compounded by less dangerous, but just as uncomfortable problems as poor teeth and poor eyesight. In such a context, Christmas could be a welcome diversion. Most young working-class children could expect a stocking with some combination of fruit, a new penny, nuts, sweets and maybe even a piece of coal (which was supposed to bring luck). Some parents padded out stockings with newspaper to ensure that their meagreness was not emphasized but many children could also expect a better dinner than normal and a small toy, even if it had been made by father rather than bought.[122]

The interwar years were far from the period of universal working-class despondency that they are sometimes imagined to be. For those in regular work, it was actually a decade of some prosperity, and many working-class families benefited from falling prices and the availability of cheap credit. This enabled some working-class families to buy their children handsome presents, as well as to enjoy something of a Christmas feast. Indeed, like their middle-class equivalents, working-class newspapers ran cartoons about the pressures of Christmas shopping and even the Communist *Daily Worker* published Christmas recipes.[123] The results were described in a 1937 South Wales novel:

> The miners made much of Christmas here. For the past week the front room in each house had been locked against the children, festooned with paper streamers, toys hidden in drawers of the chest and a steady accumulation of good things to eat, cake, oranges, sweet sugar biscuits, all brought with the club money paid out at this time of year, laid upon the table.[124]

Mass Observation noted how in Bolton the working class temporarily satisfied their normally thwarted desire for 'abundance and riches' by stacking their coalhouses high, freely giving presents and buying more food than was needed.[125] A Yorkshire miner recorded that after twelve months of regular work, Christmas was much looked forward to as a time for treats and a rest. He could not afford chocolates, rich cake, turkey, pudding and pork pies all-year round, but he always had a change of fare at Christmas and felt that he deserved it.[126] Because people felt this way, there were times when the economy seemed to have little impact on the festival. 'Money may be short but it is always found at Christmas,' said a Bolton sweetshop owner in 1938. A toyshop in the town even noted that poorer customers – 'clog and shawl types' – spent more than those with cars.[127] The son of a Derbyshire miner summed up his interwar festive memories: 'Although we were poor I had good presents.' For his family, Christmas was a day of 'fierce pleasures' rather than 'temperate enjoyment'.[128] Such behaviours were rooted in something noted in Richard Hoggart's 1950s study of the traditional working class: after essentials had been paid for, there was a general desire to spend on extravagances and things to enjoy rather than more functional and useful goods.[129] That was particularly evident in the fancy boxes people chose for their Christmas chocolates, despite the fact that more chocolate might be obtained for the same price in packaging that was less pretty.[130]

The required money might come from sacrifices such as cutting down on small luxuries or even the regular shopping. In 1927, the *Daily Mail* noted that 'the tradition of Christmas is more sacred than the claims of creditors' and claimed this was causing families to fall behind on their hire purchase schemes and loan payments.[131] But more common was for the mid-century working class to save for Christmas rather than default on their debts. Since the Victorian period, those workers with disposable incomes that allowed them to save spent one half of the year putting aside money for Christmas and the other for a summer holiday. In 1949, a study of workers noted that Christmas stood alongside clothes and holidays as the most frequent reasons for saving.[132] Some savings clubs specifically used Christmas to attract business. In 1922, for example, the Walthamstow Democratic Thrift and Loan Club was promising to 'ensure' members 'money to spend at

Christmas'.[133] More common were the Christmas savings clubs that were run by organizations as varied as factories, shops, pubs and churches. Some required regular contributions or were for specific items such as a turkey, goose or chocolate. Others just saw people pay whatever and whenever they could and then take out a lump sum. A Bolton sweet and tobacco shop owner told Mass Observation in 1938 that his savings club opened after the September holidays and that people began with the best intentions of paying in a 6d. or a shilling a week. However, this quickly dropped off to little or nothing, meaning that by Christmas the typical pay out was only 4 to 5s., which mostly went towards buying boxes of chocolates.[134] A woman from a Liverpool slum told an investigator in the mid-1950s that from September onwards she paid 2s. 6d. a week to the grocer, 2s. to the greengrocer and 1s. to the newsagent from whom she bought her presents. She neither received nor expected interest in these savings and said these payments were the only way she could get extras for Christmas dinner.[135] Other seasonal saving schemes were linked to sickness clubs that paid out any money left over at the end of the year to members to spend at Christmas.[136] The overall scale of saving was evident in Swindon, where in 1936 it was reported that nearly £20,000 had been paid out in the district, with the typical pay out being between 19s. and 30s. The local paper said this allowed 'those little extras and luxuries which alone can give Christmas its true meaning'.[137] Such clubs became part of the Christmas economy in themselves. In the 1930s, to the annoyance of local shop owners, some workers started their own saving clubs, earning small commissions by collecting people's money and then buying goods such as chocolates for them direct from wholesalers.[138] Nor were the clubs free from problems for those actually taking part. The secretary spending or running off with the monies collected was a reoccurring joke in popular culture. There were occasions when it did actually happen, leading to ruined Christmases, suicides by the perpetrators and calls for parliamentary regulation.[139]

Maybe a third of the interwar working class did not have any financial security and saving a good sum was certainly beyond the fluctuating numbers of unemployed and those in irregular work. Their Christmas was quite different. In some families, treats went no further than some fruit, nuts and a few sweets in the children's stockings.[140] One unmarried 31-year-old electrician from Farnborough recorded in 1937 that with his father out of work, his mother gave him clothes as a present before the day 'and the whole matter' was forgotten by the 25th.[141] Nor could the unemployed enjoy the break that Christmas provided others, since their problem was too much free time rather than not enough. Even visiting friends or family could be difficult because of the fear of offending informal codes of reciprocity in hospitality.[142] A. J. Cronin's 1937 novel *The Citadel*, which drew on his experiences as a doctor in a Welsh mining community, described one sick man's Christmas with an almost bare kitchen, a low fire and a branch of fir in a bucket serving as a tree. On it was three small candles and beneath it the Christmas treat, three oranges. Dinner for the man, his wife and four-year-old daughter was two beef faggots.[143] Other children from such backgrounds might rely on relatives for their only presents. A London man remembered that after a bad year for his father his stocking contained cinders from the grate and a piece of rock-hard bread. The fact that his parents gave these 'gifts' at all perhaps suggests they thought it important that something was given. Not everyone got even that. Another man remembered of his interwar fatherless childhood: 'You hung your stocking and if you got anything in it you were lucky. We used to have what the other people chucked out afterwards.'[144]

Charity did give many a better day. The interwar period saw fundraising across Britain to give the unemployed and their families presents, meals, hampers or just the chance to attend a concert to raise the spirits. The *Daily Mail,* for example, raised money in 1928 to buy 127,000 hampers for unemployed miners and their families, giving people, as one female recipient put it, 'a real good feed'.[145] One woman remembered that during her interwar Liverpool childhood her family received a charity parcel containing a turkey, oranges, potatoes and sweets. The children were 'nearly hysterical with excitement', although with no fire the family had to cook the meat at someone else's house.[146] At school too there could be festive excitement, sweets and a tree. A London man recalled attending several different Sunday Schools just so he could get the festive treats they offered.[147] As George Orwell argued in *The Road to Wigan Pier* (1937), for those living in poverty these small luxuries were very important.[148] One Bolton woman told Mass Observation that she and her unemployed husband had no money for presents for each other, but still got a little something for the children, who also got a present from the local paper. They put up a few decorations so it looked like Christmas and thought the day a small moment of happiness for the children.[149]

However much such efforts were appreciated and added a bit of colour to the poor's Christmas, it could not take away from the frustration that children in particular could feel. In a 1914 children's story, an orphan remarks that Santa 'ain't got a mem'ry for the likes of me and Poppy. It's rich kids as his pack's full for, what has more now than they knows what to do with.'[150] Oral evidence too points to some resentment among poorer children of the better presents their peers received. One man remembered of his interwar Liverpool childhood that while he was always given clothes, he longed for toys.[151] Richard Burton remembered of his Welsh childhood that receiving a second-hand present was considered 'shameful'.[152] Parents, too, felt the deprivation when they could not afford a special meal and might even shy away from visiting friends or family because they could not take anything with them.[153] The wives of some unemployed men laughed when a neighbour wished them a merry Christmas because there was nothing to be merry about.[154] The Labour MP for Chester-le-Street was probably right when he told Parliament in 1938 that Christmas would 'be a grim, gloomy and cheerless time for the great bulk' of the unemployed.[155] In 1922 one local newspaper went as far as claiming that 'Thousands will probably wish themselves dead this Christmas because they have no work'.[156] This was not simply hyperbole. A policeman recalled a 1930s incident of a London man who lost his job but did not tell his wife and pretended to go to work every day. That lasted until she said she wanted to go Christmas shopping, something which prompted him to throw himself in front of an underground train.[157]

After the war, the financial burden of Christmas did not disappear for the working class. Its drain on people's resources was evident in the fact that in 1946 average weekly saving in the country was £10 million but in the week before Christmas it fell to £2.67 million.[158] Even after austerity slowly gave way to affluence in the 1950s, Christmas still meant sacrifices and saving. As a 1959 episode of *Hancock's Half Hour* put it, 'I've denied myself pleasures all year to have a good Christmas.'[159] Poverty and financial hardship might no longer mean malnutrition and health-threatening housing, but they certainly had not disappeared, especially among the elderly. There were still people who were unable to afford turkeys, and who scoured the shops for cheap toys or waited until Christmas Eve to buy presents in the hope that prices might go down. Essential clothes continued to be common presents for both children and adults.[160] As unemployment emerged as a social problem again in the 1960s, Christmas became an even bigger burden. In 1966, for example, the press reported that redundancies and shorter working hours in Birmingham was curbing Christmas shopping, although people were keen to make sacrifices to ensure their children still got presents.[161] Such sacrifices could appear rather irrational to outsiders, with some families even foregoing paying the rent in order to buy presents.[162]

The motive for such actions could be found in a 1970 report that found that Christmas could create feelings of failure and inferiority and intensify the isolation of the poor.[163] Although they faced every day their inability to take a full part in consumer culture, the expectation that Christmas should involve spending made it a time when poverty was most deeply felt, especially by those with children who wanted what their friends had or what they saw advertised on television. This led one reporter in 1987 to call Christmas for the poor, 'not so much a time of celebration, but rather an experience of arbitrary humiliation'. One man, who had been out of work for four years, told that reporter that when he saw his children's faces as they watched television advertisements he wanted to put his 'boot through the screen'.[164] For single parents it was particularly difficult. As one divorced cleaner put it in 1975: 'Christmas is hell. The children are home for three weeks and I have to provide heat and meals for five.' Her children had sausages for their Christmas dinner and second-hand toys for presents.[165] In 2011 a charity was told by one woman: 'I don't enjoy Christmas at all, not one bit ... It's just another day to spend money. ... Because you don't want it to be like when you was at school and you're going to school lying and telling them that you've had loads of stuff, when you've had nothing.' The Joseph Rowntree Foundation calculated that £505 was the sum required for a socially acceptable Christmas for a two-child family, of which £460 was for presents for the parents and children. Another survey of low-income families put the cost at £182. That sum represented a very basic celebration, but it was still almost double the weekly income (after housing costs) of respondents.[166]

Savings clubs continued to offer something of a solution, but they became far less widespread in the 1950s than they had been before the war. Their provision shifted from local institutions to national companies but they often provided poor value. Savings clubs offered no interest, while schemes where people paid advance instalments for presents and food charged buyers significantly more than had they been able to afford the goods in cash. Too often they were another example of how the poor were being exploited because they were unable to get credit or afford upfront the costs of everyday goods and services. More people, however, did their own saving for the festival and the Royal Bank of Scotland estimated in 2004 that half of adults were using savings to cover the cost of Christmas.[167]

Those who could not afford to save could borrow. The growth of hire purchase in the 1950s had allowed people to buy bigger presents and taken away the traditional shame of owing money, thus helping usher in a culture where debt was normalized. This was not entirely new since local stores had always offered unofficial credit to regular customers, but undoubtedly hire purchase changed how people thought about borrowing. Indeed, in the 1950s and 1960s financial companies would knock on doors in working-class districts offering loans for the festive season.[168] Mail order catalogues were another important route for people to buy presents and pay by instalments. The main mail order firms' share of non-food retail sales peaked at almost 10 per cent in 1979, but they were gradually subsumed by credit cards and then the internet.[169] Credit cards, first introduced in Britain in 1966, allowed all manners of food and presents to be bought on tick and for the cost of Christmas to be spread out over the year. Important here was the 1974 Consumer Credit Act, which allowed women to borrow without a male guarantor. Rather than being associated with the shame of debt, owning a credit card became a status symbol in itself in the 1970s. The costs, however, were still a burden to many and for some the results could be catastrophic. Christmas was only one small cause of rising consumer credit, but a 1972 survey suggested half of housewives knew it would leave them in debt. A 2004 survey suggested that more than a quarter of people were borrowing to pay for Christmas.[170] Whether this was a genuine fall or evidence of the vagaries of consumer surveys, Christmas debt was undoubtedly a burden for some. One Northern Irish parent complained in the early 1980s, 'You're paying from one Christmas to the next.'[171] Still, a credit card was better than the doorstop or payday lenders who could charge interest rates that were difficult to believe could be legal. Christmas thus left the financially vulnerable even more vulnerable than normal. It was not even that people's usual borrowings were profligate. After struggling with the financial aftermath of a house fire, the family of a Glasgow bus driver had Christmas dinner in 1972 from a hamper bought on credit. It contained tinned fruit, vegetables and tinned chicken. Their children had few presents and there was no television for entertainment. The mother said her heart was breaking.[172] It was no wonder then that charities continued to try and do something for the poorest. Food parcels were not what people associated with the late twentieth century, but they remained the only way some could enjoy a Christmas meal.[173]

People continued to respond to the challenges with a degree of resourcefulness and even heroics to ensure that children did not go without. They scrimped and saved, even in some cases buying presents nearly a year ahead in the January sales.[174] In the 1970s the break meant two weeks' worth of benefits were sometimes paid at once, leading some recipients to spend it all on Christmas and then 'starve' for a week.[175] One researcher found a Christmas economy on a housing estate where presents were stolen to order.[176] Throughout the century, even middle-class families developed strategies to limit the season's costs. Some families agreed limits on what could be spent or banned presents for adults. Others had a store of unwanted raffle prizes, acquired bric-a-brac and unwanted Christmas and birthday presents that they could give away in December to save money.[177] But such schemes were much easier in families that had disposable incomes or places to store gifts. For the poorest in society, poverty was undoubtedly curtailing Christmas, denying them presents, a Christmas meal and a tree. By 2006 the British Retail Consortium was claiming the average household spent £975 on Christmas. In November that year, the average Job Seekers' Allowance weekly payment to someone with dependents was £92.99.[178]

Yet relative prosperity remained a far more common condition than poverty. The working-class affluence of the 1950s was neither new nor universal, but it was more far reaching than the prosperity that had begun to emerge between the wars.[179] Central to the rising incomes of working-class families was the growth of female employment. By the mid-1960s around half of married women were in some form of paid employment. Wages were also rising faster than costs and, between 1950 and 1973, the purchasing power of those on average incomes doubled. Poverty did become a topic of significant concern again in the 1980s, but while there were 3 million on the dole in the middle of that decade, there were nearly 20 million in full-time employment and another 6.7 million in part-time work. Between 1971 and 1990, there was nearly a three-quarter increase in the disposable income of the average household.[180] Rising prosperity encouraged greater levels of individualism and a desire to consume. One sociologist argued in 1961 that workers wanted 'little things instead of big things' and they wanted them for themselves rather than society at large.[181] Christmas was one way that this desire found fruition, especially among parents who were determined to give their children what they had not had. This meant multiple presents and while it is difficult to generalize there is definite evidence that working-class Christmas spending began to outstrip that of the middle class. In 1959, for example, toy manufacturers were claiming that working-class children were typically given more toys (though fewer books and records) at Christmas than their middle-class counterparts, while *The Economist* reported that 'A really expensive doll is liable to sell as well in a dock area as in Harrods'.[182] There could be considerable pride in some families that they had been able to save enough to ensure a big tree and plenty of presents for the children.[183] One man remembered how he and his wife used 'to go overboard' on presents: 'There would be soldiers by the hundred, cowboy's outfits, nurse's outfits, and later on Scalextric. There'd be so many toys we'd hide them behind the sideboard, and we'd have to move it out from the wall so that there was enough room to put them behind.'[184] In 1963 some shoppers were telling television reporters that they spent up to £70 on the children alone, a sum worth over £1,241 at 2012 prices.[185] Nor did the discrepancies of class spending disappear. By the end of the century anthropologists were noting that the working class was more lavish in its Christmas expenditure, while the various sections of the middle class were more concerned with being seen to have the right taste, which might mean rejecting significant spending as ostentatious.[186] A 2007 survey also suggested that C2s (skilled workers) spent more on presents than other groups including ABs (managers and professionals).[187] Those below skilled workers on the social scale could not afford such levels of spending, whereas those above probably did not feel the need to embrace such levels of conspicuous consumption. Indeed, Christmas spending was now sometimes showing a degree of indulgence or even recklessness. In 1998 a survey suggested that a fifth of people did not set a budget for Christmas at all. Although one in ten expected to underspend on their budget, another one in ten said they would spend what was needed to have a good Christmas.[188] In a 2011 survey of low-income parents, over half of respondents thought it was important to save for Christmas, but a third thought it was important to have a good time and think about the cost later.[189] The danger of this was that people could sometimes feel they always had to match or outdo the previous year's presents. This could lead to what retail commentators called 'extreme Christmas shopping', getting carried away and spending more and more.[190]

Commercial excess and significance

A 1990 *Punch* cartoon joked that 'the commercialization of Christmas is one of its most enduring traditions'. Complaints about the festival's commercialization were raised throughout the twentieth century and represented far more than the opinion of an idealistic or grumpy minority. A 1969 opinion poll found that 83 per cent of respondents thought Christmas was too commercialized, while 64 per cent thought stores started selling festive goods too early.[191] Some even believed that commercialism had reached such excesses that it could not last in a rational society. A 1959 article in *The Spectator* claimed, 'It seems unlikely in the nature of things that Christmas will go on being so tremendous a commercial success indefinitely. It imposes too much strain on too many people for there not to be a reaction against it. The chances are that in fifty years it may be on the way out as the universal orgy.'[192] Moreover, throughout the period, there was a belief among all ages that Christmas was more commercialized than it had been in their youth, although an awareness that such complaints were recurrent was rarely present. Yet that did not mean that the commercialization of Christmas was not growing. There was, as even a casual glance over contemporary sources shows, more advertising, a greater tendency to buy things rather than make them, and greater levels of spending on non-essentials. As *The Economist* realized as early as 1953, in all these things Christmas was just reflecting wider trends.[193] Consumption, and the encouragement to consume, increasingly defined people's lives. Between 1950 and 1980, after inflation is taken into account, spending on food, drink, clothing, household goods and consumer durables in the UK grew by nearly 60 per cent.[194] Christmas might be a particularly potent example of this growing consumerism, but it was just that, an example.

That did not stop people complaining. Some of this was simply people not liking how much Christmas cost them as individuals. The laments tended to date from before or after the day itself, while on the 25th people were just enjoying the fruits of their spending. Before the war, anger at the commercial Christmas was also encouraged by the fact that income tax was due on 1 January, which meant it was a time of significant bills for even the wealthiest.[195] Yet what exactly people were upset with diverged widely and the disgruntlement seemed to be grounded in much wider dissatisfactions with the state of society. A few, for example, regarded the commercialization of Christmas as another unwelcome symbol of the Americanization of British culture.[196] By the late twentieth century, others saw it as a symbol of the excesses of a throwaway society. Two historians even suggest that the middle-class lamentations on commercialization owe something to the loss of an opportunity to give ritually 'to those beneath them in the social scale'.[197] Christians, of course, complained throughout the period that the emphasis on present-buying obscured the religious significance of the day. The novelist and playwright Clemence Dane, for example, claimed in 1925 that commercialism led people to forget that Christmas was originally about simple things and 'a poor man's feast', a time when a child was born in a stable.[198] More than fifty years later, another writer, angry at the commercialism and excess, concluded: 'That these pagan rites should be linked with the name of Christ … I find obscene.'[199]

One of the most common complaints about the commercialization was that the spirit of giving that the festival was supposed to represent had been transformed into a rather mechanical and cynical exchange, where people decided how much the recipient deserved to have spent on him or her.[200] Such feelings were exacerbated by the knowledge that those who did not return gifts might be crossed off the following year's list. Even members of the working class in the 1930s could report that they often felt obliged to buy presents for people they knew they would be receiving something from and a suspicion that somehow this feeling was down to the shopkeepers' propaganda. Indeed, the sense that gifts were simply a transaction meant one young man told Mass Observation in 1938 that he and the friend he exchanged books with might as well just have bought them themselves. A year earlier, another young man reported that he and his friends had simply decided not to give each other presents because the whole process had become about reciprocity rather than generosity.[201] With people throughout the period asking for specific gifts, there was also a sense that it was all about receiving rather than giving. Thus, in 1925 there was a complaint in the *Daily Mirror* that people expected something they wanted and were 'vexed if they don't get it'.[202] The giving of money or even gifts that required little thought did not help deter such beliefs. Nor did how some treated their gifts. By the late twentieth century, people were increasingly happy to exchange or sell gifts they did not want, despite the fact this undermined the idea that it was the thought that counted. One 2013 survey even suggested that 40 per cent of women exchanged or returned presents given by their partners. By the end of Christmas Day 2010, more than 366,000 people had listed unwanted gifts on eBay.[203]

Others, however, were simply concerned that they were being exploited by retailers overcharging at a time when they wanted to buy things.[204] There was a sense that Christmas was some sort of commercial conspiracy where people were obliged to buy things, thinking they were giving rather than consuming. In 1936 Aldous Huxley even suggested that newspapers fostered the idea of festive goodwill just to promote present-buying.[205] In 1946 one letter writer complained Christmas was nothing more than 'an annual shopkeepers' benefit', which was terrifying for fathers who had to pay for it all and caused women to go on a 'desperate search for gifts and eatables that will look adequate but not bankrupt the house-keeping account'.[206] Some manufacturers did indeed try to define their products as integral parts of Christmas. 'What is Christmas without Crawfords?' asked an advertisement for shortbread in 1955.[207] The volume and tone of such advertising was responsible for much of the belief that Christmas was too commercial. Advertisements encouraged people to make their relatives and friends happy and to buy even for difficult aunts, creating a sense that not to buy presents was somehow mean or unkind. But they also spoke to buyers' fears about the whole process of festive shopping. In the 1980s for example, a television advertisement for Boots stressed the variety of gifts it had in a single store and promised to 'take the rough and tumble out of Christmas shopping'. 'Trust Yardley to solve your problems this

Christmas,' declared another 1982 television advertisement, in which a shop assistant tells Santa what to get his relatives. Quite what influence advertising has had on the public is a difficult question, but it is not unreasonable to assume that it helped set a cultural agenda in areas where other factors were also pushing in that direction. Yet Christmas advertising was actually usually less manipulative than at other times of the year. One 1968 observer was right to point out that many adverts did not feel they had to appeal to fear, sex, health or vanity to entice custom. They simply described the wares being sold. In other words, the commercialization of Christmas was a response to demand and not the invention of advertisers who instead were simply guiding people in a direction that they were already heading.[208]

In 1958 one writer remembered that well before the war older people were complaining how tawdry and commercial Christmas had become: 'but in their most disgruntled moments they had never imagined anything like this steam-roller, gathering momentum all October and November, with the London streets disguised as toy bazaars, and false Father Christmases popping up in every store.'[209] The beginning of Christmas displays in shops and advertisements was the key marker that the Christmas season was approaching and the perception that it was getting earlier each year was probably the most common lament about the festival's commercialization. Yet even in the late Victorian period advertisements for Christmas goods were common in November and people in the Edwardian period were remarking that Christmas seemed to be starting earlier and earlier.[210] Although there was no agreed date among retailers on when festive displays and advertising should begin, there is little evidence of a clear pattern of Christmas reaching the shops earlier and earlier. In 1921, Christmas shopping was reported to be in full swing in Knightsbridge in mid-November.[211] The middle of November was fairly typical for Christmas decorations to go up in stores across the country, but some did start earlier. On 30 October 1933, *The Times* was reporting early Christmas displays in large London shops and noting that the Queen had begun her shopping. The war and subsequent austerity curtailed this, at least temporarily. In 1952, it was noted that Christmas was now concentrated in the week or two before the day itself and the time of its stretching back into November was gone. That did not last. A year later, there were reports of a Christmas tree being put up outside a Leeds store in October. In 1959, the first decorations in Oxford Street went up on 22 October.[212] Even some children were put out at the fact that Father Christmas had already been seen in some stores in October. 'Christmas is lasting too long these days,' remarked one woman to a television reporter in that month 1959. In the same year, Coventry City Council responded by banning shops putting illuminated trees up outside before 1 December.[213]

October may have been widely thought as too early for Christmas, but this was not a unanimous opinion. In Coleford (Gloucestershire) town centre, decorations started going up on 12 October 2008. Some traders were upset, but one shopper told a paper that the decorations were 'splendid', and it was better to enjoy them for three months than three weeks. Throughout the period retailers claimed that early starts were a response to consumer demand. In 1926 Selfridge's was justifying Christmas preparations in November by saying that anticipation was much of the enjoyment and that people liked it.[214] In the 1930s there were people thinking all year of what presents to purchase and making lists of anything suitable they saw in the shops.[215] As pockets deepened, this extended to some people actually buying presents all-year round. This was partly because they enjoyed shopping, but it also spread the cost and avoided the pressures associated with shopping in December. A 1973 survey found that 56 per cent of respondents had started thinking about Christmas shopping by 8 November and 28 per cent had actually bought some presents. In 2002, Debenhams, which put up its Christmas display on 20 October, claimed that if it did not do this it would get hundreds of complaints, while Marks and Spencer claimed that half of its customers wanted to buy Christmas items in October.[216] Whether people approved or not, there was little way to avoid the arrival of Christmas in the shops and television advertisements. Shops may have claimed they were responding to the demand of some, but in starting their Christmas displays so early they undoubtedly extended the season in everyone's minds.

People were upset about the commercialization of Christmas in ways they were not about most other aspects of contemporary culture because they held the festival to be special. In particular, its emphasis on charity and giving was supposed to be the very antithesis of materialism, commercialism and consumerism. However, it is difficult to agree with those who said that this Christmas spirit was increasingly being subsumed by commercial forces. For a start, the complaint that it was all about buying presents was recurrent throughout the century. More importantly, it misunderstood the nature of gift-giving. Researchers from 1930s Bolton to late twentieth-century America found that many people buying gifts concentrated on the joy the presents would give to others. Materialism itself was thus not central to the importance placed upon gift-giving, but rather what was important was a sense of Christmas spirit and ritual.[217] People tended to see presents in terms of love and friendship rather than as transactions, and most enjoyed the processes of choosing and giving. Others may have been giving gifts because they felt they ought to but that sense of obligation came from personal relationships rather than commercial pressures. Moreover, from removing price tags to wrapping the present up or pretending it came from a benevolent mythical figure, people employed strategies to personalize the process, distancing it from consumerism and the idea they were simply passing on a commodity.[218] People also shunned talking about price. One anthropologist claimed that in the upper middle classes discussing or bragging about the cost of a present, even in very vague terms, was crass and vulgar. Other sections of society may not have thought in quite these terms, but they still did not behave as if presents were transactions. Even where givers included a receipt, it was due to a desire to ensure the recipient ended up with something they wanted, rather than because a transfer of goods was taking place.[219] Indeed, some families developed elaborate traditions that consciously or otherwise ensured people got what they wanted, but without making the whole process seem too much like a transaction. One 1930s middle-class family in Cheam produced a list of what people wanted, from which relatives bought one practical thing and 'if possible' something frivolous for a shilling or two. The parcels were then put in pillowcases and credited to Father Christmas.[220]

Thus, those anthropologists who argued Christmas tamed capitalism, turning the anonymous purchase of commodities into a sociable exchange of gifts, were probably right, although those who argued that this made consumption sacred were probably going too far.[221] Instead, what present-giving could do was reaffirm and express social bonds and relationships. Indeed, the sometimes unpleasant nature of Christmas shopping made the gifts it led to more worthwhile, as they were something that had been achieved in the face of commercial forces. Carrier even suggests that Christmas represents people demonstrating to themselves that they can make a family in 'a world of money'.[222] We should, of course, be careful of exaggerating the altruism that Christmas represented. Gift-giving was still also a way for some people to express their taste and status. They might even hope for a reward, and some advertisers did promise that. A 1964 advertisement for handkerchiefs, for example, told women that if they gave a certain brand to their men they would be 'thought the world of' and considered 'queens for keeps', while early 1970s Christmas adverts for Badedas bath products even implied that its use would lead to sex for the men who gave it to their partners.[223] Yet few human actions have single, simple motives. Gift-giving could be both altruistic and selfish at the same time. There was also, of course, the potential for Christmas gifts to have no impact or even a negative one on relationships through being too cheap or expensive, too formulaic, not thought through or even offensive.[224] The thought alone was not always enough.

Whatever its causes and whatever it represented, Christmas mattered to the British economy. In 1923, the Early Closing Association wrote to the prime minister to object to the possibility of a December general election, which it worried would disrupt Christmas trade.[225] For the same reason, in December 1928 the Conservative candidate actually suspended his campaigning for the Northampton by-election scheduled for early January.[226] Christmas did probably generate spending levels that otherwise would not have happened and at the very least kept money moving, both in terms of retail and production.[227] Before the Second World War, this led to attempts to make Christmas spending some sort of civic duty at a time of global economic problems. In 1932, for example, the Regent Street Association was telling readers of *The Times* that doing one's Christmas shopping early would increase orders from tradesmen, boost manufacturing and ease unemployment. Two years later, one MP even introduced a bill which sought to have a two-week period before Christmas when schools would be closed and shopping restrictions would be lifted, in order to boost trade and employment through seasonal shopping. Such messages faded after the war, but they did not disappear, even if not everyone bought into the claims. C. S. Lewis thus asked in 1957: 'Can it really be my duty to buy and receive masses of junk every winter just to help the shopkeepers?'[228] There were even new hints that a sense of rights was replacing a belief in duty in the popular imagination. In 1978 a warehouse worker complained to the Equal Opportunities Commission when his employers denied him the half-day off they gave female employees for Christmas shopping. Another sign of this shift was the disappearance by the 1970s of the annual reminders to be polite to shop assistants.[229] The customer was now king and it was up to companies to win his, or more commonly, her custom.

Quantifying the exact importance of Christmas was impossible because there would always be some retail activity in December and it was difficult to determine and record what exactly was being spent on festivities. Early attempts varied significantly. In 1937 *The Times* was estimating that Britain spent £100 million on Christmas. The arbitrariness of estimates was evident in the fact that a year earlier another report reckoned Christmas trade was worth £25 million, of which £15 million was on goods that would otherwise not have been purchased. More accurate estimates came through the extra currency that the Bank of England had to put into circulation to cope with the withdrawals from banks and savings clubs, as well as the demand for shiny pennies. In Christmas week 1937, for example, there was 28.9 per cent more currency in circulation than in mid-November.[230] By the 2000s official surveys were showing that average UK household spending rose by around 13 per cent in December. Retail sales in November and December were then accounting for a fifth of the annual total.[231] These were the only months when retail sales in non-food stores exceeded those in supermarkets and other food shops.[232] Although these figures are not strictly comparable, they do offer a tentative suggestion that the proportional economic contribution of Christmas might have subsided in a context where year round household spending had grown significantly. Yet the total volume of Christmas spending was undoubtedly bigger than it had been. By extrapolating from an opinion poll's estimates of individual spending (an average of £592 per adult), one financial website calculated in 2012 that UK spending on Christmas was as high as £29 billion.[233] Accounting for inflation, this was more than five times larger than the most generous pre-war estimates of Christmas spending.

Whatever the overall situation, throughout the period retailers selling things that might be given as gifts were certainly aware of the festival's importance to their fortunes. The Christmas card trade alone was estimated at £250 million in 1991.[234] In December 1952, the larger British stores sold 11 per cent more groceries, 50 per cent more clothing and footware, 50 per cent more headware and 75 per cent more chemist goods than in a normal month. In 1959 British toy manufacturers were reporting that they sold 40 per cent of their output in December.[235] In the late 1990s department stores were reporting that their turnover doubled in the two months leading to the festival. A cosmetic manufacturer estimated that Christmas accounted for as much as 60 per cent of sales in his industry.[236] As the conventions over what should be given as gifts loosened, the festive impact reached a broader range of retailers. A survey by the London Chamber of Commerce found that Christmas accounted for an average of 30–40 per cent of the annual turnover of retailers in central London, although for some it was much higher.[237] The British Retail Consortium claimed many retailers derived up to 60 per cent of the turnover from the November to January period.[238] Research in Southampton in 2007 calculated that 86 per cent of visitors to the city between November and January had come to Christmas shop and that the value of Christmas to the local economy was nearly £734 million.[239] Those retailers and products that were not associated with Christmas could also try to cash in on this trade and one 1936 observer noted how even fishmonger shops in Gloucester were dominated by turkeys.[240] In 1985 Hellmann's ran a television advertisement which suggested using its mayonnaise on Christmas turkey leftovers, with the tagline, 'Don't save it for the summer'.

However, all sorts of doubts remained surrounding the season's impact on retail. It is unknown whether Christmas was simply concentrating the spending of disposable income rather than spreading it out over the year. There were also questions over whether the festival did much to sustain British manufacturing and over its negative impact on a few parts of the service sector. A boot repairer in Bolton, for example, noted in 1938 that his trade fell away before Christmas because there was only so much money around.[241] Christmas could also cost firms money in other ways. Small retailers might give gifts to their best customers and receive presents from their suppliers in turn.[242] Thus, despite the costs Christmas generated, between the wars working-class shoppers could also expect a little reward, such as a pudding or a few extra groceries, from the shops they gave their custom to.[243]

The positive impacts of Christmas were not limited to the increased business done by the shops. Christmas also injected money into the economy through seasonal bonuses, overtime pay and temporary jobs.[244] In December 1935, the distributive trades alone took on nearly 17,000 more people than the month before.[245] A 1924 government report on unemployment noted how it fell in industries as varied as shipping, transport, textile manufacture and pottery because of seasonal trade. However, the downside was an increase in unemployment after the Christmas activity ended. On 31 December 1923 unemployment in Britain was reported to be 113,129 higher than a fortnight before.[246] That situation did not change, although the temporary jobs created became more concentrated in large retail firms.

In October 2012, the *Daily Mirror* found some 73,000 being advertised or promised.[247]

This all made Christmas shopping a symbol of how well the economy was doing and the state of Christmas trade became a stock news item. In 1931, at the height of the depression, a cinema newsreel noted that the busy shopping scenes were an encouraging sight and it hoped people were buying British. These kinds of remarks continued after the war too, with the state of trade being used in the early 1950s to discuss the gradual return of afflu-ence.[248] By 1984, it was even being used to illustrate the north–south divide and the impact of the miners' strike.[249] Such reflections happened at a per-sonal level too. Christmas could be an opportunity to see some of the bene-fits of improved personal circumstances or the impacts of worsened ones.[250] The season thus proved a turning point in the 1984–5 miners' strike when, despite the charitable distributions of toys and turkeys, the festival intensi-fied the sense of sacrifice and loss among miners and their families. The fight went out of many and, in the period before and after Christmas, many returned to work.[251] A concentrated period of spending meant the festival also made people aware of inflation.[252] Yet, while Christmas spending was obviously affected by the state of the economy, it was also rather resilient to it because it was a time that mattered to people. Reports of consumer spend-ing on Christmas bucking economic trends were common but not universal and sometimes subject to regional variations. In 1931, for example, shops were reporting that few people were not giving presents, although most were choosing things at lower prices.[253] Similarly, amid the inflation crises of the early 1970s, there were mixed reports of the impact on Christmas. While some news items pointed to people shopping without much restraint, others maintained that spending was down, especially on luxury presents for adults.[254] Once again, Christmas was showing how understanding what was happening in the economy was open to very varying interpretations. All the historian can be absolutely sure of was that Christmas was a commercial phenomenon as much as anything else.

Conclusion

Shopping was an integral part of the Christmas experience, but it was not always a pleasant part. Even those who enjoyed the bustles and pressures of Christmas shopping could be uncomfortable about the amounts they were spending and wonder whether the 'true meanings' of the festival were being overshadowed. A survey in 2000 suggested that more than half of the people struggled with choosing gifts and more than 30 per cent found Christmas shopping traumatic, with queues, crowded shops and parking being cited as the most common causes. Nonetheless, just over a quarter of women and 11 per cent of men actually looked forward to it.[255] Polls also pointed to hugely varying levels of personal expenditure at Christmas time, levels that were not always related to people's ability to spend, while a 1973 survey estimated that just one in ten adults, mostly the elderly, did not give gifts.[256] Throughout the period there were those who spent heavily on the festival and those who spent very little, just as there were those who easily afforded their celebrations while there were others who had to scrimp, save or borrow. Such perspectives lend some credence to the historian John Benson who cautions against describing Britain as a consumer society because consumerism took on so many different forms and worked very differently for different groups and individuals.[257] Yet, consumerism was still an inescapable and integral feature of twentieth-century Britain. People may have consumed in different ways, but everyone did consume. With people throughout the period allowing offspring to choose presents, sometimes from a catalogue or sometimes at the shop, even very young children were consumers.[258]

Whether consumerism liberated or entrapped people is a matter for debate.[259] It could create a sense of empowerment through the pleasure associated with choosing how to spend, and it presented people with an

PLATE 5 *Christmas shopping crowds, Oxford Street, London, 17 December 1966. Keystone-France/Getty.*

opportunity to define themselves through what they bought and gave. Yet the consumption of the working class annoyed some intellectuals, who deplored what they saw as a dumbing down of cultural aspirations or a poor substitute for meaningful work or the bonds of tight-knit communities. It made some left-wing intellectuals particularly uncomfortable; they read into it a greed and individualism that undermined traditional working-class solidarities. Certainly, in the 1950s and 1960s there was a 'rugged individualism' among affluent workers. They were aspirational for themselves and for their children and sought to be free from authority and want.[260] Christmas and consumption in general was an expression of this. Yet the decline of working-class solidarity can hardly be blamed upon consumerism alone. Individualism predated people's ability to demonstrate that through spending. Consumption was also not about wanting to become middle class or abandoning one's roots. Instead, it was about breaking free of old constraints and living more comfortable lives.[261] Nonetheless, the comforts that spending brought did lessen the need for collective action and communal socializing. In this sense, consumption did make people's lives better, but also contributed to a loss in working-class community and political influence. Few thought of that in such explicit terms, but it is likely that this was an exchange that many would have willingly made. But there were other costs too. In 1999 one doctor reported how January usually brought a 'steady stream' of patients, some of whom were depressed that they had spent a lot of money, bringing debt and a lack of gratitude.[262]

Christmas also encapsulated how the choices people had at their disposal were within a framework that required people to spend if they wanted to live and eat and encouraged them to do so at levels and in ways that would affirm or change their status in the eyes of themselves and others. Given these pressures, it is difficult to see consumerism as something liberating for those were unable to consume much. Thus, as Hilda Ogden summed up in a 1987 episode of Coronation Street, Christmas was a good time for the 'haves', but not so good a time for the 'have nots'.[263] Extreme poverty became less common in the welfare age, furthering the homogenization of the Christmas experience across Britain, but at no point did it have to mean an unhappy Christmas. Some people did enjoy themselves on little money and it could be a rare moment of happiness in otherwise difficult lives.[264] Zweig's late 1940s study of London workers found it was perfectly possible to be happy and poor but he also found that personal relationships were fundamental to happiness.[265] And, above everything else, Christmas, including people's purchasing activities, was about celebrating and affirming relationships.

Moreover, choosing was not the only pleasure to be had in spending. In a 1945 novel a prosperous businessman buys crystallized fruit and oysters to take home for Christmas. Neither he nor his family actually liked crystallized fruit very much but 'it had been there on the counter and he was in the mood for buying things'.[266] People just enjoyed buying things and the critics tended to forget how liberating that could feel. Annoyed at those complaining about the commercialization of the festival, a Sussex newspaper editorial argued that shop displays brightened the lives of 'those accustomed to drab surroundings'.[267] For those without much, a present of chocolates or a handkerchief was a genuine moment of pleasure. The simplicity of gifts might have faded, but the intention did not. However much some people disliked what they regarded as the commercialization of Christmas, others enjoyed the 'shebang', from the buying to the giving and receiving. Thus, one Yorkshire miner noted in 1937 how animated people were choosing small cheap gifts in Woolworth's, and that these gifts would bring much pleasure.[268] Terry was right to declare in a 1980 episode of *Terry and June* that 'Christmas is the reward that we give ourselves for getting through another bloody year'.[269] The pleasures were felt by the rich too. Lady Asquith may have been the daughter of an Earl and the daughter-in-law of a recent prime minister, but she seemed rather happy recording in her 1917 diary the £7 in her stocking.[270] In a 2002 survey only a third of the respondents reported that they did not like the festival's commercialization and slightly fewer reported fearing spending too much.[271]

Christmas did give this minority an opportunity to express their discomfort with the consumerism of society. In the early 1990s in the United States, a Buy Nothing Day emerged in response to the general concerns surrounding consumerism and Christmas. It quickly spread across the world, being held in the UK at the end of November, the start of the main Christmas shopping season. Others made more personal stands. Politician Edwina Currie recorded in her diary in 1987 that the commercialism of Christmas made her 'nauseous'. She had a 'deal' with her children: they did not get presents, but she took them to the sales afterwards.[272] Far more went along with the traditions, but that did not mean they were entirely comfortable with the festival's commercialism. Nor were those who claimed that Christmas had become more commercial wrong. There was probably more advertising and higher levels of expenditure and consumption. Yet this was not just true of Christmas but of society in general and the festival was simply symptomatic of a wider shift rather than some free-standing anomaly. Moreover, as shopping shifted to multiple stores, Christmas also seemed more commercial just because people were shopping for it in bigger shops, with bigger advertising budgets than in the past.

Commercialism was one of the reasons why the festival survived and prospered. Advertisers ensured the festival dominated the media in December, encouraged people to spend and reminded them of what was coming. Yet commercialism did not undermine the family and charitable elements of Christmas. Family ties were reaffirmed through the process of buying gifts, while charitable donations were often made on shopping expeditions by people perhaps feeling a little guilty at what they were spending on their family. Indeed, as the twenty-first century progressed, some advertisers turned to promoting the emotion of Christmas rather than any specific product. John Lewis' 2011 Christmas advert, for example, said nothing at all about goods, but instead showed a small boy desperate for Christmas to come so he could give his parents a present. The tagline was 'For gifts you can't wait to give'. It literally brought some viewers to tears and two years later had had over six million views online. Although some were cynical about such ploys, consumerism was simply not at odds with the other meanings of Christmas. Intentionally or otherwise, it was an act of generosity, a way to express family and social bonds. Nor was it necessarily at odds with the religious and charitable elements of Christmas. People could and did buy goods where the proceeds or profits went to a good cause.

Whatever the relationship between commercialism and Christmas, what is certain is that on Christmas Day most shops and businesses stayed closed. Indeed, whereas the Sabbath lost its power over consumerism in the 1990s, a Christmas Day (Trading) Act was passed in 2004 to prevent larger shops opening. However much Christmas was decried as a symbol of out of control commercialism, the 25th of December was actually the quietest consumer day of the year. Yet even then, some £76 million was taken out of UK Link cash machines on 25 December 2012. Moreover, the internet was making shopping easier than ever and an estimated £300 million was spent online on Christmas morning 2012.[273] People's appetite for consumption was insatiable.

CHAPTER TWO

The family Christmas

In his 1934 Christmas Day broadcast, George V said that Christmas was 'the festival of the family'. It was a statement of the obvious, but it was also a very powerful image. Family was the building block that society was built on and it was the unit most people lived in and aspired to. The importance that people placed upon family meant there was considerable concern after 1945 at what people thought was its decline. Sociological factors seemed to be undermining it, as people moved around in search of work, old working-class communities were broken up or moved by slum clearances, divorce rates rose, and increasing numbers of women got jobs and thus no longer lived lives dominated by domestic responsibilities. People often felt the very concept of family was undervalued too. It was never explicitly attacked by anyone of any political stature but the growth of the state, business and trade unions often created a sense that the ordinary bloke and his family did not count for much anymore.

Thus, as the twentieth century progressed, Christmas seemed an increasingly rare time when family clearly mattered. It was a time when relatives came together and retreated from the pressures of work and the outside world. They expressed their ties through gift-giving and by following their own interpretations of wider customs and rituals. One 1922 writer argued the festival's 'real charm' lay in how it brought different generations together in a fashion where dignity and conventions were cast aside in favour of everyone having fun together.[1] In 1960 *The Times* claimed that what family life owed to Christmas was 'altogether incalculable'.[2] Psychologists too saw in Christmas an idea of resolving family discord and argued that this was its 'perennial attraction'.[3]

The festival may have seemed an ideal of family harmony, but the reality was more complex. Spousal arguments, complaints from awkward aunts, teenage tantrums, or embarrassed silences with in-laws or step siblings all meant that family get-togethers were not always pleasant occasions. For wives and mothers, Christmas often meant a considerable amount of work and preparation that was not always appreciated. Both sexes could get depressed when television replaced the family games they remembered of their youth or when sibling gatherings stopped with the death of elderly parents.[4] Christmas could thus represent the wider notion of family decline in microcosm. Yet family itself was not a straightforward concept; for some it meant the immediate nuclear unit, while for others it was always an extended entity. Again, Christmas could bring disputes and tensions over this into focus.

Pleasant or otherwise, the stories of Christmases past entered family folklore, that web of memories that defines and binds families together. Moreover, while the unhappy may often be the most visible and audible in society, they are often the least representative. On the whole, people's memories of Christmas were pleasant and nostalgic, dominated by recollections of presents, television and family.[5] Families might not have often lived up to an idealized notion of happiness and harmony, but most, whatever shape they took, were loving units that provided emotional stability and security. It was for this reason they remained at the heart of society. By the twenty-first century, families may have taken different shapes to their earlier forms, but their roles and functions were as strong as ever and Christmas played its part in cementing their unity.

PLATE 6 *Family Christmas tea, 1919. Topical Press Agency/Getty.*

Family gatherings

It was the Victorian middle class that had turned Christmas into a festival of the family. For them the festival was a celebration of kin and domesticity. Dickens captured this in his *Christmas Carol*. The Cratchits' love meant they were happy despite their poverty and when Scrooge comes to his senses, it is not to his employee's house he heads but to his nephew's. Family gatherings were common for the interwar middle classes too. They might not have lasted the whole day, but it was certainly common for extended families to come together and for adult children to celebrate with their parents. For example, in 1937, an eighteen-year-old student in Hove recorded that his family always came together at his grandparents' house, about a mile away, where the gathering was swelled by various friends. This may have been what was expected, but it did not mean people of that age group liked it. That same year, a 28-year-old woman noted that the younger generation would like to abandon the traditional family Christmas, but kept it up for the sake of older relatives. Similarly, a former student in Cardiff noted that most of his friends thought they had to stay at home with their family at Christmas. Few of them did this for the whole day, but he thought there was a slight feeling of guilt when this unwritten rule was broken.[6]

For the masses, the dynamics were rather different. Many Victorian working-class families had strong contact on a regular basis because they lived very near each other, but that traditional pattern was gradually being undermined as people moved around in search of work. Thus, just as was the case for the middle classes, as the festival grew in importance at the end of the nineteenth century, so too did the number of working-class people who travelled back to see their families. This was enabled by rising real wages, the spread of the railways, Christmas Day trains and the creation of Boxing Day as a public holiday in the 1870s.[7] The interwar depression furthered that pattern, as the industrial districts of the north, central Scotland and South Wales haemorrhaged their young and unemployed to the more prosperous Midlands and south. Such were the levels of movement that one Yorkshire miner noted that many people had left his village to return home to other coal districts for Christmas. But, of course, not every family actually wanted to get together. In 1937, a Farnborough electrician recorded that some families were simply not 'clannish' – his extended relatives did not meet up or interest him.[8]

Quite how common it was for adult children or siblings to return to the family home is not something for which there exists clear evidence. Some historians claim that by 1914 a family gathering at Christmas was still not the norm for probably a majority of the working class. After all, money was limited for a large meal, cooking facilities were inadequate and houses were small.[9] As living standards improved, for those in work at least, family gatherings do seem to have become more common, especially for those families where no overnight stay was required. By 1941 Mass Observation was arguing that family gatherings were a 'feature of the usual Christmas procedure'.[10] Even in some families that lived relatively near each other, Christmas could be the only time of year children saw their grandparents.[11] Some working-class people recorded in the 1930s the social pressure that existed on people to get together with their families, even if they saw their family all the time. One warehouseman recorded in 1937 how those whose families were dispersed enjoyed the reunion, but for him it was 'just another tea down home'.[12] The problem of space remained and a miner's son from near Stoke remembers his extended family eating Christmas tea in shifts because there was not enough room. Chairs and cutlery might have to be borrowed and people could eat in different rooms or sitting on armchairs rather than at the table.[13] A 1950s study of a Liverpool slum found that Christmas 'dos' were important, but might simply be a visit to Mum on Christmas Day.[14] Indeed, gatherings often did not entail eating Christmas dinner together, thus sidestepping issues of cost and space. Perhaps with a degree of exaggeration, one Lowestoft woman, whose mother had eleven siblings, reminisced about her extended family's pre-war Christmas Day gatherings – there were forty people in the front room and five children were meant to sleep in one bed. 'It gave you a sense of such security; you felt you were related to everybody.'[15] The space issue was not always much better in middle-class families. The autobiography of one writer recalls breaking under the strain of Christmas 1938. There were fourteen people in his bungalow and just one toilet; the continuous sound of its use drove him to irritation.[16]

Sociologists in the 1950s East End found that family gatherings were most common while parents were still alive. After that the levels of contact between siblings might drop significantly and traditions of the extended family meeting for Christmas would often come to an end. But they also noted how the practice of adults returning to their parents' home for Christmas was a way of reaffirming membership of the family.[17] A 1960s study of middle-class London found similar patterns, with more than two-thirds of households studied having relations who visited at Christmas, whether that was for dinner, tea, a cocktail party or to stay. It also noted that family members absent from a reunion might be telephoned during it. There was a belief that family mattered and that it gave the children a sense of security. There was much variation in how far ideas of family extended to invitations and this was influenced by logistics and how well people got on as much as anything, but there was also a sense of duty that relatives living alone should be invited.[18] A study of the working class in the late 1950s argued that family relationships improved with growing affluence, because people had happier childhoods, fathers took greater roles in bringing up the children and relatives became more a source of help than burden. It also noted that because families were becoming more dispersed around the country, there was less fear of family interference and censorship, which encouraged the reunions that affluence enabled.[19]

Family dispersal was happening in all classes in the post-war period. For some, the cause might be moving in search of work, especially among children who had been able to climb the social ladder thanks to a grammar school education. But it could also be down to the population movements brought about by slum clearances and the building of new housing estates. Such dispersals meant festive gatherings were not assured or automatic but where they did take place they often became more sustained, a trip of a few days rather than a few hours. They were made easier by rising levels of affluence and car ownership but any gathering was still limited by the question of where to put people, especially if an overnight stay was required. Meeting at hotels could be a solution to both space and geography but this was increasingly unfashionable after the war and at odds with the festival's emphasis on home. The problems of space did at least ease as the size of families decreased: the average number of children fell steadily from 3.4 for those married in the Edwardian period to 1.8 in 2012.[20] But more family gatherings meant a new dilemma emerged for couples who now had to decide whose set of parents to spend the festival and associated days with. As a 1986 writer put it, 'The simple enquiry about your whereabouts and the company you'll be keeping on 25 December oozes with sour layers of family history.'[21] Those with children tended to stay at home and ask people to come to them, although that could still cause tensions over which set of parents to invite.[22] Such issues were intensified by the growing number of divorces and remarriages. By the late 1970s, 11 per cent of all dependent children, nearly 1.5 million of them, were living in one-parent families.[23] Some children of all ages could even end up eating two different Christmas dinners in a day to ensure their company was shared between divorced parents. But there were other parents who did not get to see their young children on Christmas Day at all. Whatever arrangement was used, the vast majority of people of all classes did spend the festival with family. A 1951 poll found that only one in ten were not going to spend Christmas at home, while in a 1969 survey 88 per cent of respondents said they would be spending Christmas with family and only 5 per cent on their own.[24] Those polls did not, however, interrogate what people meant by family and missed how for most people the concept did centre on the nuclear rather than extended unit. This was clearer in a 1972 poll that found that half respondents were spending Christmas Day itself just with their own household.[25]

In 1937, a 28-year-old female press assistant recorded that her family did not really enjoy Christmas because 'we are all rather solitary individuals and like reading or getting on with our own hobbies. We find it hard to adjust ourselves to the sudden spasm of sociability which seems to be demanded of one at Christmas.' Her mother, however, was an exception and it was for her sake that the family came together for two or three days at Christmas.[26] Across the century, in the families where people who did not live together came together, it was often because it was 'the thing to do' and relatives expected it of them, another Christmas tradition and ritual. But that did not always mean it was a pleasurable experience.[27] A 1961 novel suggested that at Christmas people lost their status as individuals and adults, becoming 'mere units' within a family, put in their place and sent back to 'the nursery or cradle, almost'.[28] Domestic rows at Christmas became so common that they became a familiar source of humour. A 2012 novel could thus quip: 'The whole day had gone reasonably well considering most civil wars can trace their origins back to a difficult family Christmas.'[29] Spending prolonged time with one's family could make people aware, or simply remind them, of their relatives' faults. On Christmas Eve 1948, one diarist recorded that he 'wondered how I could possibly survive Christmas: my father's thin jokes, my mother's fuss about the cooking, Deenie's fuss lest the robin might not return to its bird-bath and her radiators freeze during her absence from home'.[30] In some families, things started well but tensions grew as the holiday continued, especially if too much alcohol was involved. By Boxing Day, the whole dynamic might change, as people unused to living with each other struggled without the distractions of the rituals of the day before. For those whose personality or politics did not fit in with the dominant values of the family, Christmas could be a particularly trying time, which might involve much biting of one's tongue. One twenty-year-old student recorded her unhappiness after a family gathering for Christmas 1937: 'All rather false, as they hate and despise me, and I loathe being here.'[31] Half a century later, a few students could even be found staying at university for the whole Christmas break because they were alienated from their families. These may have been extreme examples, but they highlight the intergenerational tensions that could exist as a result of different values. Although people were always individuals, there is evidence to support the popular idea that the middle-aged were more anxious, cautious and conservative than the young and tensions between middle-aged parents and teenage children seem to have become more common as the century progressed.[32] Leaving home could therefore be a relief to both sides but Christmas brought back what people had escaped. Roy Strong's 1969 Boxing Day diary entry, for example, was devoted to lamenting and criticizing his father's life, behaviour and even appearance.[33] Such tensions went in the other direction too and encounters could lead old people to be annoyed by their younger relatives and the young in general.[34] However, parents did seem to be better than their children at the unconditional love family was supposed to be about.

Although family arguments were a staple of festive television comedies, they were not always funny. In 1999 one doctor noted how January usually brought a 'steady stream' of patients 'trying to come to terms with the fact that Christmas brought them misery instead of magic'. Their problems related to eating, shopping or sex and were often compounded by what he called 'spouse saturation syndrome', where people grew frustrated from unrealistic expectations of their partners.[35] As early as the 1970s, the Samaritans were putting on a special service for Christmas. In 1975, a Lancashire refuge reported that 'in our world it is the worst battering season of the year, if only because of the financial pressure and booze'.[36] By the twenty-first century, reported domestic violence could spike by as much as a third on Christmas Day. Home Office statistics showed between Christmas Eve and 6 January the murder rate was then around 25 per cent higher than the average for December and January.[37] Divorce lawyers too were recording Christmas Day emails and website visits from people who appear to have decided that their marriage was over.[38] Avoiding seasonal family tensions was thus a matter of serious concern throughout the period. One 1915 writer even maintained that the best way of keeping the Christmas spirit was not to insist that it had to be a family festival.[39] More prosaically, as early as the 1920s there were articles on games and activities that could be used to stop family get-togethers becoming strained.[40] Other people simply put on a 'facade of contentment' in order to keep the peace.[41] The result could be, as Agatha Christie's Poirot noted in a 1938 novel, 'a great amount of *strain*. People who do not *feel* amiable are putting great pressure on themselves to *appear* amiable!' He thus maintained there was a great deal of hypocrisy at Christmas, even if it was for honourable reasons.[42]

We should be wary of thinking that every family was like this. Moreover, given how arguments were hardly unique to Christmas, especially in families beset by financial or marital problems, the festive season could actually be a respite from turmoil and not a trigger for it.[43] Even within families where there was strife, there was still also usually love. If there was not, no amount of social convention would have been enough to pull them together, especially in a society where divorce was socially acceptable and family had come to mean many different things. More common than arguing was having a rewarding time. Christmas could be an opportunity to renew old acquaintances or get to know new in-laws.[44] Or it was simply, as the *Daily Mirror* put it in 2007, 'about having a laugh with the people you love'.[45] That might seem sentimental to the cynical but many people felt it. In 1937, a 34-year-old London housewife with a young daughter summed up her day: 'No quarrelling. No discontent, No spite. No disappointment. A happy Christmas.'[46] In a survey sixty years later, just 18 per cent said that family arguments was a cause of Christmas dread, while just 6 per cent said the same of either visiting the family or having them to stay. These were similar figures to the 6 per cent who feared the television breaking down and the 17 per cent who worried about the central heating breaking.[47] Research in the United States found that people reported greater levels of happiness if their Christmas was dominated by family or religious experiences rather than by spending and receiving presents. It also suggested that while most people were happier at Christmas than at other times, levels of upset were not different to other times of year.[48]

Indeed, Christmas not only made most families happy, but also helped define and bond them. It created a break in the working year to ensure that the good intentions of keeping in touch were actually acted on. It was an opportunity to remember those no longer alive, cementing a sense of family continuity.[49] The festive rituals families established also helped develop their sense of identity – whether that was where they hung their stockings, when presents were opened, or what entertainments were enjoyed. Christmas stories became a shared family memory. They were retold each year and embodied in photographs, homemade decorations and treasured gifts. New parents could gain a sense of forging their own family identity through merging the traditions of their respective childhoods. Christmas was thus not just a reflection of the importance of family in British society, but also helped make and maintain that importance.

Children

In 1948, the poet Cecil Day Lewis declared 'when we have children of our own, we soon find ourselves taking Christmas seriously again, co-operating with them in the shaping of a new model Christmas Day, which in its turn modifies, replenishes and marries with the Christmas of our own childhood, till memory can hardly tell the old and new apart'.[50] Since its Victorian reinvention, Christmas had been a celebration of childhood both past and present. This extended to a popular recognition that Christmas could connect adults with their own childhood and create opportunities to give children happy memories for future life. Indeed, the festival's revival owed much to the changing value placed upon childhood in that period. This extended beyond legislative developments that protected children from work and extended their education, to a celebration and even indulgence of their imagination and childhood in general.[51] The seasonal focus on children was also enhanced by the endorsement of churches who linked their preaching and theology to celebrations of childhood. This was not a cynical move – after all, the religious focus of the festival was the celebration of the birth of a child – but it did help legitimize the wider emphasis on children brought about by the veneration of childhood and encouraged by commercial forces seeking to sell toys.[52]

After the Great War, there were further social changes that encouraged the focus on children at Christmas. The decline in family sizes that followed the Victorian period helped ensure that children could expect more attention from their parents than generations before. By the interwar period, two or three children had become the norm and one impact of this was that children spent more time at home, even if the streets remained their primary playground. This was not just because there was more space at home, but because those homes were increasingly more comfortable and, with the wireless, more entertaining too.[53] There were also cultural pressures to encourage more intimate relationships between children and parents. Inter-war parenting manuals depicted children and their passions as something to be enjoyed rather than suppressed and controlled. This naturally extended to Christmas and as early as the 1920s there were

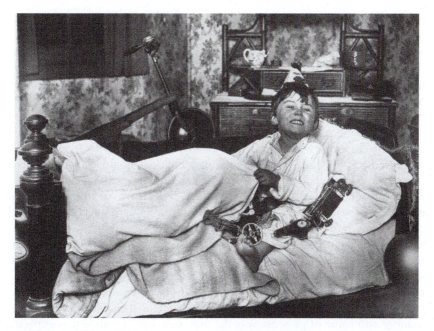

PLATE 7 *A child on Christmas morning, 1925. Kirby/Getty.*

articles stressing the importance of choosing the right gifts for children and involving them in the festive preparations.[54] This was a recognition of their individuality and the importance of fostering that. The *Evening Standard* noted in 1933 that 'the done thing' now was to take children shopping, so they could choose their presents.[55] The mass of parents may not have been able to indulge their children in the fashion of the middle class but that did not mean they did not have the same aspirations to ensure their children were happy and that was an important driver in the monies that people willing to spend on the festival. During the Second World War too, Mass Observation were told by a number of respondents that the only reason to celebrate Christmas in the circumstances was for the sake of the children.[56] Moreover, people drew genuine pleasure through seeing their children happy.[57] Children were something to be enjoyed rather than just nurtured.

However, the material shortages in many working-class families con-strained what could be done to make children happy. Even when it came to food, it was often the breadwinner who had the first claim, simply because the whole family depended on the income generated by his manual labour. In the 1930s, observers claimed that some men even locked their children out of the house on Christmas Eve to stop them taking the next day's food, while they spent a long evening in the pub.[58] However, in the 1950s and 1960s, there does seem to have been a cultural shift in working-class fami-lies. The child increasingly became the focal point of the family and con-temporary sociological studies noted the significant pride people had in their children. Children were treated less severely than their parents had been and there was significant investment of time and resources in their emotional well-being.[59] Family consumption moved away from prioritizing the breadwinner towards parents making sacrifices to allow the children to have more toys or better food. Helped by rising family incomes and better housing, children might now have their own room and pocket money was becoming the norm. Rising wages also meant they no longer had to start earning as soon as they were old enough, and it was not unreasonable to expect bright children to climb the social ladder, thanks to free grammar school education. Indeed, it was because children could lead better lives than their parents had that those same parents were willing to make sacrifices and endure hardships to help their children.[60] All this might have meant there was less need to indulge children at Christmas time – after all they now more indulged throughout the year – but what it actually did was lead to children being better treated at Christmas. They increasingly received multiple presents and were free from an expectation that any present they gave back should be of equal value. Christmas seemed to become a route to ensuring the happy childhood that both psychologists and ordinary families believed was important.[61] Affluence enabled that and the growing number and value of presents was the outcome. But gratitude was expected and that brought its own reward. One man remembered of being a generous parent in the 1950s: 'The kids would come up to us and say, "This is the best Christmas we've ever had," and that would make it all worthwhile.'[62]

Youth's centrality to Christmas was given state recognition when there was a children's competition to design a festive stamp in 1966 (although stamp collectors thought this undignified and wrote to the press about the disgrace it was bringing).[63] That decade also saw a growth in the idea of that children had a right to be safe and well treated. Public places gradually became more child friendly and even breast feeding in public became generally acceptable. Childhood itself was also getting longer and in 1972 the school leaving age was raised to sixteen. This desire to recognize and protect the rights of children had the side effect, however, of making children less and less free. The streets gradually became seen as threats rather than playgrounds. In 1971 research suggested that around 80 per cent of seven- and eight-year-olds were allowed to go to school on their own but two decades later this had fallen to fewer than one in ten, while half of nine-year-olds were not even allowed to cross the road on their own.[64] Children's free time was also increasingly geared more towards organized activities instead of unstructured and unsupervised play. The late twentieth century thus saw children richer in material goods and attention than their parents had been but poorer in the freedom to discover the world beyond their more affluent homes. They even saw their parents less as divorce became commoner and more and more women worked full-time with nurseries and nannies taking on some of the childcare that had traditionally happened in the home. In such a context, indulging children at Christmas became a subconscious compensation. Guilt is not unusual as a motivator in contemporary consumer behaviour, but in some ways this was a return to the remorse of the nineteenth-century middle class, for whom expensive presents had helped fill a perceived void of diminished social contact between parents and children.[65]

Few children's presents were completely free of the assumptions and aspirations of parents either. Thus, the twelve-year-old son of a Tylorstown teacher recorded in his 1952 diary that he woke at 4.00 am and received nineteen books and a stocking.[66] Of course, educational presents could still be rewarding and even fun and it certainly was not just books that were laden with improving undertones. Lego and other construction toys were thought to develop creativity, while board games were supposed to bring families together. Other toys were shot through with the gender assumptions of parents and the toy industry. An oral history study of working-class women who grew up before 1939 found that those who received toys at Christmas always mentioned dolls first, leading a historian to argue they were being 'conditioned' into being mothers.[67] Even in the late twentieth century, girls' toys remained highly gendered, dominated by pink colours, and caring or creative methods of play. For boys, meanwhile, sporting goods, toy soldiers and guns were always common illustrating how stable certain assumptions about masculinity were. But none of this meant that people did not also try to buy things that their children would like and Christmas was as much about celebrating childhood *per se* as it was about trying to shape it.

There may have been sociological reasons underpinning how children were treated at Christmas but that did not mean it was not a magical time for the young. Part of this was the excitement of the anticipation. It was something to look forward to and countdown to. Advent calendars ritualized that process and their late twentieth-century shift from revealing a picture each day to giving a chocolate or even a toy was another sign of the growing indulgence of children. Central to what people were looking forward to was the festival's otherness; even for most interwar working-class children Christmas represented a significant contrast to everyday life. The food was better than normal; there was the fun of decorations in the house and, of course, there were presents. Even a stocking of a new penny, some nuts and an orange was a significant luxury. As one interwar recipient of such booty remembered: 'What magic to find to waken and find that Father Christmas had not forgotten us – that someone cared!'[68] In such cases, it was clear that the magic came from simply receiving any sort of gift. However, measuring joy is very difficult and the excitement of children from more affluent backgrounds was also substantial. A man interviewed in the 1980s clearly remembered the joy of receiving a train in 1926: 'It was a feeling which has never in fact left me from that day to this, and thrill of it I can still feel inside me.'[69]

It would be quite wrong to dismiss such feelings as greed or consumerism, not least because many younger children believed that the gifts had come from the magical figure that was Santa Claus. Christmas was a rare personal encounter with magic for children who lived in a real world. Of course, the nature of that reality shifted over time. In the early twentieth century, life for working-class children could be hard, deprived and even brutal. There was little attempt to protect them from the realities of growing up poor, but there was also considerable ignorance about adult life and the wider world. There was a widespread belief in a God that must have seemed mysterious but this brought little material reward. The magic of Christmas was thus not rooted in the existence of wonderful ideas and individuals alone but in the evidence it provided through Santa of the existence of a benevolent external figure that did make life better. As the century progressed, material deprivation declined and knowledge increased. Growing secularism meant less emphasis in daily life on magical figures that stood beyond humanity. Awe and wonder were now something communicated via the television set. Even the night sky, which had its own sense of magic that encouraged people to consider their individual insignificance, became less visible. Christmas helped fill that void, bringing children into contact with a magic that was otherwise absent in their lives. Popular culture certainly encouraged young children to see Christmas as a magical time. In family films, snow was the norm, reindeer could fly, everyone was happy and it was all led by a cuddly, larger than life benevolent figure at the head of an army of hardworking chirpy elves. Even those tales that subverted this image tended to see balance restored at the end. Nor were such images bound by conventions and there were always updates (such as *Holly the Christmas Fairy* whose job is 'to make sure that Christmas is as sparkly and happy as possible'[70]) that kept to the broad parameters of what Christmas meant but spoke in a language that contemporary children related to.

It was adults that had created this magical world but they were often uncomfortable with it because children's reaction was not always the simple innocence they hoped for. In 1915, Lady Cynthia Asquith recorded in her diary: 'Got up early to see the children opening their stockings. It was like the nightmare of a spoilt child.'[71] That year there were other complaints that children did not always appreciate Christmas because they were becoming more precocious than they used to be.[72] People found themselves torn between, as one 1968 writer put it, a belief that Christmas was for children and despair at their 'flushed over-excited faces pink with predatory lusts'.[73] Such concerns over how self-centred and greedy the festival could make children grew, as the general attention and the number of presents bestowed on children multiplied. Christmas lists and requests meant there were interwar concerns that young were sending in their orders as if Santa was a tradesman. In 1921 the *Daily Mail* complained that children not only expected presents but criticized them and sometimes did not bother remembering who had given them what.[74] Extended family felt it too. By 1951 a man was complaining about 'little children trained by their mothers to expect something from all uncles, real or not, who regard me, about the middle of December, in a new calculating way, weighing up whether I am worth a toy train or a box of bricks'. That same year, a letter to the *Daily Mirror* complained of people buying expensive toys for their children, saying that children should be taught that Santa only brings presents that fit in a sock.[75]

The response to such concerns took a number of different forms. There were some rich fathers who disapproved of giving presents to those who expected them for fear of making children extravagant.[76] A 1934 manual on common sense in the nursery opined the importance of ensuring Christmas was not just associated with receiving toys and recommended that from the age of two-and-a-half children should give presents and understand what they were doing. To help teach them gratitude to their parents, it advocated avoiding the 'all too common' mistake of letting children think Father Christmas brought all the presents. To prevent a 'grasping attitude', it recommended that children not be allowed to use their father's stocking or a pillow case because their own sock would not hold enough.[77] Making children buy presents for their parents and perhaps other relatives too seems to have become relatively common in middle-class families by the 1950s but it quickly grew in all families where children received pocket money.[78] Forcing children to wait to open some of their presents with the rest of the family, rather than simply ripping everything open upon getting up, was another way to teach children control and gratitude. Making children write thank you letters was yet another response that developed in the middle of the century and one that turned into a chore that no one much liked, children or the parents who had to supervise it. In another example of people feeling children were getting less grateful, there was also a sense that the habit of thank you letters declined at the end of the twentieth century.[79] Others held festive parties where the children were consciously not the centre of attention. A 1951 article in the *Daily Mirror* about such parties argued that children had to realize that Christmas was not just for them and that there were times when they would have to be quiet.[80] But these were small steps and most parents simply went along with the tendency to indulge their children, even when they were uncomfortable with the outcomes. Chris Mullin, Labour MP for Sunderland South, recorded in his 2002 dairy that he did his best to look cheerful while his daughter grudgingly kept a list of who had given her what. He found it 'a deeply depressing experience watching children who have everything piling up new possessions' and was relieved when it was all over.[81] Such were the feelings of helplessness that by 1969 *The Times* had a child psychologist writing on how to survive Christmas with children.[82]

The selfishness of children should not be exaggerated. A few of the complaints were little more than the moaning of adults who just did not like Christmas or maybe even their children. Before the Second World War, some people were grumbling that their children came home from boarding school for Christmas, bringing with them expense, noise and bustle.[83] In 1945 Evelyn Waugh recorded in his diary: 'By keeping the children in bed for long periods we managed to have a tolerable day.'[84] Moreover, it was unrealistic to expect children to have the emotional maturity not to express their feelings about Christmas in terms that concentrated on what they were given. To their credit most did tend to be rather realistic in what they asked for. During the Second World War, for example, one girl's letter to Santa, simply asked for 'any little thing you can spare'.[85] Such realism does not need to indicate that they did not really believe in Father Christmas but rather that they knew that the world was unfair, with some people being lucky and others less so. Nor did their delight in presents mean that they could not be religious, think of others or enjoy the family-centred nature of the day. It was not just the gifts that made children happy but whole event and context – the anticipation, the ritual and associated trappings, and the fact that it was all done with parents, who, for once, were perhaps not otherwise distracted. Moreover, it is surely not unreasonable to suggest that even the Manchester boy who wrote to Santa in 1953 asking for a flying saucer and two guns that fired real bullets was grateful for whatever he received in the end.[86]

As children grew older their relationship with Christmas changed. Although youth culture became more distinct in the 1950s, there was also a teenage culture in the first half of the century, which had its own sense of style and distance from older people.[87] The close contact over a sustained period, meant that, like holidays away, Christmas was a moment when teenagers were acutely aware of their families. For some this was a pleasant experience but for others it was not, particularly only children who found themselves cut off temporarily from contact with others their own age. In 1937, one London woman was told by her middle-class teenage male cousin that Christmas was like Sunday: there was nothing to do between the eating. He concluded by saying, 'You don't live on Christmas day. It's only existing.'[88] There was also a wealth of opportunities for teenagers to be embarrassed or offended by the fashion or musical tastes of relatives who bought them presents, or by the expectations that they join in what could be perceived as childish family games.[89] Rejecting or laughing at Christmas was not uncommon as a way of signally a new adulthood and maturity. In 1919, unimpressed with family games, sixteen-year-old Evelyn Waugh recorded in his diary: 'Like birthdays, Christmas gets duller and duller. Soon it will be merely a day when the shops are most inconveniently shut.'[90] Research in American shopping mauls in the 1980s found that this was evident in encounters with store Santas. Teenage girls flirted with him, while boys could be quite hostile and mock him. In doing so, both sexes were rejecting their childhoods and proclaiming their adulthood.[91] One reason why teenagers were keen to do this was that childhood itself was actually getting longer. If its end was marked by the school leaving age then it was set at fourteen in 1914, fifteen in 1944 and sixteen in 1972. This meant there was a longer period when teenagers were not financially independent or recognized as the young adults they felt themselves to be and a family Christmas, with all its associations of childhood, reminded them of that. But that did not mean they could not enjoy the festival, and not just because it meant presents. By 1980, the *Jackie Annual* was telling girls that Christmas was 'a great time for meeting boys, as there are lots of parties and lots of mistletoe about too'. It promised that if it snowed there would be lots of boys in the park and advised going carol singing because it was a chance to hold hands in the dark. The advice for those who wanted to get rid of their boyfriend was to return all his letters and presents in a stocking or to ask him if he would be the fairy on the top of your tree.[92] As they grew older, a Christmas Eve in the pub became more important for many young people than the day itself, leading *The Likely Lads* to declare in 1964 that waking up on Christmas morning and reaching for an aspirin rather than a Rupert album was a moment in every bloke's life.[93]

Men and women

Of all the changes in British society since 1914, the position of women in public life was perhaps the most significant. The wake of both world wars saw women celebrated as the foundations of a domestic ideal, but by the end of the twentieth century, girls expected to have a career and to be treated the same as boys. It was a norm for married women to work and discrimination in the workplace was illegal. Women could be found in just about every position of influence and power in society. A woman was head of state and one had been prime minister. But gender equality remained a mirage. In the workplace men were still dominant; in the home women still bore the greatest burden of housework and childcare. Christmas, and especially the question of who prepared the dinner, was a clear illustration that women were still regarded as the chief homemakers in society. Yet their role in the festival was not just as the worker; they were also central to organizing and promoting it. This was viewed as another example of women's altruism. Before the Second World War, local and national newspapers acknowledged the strains of festive preparations, telling readers that it was women who made Christmas better for everyone else. For example, one writer in the *Daily Mail* remarked in 1935, 'We know very well who it is that, in most of our homes, keeps alive the Yuletide tradition of kindliness and good will.'[94] Indeed, without them, the family Christmas would have looked very different and *Coronation Street's* Hilda Ogden was quite right to remark in a 1987 episode that 'it's women what keep Christmas going, always have done'.[95] Research in Canada in the 1980s found that women felt obliged to buy presents for the wider family, whereas men only did for their immediate family.[96]

Yet, as one American study of the festival noted, it was a mythical man who was seen at the festival's spiritual heart and he even received the credit for the presents that women had bought.[97] The more radically minded feminist might see a conspiracy here, especially when advertising encouraged women to see both their festive and everyday roles as a provider for others. A 1925 advertisement for porcelain-enamelled kitchen tabletops noted that 'a housewife's Christmas is largely spent in providing enjoyment for *others*. Only when her work is finished – when she has cleared away – washed up and cleaned up – can *she* enter into the festivities … if she is not too tired.' It claimed a new tabletop would make the cleaning up easier.[98] A 1930 advertisement for a restorative tonic told women that with Christmas coming they must build up their strength: 'For your own sake as well as for the sake of those happiness depends on you'.[99] Mid-century cookers were similarly marketed with the promise that they would mean women could spend more time at Christmas joining in the fun and games.[100] Of course, no advertisement trying to sell a labour-saving device was going to suggest getting someone to help instead but women's publications also took the line that preparing for Christmas was a female realm. One reassured readers in 1930 that taking an interest in festive preparations and domesticity was quite fashionable for modern women.[101] In 1936 *Woman's Own* even proclaimed 'If you *love* Christmas and all that it means, you won't mind extra work'. In 1958 it told readers that just fifteen minutes relaxation in a whole day should be enough to keep them healthy at Christmas. Throughout the period, such publications emphasized the importance of planning celebrations.[102] The intention was to help women cope but the implication was that Christmas had to be a major logistical operation. A 1965 annual, for example, included an eight-week plan for Christmas preparations and told readers that gift shopping should be started seven weeks before the big day.[103] That was typical of how women were being told how to do Christmas in books or newspaper and magazine columns that on the surface simply offered Christmas advice but were actually rather dictatorial. Of course, Christmas guidebooks were not explicitly aimed at women, but it is difficult to imagine that the intended market was not women, particularly when the photographs within them were always of women and children. Published advice certainly pushed women to take on more work than was necessary. Thus, in the 1930s, women's magazines encouraged women to make not just the food but gifts, decorations and outfits too and to ensure that they looked their best. In 1949 the *Daily Mirror* told women to go to bed early on Christmas Eve and suggested that readers try and make a realistic snow scene on the icing of the Christmas cake. In 1966 *The Times* told readers that 'There is no excuse for giving a badly wrapped present'.[104] In 2010, a book entitled *The Best Christmas Ever* claimed coordinated colour schemes for wrapping presents were important. A 2008 publication, *The Perfect Christmas*, even told women to clean the whole house before Christmas, room by room, although it was careful to instruct that the rest of family should help too.[105]

By the twenty-first century, women's magazines were at least placing less emphasis on a perfect Christmas and acknowledging the problems and stresses. Yet the narrative of advice and guidance they offered was often contradictory: drink and eat to excess but control your intake, spend what you want but do not overshop, organize and plan but getting things wrong is fine, do it all yourself but do not be pressurized into being a superwoman.[106] One book, based on a BBC television series, offered the advice:

It's great fun and much more satisfying to make your own decorations, cards, cakes and presents, but Christmas is such a busy time of year that I'm all for cheating as much as is necessary to cope. There's no point in struggling to do everything yourself if it means you're going to end up too stressed and exhausted to enjoy yourself.[107]

Yet the book was still full of guides on making your own presents and decorations, food and entertainment. There was no 'you must do this' but clearly an expectation that wives and mothers at least have a go. Published advice also reminded women why they should put in the effort. It was certainly not for themselves. The 1964 *Woman's Own Christmas Annual* told readers that dinner was more than a festive meal: 'Look around the faces at your table and you will know the full joy of creating it.'[108] Similarly, Christmas books repeatedly stressed how effort and detail would make the festival special for everyone. One 2010 book promised to 'inspire you to share the kind of Christmas that memories are made of'.[109] In other words, it was up to wives and mothers to ensure their families had good times to look back on.

The result of all this advice was a pressure on women. Even if they had not read the female columns of newspapers or a book on Christmas preparations, the advice soaked into cultural expectations and was reinforced by the ubiquity of advertising and the conversation of other women. The Christmas stress of wives could even make the problem pages of newspapers.[110] One man recalled that his mother had such high expectations of Christmas that the meal was tension-laden and a wrong word could easily cause a blazing row between his parents.[111] Even women in powerful positions felt the pressure. In 1974, Barbara Castle, the Secretary of State for Employment, recorded in her diary that it had been one of the happiest Christmases ever. Most of her family were there, her 'food was fine; everyone behaved perfectly'. But preparing it all was strenuous and she reflected 'how I got through all the work I will never know. Christmas is exacting enough when I am not a Minister and when I can get the domestic help I can't get now. But my aching feet did not spoil the fun.'[112] By the late twentieth century, family memories of mothers and grandmothers preparing huge Christmas feasts without processed or prepared ingredients increased the pressure on women.[113] One academic has argued that there is a 'Christmas imperative' on women to not just make a perfect Christmas but to recreate the Christmases of their childhood, something they were pushed into by the media and consumer society.[114] Research in the early twenty-first century found that women could see Christmas not as an occasion of excitement but of hard work and some were even 'driven to anger by the seasonal clutter of cards, wrappings and gifts'.[115] One 2008 book claimed that around the second week of December it was common to hear women proclaiming: 'I hate Christmas – to me it's just a load of work and hassle on top of everything else I do around the house. And furthermore. No one else lifts a finger. You just sit back and think the fairies do everything.'[116]

The scale of effort involved should not be underestimated. Even before the food preparation, many women had cleaned the house and polished the cutlery. Making the table look nice was important to many women to the extent that some colour coded its decorations and linen. Most of Christmas Eve could be spent pealing vegetables, baking, decorating, and making soup, stuffing, and desserts.[117] One 1964 guide on how to do Christmas dinner for eight had the woman in the kitchen from 9.45 am to 1.15 pm on the 25th, when the advice was for her to remove her apron, tidy her hair and relax for ten minutes.[118] In 1986, one fifty-year-old described her Christmas to Mass Observation. At 8.00 am on Christmas Eve she was doing last minute food shopping. An hour later she was preparing the turkey. Later that morning she was cleaning, preparing more food and visiting elderly ladies. On Christmas Day she was up at 7.30 am and had telephoned relatives and visited her parents' graves before returning to prepare vegetables at 10.15 am. She washed up straight after lunch, a chore much bigger than normal after a mammoth and complex dinner. By 11.00 pm she was making yet more food and then tidying again before bed at 1.30 am.[119] Technologies such as better ovens and dishwashers eased some of the burdens but their spread was much slower than their current ubiquity suggests. Even in 1990, only 13 per cent of British households had dishwashers.[120] The rise of convenience food had far less impact because there was a pride in making one's own. A 2004 survey found that one in five women were spending ten hours on the Christmas dinner, with only one in four getting any help from their partners.[121]

By the 1940s women were increasingly expecting some help around the house and resentful when it did not materialize.[122] But mid-century developments should not be exaggerated. There could often be a reluctance to let their husbands help too much. This was partly from a sense of fairness when they were not in paid employment but it also owed something to a desire to retain control of the home and their sense of housework as a skill that was both unmanly and something that men might not actually possess.[123] Indeed, women had considerable pride in their cooking skills and some sent their family out for a walk 'with relish' so they could be left to prepare the Christmas lunch.[124] Yet the result was that some women did not get to enjoy the meal properly. One woman told Mass Observation in 1937 that she did not want to eat too much of the dinner because by the time it was served she was fed up of the smell.[125] A man (born in 1961) remembers that his mother did not even sit down until everyone else had finished their lunch.[126] The singer Morrissey remembered that his Irish grandmother in 1960s Manchester would not set a place for herself at Christmas dinner, eating after everyone else.[127] Of course, particularly as the century progressed, there were always variations in domestic arrangements. There were men who took pride in washing-up or even in their ability to cook a turkey, but it was a sign of the strength of traditions that more wives did not follow the woman who recorded in 1986 that she cooked a 'straightforward' roast pork with satsumas to follow because she did not 'like to be in the kitchen missing all the fun'.[128]

Few followed this example because Christmas preparations, and especially the food, were something that women claimed ownership of, for all its pressures. Although numerous media forms certainly encouraged married women to think that their personal happiness was entwined with the needs of their family, it would be wholly misleading to see this simply as the product of social and cultural expectations. Mothers drew genuine satisfaction from seeing others happy and home making was a rewarding exercise in itself. The effort involved in the chores could make them a sign of love in themselves.[129] Thus, women's festive efforts were a conscious attempt to show their love for their families. This was true of both the beginning and end of the period. Mass Observation found that in late 1930s Bolton the happiness of many working-class women was entwined with the happiness of their family members and their role in ensuring that happiness.[130] One magazine claimed in 2009 'when you gather the people you love under one roof, your instinct is to pack them so full of food and love that it will last the whole year'.[131] Women were thus as much victims of their own expectations as victims of the cultural pressure on them. One 1945 novel noted a middle-aged wife had seemed to spend most of an 'exhausting' day 'either cooking or serving food or washing-up' and claimed that all over London there were other women 'similarly slaving away as chefs and pastry-cooks, everyone of them obstinately convinced that Christmas without other people's overeating wouldn't seem like Christmas at all'.[132] Such excesses perhaps even grew as the material resources of a typical family improved. By 1986, a book by Jilly Cooper was claiming: 'Women tend to behave as though they're taking a degree in Christmas and that the world will end if they get a third in sprouts, a fourth in bacon rolls and fail bread sauce totally.'[133] In a 2010 novel a wealthy working mother reflected:

I love it so much, and I want it to be lovely, so redemptive, so right. There's no point in doing it craply, is there? I know people who do do it craply, sitting there miserably with their substandard presents and their overcooked titchy bird, but that's not how I roll. The idea of that kind of Christmas makes me want to cry: I can't bear even to watch pretend people doing it on television. It's not that I want it perfect in the Martha Stewart sense – I don't even own any matching crockery. I just want it to be ... nice. Warm. Living. Joyous. All those things. Christmassy.[134]

Those women without the time to go to excessive lengths could even feel deprived. In 2005 a working mother complained to the *Daily Mirror* about how she had to listen to say-at-home mothers saying they had bought and wrapped all their presents by August.[135]

Women were also clearly aware about what was happening. One reflected: 'I think you have to be careful not to get too caught up in things being beautiful and perfectly presented. It's all about having a good time and relaxing, not having the perfect everything … They [the family] don't remember what napkins you have got on the table.' Yet, she still told researchers that she got a bit carried away with the Christmas preparations.[136] The contradictory Christmas messages women were subject to and the contradictory ways they perceived their roles is not surprising. Both feminism and economic forces had created a situation where women expected to be able to do everything. They were told that they could have a career and be a homemaker. They were told that the attention they gave their children was crucial but also that they should be leaving the children to go to work. The pressures this could create were immense and when people did not meet them the result was disillusionment and frustration. In such a context, Christmas was a time when women could prove to themselves that they were good homemakers and at the heart of their families' welfare and happiness.

Ironically, it was two television advertisements that came closest to the experience of most mothers at Christmas. A 1985 advertisement for Oxo showed a mother trying to make Christmas dinner while the rest of the family messed around or disturbed her. She set a beautiful table and cooked a huge meal, but her family seemed rather oblivious and her daughter simply said, 'Mummy made the gravy.' Yet the knowing smile from the mother showed little resentment, safe in the knowledge that she and all the female viewers knew who had really made Christmas. In 2012 Asda ran an advert that featured a stressed mother running the family's celebrations and the slogan 'Behind every great Christmas there's Mum'. It was not an isolated example in supermarket advertising and received some middle-class criticism for being sexist, outdated and insulting, but more commonly there seemed to be an appreciation that women's hard work was being recognized.[137] For all the advances of feminism, Christmas showed that in the majority of houses women remained at the heart of their domestic operations.

Husbands' responses to the Christmas efforts of their wives were as varied as should be expected of half the married population. While some got angry at how much their wives spent, others just ignored it or forgot say thank you.[138] A few fully appreciated the efforts of their partners. In 1975 Tony Benn recorded in his Christmas diary that his home was a 'great family centre and it is all a result of Caroline's love, her care, her attention to detail. She is a remarkable woman.'[139] Whatever the women were doing, Christmas was also a time shaped by ideas of masculinity. John Tosh has argued that while Victorian fathers had important domestic roles, their masculinity could also be unsettled by the female dominion of the home.[140] Similarly, the control many women exerted over Christmas could marginalize men. Of course, few minded being banished from the kitchen on the day itself or excused the trials of shopping but the preparations could still leave them feeling excluded and annoyed. The father besieged by bills brought about by women's Christmas activities was a common source of interwar humour.[141] One letter writer to the *Saturday Review* in 1937 complained that women of all ages were turning Christmas into something that upset households.

> For days before Christmas every room seems to be given up to warehousing mysterious packages, female members are busy making lists of all the individuals they have ever met who are likely or they think are likely (not always the same thing) to remember them in some way or the other at this season, and the mere male is 'shoo-ed' into silence if he asks awkward questions, is summarily and severely dealt with if he disarranges the mountains of packages to look for a straying pipe or other prized possession and is expected to be ready at any moment to act as transport mule for the conveyance of the multitudes of parcels to their Post Office destination and, incidentally, blithely to pay for their postage.
>
> No doubt this all helps Christmas trade and the Post Office receipts, but where does the 'peace,' also associated with this season, come in for male members of the household?[142]

But had women not organized Christmas then it would not have happened in many households. This was evident in the 1937 Mass Observation return of a railways draughtsman from Oldham which recorded that his wife had been ill so Christmas meals were little different to a normal day.[143]

Not every father in the middle of the century was insecure and grumpy about Christmas. It was, after all, a break from the stresses of their jobs. Indeed, men could be as strong as women in their expectations of Christmas. In 1926 the *New Statesman* claimed that

> On Christmas Day all men – or, at least, nine men out of ten – are Conservatives. They would be disappointed if the smallest detail in the ritual of the day were not adhered to. They demand the same food as they have eaten on all previous Christmas Days, the same decorations of holly and mistletoe, the same foolishness of crackers and paper caps. They feel that in this they are doing something that has been done for a thousand years, and it is as though their ancestors as well as their children were seated with them at the table.[144]

Indeed, rather than see Christmas as something that upset men's natural control of over things, the festival could actually be seen as an opportunity for men to assert their position as head of the household and a caring father. This might come from something as simple as carving the turkey to playing with the children while the women cooked. Contrary to popular perceptions, early twentieth-century fathers of all classes were not above playing with or looking after their children and some could be openly affectionate and loving. Indeed, even acting as the breadwinner could be seen as an act of devotion to family.[145] In the middle of the century, there was an increased emphasis on men's place in the home and family, even if this did not fully embrace domestic work and chores. Sharing and taking part in family life increasingly became expected and sought out by men of all classes. Childcare may have been a woman's role for much of the twentieth century but men were expected to play with children. They were better able to do this thanks to the fall in the typical working week from fifty-six hours before the Great War to around forty after the Second World War.[146] Indeed, the role of fathers in creating stable family life was widely accepted. This was true of all classes, although, working-class men, who could rely on manual work to assert their manliness, might sometimes feel more secure taking part in less traditional male activities than their white-collar peers.[147] Research in the 1950s suggested that men more than women regarded parenthood as an ingredient of a happy married life.[148] Interwar seaside holidays also saw fathers take a lead on playing and entertaining the children and that was part of the attraction of the break for them. The same was true of Christmas: it gave men the time and licence to demonstrate and enjoy their commitment to family life.[149] Thus, while women were cooking, fathers, uncles and grandparents often played with the children. Some developed their own annual contributions to the festivities, dressing up as Santa, doing tricks or even preparing their own dish. In the 1920s J. R. R. Tolkien wrote elaborate letters to his children from Father Christmas and his helpers.[150] Between the wars, there were even magic sets specifically aimed at fathers who wanted to entertain others.[151] Indeed, some men took play so far that they took things over, particularly with toys such as train sets that appealed to their boyish side.[152] The festival's emphasis on joviality and being a little silly protected them from any real or imagined suggestion that their masculinity was being undermined by playing. So, too, given the fact that men might 'perform' their masculinity differently in public and in private, did the fact that the family Christmas took place away from the gaze of workmates and neighbours.[153] But Christmas also gave men the chance to demonstrate their love through more traditional manly activities such as making presents, something which also gave families access to far grander toys, such as castles or dolls' houses, than they could have otherwise afforded.[154] One Shropshire woman remembered of her childhood early in the century: 'I get a great feeling of warmth and love about all this. My mother I loved dearly, but my father was a distant, rather terrifying figure who was often not at home, and with whom we associated naughtiness and spanking and a loud cross voice. He was not like this on Christmas Day. In retrospect this early morning bouncing on the bed and having fun with Daddy, has acquired a nice, cosy, relaxed atmosphere.'[155]

Just because men were at home 'does not automatically imply involvement or engagement' in domestic activities.[156] Some men could also be prone to find Christmas rather difficult, partly because of how different it was to their normal routines. Some had to force a degree of joviality or even take something for it. Advertisements for different liver salts in the 1920s told fathers that being sorry for themselves could spoil Christmas for others and that they owed their family 'a happy face'.[157] After his guests had left at around 11.00 pm, comedian Michael Palin noted in his 1976 diary: 'I think I've learnt to handle these family Christmases a bit better. I feel tired, but not heavy, fat or blotto with it.'[158] Others just found it difficult to stop thinking of work. Some people with powerful and stressful jobs clearly struggled to switch off or entirely escape work for anything beyond Christmas Day itself and even then that day might be interrupted.[159] On Christmas 1999 Tony Benn rang Ken Livingston to ask about his running mate for the London mayoral elections.[160] A few family men simply opted out. One woman recorded in her diary for 25 December 1960 that, despite having visiting family, her husband, 'the horrible rat', had stayed in bed all morning and then gone to the pub in the afternoon. She summed up: 'I've never, never, had such an awful time.' The previous day it had emerged that he had cancelled one of the two desks she had ordered as presents for her daughters, leaving just one between them. He tried to pretend it was a shop error.[161] In 1943, Nella Last's flu-suffering husband did not get her anything and even used the family sweets ration for himself. She was not impressed and fumed in her diary about her thirty-two years of slavery looking after him.[162] Such pictures were more significant than the outcome of individual personalities; they confirm the position of historians who argue that the increased domesticity of fathers had limits and the dangers of suggesting that all men were family-centric.[163] No amount of cultural change would change the fact that some men were just selfish.

Beyond the family

In the Edwardian period there developed a culture among the well-off of spending Christmas at the seaside, in a city hotel or even out of the country. Some of these people were simply those without family looking for company but others took children with them. The trend grew in popularity between the wars as some hotels put on lavish dinners and elaborate programmes of entertainment and dancing. Some Lyons restaurants offered Christmas Day dinner for 3s.6d., which *Woman's Own* said was less than it would cost to eat at home. Some justified Christmas in a hotel as a way of allowing children to spend the festival with others their own age but, just as in the Edwardian period, others argued that it marked a decline in traditional values. In 1931, for example, one writer claimed that a generation ago Christmas had been a Christian festival of the home and that avoidable absence from the home was 'regarded as a symbol of family disunity and egotism'. He blamed what he saw as a new trend and the associated selfishness on materialism and Christian decline.[164]

More convincing were those who offered more prosaic explanations. In 1934 one middle-aged writer put it down to the housing shortage which meant many lived in hotels and the growth of the motor car which freed people from train, bus and tram services that stopped at tea time. He concluded that 'folk who once made Christmas for themselves go away to have it made for them'.[165] That same year, the Travel Association of Great Britain and Ireland estimated that the number spending Christmas in a hotel had more than doubled in five years. It thought this was due to not just cars but also the growth of people living in flats and the labour involved in hosting Christmas. Others put the trend down to a decline in servants and women wanting a break from chores.[166] Rising affluence and better transport saw a further apparent growth in people spending Christmas away after the Second World War. On Christmas Eve 1955 nearly a thousand cars crossed the channel from Dover. 23 December 1971 was British European Airways' busiest day of the year, and the airline carried some 90,000 passengers. Twenty-five years later, the media was reporting that half a million people were leaving Britain for Christmas.[167] No longer was the Christmas away the luxury of a wealthy middle class.

Reporting in 1958 on the increase in people flying to hotter climates, *The Times* was told it was people wishing to escape 'the sentimentality' of an English Christmas, and yet one travel agency still flew out a supply of Christmas puddings for its customers in Spain.[168] The trend thus neither marked a decline in Christmas nor family. Some people's Christmas getaway may have been at the expense of an extended family gathering but the norm was always to spend the festival with the immediate unit anyway. Moreover, the whole purpose of some hotel gatherings was precisely to have enough space to allow an extended family gathering. Few went away alone and those who did could enjoy being with other people.[169] Indeed, although the numbers going away for Christmas rose in the second half of the century, concern about this virtually disappeared and the reason for this was quite simply how secure the family Christmas was.

For those without close family, Christmas was a difficult time. In a 1960 novel, a single pregnant woman who was estranged from her father, remarked that Christmas 'wasn't a thing you could ignore, and being alone at it was to combine the worst elements of being alone at any other time, and multiply them by two hundred and fifty'.[170] Even people with a circle of friends could still find themselves alone at Christmas because they did not feel they could impose themselves on others' family. For some, it was circumstances such as war or even prison that left them alone. But whatever the reason, for those alone Christmas could be 'an occasion to be got through as quickly as possible', as a 1977 novel put it.[171]

Although it was generalizing, one left-leaning publication was not too far out when it claimed in 1979 that 'Christmas is a rotten time: for the divorced, for single parents, for the isolated elderly, for the poor and the mentally ill'.[172] A 2000 poll found the divorced, widowed or separated were twice as likely as the national average figure to feel depressed at Christmas time (although almost two-thirds did not feel that way).[173] Married couples unable to have children also found it a difficult time, as did those who simply wished they had more children. Christmas could be particularly sad for the bereaved and cemetery visits were common on day itself.[174] In 1916 the novelist H. Rider Haggard, who had lost family members and the sons of friends in the war, recorded in his diary: 'a sad, sad Xmas for many. I had not the heart to drink healths after dinner. That old custom reminds one of too much.'[175] People also felt the pain of what they might have had rather than what they had lost. In 2013, a recovering heroin user looked back on his Christmases in hostels and wrote: 'It was all very well meaning and I had a laugh or two there. But it just reminded me of what I didn't have: a normal life and a normal family.'[176] Thus, even for those not physically alone, Christmas might reinforce a sense of isolation or loss. In 1957, Kenneth Williams, an unhappy homosexual, wrote in his diary: 'It is always this time of the year that I yearn for the thing which life has never given me – physical love.'[177]

Social concern about those alone at Christmas focused on the elderly. Indeed, the festival made society feel distinctly uncomfortably about how

PLATE 8 *Salvation Army Christmas dinner for homeless men, 1929. Time Life Pictures/Getty.*

its older members were treated. On 25 December 1981, fifteen elderly people were even found dead in their homes in the West Midlands, with the cold believed to be the cause.[178] Concerns that the elderly were neglected by their adult children were recurrent throughout the century but became particularly prevalent after the establishment of the welfare state. Indeed, between 1938 and 1980 the proportion of old people in public institutional care increased by over 140 per cent.[179] One 1968 writer claimed that the welfare state had killed the extended family Christmas because it meant people thought that the state would look after their elderly relatives. He pointed to an old people's home in London as evidence. Half the thirty-seven residents could have gone to their married children for Christmas but only five had done so. The manager said the families of the rest 'didn't want to know'. But he also noted that there was good atmosphere and happiness in care homes at Christmas and they had their own communal feeling with people feeling content with the routines and familiarity.[180] Similarly, one nurse noted in 1986 that all her elderly patients had new dresses and had their hair done for Christmas. Many were 'as excited as children'.[181]

It was those living outside care institutions that were most likely to be alone on Christmas Day. Thus, in 1962, an article on gift-giving advised that 'The most you can give any old person is your company'.[182] Age Concern claimed in 1974 that the elderly received more attention at Christmas than any other time of year, but that it was 'a sad indictment of society if people really think loneliness can be cured by a Christmas pudding or gift of talcum powder'. Moreover, the intended kindness of others could actually make things worse. In 1966, one 76-year-old in London, whose husband and son were both dead and who lived alone in a bedsit, told *The Times* that she was normally by herself at Christmas, but when she was invited by friends to their homes she suspected it was only because they knew she was lonely. Being with other people then just made her feel more lonely.[183] In 2011, *The Sun* ran a 'Care for the Elderly This Christmas' campaign that urged people to befriend someone alone. It featured a 78-year-old woman unable to leave the house because of her osteoporosis. She was lonely and isolated, with no family and unable to visit her dwindling number of friends because of her health and finances. For Christmas she just wanted someone to talk to.[184]

Such stories contributed to a myth that suicide rates peaked at Christmas. That was not true anywhere in the Western world and it cannot also be assumed that simply being alone or isolated was always a cause for concern.[185] Just as they did all-year round, the television and radio helped people feel less isolated at Christmas and as early as the 1920s, the BBC was claiming this as a good reason for festive broadcasting.[186] In 1937, a 59-year-old chemist from Luton told Mass Observation that he spent the day at home alone, pottering, doing experiments and reading. He spoke to no one, but said it was the most satisfactory Christmas for many years.[187] A 1951 letter writer to the *Daily Mirror* complained that he was invited to parties because people assumed he was lonely and miserable, but actually he just wanted to be left alone.[188] Moreover, most elderly people were not actually alone. In 2012 one charity estimated 500,000 were, but this was half the number that lived alone, while the total number of people in the UK who were sixty-five and over was then more than ten million.[189] In 1955 an ITV news report drew attention to elderly people at Christmas. One woman who was going to be on her own that Christmas said it would bring back memories, some sad and some happy. Another found it a time of happiness because people were good to the elderly. She was getting a lunch from the local vicar, although she and her husband would have no other visitors.[190] Such small gestures may have made their Christmas better, but it is difficult not to conclude that Christmas revealed how neglected the elderly of the post-war UK were. The state may have looked after their physical needs and a few might not have wanted much more, but the fact that hundreds of thousands of people did not speak to anyone on Christmas Day showed that the festival's spirit had its limits. Indeed, it was the power of the ideal of the family Christmas that made the situation of those without it so tragic.

Conclusion

In 1962 *Woman's Own* ran a feature about what a family would be dreaming about on Christmas Eve. The wife was worrying about whether she had

PLATE 9 *A family Christmas, 1946. Fox Photos/Getty.*

enough milk, where she put the holly doilys, whether the children would wake too early and how her mother-in-law would behave. She was annoyed at her husband for mixing his drinks at an office party, spending so much on their daughter's present and taking so long to put up the fairy lights. But she was proud of her mince pies. Her last thought was to get more milk in. The husband was regretting how much he had drank at the office party and thinking over how the family tradition had started that he would eat a mince pie straight from the oven. He was pleased he remembered to tell his wife they were the best yet, even though they tasted awful on top of the alcohol. He was also rather pleased with the alternate red and green lights he had rigged up and was confident that his children would like their presents, although he was glad his wife did not know how much he had spent. His last thought was to get more beer in. The children, meanwhile, were simply wondering whether Father Christmas had been yet.[191]

Although Christmas was often a highly gendered and sometimes a tension-laden occasion, it also played an important role in bonding families together. Indeed, surveys showed people saw the festival more as a family event than a religious or commercial one.[192] This had much to do with how the growing length of the holiday and the decline of public entertainment and church meant people spent more time at Christmas at home. But the family festival also continued to owe much to gift-giving. Presents were a complex mix of social obligation and personal choice, 'a means of both reflecting and constructing social relations'.[193] To say thank you for another year of domestic support, men might often spend more on their wives and partners that they expected in return. Cousins, nieces and nephews, uncles and aunts, and godchildren could all be remembered through a gift, despite a lack of contact the rest of the year. In such cases, an American sociologist argued that gift-giving dealt with 'important but insecure relationships', confirming and developing goodwill where it was needed but not secure.[194] Christmas could even be used to transfer financial resources within a family that might be awkward at other times. Such utilitarian interpretations rather obscure the love that also lay behind gift-giving. For some couples, Christmas was a romantic occasion. For, example in 1937, a 29-year-old warehouseman recorded his wife's excitement at their exchange of gifts. He always gave her something she asked for and several small presents as surprises. They also posted cards to each other. In one Yorkshire works, an employee recorded in 1938 that people there seemed to be saying they were looking forward to Christmas because they would have sex.[195] By the 1990s, there were more conceptions at Christmas than at any other time of year.[196] Even pets could have their place in the family confirmed through a gift, a practice that was noted across the century.[197] In contrast, giving presents to friends, which was quite common in middle-class circles between the wars, seems to have become less usual towards the end of the century.[198] One reason for this may have been as people had more money to spend, the sacrifice signified by a gift lessened and thus so too did its meaning.

In 1964, one woman thought the problem with present-giving was that it was becoming too wide: 'Once you draw the net too wide, it becomes like commercial Christmas cards, of no value at all.'[199] By concentrating presents on family, their meaning was heightened.

There were other ways Christmas cemented the bonds of family. Between the wars, Christmas was a popular time for working-class weddings because people had the time for both a party on the day itself and a honeymoon on the day after. More commonly, families actively did things together at Christmas, such as playing games, talking, and having sing songs. It was often bemoaned that television and the wireless undermined these interactions but that does not mean they did not happen. People did not always just watch or listen silently or passively. They talked about and over programmes. Sometimes they just ignored it, or read, knitted or played at the same time. They may have argued over which channel to put on but they also learnt about each other's tastes and lives. *Top of the Pops*, for example, may have annoyed the older generation but it also gave them contact with the culture of their children. Many families also developed their own special rituals and traditions. In the late 1930s, a Bradford family had a ritual of knocking on their own front door at midnight and declaring 'I wish you a merry Christmas and a happy New Year, a pocketful of money and a cellar full of beer.' This was a self-conscious continuation of something they thought dated back generations.[200] Other families had present-opening rituals, such as opening them in turn, sitting in particular seats or publicly trying to guess what was inside in the wrapping. Even if the ritual was not so formal, many families required members to open presents publically, emphasizing the fact that this was an exercise that reinforced social relations.[201] Modern technologies even allowed the process to be recorded and re-watched in years to come. The advent of video recorders in the 1980s also created an annual tradition in some families of watching a favourite seasonal movie. Like the use of family sayings and nicknames and the decor and ornaments that turned houses into homes, such rituals were something that said 'this is who we are and this is what makes us that'. As the power of the external rituals of religion or community faded and the shapes of family changed, with some not even sharing the same name anymore, such rituals became all the more important. One historian thus summed up, 'What sets our age apart from all others is that each family is now the creator and custodian of its own myths, rituals, and images.'[202]

The bonds of family that Christmas expressed were complicated by ideas that there was an obligation to give presents to certain relatives. Thus, in a 1955 teenage girls' play, an aunt remarks 'No, child, it was not kind of me. People do a lot of things at Christmas which they would not think of doing any other time of the year … What you think of me if I didn't give you a present?'[203] Few would have actually said that openly in real life but there were certainly occasions when Christmas undermined family. It was a time when people not always used to being together had to cope with complex meals, overcrowded houses, excited children, too much alcohol and each other. So common were these challenges that even the BBC broadcast a radio programme in 1946 advising listeners on how to cope with Christmas.[204] In extreme cases, such tensions led to severe arguments, violence or family break up but it is difficult to believe that Christmas was the actual cause of such outcomes, rather than a symptom of or catalyst for much deeper pre-existing problems.

The centrality of family to defining Christmas was evident in the Second World War when people's enjoyment was curtailed by the absence of loved ones. Respondents told Mass Observation that family members being away in the forces made Christmas a sober and sadder affair. In 1941, a young woman who spent Christmas in a hotel because her sister could only get one day off, recorded that it had not felt Chrismassy despite the presence of turkey, Christmas pudding, mistletoe and crackers. There was 'always something missing' she mused. It was her first Christmas away from home. Yet the same survey found different cases where people were able to enjoy themselves and even forget the traumas, bereavements and burdens of war. The report concluded that individuality was paramount to people's experiences: 'War does not reduce people or swamp them in an overall mediocrity.'[205] That same individuality was also true of Christmas in peacetime. The majority of people valued family but there were always variations in what that actually meant in festive practices.

One anthropologist has argued that the centrality of family to the festival is misleading. It is a construct that people value precisely because family is actually in decline in wider society. The family Christmas is thus, in this interpretation, an inversion of reality. In contrast, another anthropologist argues that Christmas matters so much precisely because it is an embodiment of the importance of family in society.[206] Of course, both positions can be simultaneously true. There was widespread concern in the second half of the twentieth century about the decline of family. Divorce was the prime culprit but those who valued marriage also bemoaned a fall in the numbers turning to that formal rite. Yet, it is difficult to accept that family was on the wane. Rather, it was evolving, both in form and dynamics. Compared with before the war, immediate families were actually spending more time together. Shorter working hours, more comfortable houses filled with better toys and entertainments, and the shared pastime of watching television, meant immediate families were at home more. Yet central heating, multiple televisions and bedrooms full of toys, books or gadgets meant families increasingly did not actually congregate in the same room. Even when families watched television together, it did not mean they actually always interacted that much.[207] Notions of sexual equality may have become mainstream and mothers may have increasingly also been in paid employment but women remained at the heart of both the ideals and realities of domesticity. Many families also now looked different, sometimes comprising unmarried couples, or step parents, children and siblings, or even same-sex partners. Yet, whatever shape they took, most were still units that provided the love and support traditionalists so valued in older notions of families. This was why most people still aspired to have their own family.

All this meant there was still a role for Christmas. It was the ultimate extension of a leisure life that was increasingly focused on the home. It allowed people to celebrate an ideal of themselves and family harmony. It was a time when they came together, celebrating something that was otherwise marginalized in the day-to-day pressures of living. As people developed a sense that time was precious in the later twentieth century, Christmas became even more important. It even allowed the working mother to show she was still capable of fulfilling older ideals of nurturing and providing for her family and for those same people to show her the gratitude that they usually forgot. There was a remarkable degree of continuity across the century in these regards. Indeed, one of Christmas's most powerful historical messages is that amid a sea of social and cultural change it, like families themselves, was a beacon of continuity and stability.

CHAPTER THREE

The rituals of Christmas

One man remembered of a Christmas dinner for British troops in 1917: 'War-hardened veterans to whom high explosives had been for years part and parcel of their daily lives, screwed up their eyes in fearful expectation of the ex-detonation of a cracker, just as they did when they were children.' An airman remembered that on the Western Front that year everyone in the British forces tried 'to go through the old routine no matter what was happening'.[1] For these soldiers, Christmas offered a connection to normality, which they exerted through adhering to the rituals and customs that helped define the festival, made it different to other holidays and injected it with luxury, fun and wonder.

Such rituals were followed out of a sense that they were historic practices and that Christmas itself should be traditional. As a Jeeves and Wooster story put it, many people consciously sought to have 'a real old-fashioned Christmas with all the trimmings'.[2] This dedication to tradition ran far deeper than Christmas. It was rooted in a widespread popular reverence for days gone by, real or imagined. This was particularly clear between the wars when some celebrated Christmas as part of their commitment to 'Merrie England', just as many of their Victorian forefathers had.[3] More common, however, was a less defined commitment to old-fashioned ways of doing things. In the early and mid-twentieth century, much of Britain was a deeply conservative society, something apparent in the masses' lack of political radicalism. Even after 1945, there could be distrust of modern things and a fond appreciation of the old-fashioned.[4] In a shifting and uncertain world, the past was a refuge that seemed safer and more straightforward than the present. Christmas was part of these cultural currents and the continuation of its traditions is evidence of conservatism's legacy in a more modern world. But there were also forces of modernization encouraging conformity to the dominant Christmas rituals. The media in all its forms – advertisements, radio, films, newsreels, television and so forth – all played a part in informing how Christmas was celebrated. They told viewers, readers and listeners how others, particularly the famous, celebrated and encouraged aspiration and conformity. But the media was also influenced by those same rituals it promoted and most Christmas advertising in particular was rather conservative.[5]

The endurance of many Christmas rituals also owed much to how imprecise they were in their meanings. Their specific origins mattered little to most people and their popularity was rooted in the simple fact that they were traditional. People may have been interested, for example, in the fact that Christmas trees may have had pagan roots, but that was not why they put them up in their homes. People did, however, think about what following rituals might say about themselves. The materialism of Christmas traditions meant it was entwined with status – consumption was usually as much about signifying taste and wealth as it was about purchasing something to eat or enjoy. Indeed, as the traditional markers of class faded and blurred, consumption probably became the most important signifier of status that remained.[6] For some, Christmas was another opportunity to display one's superior's taste, but for others, it was an opportunity to make a gesture. Finances might be short but, like the annual holiday, Christmas was a time to show you could indulge yourself and live life in style, making up for the humdrum existence the rest of the year round.[7]

However, much of Christmas took place behind closed doors and thus the primary audience for festive displays of taste and status was one's self and one's family. This did not make them any the less significant. For the working classes in particular, the festival was an opportunity to reassure themselves that they shared the tastes and pleasures of both their so-called betters and the wider community at large. Thus, between the wars and in the early years of post-war affluence, the working classes embraced the rituals practised by the middle classes such as trees and turkey dinners. Indeed, those who did not celebrate Christmas were making something of a statement that they lay outside mainstream culture. One anthropologist has pointed to the consensus in his profession that 'rituals are symbolic performances which unite the members of a category of people in a shared pursuit that speaks of, and to, their basic values or that creates or confirms a world of meanings shared by all them alike'.[8] This might sound rather grand, but it points to the fact that participating in Christmas was a conscious decision. People did not simply 'do' Christmas without thinking, although they might not think much about why they were doing it. Things had to be bought, decorations had to be put up and the children had to be told stories. Some people even bought one of the many books that told readers about 'how to do' Christmas. In other words, people chose to go along with festive rituals.

It was possible to use rituals to signify simultaneously membership of a wider community and status within that community because Christmas customs were actually very loose in their requirements. Adherence simply meant sending cards, giving presents, putting up a tree and decorations, telling the kids presents came from Santa and having a special meal. Yet, as this chapter shows, how those things were done was up to the individual. The power of Christmas rituals thus lay both in the way they signified an adherence to tradition and a dominant culture and the freedom they simultaneously allowed to highlight a personalized position within that culture.

Cards

In 1971 a woman wrote to *The Times* at the start of November to say she had already received her first Christmas card of the year.[9] No matter how much anyone tried to delay or put off Christmas, there was no guarantee that one's friends and relatives would do the same and the appearance of the first card could be a signal that the season had arrived in the home rather than just in the shops and on television. A few hardy souls shopped for Christmas throughout the year, while others began preparations in October when they made a cake.[10] But such acts could be excused as forward thinking or saving money or effort. The Christmas card, in contrast, was a marker of when Christmas really started for people, and it was not dependent on when the shopkeepers wanted the season to begin.

Christmas cards were also another Victorian invention, beginning in the 1840s and taking off in the last thirty years of the nineteenth century, firmly establishing themselves as a middle-class habit.[11] Financial pressures and dilemmas over what was appropriate dented the card trade during the First World War and a number of manufacturers went bankrupt.[12] By 1923, it was being reported that card sending had still not fully recovered but festive mail was voluminous enough to require the employment of 30,000 temporary postal workers. A year later, the Royal Mail was reporting its load at Christmas was typically 50 per cent higher than the rest of the year.[13] Yet it is difficult to know quite how widespread card sending was before 1939. In an era when some struggled to feed their families, it was never going to be a priority, but for those of restricted means there were bargain boxes of cards, sometimes advertised with no reference to what was on them at all.[14] One woman remembered of the 1930s that maybe a dozen was the typical number sent in her Hertfordshire village.[15] Mass Observation's 1938 Christmas questionnaire found that some people only sent a handful of cards, and some none at all, but others dispatched more than seventy. That year, an estimated 470 million were sold in the UK, which hardly suggests a ritual limited to the middle classes. The Second World War again set the tradition back. There were some who felt that, given the paper shortage, sending cards was inappropriate and in 1942 one magazine felt it had to point out that most cards were old stock rather than newly manufactured.[16] The practice quickly recovered after 1945 however and became more widespread as the working classes grew more affluent. According to one historian's figures, the numbers sent had increased by 1949 to 590 million, 775 million by 1954 and 992 million in 1974. By 1993 the *Sunday Times* was claiming that 1,500 million were sent in Britain.[17] However, such large estimates are inevitably exaggerations and seem to be confused with the total volume of Christmas mail. A 1952 estimate put the number of cards sold at 100 million, a fifth of the entire festive mail, while a member of the Greeting Card and Calendar Association council estimated that 500 million of the 734 million items posted at Christmas 1955 were cards.[18] Opinion polls offer more meaningful suggestions. Gallup suggested that the average number of cards bought rose from 24 in 1955 to 32 in 1986. In contrast, a 1985 survey suggested the average family sent 68 cards.[19] Perhaps all that can be concluded for sure is that the practice grew in both adherence and volume.

Throughout the century there were no agreed social conventions on who cards should be sent to. Individuals did, however, have their own rules. Some objected to sending them to colleagues or neighbours who were seen nearly every day. Others did not send them to family who were absent for most of the year but would be seen on the day itself. Even how cards were displayed could be subject to a hierarchy, with, for example, those from close family on the mantelpiece, those from other members of the family hung on the chimney breast and those from everyone else hung elsewhere in the room.[20] Some tried to opt out of cards altogether, although they might be then guilt-tripped back when they started to receive cards. Indeed, the importance of reciprocation meant an unexpected card could cause some stress.[21] This was not paranoia; offence did seem to be taken and some people kept a running list of who to send cards to, crossing off anyone who did not reciprocate. For many, a card was the only annual contact they had with friends and family who had moved away. In 1937, a Marlow housewife recorded that of the dozen cards she and her husband received, one was always from an army pal that her husband had not seen since the war. Since cards were sent to people with whom all other contact might have ceased, not receiving one back could also lead senders to wonder whether if someone had moved away, got divorced or even died.[22]

Despite such uncertainties, Christmas cards helped establish and renew bonds in and outside family. In 1942, one woman wrote in her diary: 'Maybe it is only a card, but it sends one turning back the pages and thinking of the things that belong to the sender. As one gets older and there is so much background, one can't be dull, but can just open the heart's store, look round the shelves, take down the memory and live it over again. Grand!'[23] A 1945 novel, set just before the war, noted that most of the girls in one office had exchanged cards, even though they shared tea breaks twice a day. Yet 'for the past two or three days they had been behaving as though they had been parted for years ... distributing views of snow-bound coaches and lighted taverns and children tobogganing and robins and boys bearing holly and old bellmen crying "Oyez", as though Noel and the 18th century were the same thing, and life depended on celebrating both'. They then displayed these cards at work as 'tokens of popularity and good-fellowship'. The novel also highlighted how the sentimental messages within cards expressed their social function very overtly – a lot of 'let-us-join-hearts-even-if-we-can't-so-much-as-touch-hands' as the writer put it. This was especially true of the cheaper cards, and the same novelist concluded: 'For a penny you got real heart-cry, with a quite decent quality envelope thrown in.'[24] It was easy to be snide about such tastes but they were no different to the working-class penchant for sentimental songs and films that raised a smile and offered a temporary escape from reality. Moreover they, like Christmas cards, encapsulated values and emotions that people actually cherished.[25] Cards did not lose this function. In the twenty-first century, a poverty charity found that boxes of cards from pound shops enabled low-income families to keep in touch with friends and helped their children integrate at school and understand the importance of giving.[26]

People also genuinely enjoyed receiving cards, especially in the era when fewer were sent and there were less other material symbols of the festival to take up one's attention. For the Victorians, cards, even cheap, gaudy mass-produced ones, were often things of beauty and value. As Pimlott remarked, 'The Christmas card was a small present in itself, and often chosen and cherished as an object of beauty and intrinsic worth.' To him, they allowed for 'unconscious self-expression' and a 'release for emotions which were normally inhibited'.[27] Even in the 1980s, there were housewives who would rearrange the cards on display every few days so a different selection could be admired.[28]

As they had been in the Victorian era, cards could be microcosms of their age.[29] In 1914 there were both cards that sent messages of peace and goodwill and those with patriotic messages.[30] By the 1920s the designs on sale included motor cars and aeroplanes. A fashion for larger cards emerged in the mid-1950s, perhaps as a material expression of the emerging affluence.[31] By the 1960s, there was pop art and mini-skirted girls in Father Christmas costumes. Political messages and humour had also found their ways on to cards from the nineteenth century onwards.[32] In 1977, the National Secular Society even had cards with the message: 'We all loathe Christmas but it comes only once a year and is soon over.' Fashions, of course, created the danger that you might receive the same cards you were sending. One manufacturer introduced musical 'Jingle Bells' cards in 1958. They became a best seller but production had to stop because nearly everyone had one.[33]

The more contemporary designs that existed were not guides to what sold and the market was actually very varied. A 2010 survey found 5,363 different designs on sale in major British supermarkets, less than 1 per cent of which had religious themes.[34] A 1933 trade magazine suggested that most people wanted cheerful cards of 'pleasing and more or less familiar design'. That meant a majority of cards were rather conservative, conforming to the jovial, wintry and historic ideas of Christmas. Thus, in

1952 the most common design was said to be coaching scenes.[35] Middle-class tastes however were more varied. In 1946, a Sussex country rector recorded that of the 114 cards he received three were religious, whereas there were twenty-six pictures of houses/cottages, eighteen of dogs, fourteen of horses and coaches, seven of birds, nine of scenery and ships, five original drawings or paintings and six personal photographs or poems. A further five were facetiously jovial, two of which he thought were of a very moderate taste.[36]

Amid such variety, the author of a 1954 book on cards claimed that there were annual complaints about the 'comparative rarity' of religious depictions. In fact, even in the Victorian period, religious cards had not been the norm and there was little to suggest they were in decline. If anything the opposite was happening and people used cards to emphasize the religious significance of the festival as concerns about its secularity increased. In 1962, a manufacturer, who produced 14 per cent of the cards sold in England, told the press that religious depictions represented 12 per cent of his sales. He claimed that holly and robins were out and his current bestselling card was a map of the Holy Land. Indeed, he felt that these cards were 'putting Christ back into Christmas'. By 1966, it was being estimated that about a quarter of Christmas cards were religious.[37] Yet this still meant that three-quarters were not religious and cards remained a potent symbol of the secularity of Christmas.

The religious ideal however was visible in the emergence of charity cards after the war. By 1956, UNICEF alone was selling 1.25 million of them in Britain. A decade later, a hundred charities formed the Charity Christmas Card Council to improve their reach and sales. By then they were selling around 100 million cards, roughly a seventh of the total.[38] Manufacturers suggested it was those of a higher social class that were most likely to send charity cards.[39] This was partly simply because they were most able to afford to combine a necessary purchase with a gesture of charity. Some perhaps sent charity cards because they feared being judged if they did not. Nonetheless, not all were happy about the pressure. In 1971 a letter to *The Times* complained: 'Now that it is immoral to mail any Christmas cards which do not remind of the maimed, the maladjusted or the mad, is it not time to remove the Merry from Christmas?'[40]

This letter writer was well aware that what was on the cards one sent said something about the sender, whether intentional or not. Cards thus inevitably became entangled with interpretations of taste. In 1920 a writer demanded to know why artists allowed 'the general level of Christmas greeting cards to remain so deplorably low'. For him they were 'insignificant prettiness and foolish sentiment and feeble technique' and designed by 'bright "flappers", quavering spinsters and fourth-rate magazine illustrators'. He thought the custom of sending cards was on the wane, although still observed by all classes, and that it should be used to spread art to the masses and raise standards of taste.[41] Less elaborately, an architecture student recorded in

1937 that he found most Christmas cards 'too ugly'. For others, it was not the quality of the art that rankled but the subject matter. In 1950, even an editorial in *The Times* was calling for an end to outdated stagecoaches and photographs of the sender, his family or home.[42] C. S. Lewis complained in 1939: 'What in heaven's name is the idea of everyone sending everyone else pictures of stage-coaches, fairies, foxes, dogs, butterflies, kittens, flowers, etc?'[43] In 1967 the director of the National Portrait Gallery claimed that

> few things provide such a devastating index to the English class system. From the photograph of the backwoods county family at the meet to the working-class vision of crinoline ladies staggering through ten-foot-drifts to distant churches, from the greeting in every language from Swahili to Serbo-Croat of your international do-gooders to your printed addressed jobs with logs blazing away in a rookery-nookery fireplace of stolid stockbroker belt, they epitomise a number of separate class dream worlds.[44]

But there was much snobbishness in such attitudes. The reality was that before television Christmas cards were a rare encounter with art for the working and lower middle classes. They might have the odd photograph or print hanging on their walls, but they did not live in an image-saturated environment. In a humdrum world, the masses enjoyed things that were lavish and extravagant.[45] What outsiders saw as vulgar, could be to the working-class recipient something charming, fancy and even exotic. One 1948 observer noted the care with which people in a village shop chose their cards. He was not impressed by the verse or art, but argued that 'it is surely a useful thing that simple people should take trouble to distinguish between one card and the other, and surely the mental movement required to make such distinctions is an essentially aesthetic movement'.[46]

People picked their cards carefully because of their awareness of how they might be interpreted. A few people between the wars even bought their cards in November to ensure they got the ones they wanted. Some were guided by the picture, others by the verse but some did choose randomly.[47] In a 1924 short story, a woman embarrassed by receiving cards on Christmas Eve from acquaintances not on her list, heads out to buy some to return. She found all the 'decent' ones sold and the only stock left depicted Christmas puddings or 'comic men with jovially red noses kissing vinegarish females of uncertain age under the mistletoe'. These were not things to send refined and teetotal friends. They cost at least a penny, compared to 4d. for the one she liked, an old-fashioned carriage in the snow. A middle-aged woman remarked to her: 'They don't seem to produce the charming Christmas cards nowadays that they used to years ago.'[48] In 1962, one woman wrote that she classified her card list: 'simple religious for some children, innocently frivolous for others; religious plus text for ecumenical uncles; neat not gaudy for old teachers; old masters for aged relatives; good designs for best friends'.[49] Others were more concerned about what the cards said about their affluence than their taste. In a 1935 novel, middle-class inhabitants of a small seaside town studied all the cards for sale in the local stationers so that they knew how much the senders of cards they received had spent.[50] A woman born in 1946 remembered that her parents would not hand deliver local cards for fear of it being thought that they could not afford a stamp.[51] In 1967 *Coronation Street's* Hilda Ogden was even said to rub out the cost and write a higher one on her Christmas cards before sending them. She judged the ones she received on their size.[52]

No matter how ingrained the habit of sending Christmas cards was, something of its magic began to fade as the century progressed and the numbers sent multiplied. As early as 1934, a Bath newspaper called it the 'emptiest of vapid formalities'.[53] In 1959, the Federation of British Industries noted some firms were no longer sending cards because they felt it had become too routine and commercialized. Individuals too were beginning to see cards in a different light. In the 1960s a few took out newspaper notices to say they would be not sending any but instead would be making a donation to charity.[54] Practical considerations undermined the practice too. The telephone reduced people's reliance on letters to keep in touch and thus reduced the importance of the cards letters were sent with. In 1975 increased postage costs and the refusal of the Post Office to introduce special rates for Christmas cards were estimated to have caused a 20 to 30 per cent fall in card sales. The increasingly early arrival of some cards did not help. Some remembered their pre-war childhoods of excitedly waiting for the postman on Christmas Day but the 'post early' campaigns meant most now arrived far earlier. Before the war, many had simply ignored these slogans. In 1936 in Bristol alone, 969,000 letters were posted on Christmas Eve and over 646,000 were posted after lunch.[55] After the war, the increasingly strained postal service could not guarantee such fast deliveries and this made people avoid sending their cards too close to Christmas Day . Yet, when Christmas Day deliveries were abolished in 1961, some objected, claiming that cards that arrived early were forgotten whereas timing something to arrive on 25 December was 'thoughtful'.[56]

As society got more affluent, sent more cards and placed less value on the practice, people also seemed to devote less time to choosing and even writing their cards. Multiple packs and boxes were the norm by the middle of the century. Card manufacturers claimed that people still carefully chose cards for close relatives and friends, but sent standard and cheaper ones to others on their list.[57] Whereas how to address a card could be the query of a 'problems page' letter in 1950, there were complaints in 1960 about people sending cards printed with the name and address of the sender but with nothing written inside them. In 1993, the *Sunday Times* was lamenting the existence of cards with pre-printed messages for school friends, bosses and all manner of relatives, suggesting that consumers were increasingly reluctant and unable to spell out things on paper.[58] Such short cuts meant what could have been a personal experience often became just an expected ritual. Photocopying and computers encouraged people to replace individual letters with a standard one inserted with every card. Detractors sneered at the boasting and impersonal nature of these round robin letters, although the perfect world they often depicted was not out of sorts with the idealized nature of Christmas itself. Yet they were a cause of genuine anxiety, as people compared their own lives to the perfection they read about from others.[59] By the twenty-first century, email meant the letters and cards might not even be physical things anymore, although that too was disapproved of by the traditionalists.[60] Not helped by rising postal costs and the emergence of social media, sales of cards were slowly falling in the 2010s and there was a despondency in the greetings card industry which relied on Christmas for 10 per cent of its UK sales. Between 2009 and 2012 alone, its festive sales fell from £172 million to £164 million.[61]

Decorations

Perhaps a majority of people started receiving cards before they put up their decorations. Between the wars, decorations were dominated by greenery such as holly, ivy and mistletoe. Their use was a legacy that predated the Victorians and carried with it the remnants of early modern superstitions. Putting decorations up before Christmas Eve was thought to bring bad luck, while burning them afterwards was meant to avoid ill fortune, although there were geographical variations in when this was supposed to be done. Everywhere, however, the practice of burning green decorations was fading from fashion in the early twentieth century.[62] In 1921 a magazine article noted that taking green decorations down before Candlemass Day (2 February) was supposed to be bad luck, but it accepted that in most private homes they were gone by then because they had withered. It reminded readers of the variety of superstitions that promised misfortune to those who left them up too long, including the threat that the fairies that lurked in decorations would turn into elves of mischief.[63] The fact that such knowledge could no longer be assumed is evidence in itself that superstition was fading in a world of science and mass education. Nonetheless, there were still those who stuck to these traditions and transferred them to the modern decorations that replaced greenery. In the 1940s, for example, there were Welsh women saying it was unlucky if a man put up the decorations.[64] Indeed, as a Portsmouth newspaper pointed out in 1938, such superstition may have been much laughed at but it was still common and followed, even if only out of a sense of tradition.[65]

One plant had particular connotations with Christmas and its own set of traditions. Perhaps as a remnant of some sexual rite, mistletoe combined Christmas greenery and the festival's importance as a time when conventions could be broken, this time in the stealing of a kiss. Pimlott was right to argue that mistletoe was popular among the Victorians because it 'provided an outlet for impulses which had at other times to be restrained'.[66] It was hung in workplaces, pubs and cafes and as late as 1947 a writer could claim that girls were not supposed to refuse a kiss under it.[67] Again, there were local variations surrounding the tradition. In the 1950s researchers recorded sayings such as a girl who had not been kissed under the mistletoe would not be wed that year and the first man to kiss a girl under it must give her a pair of gloves.[68] By then, however, the popularity of the plant was much reduced from its Victorian heyday. This was partly because of the falling numbers of the fruit trees it grew on and by the 1930s Britain was having to import mistletoe from France.[69] In 1925 one writer noted that mistletoe had fallen into disuse to some extent but he did not mind too much, noting 'If the girl wants you to kiss her, mistletoe is no advantage: if she does not, it is no excuse.'[70] Well into the 1950s, some women certainly continued to feel obliged to receive a kiss under the mistletoe but in the less formal post-war climate this meant less and less, which meant the tradition gradually faded further from popularity.

In fact, the use of all green decorations faded somewhat as the century progressed. Urbanization meant fewer people had access to them and by the First World War both the middle and working classes had begun to supplement or replace them with things made from glass or paper. By 1927, one Scottish newspaper was even claiming that synthetic holly and mistletoe was

PLATE 10 *Christmas decorations on HMS* Mermaid, *1916. Paul Thompson/FPG/Getty.*

as common as the real thing.[71] But greenery from the garden and elsewhere was still used inside the house throughout the period. Indeed, one 1947 writer claimed that Christmas put urban children in touch with seasonal change, partly because they went out to look for green decorations.[72] In 1940, a middle-class Swansea man used berries, leaves, ivy, gorse and rose hip sprays to decorate his home. These were added to frilly paper decorations, 'rather flattened' paper chains, coloured glass balls and coloured candleholders. They were hung in window recesses, on the stairway, in the passage, over pictures and on the mantelpiece. He recorded in his diary that the effect was 'quite colourful'.[73] This combination of bought, homemade and green decorations was probably quite typical in the middle of the century. A man recalled that in most windows in 1930s working-class Tyneside hung 'wooden barrel hoops wrapped in greenery, from which glass baubles and tinsel were suspended'.[74] In Cheshire, similar decorated contraptions, made from two hoops pushed together, were known as Christmas bushes and were hung from ceilings and used instead of trees.[75] Tinsel (made from aluminium paper), glass balls and paper chains, bells and stars could all be bought cheaply in bazaars and multiple stores such as Woolworth's. One working-class woman remembered that during her 1930s childhood the decoration was just 'tatty paper chains which we had saved for years'. Nonetheless, their appearance was still 'like greeting old friends again'. Another remembered that in her deprived Edwardian childhood, homemade paper streamers had given her house a sense of life.[76]

In the 1950s growing working-class affluence saw decorations become more extravagant, a riot of bright and shiny materials. This was rooted in that class' taste for interior decor that was elaborate, colourful and chintzy.[77] The fact that decorations had no practical use perhaps made them particularly attractive to a working class that wanted to indulge itself. Technology and the lure of the modern helped too. Just as many families were replacing the traditional features of their homes by removing cornices, fireplaces and panelled doors, so too did Victorianesque decorations lose something of their dominance. On trees and mantelpieces, candles gave way to electric lights. Silvers and golds pushed out traditional greens and reds. Aerosols allowed spray-on snow to be spread everywhere. Plastics supplanted glass and paper and led to a whole range of new decorations and Santa and snowman miniatures. In 1960 *Woman's Weekly* was telling readers to be wholehearted in their decorating because it gave the home a festive spirit. They should pack away some pictures and ornaments to make room and combine something new with the treasured decorations used every year. In the 1960s observers were noting that the greater interest in home decoration led people to seek more originality in their Christmas displays, bringing in the likes of spring flowers or even pineapples.[78] By the late twentieth century, new technologies meant there were decorations that flashed and played music. For those who wanted to, homes could be turned into bewildering displays of kitsch, colour, noise and light.

Some read deep meanings into these practices. In 1956 a *Daily Express* editorial declared that 'Decorations are an essential part of the gaiety of Christmas. Familiar scenes are made bright and exciting. The whole family is drawn closer together – bound by the fragile links of a paper chain.'[79] An anthropologist claimed that Christmas lights 'illuminate and gradually dispel the dark cold and austere outside, making it bow to the sociality within. From this base it reaches out with the aim of incorporating some larger humanity in a divine or global sphere.'[80] That might sound rather pretentious but ordinary people certainly could think there was nothing ordinary about their decorations. A Barrow housewife recorded in her 1942 diary: 'To other people the glittering balls and ornaments would look like rubbish, but I'd not change them for gold and jewels – they are alive – with "memories that bless and burn".'[81] Pulling the decorations out of storage and reassembling them was a tradition in itself. They might not be much noticed when actually hanging on the tree or mantelpiece but the first handling of them could lead to bursts of nostalgia.

Most common, however, was for people to see decorations as signifiers of taste. Some interwar middle-class families limited their decorations to cards on the mantelpiece and holly and mistletoe in a vase or on picture frames. Even some working-class families then thought paper decorations were rather 'common'.[82] People's sensibility to this increased as the decades progressed. The 1950s and 1960s fashion for DIY encouraged people to see arrangements and homemade decorations as some sort of conspicuous consumption, a sign of taste, time and talent.[83] In 1961 the Countess of Bandon contrasted the 'tatty' paper decorations of her childhood with her own 'beautiful and dignified' arrangements of holly, ivy, yew and coloured balls, none of which she would let the children help with except for those placed on the tree.[84] There was advice aplenty for those seeking to achieve such effects. In 1922, for example, the *Daily Mail* told readers that decorations should be limited to one or two rooms and the entrance hall. In 1934 it was recommending pink and silver or green, red and gold as colour schemes for the Christmas table.[85] Ladies groups had talks on tasteful and 'ingenious' decorations and television was soon pitching in with similar advice.[86] As home improvement became something of a British obsession at the end of the twentieth century, the advice grew more elaborate. One 2000 book suggested five different decorative themes: white, traditional, exotic, contemporary and country.[87] Other books told readers to decorate with style and panache, and promised something 'truly special' without any need for much time or special skills.[88] For those who could afford it, there were companies who would do the decorating. Most of their work was for commercial venues but one, whose client base was typically high-income families, noted: 'Our typical residential customer is someone who values their private time with friends and family, who doesn't want to deal with the hassle of decorating but wants a beautiful looking home for the festive period.'[89]

Yet even newspaper articles offering advice on tasteful decorating could still conclude, to quote one 1934 local newspaper, that 'The tinsel and the coloured paper are not to be despised; they are the symbols of the spirit which wakes anew each Christmas and which only the disgruntled would like to see discontinued'.[90] Some were forced into such decorations because in a children's festival their offspring's demands for colour and sparkle won out over parents' more sober tastes. Yet what might seem tacky and kitsch to some was a source of joy to others. Indeed, some self-consciously took pride in being gaudy. In the 2000s, one childless woman in her thirties told a researcher: 'We really doll the house with lights and tinsel and everything tacky.'[91] Even this could be unvoiced status-seeking since allowing your normally stylish home to become temporarily garish showed visitors a sense of fun and an ability to not always be too serious.

Some people, however, did not decorate at all. Between the wars, decorations were an expense some could not afford, while in a 1938 survey there was some sense that decorations, beyond maybe a few greeneries, were pointless if there were no children at home.[92] After the war, it was young adults and the elderly who were most likely not to decorate, whether through a sense that Christmas was behind them now they were no longer children or because they were not likely to have anyone around to see the decorations. A few did not do it because they just did not like decorations or found them, as a character in the 1952 film *The Holly and the Ivy* put it, 'peculiarly depressing'. In 1967, the director of the National Portrait Gallery was even horrified by the 'aesthetic dross' of Christmas decorations at a time when British design was supposed to be leading the world.[93]

By the late twentieth century, perhaps more common than horror at the aesthetics was horror at how early some people put up their decorations. In 1978 one Christmas historian wrote that the decoration of the home was 'widely left' until the 24th.[94] If that was true then, it was a custom that was quickly undermined but even before the 1970s it was far from universal. Even in the 1940s there were examples of people decorating the house in early December.[95] One 1975 book claimed that traditionalists said decorations should not go up before 6 December (the feast day of St Nicholas), whereas purists maintained Christmas Eve was the date.[96] In a middle-class backlash, anything before December was increasingly regarded as very poor taste, while leaving it late was fashionable. In 1984, *The Times* claimed the country was divided into two classes: 'those who start to celebrate Christmas at the end of August and end their festivities on Christmas Day, and the others who start theirs just as the first group are stopping'.[97] But even among the middle classes the Christmas Eve date was then falling away, although it was not replaced with any agreed alternative. By the late twentieth century, decorations may have gone up earlier, but they were coming down earlier too. The tradition of retaining them till Twelfth Night fell into abeyance, partly because the religious significance of the twelve days of Christmas faded and partly because there was no agreement on whether Twelfth

Night was the fifth or sixth of January. Both dates were generally replaced with any convenient date just after New Year.[98] Yet we should be aware of exaggerating the earlier conformity to the tradition of taking them down on Twelfth Night. One Hertfordshire woman remembered of the mid-1950s that decorations came down quickly after Boxing Day.[99] Thus, perhaps the only thing that can be said for certain about the time decorations were up for was that it was a personal decision taken within broad parameters of tradition and taste.

The question of when decorations went up became a public rather than private one as more and more families started making their decorations visible to the external world. At one level, this might be interpreted as another attempt to show off one's good taste or adherence to a dominant cultural practice, but it can also be seen as a genuine attempt to share the aesthetic and heart-warming qualities of decorations. This was not a new development; the Victorians had put greenery on the outside of their homes, but this custom had fallen away by the middle of the twentieth century.[100] In its place emerged a new tradition of placing wreaths on doors and decorations in the widow with the curtains open so passers-by could see inside. A 1960 novel described a London suburb:

> In the windows of some of the dark, staid villas, usually so depressingly uniform, were the marks of individualism – small trees speckled with colour, or a silver ball with streamers, or a holly wreath, or nothing. Even the absence of a Christmas token seemed like a personal statement and stirred the imagination to wonder why.[101]

In the last quarter of the century, external electrical lights were often added to such domestic displays. As with so much of Christmas ritual, it is difficult to be certain how widespread all of this was. At around 7.30 pm on Christmas Eve 2013, on the suburban streets around where I live in Cardiff, roughly a third of houses either had external decorations or the curtains open so that internal lights and decorations could be seen. The majority of external decorations were simple trails of lights, usually white, or wreaths on the front door. That was probably not untypical. While a significant minority chose to show off and share their festive spirit, a less noticeable majority did not.

When, in 1964, an American family put extravagant decorations, including a rooftop Santa, on their Surrey house, some of the neighbours complained and the incident made the national television news.[102] It was the 1990s before such external displays became common, popularized perhaps by depictions in American films such as *National Lampoon's Christmas Vacation* (1989). Householders competed with each other to produce outlandish displays of pulsing coloured lights and plastic inflatable depictions of both Christmas iconography and almost random objects such as teddies, trains and ladders. Some even held their own lighting ceremonies.

One BBC investigation argued that reactions to such displays were divided roughly equally between welcoming, hostile and ambivalence.[103] However, the hostility they attracted could be very strong, even to the level of disgust. The displays were concentrated in working-class urban districts and some called them 'chav bling'. This sense of superiority was rooted in the hostility that could exist towards sections of the working class and the former council estates and other areas of low cost housing where the displays were usually found. Critics regarded the displays as not just lacking in taste but in sense too, viewing them as a waste of money and electricity by profligates unable to afford it. Research in Manchester and Sheffield found that the householders responsible tended to be middle-aged or older and not working. They were not defensive about their displays but proud of the colour, exuberance and humour. Most importantly, they thought it a conscious celebration of Christmas, an attempt to spread cheer and joy to others in the community, something which they were proud of. Some added to this altruism by putting charity boxes out along with the extravagant decorations.[104]

Christmas trees

The centre piece of decorations was, of course, the Christmas tree. Armstrong claims that 'they created a new spectacle in the home, transforming the interior and adding to the experience of a special occasion through the creation of an environment that was familiar yet different'.[105] A 2008 book declared: 'Christmas wouldn't be Christmas without a beautifully decorated tree.'[106] Many people, and certainly those with children, would have agreed but the tree's development had actually been a rather protracted affair. By the outbreak of the Great War, Christmas trees were fairly standard in middle-class homes but in working-class houses they were far less common. In 1918, *The Times* noted that Christmas trees' German associations meant they were not in vogue that year, but that did not last and the interwar period saw a growth in the number of working-class families buying trees. In 1926 the growth in demand was being estimated at 10 per cent a year. Indeed, *The Times* claimed that 'Poor families in Lewisham and similar districts are just as particular about the shape of their trees as people in Belgravia'.[107] This was not just a replication of middle-class tastes. Supply was increasing as the Forestry Commission, set up in 1919, planted more conifers. People also saw trees in public places, such as shops, schools, parks, squares and hospitals, and in films, and that reinforced their desire to have one.[108] But before the war, the Christmas tree was still far from a universal norm. In 1937 a London teacher recorded that he had seen a large number of trees through people's windows on his Christmas Day walk. But the fact that he thought this worth recording suggests it was not a deeply engrained or automatically expected habit.[109] Of the thirty respondents to Mass

Observation's Bolton Christmas 1938 questionnaire, a survey dominated by the working and lower middle class, twenty-one had put up decorations in their home but only five had trees.[110] In 1930 a London Christmas tree seller claimed that the market was stronger in the Midlands and in the north because the London child was 'getting too modern', perhaps not believing in Santa Claus or not liking trees because mechanical toys could not be hung on them. Some estimated the number of trees put up in Britain before the war at 4 million, a significant figure but still one that indicated it was a minority habit.[111]

Trees on sale before the war varied in price from 6d. to £15 and in size from a matter of inches to 25 foot. Of course, very few had a house that could take anything that size and the cheapest were just ornaments for the sideboard or table.[112] In 1924 sellers were saying that the day of the big family tree had passed and the vogue was for small ones that could be placed on tables.[113] However, after the war there was a shortage of trees, caused by more pressing needs for timber and import restrictions to prevent disease. The large tree thus became an aspiration, creating a black market and some outrageous prices. In 1946 it was reported that 8-foot trees were being sold for £39 18s.[114] In 1951, the last year of supply problems, a survey found that just two in five respondents had erected a tree. That year, a middle-aged, middle-class Sheffield couple bought a tree for the first time and invited all

PLATE 11 *Christmas trees and mistletoe, 1923. Hulton Collection/Getty.*

the neighbours in to see it, suggesting that it was relatively unusual. Over the course of the 1950s and 1960s, better supply, more spacious housing and greater levels of affluence saw the Christmas tree become the norm in working-class families. By 1986 opinion polls were suggesting 79 per cent of people had Christmas trees, compared to 47 per cent in 1953.[115] If research in America was applicable across the Atlantic, then most of those who did not have a tree were either elderly or childless.[116] Cost and space however remained a problem for some. A 1970 report by Shelter, for example, noted the case of a young woman living in a single room in Liverpool with four children. She simply had no room for a tree.[117]

A 1971 news report claimed that if a tree dropped just 1 per cent of its needles there would be 2,000 to sweep up. Trees were treated to minimize this problem, but this could not stop the competition from artificial versions which offered a more regular shape without any of the mess. The first artificial trees made in England were said to date to 1932, but their convenience was outweighed by the fact they were not 'Christmassy' enough, at least according to the *Portsmouth Evening News*. It was not until the 1960s that they became popular, by when their material was in keeping with fashionable home decor, thus enabling people to show their modern taste. The fact that they could be cheaper helped too. By 1971, it was being reported that real tree sales had slumped and an estimated half the market had gone over to plastic ones.[118] However, in the 1980s real trees became fashionable again, partly because a feeling emerged that artificial ones were rather working class.[119] Estimated annual sales of real trees in the 1980s were 4 million but a quarter of a century later this had reached 6–8 million.[120] Research was then finding women who toyed between the perceived higher status of a real tree and the practicality and cost-effectiveness of an artificial one.[121] Such decisions were not helped by environmental confusion over whether it was better to buy a plastic tree that would last but cause pollution in its construction or a new real one each year. By the twenty-first century, the cost of real trees had slid upwards, and this, along with concerns about allergies, led home decor experts to declare that fake trees were no longer 'social death'. They did, however, suggest people buy white or silver trees rather than ones designed to look real.[122]

Before the advent of plastic decorations, trees were decorated with tinsel, glass balls, cotton wool, ribbons and chocolate coins, with an angel or fairy on top. There was even a brief fashion for colourful spray painted trees in the late 1920s.[123] It was candles, however, that dominated the decoration of interwar trees. Indeed, in some homes their lighting could be a rather formal occasion which the family would gather to watch.[124] Candles were, however, a fire risk and the spread of domestic electricity in the interwar years brought greater use of 'fairy lights', some of which were even shaped as small Santas and the like. By the late 1930s newspapers were claiming that few risked lighted candles anymore.[125] Whatever the source of the light, there was something magical about a decorated tree and the way it transformed a room, even for those accustomed to material luxury. In 1925 one magazine proclaimed:

> To hear the cry of joy when the curtains are drawn back by Father Christmas in person, to reveal the tree in all its glory in some squalid slum, where its advent is the great event of all the year, is worth the longest, dreariest underground journey. Even in luxurious drawing-rooms the same spell is exercised – at least, over the very tiny ones – at the sight of the vision splendid ... It is, indeed a poor heart that does not rejoice when the tree shines forth amid a circle of smiling faces, whether their owners wear smart or shabby frocks.[126]

Even nearly a century later, an investigation of low-income families found that the delight a tree could give children helped make up for a lack of presents.[127]

An American historian has suggested that the 'Christmas tree is every childhood wish and fantasy fulfilled, and a reminder to every grownup of a time when dreams really could become true'.[128] That might sound whimsical but some people invested considerable effort and emotion in getting their trees to look right. A 2004 survey suggested that one in five women spent five hours decorating them, although only 1 per cent of men were willing to do the same.[129] A woman in her forties told researchers: 'I'm very particular when it comes to my tree ... I'm almost territorial.' For some this extended to not letting their children decorate the tree. Researchers even found one woman who ended up with six trees, because each of her children wanted their own, while she wanted to decorate the main family one.[130] Yet other families decorated together and not to do this could be seen as churlish given how much children enjoyed the activity. Indeed, sharing the activity was a tradition in itself. People appreciated this ritual and were often very aware they were building memories.[131] Children often made tree decorations that were used year after year, even when their makers were grown-ups; the decorations served as a reminder of what had been or as a link with them when they were not at home that year. And if the children did mess up the decorating, it could always be rearranged more tastefully after they had gone to bed.

Another central function of the Christmas tree was to provide a place where presents could be arranged. Christmas presents had traditionally been put on the tree branches, but the increasing size and volume of gifts made this impossible and instead it became the post-war norm for wrapped gifts to be stacked up around the base of the tree. To maintain tradition, some families however developed tree presents, small gifts that were small enough to wedge onto the tree itself. Presents themselves were nearly always wrapped. Even if something was too big to wrap then a symbolic bow or card was added to it. Wrapping had the practical use of adding surprise and distancing the gift from the idea that it was something bought. It was also an example of the extravagance of Christmas and is another indication of how widespread conformity to festive rituals was.[132] This does not mean the wrapping ritual stood still and after the war the festive wrapping paper that Woolworth's had popularized in the 1930s quickly replaced brown paper for nearly everyone.[133] Nor was the ritual uniform in how it was applied. Some wrapped quickly and carelessly using paper bought for its price rather than pattern, while others had colour schemes and elaborate bows. There were those too, especially people who remembered the shortages of war and austerity, who rescued the paper after a gift was opened and ironed it for reuse the following year.[134]

Santa Claus

The modern Santa Claus originated in the United States in the 1820s but on being imported into the UK, he merged with the English Father Christmas, an unruly and sometimes even debauch figure who symbolized festive celebrations. When that happened is less clear, but the habit of British newspapers to cull information from American equivalents meant he was occasionally being described in the early 1850s.[135] Whether it was through people simply copying what they read in the press or in letters from relatives who had emigrated, Father Christmas or Santa Claus was widely being cited by the 1880s as the filler of stockings in many families. That process had been accelerated by the use of his image in advertising and in department stores but the tradition was still evolving. Oral evidence from the Edwardian period shows that stockings were not always linked to him.[136] In 1914 a Welsh-language newspaper referred to him as belonging to the English, although other papers show he did appear at Welsh parties and stores. In 1919 another Welsh-language newspaper was urging readers not to reject him because he had an English name.[137] Elsewhere, the Great War did not help his cause. In a 1919 newspaper story, a poor widow tells her children that Santa is German and that no British boy would want a present from him.[138] But his spread was unstoppable and a 1931 writer declared: 'it looks as if he might yet reign all over Christendom as the King of Christmas.'[139]

It was the 1920s to 1940s that saw a series of older customs surrounding him cement themselves in the popular practice of all classes, encouraged by published children's stories and cinematic depictions such as Walt Disney's *Santa Workshop* (1932). Santa became accepted as the giver of stockings. He was widely thought to arrive on a reindeer-pulled sleigh and entered homes via the chimney. Indeed, some families even had it swept for his visit. Parents might, especially in the north, get their children to leave out crusts out for his reindeer and a sherry, mince piece or even a cigarette or money for Santa himself.[140] The Victorian habit of writing to him also continued to grow, although the addresses used varied from the home's own chimney to the North and South Poles and Switzerland, Toytown, Fairyland or even Whitehall.[141] Some individual postmen wrote back and there were various official recognitions too. In 1952 Hull Corporation set up a service where Santa could be telephoned and he received more than 3,000 calls. In 1966 a man began a business answering children's letters to Santa (at a charge of 2s. 3d.) but he ran into opposition from Father Christmas (Presents) Ltd, which has been set up in 1948 and claimed the name.[142]

The fact that that there was no agreement on his address demonstrates the variations that always existed within the agreed framework of custom. Some children left out pillow cases rather than stockings. There were variations in where they were left too. One woman remembered that early in the century her parents put the stockings in the kitchen to avoid the children waking early, finding presents at the foot of the bed and then rampaging around the house.[143] Throughout the period, parents and writers did not always tell quite the same stories about Santa either. A 1923 British newsreel cartoon depicted his sleigh being pulled by a star rather than reindeer and showed him using a magic wand to make himself small enough to fit down the chimney.[144] In some families he just brought children's stockings, but in others it was every present, including those for adults.[145] There was no conformity or rules either in what went in stockings. As one reporter noted in 1970: 'they can either be frivolous or soundly practical, widely expensive or thoroughly cheap but they must be small enough to slip easily into a

PLATE 12 *Christmas stockings, 1955. Evans/Getty.*

football sock.'[146] Many parents did, however, replicate gifts they had found in their own childhood stockings, most notably fruit and chocolate money, long after such items were no longer unusual treats. As for the Victorians, Santa could be explained either as a magical bringer of gifts and indulger of children or as a moral figure that rewarded good behaviour but would not spoil. Researchers in 1950s British schools found many children believed he came before Christmas to collect messages, while his helpers were as diverse as fairies, pixies, elves, golliwogs and midgets. The researchers also recounted that many children thought Father Christmas and Santa were different people.[147] They did not explore quite what the difference was but it illustrates how the different names, myths and iconography could confuse small children. After the Great War, there were some who objected to the name Santa Claus because it was thought to be Germanic. Others, however, thought the name more apt because it linked the tradition to Saint Nicholas, while a Cheshire vicar argued in 1939 that Father Christmas was too anaemic to be acceptable as a name.[148] Yet, after the Second World War, this name seems to have become more common, probably because of the mid-century distaste about the Americanization of British culture. Aspects of the tradition's evolution were very subtle. Calling up the chimney to him, common before the First World War, was replaced with the safer practice of posting letters. Before central heating, jumping out of bed to look at the stocking in a cold bedroom was less appealing than it was for later children. Thus one writer in 1948 asked 'What child does not wake up early on Christmas morning, savouring the warmth of bed, deliciously postponing the moment when he will throw aside the bedclothes and feel in the darkness for the loaded stocking?'[149] His route of entrance also had to evolve after chimneys became less common with the spread of central heating and the restrictions enforced by the 1956 Clean Air Act.

How people imagined Santa also evolved. His visual appearance settled down in the Edwardian period, with a beard and hooded fur-trimmed coat or robe being norms, although less set and less smart depictions did continue.[150] Thus, readers of a 1920 story that described him as 'an old man in a scarlet robe, with a long white beard and the kindest face in the world' would have been familiar with that image.[151] Children's books were an important component in fixing his image; one 1915 story noted: 'There he was, the jolly old man, with his red coat and long white beard, just as she had so often seen him in picture books.'[152] Advertising, the most common place he was depicted, also played its part and encouraged a shift from the British idea that he wore a robe to the American imagination of him in a suit. Much of this advertising was of course in black and white but where colour depictions did exist, it was the norm for Santa to be red, even before the famous interwar Coca-Cola advertisements that are widely but wrongly thought to have invented his modern look.[153] He had already evolved into a figure that could be used to sell pretty much anything. In 1924 the *Daily Mirror* noted how he walked the streets with sandwich boards, drove a car and was even used to sell holidays to warmer climates. He could also be found in most department stores, where he might charge for a visit and a small gift.[154] The more he appeared the more established his look became and after the war depictions of him in a robe rather than suit became unusual. In 1957 one writer summed up: 'Santa Claus has stopped developing; he has arrived at a point where he serves the needs of parents, and there he sticks. Any change in Santa's appearance would bring him into disfavour, so he stays as he is; what alters is his setting.'[155]

The success of Santa was rooted in the fact that he was more than just an attractive fellow and a nice tradition. He personified Christmas for children and played a major role in controlling their behaviour. Indeed, Hamlin has argued that Santa allowed Victorian parents to escape their disciplinary role by passing the judgement on their children's behaviour to an outside figure.[156] Although Golby and Purdue are right that he no longer actually punishes the naughty, that does not quite convey the reality of the situation.[157] Although presumably no parent would now leave a stocking unfilled, the threat is always there and is widely used to ensure or encourage good behaviour. His naughty list is a staple of films and children remained well aware that Santa does not visit children who seriously misbehave.

Santa had other functions too. He brought great happiness to parents who enjoyed their children's innocent excitement and joy, something sometimes too rare in an often harsh world. Perhaps Santa was a subconscious replacement for God in a secular age that still wanted to believe there was an external force for good out there.[158] Because Santa was believed to make rather than buy the gifts he brought, he also distanced present-giving from consumerism. This allowed parents to buy their children lavish gifts without spoiling them or it might deflect the blame for poor gifts from impoverished family circumstances to this mysterious figure. The memoirs of one woman who grew up in the 1920s recall how her father told her Santa was an old man and thus could not be expected to carry heavy presents, although she was still cross that he gave richer children better presents.[159] Yet Santa was supposed to be an egalitarian figure who came to rich and poor, a view encouraged by his role in giving out presents at charity events early in the century. Freudian analyses, meanwhile, saw strange things in Santa and even the possibility that parents might encourage their children to believe so that they could feel the 'narcissism of superiority' of knowing something their children did not. Alternatively, Santa might feed parents' narcissism through taking them back to their own childhoods and a belief in Santa that they did not want to end. This is more credible at least than those who saw Santa's emergence from the chimney as symbolic of our coming into the world from the birth canal.[160]

Most parents seem to have seen Santa as a harmless white lie told to make childhood more magical and for the pleasure they derived from their children's delight. But this does not mean all went along with the fiction happily or without any concerns. There were always some who opposed

Father Christmas on the basis that it was wrong to lie to children. Others complained what Santa had come to represent tarnished the original tradition, that it was a 'pagan tale' or distracted from the festival's religious ethos.[161] In 1962 one woman wrote in *The Times* that she had ended Father Christmas with her young children because 'half-truths and make believe' would not do. She preferred to concentrate her efforts on getting them to believe 'the historical fact' of the baby in the manger and she claimed her children did not feel deprived and nor had they told their contemporaries.[162] Yet these were clearly minority viewpoints and a 1969 opinion poll found that 76 per cent of respondents thought parents should encourage their children to believe in Santa.[163]

Peer pressure was an important reason why parents lied to their children about Santa. It was difficult not to conform; to be the parent of the child who spoilt it for everyone else's children would be very dangerous socially. An American psychiatrist argued in 1951 that for Jewish parents to reject the Santa custom was to reject an important part of US culture, whereas passing it on was an indication of assimilation.[164] This argument could be extended further. Santa was a very powerful cultural norm and one that brought joy to children. For parents to reject it was one of the most powerful statements of cultural dissent that they could make, a prioritizing of their own cultural beliefs over the magic of their offspring's childhood. Even post-war authorities maintained the fiction. The Post Office replied to Santa's letters (even in the face of cost cutting exercises), broadcasters stuck rigidly to not giving the game away, advertisers were reminded by their regulator to do the same and as early as 1928 there was public controversy over a story that a Sunderland teacher had told children the truth.[165]

Yet believing was occasionally a cause of confusion and even stress. Children asked their parents to put fires out in case Santa was burnt. Some were confused by how Father Christmas could be in so many stores at once.[166] They compared the stories they were told and wondered and worried about how Santa could do everything that he was supposed to. Between the wars, the fact he was more generous to some than others troubled children.[167] The fact that he only came to homes that celebrated Christmas could also be rather confusing, especially for children of other religions who did not take part. But most children were able to rationalize this and much else. Most easily reconciled the idea that the Santas in the shops was not the same person or the real thing. Rather than let this worry them (as their parents might fear) they simply appreciated two presents.[168] They accepted the inconsistencies and illogicality of Santa, just as they tended to accept the world as presented to them. Indeed, much of what they saw around them in the adult world did not make sense. For children believing in Santa was no more incredible than believing in a benevolent God in a world they knew was full of sadness and injustice. The fact that adults told them Santa was real and produced evidence such as the remains of food left out, was a very powerful influence, especially in a world where children were told it was wrong to lie. As psychologists found, children could thus continue to believe, even as their powers of reasoning developed. Yet this does not mean they believed everything they were told about Santa and they could recognize the elements of fantasy about him from an early age, especially in terms of those they saw pretending to be him. Indeed, it might be that many never really believed in him but acted out the role because it was expected and to ensure they received presents.[169]

As rumours spread around the playground, some children tried to find out for themselves. This might involve trying to stay awake as long as possible or even hiding a letter to Santa up the chimney to see if it was taken.[170] The disbelief in him might come gradually, the result of suspicions, a growing critical faculty and conversations with friends. A study of different British schools in the 1950s suggested that most children's belief in Father Christmas lasted until they were six and sometimes longer. Spotting their parents leaving the presents out or being told by older children brought the make believe to an end.[171] Psychiatric research found that discovering Santa was not real could cause disappointment and negative feelings but these were not long-lasting or intense. The discovery could also be a relief for more logical souls who could not understand quite how he could exist. Any trauma could also be muted by the esteem that the knowledge brought as an indicator of growing up and research does suggest that for a majority of children there was some pride in working out that Santa was not real. Indeed, it could be parents who found this coming of age time more difficult, a sad marker that their children were growing up and on the road to independence.[172]

The Santa story inevitably became entangled with the wider ideas about the decline of Christmas. There were concerns in the 1930s that middle-class schools and governesses were very modern and gave children adult perspectives on the world, with the result that they saw through the Santa charade.[173] In responding to complaints that Christmas did not have the magic it once had, one writer claimed in 1971 that Father Christmas had 'never been *credible* to children. It is just that city living, no open fires, no big chimneys, some knowledge from television of the vastness of the world and the impossibility of visiting every child in it, makes it more difficult for children to suspend their disbelief and hold on to the magic.' Yet, as she noted, that was what many did or at least pretended to.[174] If anything, the Santa myth grew stronger rather than weaker with the modernization of society. His chief reindeer got a new name and character of its own thanks mostly to the popularity of the 1949 song 'Rudolf the Red-nosed Reindeer'.[175] Technological developments made Santa seem more real, even in age where children were less naive. Film and television cemented his position as the icon of the festival. They may have played around with his personality and environment, but they ensured that every child knew who he was, thus making the challenge to any parent who did not want to engage in the make believe immensely difficult. The internet even allowed his movements to be tracked and for personalized films and letters to be sent back to children. Those who bemoaned that children did not have the same innocent enjoyment of Santa that they had had were probably misunderstanding what contemporary children were like. They may have had knowledge, computer games and expensive toys in their grasp but that did not stop their awe and amazement at a myth that was enchanting as anything ever made up. Parents of young children saw that each Christmas and it was the joy he brought their children that meant they were willing to lie. No matter how much values such as truth and honesty mattered in society, the happiness of children, at least for this one day, mattered more.

Food and drink

The heart of Christmas Day was dinner. Feasting had always been central to celebrations of both Christmas and the wintertime festivals that predate Christianity. There were, of course, significant variations over the centuries in terms of what was eaten but by the Great War a number of traditions such as Christmas puddings and mince pies were well established. But more important than what was eaten was how much was eaten. One writer called the food at a family Christmas in 1938 'an almost sinful profusion of everything'.[176] That was then an exaggeration for the working-class but even their dinners were usually characterized by the fact that they featured more food than normal.

The meat that formed the heart of the Christmas dinner illustrated how traditions were still in flux between the wars. While turkey's place as a festive meat had been popularized by *A Christmas Carol*, it also caught on because the size of the bird meant it was suitable for feeding a large family gathering, while its appearance on the table was a spectacle in itself. Yet turkey was still relatively unknown by the Great War as a working-class festive meal and in 1921 *The Times* remarked that while turkey was the Christmas dinner 'of the many' it was beef that was 'of the multitude'.[177] In 1923, a dealer at a London market wondered if turkey was going out of fashion because demand was low with people preferring beef or pork for Christmas.[178] Turkey did grow in popularity as part of the general spread of middle-class Christmas traditions between the wars and its consumption perhaps became something of a status symbol, encouraged by references to it on the radio and in newspapers and magazines as the festive dish.[179] By the late 1920s and 1930s, newspapers and butchers were reporting how it was replacing other meats. In 1936, a Sunderland newspaper went as far as saying that the turkey was the 'most important thing about Christmas'.[180] *Woman's Own* tried to reassure those who could not afford the bird that pork could taste like turkey and that beef had once been traditional.[181] The shift owed much to the rise of cheap imported turkeys. In 1923, for example, the cheapest imported turkeys cost 1s. 3d. a pound, whereas Norfolk turkeys were 2s. 9d. By 1936, Canada was exporting a million turkeys to Britain for Christmas.[182] Take-up was boosted by the growing availability of smaller birds, as farmers responded to market demands and by the late 1930s the standard size of a Christmas turkey seems to have fallen from 20 to 16 or 12lb. Consumers wanted smaller turkeys because they were cheaper but also because in modern housing developments flats and maisonettes only had small ovens which could not accommodate the traditional bird.[183] Whatever their size, by 1938 more than 2.5 million turkeys were being bought meaning maybe one in five households were having it for Christmas dinner. Pictures of the birds in the days before their slaughter were now staples of newsreels and their impending doom was an established joke across popular culture's different mediums.[184]

A key appeal of turkey was that it was not often eaten at other times and thus made the Christmas meal special. However, all forms of poultry remained expensive and joints of beef or rabbit remained more common before 1939 as Christmas meals for working-class families for whom any kind of roast meal was special. Indeed, the vagaries of supplies from abroad meant meat costs could vary significantly and this encouraged people to buy whatever they felt offered the best value.[185] A Suffolk man even remembered his family having blackbird pie for Christmas dinner 1930 because his parents could not afford to buy anything.[186] One way of getting decent meat at a decent price was simply to wait until late on Christmas Eve when butchers auctioned off their remaining stock. Even then getting the money for a cheap

PLATE 13 *Turkeys and ham for sale in a London pub, 1923. Topical Press Agency/Getty.*

joint could mean going without meat in the weeks after Christmas.[187] In 1938 two different Bolton butchers noted that it was pork and then mutton that sold the most at Christmas, claiming that people ate beef the rest of the year so there was less festive demand. In contrast, another butcher in the town said turkey and pork were his best sellers, although demand for birds depended on the price. Thus, while turkey may not have yet been established as the festive dinner for all classes, prices permitting, the working classes did look for meats that made Christmas dinner special by being different. Indeed, such was the desire for a good meal that this final Bolton butcher noted that his trade trebled at Christmas.[188]

Chicken, uncommon in working-class diets before 1939, was another alternative that gained in popularity after the war, partly perhaps because it resembled a festive turkey. A 1951 poll found that three in five respondents were having some form of poultry for their Christmas dinner. A 1955 survey in Greater London found that 41 per cent of respondents had chicken and 38 per cent had turkey.[189] That decade's affluence gradually enabled people to buy chicken more regularly, which both meant it lost its specialness, and that more could afford turkey at Christmas. Supply was increasing too, as turkey farmers improved production methods to meet rising demand.[190] In 1958 an ITV reporter interviewed pedestrians who he found walking alone in London and judged the standard of the dinner they were going to have by whether it was turkey or not. Consumers seemed to expect the same by then and there were reports of 'turkey tantrums' when the cost of the birds was too high.[191] By the 1970s turkey was so engrained as a Christmas tradition that sitcoms could joke about families buying a giant one despite none of them really liking it. By the middle of that decade around 10 million turkeys were being sold for Christmas, while chicken sales were substantially down on their norms at other times of the year.[192] In 1997 polls were suggesting that three-quarters of people had roast turkey on Christmas Day, a figure still being replicated by surveys twenty years later.[193]

In 1933 Sir Robert Bruce Lockhart recorded that his Christmas dinner was 'a gluttonous and boring show with about seven courses'.[194] Such levels of feasting were unusual but most people did supplement the main meal with a number of other treats. Stilton cheese became widely associated with Christmas and in 2010, 70 per cent of all its sales in Marks and Spencer took place in December.[195] It even generated its own rituals. One man remembered an interwar family custom of examining a large Christmas stilton with a magnifying glass, looking for moving mites and then taking a spoonful. An uncle would call: 'Those who are about to die salute thee!'[196] Stilton was more ritual than luxury but chocolate was quite different, especially before the war when its consumption was still a treat. Working-class families then paid into chocolate clubs to ensure they had a box to share on the big day. The festive consumption of nuts, cakes and fruits also increased in the middle of the century, as people strove to eat both more than normal and types of food that they would not normally buy in order to make Christmas special. One Rhondda man remembered of his interwar childhood that poverty meant Christmas mocked small children's dreams but it was still an enjoyable occasion because the food was much better than normal.[197] Families were helped here by the popularity of food and drink as presents within all classes. Even Harrods advertised tea as a potential present in the 1920s. The receivers of such a gift were presumably not reliant on presents of food and drink for a bit of festive luxury but many interwar working-class families were. This extended beyond conventional luxuries such as sweets and chocolate to what the middle classes might consider everyday joints of meat. Another route to a special meal was stolen goods and an investigation of Huddersfield working men's clubs in the late 1950s and early 1960s recorded that everyone knew it was best not to ask where a Christmas bird came from.[198]

Those who could afford to spend on food did. Even in 1938 Bolton fruiterers were noting that people were prone to buy more than they needed.[199] During the war, people's desire for a large meal was kept up and they saved rations to ensure they got it. Thus, in 1940 Nella Last's working-class family had chicken, sage and onion stuffing, sausages, potatoes, sprouts and creamed celery, followed by Christmas pudding, rum sauce and cheese and biscuits.[200] The affluence of the 1950s increased people's ability to live up to such expectations. The novel *Saturday Night and Sunday Morning* (1958) illustrated what many working-class families could now achieve: 'baked potatoes, roast pork, and cauliflower, and no one spoke during the eating of it. Plates of Christmas pudding followed, rivers of custard flowing

PLATE 14 *A middle-class Christmas dinner, c. 1951. Grace Robertson/Getty.*

down the escarpments of each dark wedge.' For tea there was salad, bread and butter, trifle, Christmas cake and mince pies.[201] Even in a Liverpool slum, an investigator in the late 1950s found people saved for and placed great emphasis on a good Christmas dinner. Some were having goose, others both lamb and chicken and even the poorest families had 'a lump of pork'.[202]

The vegetables people consumed were diversifying and multiplying too. Christmas meant some working-class families might have vegetables such as parsnips that they did not otherwise eat but accompaniments were usually quite simple before the war. In 1937, one wealthy family had just sprouts and potatoes with the turkey, bread sauce and gravy, although the starter had been artichoke soup and there was champagne afterwards. That same year, a 49-year-old Marlow housewife recorded that her roast chicken was accompanied by just sprouts and jacket potatoes.[203] But post-war affluence encouraged all classes to produce plates piled high with a variety of vegetables. Indeed, one, the brussel sprout, became a tradition in itself after the war. Before 1939 they were eaten due to their seasonality but they were still uncommon enough for newspapers to recommend eating them at Christmas.[204] Again, it was the 1950s that saw their establishment as a tradition – mostly because of their relative unusualness for most of the year – and by the twenty-first century, a quarter of all British sprout consumption was taking place in December. By then surveys were suggesting that as many as seven in ten people ate them on Christmas Day but just a quarter of people finished their serving, while a fifth dreaded being served the vegetable.[205] In the face of this, the fact that they were served so widely was another example of the power of people's sense that Christmas traditions should be conformed to.

The frozen-food manufacturer Birds Eye claimed in 2013 that many people were replacing sprouts with peas.[206] The National Food Survey between 1975 and 2000 confirmed that expenditure on traditional festive foods such as dried fruit and sprouts was falling, especially among the middle classes.[207] This does not mean traditions were being completely abandoned but puddings were diversifying and there were new twists on the existing staples such as cooking sprouts with pancetta. Such dishes illustrated how, thanks to inspiration from television cookery programmes, the standards and diversity of British cooking were improving.[208] In 1990 a television recipe for chocolate truffle torte on *Delia Smith's Christmas* saw a sudden demand for the ingredient liquid glucose and within two weeks there was none left to buy in Europe. Smith was also responsible for boosting the popularity of the cranberry in British Christmas recipes (although it had been recommended as an accompaniment since at least the 1930s).[209] Influenced by the growing fashion for good cooking, some people even abandoned the turkey in favour of a goose or pheasant that would allow them to simultaneously declare their fashionability and commitment to what they imagined was an older tradition. However, some cookbooks regarded the turkey as 'non-negotiable' and central to what made Christmas.[210] Lovers of good cooking who followed this line turned to organic and free-range turkeys. They first became popular in the 1980s but by the twenty-first century they were fashion statements in themselves. In 2011, one upmarket farm selling 40,000 birds a year, allowed its stock to run around a cherry orchard, had open days so people could see the conditions, hand plucked its birds and hung them for two weeks which, according to the managing director, gave them 'an incredibly different flavour and texture'.[211]

The hold of tradition on the Christmas dinner at the end of the century was further evident in the use of family recipes. A 1985 survey suggested that a quarter of women used a passed down family recipe for their Christmas cake and that young wives were as likely to make one as older ones.[212] In low-income families, sacrifices were made to ensure there were a few traditional trimmings and treats, even if this was for just one meal.[213] For such families conforming to tradition helped mark a participation in society that was too often denied them. Across the social board, a traditional dinner was something that appealed to all generations in a way that something more adventurous, modern or foreign might not and this mattered at a family gathering.[214] Moreover, because the meal was so important to the whole festival there was probably less willingness to experiment and produce something that someone might not like or even approve of. Thus, the Christmas dinner retained its popularity, even if it had been updated in various ways. By Christmas 2012, some estimates claimed the British were consuming 10 million turkeys, 370 million mince pies, 25 million Christmas puddings and 35 million bottles of wine.[215] The figures for puddings and pies were probably exaggerated but there did exist, for the few so inclined, Christmas-dinner themed or flavoured pies, cheeses, pizzas and crisps.

A roast meal for an extended family was a complex affair, dependent on timing and skills not often practised by most ordinary cooks. Already by the interwar period, preparing the meal was acknowledged as a source of stress and considerable work. A lack of a big oven meant some working-class families had to cook their Christmas meat at the local bakehouse, although this did add to the sense of occasion and was an opportunity to meet up with others.[216] For more prosperous families, newspapers ran features on how to cook and carve a turkey and what to do with the leftovers.[217] By the 1930s Christmas was being used to sell gas cookers on the basis that they made preparing the dinner easier. Servants being on holiday could add to the stress in households where people were not used to cooking. One cookbook suggested that homes without maids skip soup so the roast would not be spoilt by delaying its serving.[218] In 1937 a 31-year-old artist from Birmingham noted her anxiety over dinner but when everything was perfect she recorded: 'I'm proud of my success.'[219] Having a maid became far less common after the war but the resulting growth in cooking experience did not mean Christmas dinner was necessarily any easier. A 1978 Delia Smith book noted that cooking a Christmas turkey for the first time, especially with guests and in-laws milling around, could 'quite a traumatic experience'. Two decades later, celebrity cook Nigella Lawson was writing that Christmas cooking could 'induce panic and depression'.[220] Such comments were common in cookbooks and were probably there to make the reader feel better but the wealth of advice available is also an indication in itself that people did want help. Indeed, there was also a market specifically for Christmas cookbooks. The first dates back to 1870 and further ones were produced in the interwar period.[221] But it was the 1990s that saw their numbers rise quickly and by 2014 the British Library was listing 203 publications in its Christmas cookery section. By then, festive television cookery shows were common too and setting new standards of Christmas aspirations, not just in terms of the food served but the kitchens it was cooked in and the family parties it was served to. The new celebrity cooks offered lifestyle guides as much as culinary instruction; 'All I wanted was a day like Nigella's' sobbed a member of television's *Royle Family* after a disastrous attempt at making dinner.[222] It was all a long way from the practical demonstrations of the first Christmas cookery shows in the 1950s but as people had got more prosperous the requirements of what would make Christmas special and different had grown too.[223]

The National Food Survey showed that between 1975 and 2000 all classes spent an increasing amount on ready and convenience foods but that there was no rise in such spending at Christmas.[224] Indeed, Christmas was a time when people actually tried to shy away from conveniences that at other times they might have used. In 1980 the British Poultry Federation experimented with new products to help those suffering in the recession enjoy Christmas. Frozen chicken burgers did not catch on as a Christmas meal but did have potential for the rest of the year, unlike the churkey, a small bird injected with chicken soup after slaughter, which briefly entered the festive market.[225] There were various attempts to produce more traditional convenience Christmas dinners that just needed heating but these were not successes. Instead, people were more likely to buy puddings, pre-peeled vegetables, or prepared meats, items that still required some assembly or cooking and thus allowed people to feel they had made dinner after all. It was a meal that was supposed to be hard work.

The effort was made because Christmas dinner was a highlight of the day and a ritual in itself. The table was decorated and set using the best crockery. Indeed, some people only used their best tablecloth and cutlery at Christmas.[226] The family of Andrew Martin, a York novelist born in 1962, used to eat in the lounge as a marker of the importance of the day, pushing back the sofa to make room. Thus, there was a sense of occasion even before the food had been served. Of course, not everyone had the same aspirations and some families still ate the meal with the television on.[227] But surely more common were those who ate, talked and then afterwards relaxed in the glow of being full and content. Such simple pleasures mattered, especially at times of trouble, as the 1940 diary of a Swansea air-raid warden recorded:

The turkey was one of the finest I've tasted – Bayney [my wife] said I say this every year. The brussel sprouts, of our own growing, had the authentic nutty flavour, and the roasted potatoes were gold-brown without and floury white within. The Christmas Pudding anointed with brandy, blazed as it should. The crackers, although last year's stock, cracked, every one. And they held toys as well as hats and mottoes. A good, happy day, with no raids by either the Germans or the British.[228]

In a 1941 Mass Observation investigation, 42 per cent of respondents were having game or poultry for Christmas dinner and just 1 per cent were having an ordinary meal.[229]

The traditional Christmas dinner was not complete without crackers. Between the wars they more commonly had rhyming mottoes than jokes inside them and Dylan Thomas remembered one of his declaring 'Let's all have fun this Christmas Day, Let's play and sing and shout hooray!' It caused the adults to roll their eyes.[230] The size and shape of crackers was then more varied than today's products. In 1924 it was reported that they were getting bigger, with two foot being considered worthwhile, although some were as big as six-feet long. Boxes could be bought for as little as six pence and they contained balloons, hats, musical toys and parlour fireworks. The 1937 diary of a County Durham factory worker made it clear how much the hats and jokes were enjoyed in his family. They even had them at breakfast on Christmas morning.[231] The son of Derbyshire miner recorded of Christmas 1934: 'We all laughed in our bellies simply because the jokes were feeble.'[232] But even between the wars, when humour was less sophisticated, there were those who did not like this particular ritual. A former student living with his parents in Cardiff noted that they drank Moussec, port, brandy and sherry with their lunch, followed by cigars, but did not have crackers or hats: 'Such things put too great a strain on our awkward domestic conviviality.'[233] As the century progressed, the ability of crackers and hats to delight probably dissipated and most were actually rather poor value, especially since there was generally no way of knowing what was inside them.[234] Thus, the fact that they sold at all was another testimony to the power of traditions.

Lighting the brandy on the pudding was another ritual that added to the theatre of the meal. Although for some, it seemed a waste of drink, for more it was a moment of cheer that could dwell in the memory. In 1961 the Countess of Bandon wrote of her childhood: 'I can hear the laughter and see all the faces of my aunts with a strange sort of green glow from the jumping flames. I can taste that horrid strong brandy which took away my breath, followed by the delicious sweetness of the raisins.' She was not alone in not being keen on the taste and the Christmas pudding was another food that was kept up more out of a sense of tradition than enjoyment. Some people simply ate a small portion because they felt they should.[235] The tradition extended beyond the mere eating. Making the pudding could start as early as October, with children stirring the mixture three times and making a wish.[236] Between the wars, some shared the expensive ingredients, grouping together to make a large batch in a washhouse's copper tub. Despite their general preference for sweeter foods, children liked Christmas puddings because coins were often put inside, the only reason some ate it at all.[237] Other families put charms in their pudding, such as silver dogs or bells, and finding one might have a specific meaning such as foretelling your marriage or wealth.[238] But the popularity of the pudding faded over the twentieth century and by 2010 surveys suggested that less than six in ten people ate the dish.[239] It was not tasty enough and too much effort to make. As early as the early 1920s there were laments that people now bought their puddings rather than made them at home.[240] Ready-made puddings helped prop up the tradition but the fact that so many of those sold were rather small showed how their purchase might be simply be made for form's sake or to satisfy a family member with a less sweet tooth or stronger affinity for a traditional Christmas.

The pudding helped make brandy a staple Christmas purchase in many families but this was also because it could be drunk. Drinking was an integral feature of many families' celebrations. Indeed, drunkenness in the streets around Christmas had been a topic of concern in the Victorian period, not least because of the contrasting image it presented to ideas of goodwill and domesticity.[241] The Queen never says merry Christmas in her broadcasts, apparently because of its connotations with drinking, and one accountant remembered being trained always to say Happy rather than Merry Christmas to elderly female clients.[242] Yet Christmas, like weddings and funerals, was one time when the interwar working class might appear drunk in the street without incurring a social stigma from respectable neighbours.[243] Public drunkenness was less of a problem by the interwar period, at both Christmas and other times of the year, but it remained a time of year when people clearly drank more, especially at home, than they would otherwise do. Indeed, the absence of drunkenness cases before Hull magistrates at Christmas 1945 was actually a cause for comment.[244] Even people who did not otherwise drink might have a tipple at Christmas and others felt it quite alright to start before lunch. By the late 1950s some working-class families were buying bottles of spirits, port and sherry to have at home, despite the fact these drinks were not drunk in pubs or at other times of year.[245] In 1943 Mass Observation found that teenagers and children were often given a small beer at Christmas time, while children might sneak a taste of whatever alcohol was around. Indeed, a quarter of those asked said Christmas had been when they first tasted alcohol.[246] In 1932 a drinks importer was noting that in his industry sales from October to December could be three times the January to March period. Perhaps to help spread the cost of Christmas in the middle of the century but also because wine was not widely available, people were buying their drink early. Statistics for 1963 showed that while beer sales spiked in the summer, wine rose by 67 per cent on the year's average in November, while spirits were 107 per cent up.[247] The growth of off licences in the 1960s made alcohol more available and lessened people's need to order things in and probably also increased drinking in the home all-year round. But the Christmas peak remained and by the twenty-first century alcohol consumption was 41 per cent higher in December than the annual monthly average. This also crossed class boundaries; whereas the middle classes normally spent a higher proportion of their food budget on alcohol than the working class, this was not true in December.[248] Drinking at home had a rather practical purpose, in that it helped raise the cheer in what could be strained family circumstances. A Coventry housewife even wondered in her 1948 diary whether the moments of bad temper and atmosphere of subdued happiness in her teetotal family gathering could have been avoided by a spot of wine.[249] But why ever they did it, drinking too much was a standard joke for the festival and dealing with Boxing Day hangovers was part of the throng of Christmas advice that newspapers and magazines offered throughout the century.[250]

In 1962, two Hatfield pubs applied to open at 11.00 am rather than noon on Christmas Day because some wives liked to have a drink with their husbands before lunch; the magistrates were shocked and their chairman announced: 'This has shaken us. This is a religious festival and the churches are holding special services at this hour.'[251] But they were out of touch with popular beliefs. A researcher in Gosforth (Cumberland) in the early 1950s found that Christmas was a rare occasion when local women could visit a pub without eliciting much comment. A late 1950s ethnography of a rural north Wales village also found that some young women went with their husbands to the pub at Christmas but would not do so the rest of the year.[252] Not all men took their wives and a morning trip to the pub was common enough for Pat Phoenix to proclaim on *Coronation Street* in 1972 that all men were too paralytic to appreciate Christmas lunch.[253] We should be weary of clichés here. In 1947 a 35-year-old carpenter complained that the pubs of Croydon were undecorated and quiet on Christmas Eve. He maintained that Christmas was not what it once was and that in the past he had seen queues outside pubs before opening time on 24 December. Other surveys suggest that pubs were quiet on Christmas Day itself but busy the night before.[254] In 1956 thirty Scunthorpe licensees even applied to close their pubs on Christmas evening, complaining that opening was a 'dead loss'. That was, no doubt, because people were at home; of all the traditions of Christmas, the fact that it was festival of the home was probably the strongest and most widespread.

Conclusion

Once the eating and presents were out of the way, people not only needed something to do but they even felt, as one middle-class woman noted in 1937, that they should be doing something.[255] It was here that rituals really diversified in the days before television. There might be a gathering of friends or neighbours but as the holiday got longer this seems to have shifted away from taking place on the 25th itself. Entertainment might come from a singsong round the piano or gramophone, from father dressing up as Santa, or children performing their party pieces.[256] More middle-class families might expect children to put on a play, something which itself could become a family tradition and was encouraged by the inclusion of suitable Christmas scripts in annuals.[257] Parlour games were popular with many (though not all) and in tune with the festival's jovial and slightly silly atmosphere.[258] Playing cards was more common, especially among the working class. Some listened to the wireless or read to themselves and others. An early historian of Christmas wrote in 1902 that 'Everybody knows that Christmas is the time for ghost stories'.[259] They continued to be mainstays of many Christmas publications throughout the interwar years but they were a fading fashion. As the *Saturday Review* noted in 1922: 'Who but a genius can make a success of a ghost story with an audience gathered round a radiator?'[260] All these entertainments did continue in the post-war period but they had to compete against the pull of television. In 1954 a middle-aged Sheffield man lamented in his diary how his Christmas guests had wanted to watch television and had to be lured away from it. 'TV seems to have a fatal allurement for young people' he summed up.[261] He liked to hold slide shows but others were less imaginative. As a character remarked in the 1974 Christmas special of *Steptoe and Son*, every year he watched television and ate and drank for three solid days because there was nothing else to do.

How families marked Christmas could become something of a ritual in itself. Some played a particular record every Christmas morning; others celebrated the start of the holiday by always watching the same film. In the late twentieth century, many children always wore new pyjamas on Christmas Eve. In a 1930s middle-class Surrey family, the tradition was that presents were piled up in a bath. A middle-class Swansea family in the 1940s had a tradition of giving 'daft' gifts such as a potato wrapped in Christmas paper or an apple, nut or sweet wrapped in multiple layers to make a large parcel.[262] Such very individualized traditions helped define families, cementing their shared sense of identity. They could also be self-conscious symbols of the collective personality of a family, a ritual that displayed their humour or tastes. When presents were given was a particular opportunity to stamp some personality on the day, especially for those who wished to express their patience and lack of greed. The timing might vary from upon waking to after breakfast, church or lunch. As the century progressed, and the volume of presents grew, some families staggered them through the day. There were also variations in how exactly the presents were opened. In some families, it was a very public affair, with people taking it in turns and allowing everyone to admire and see what had been given. Opening them all at once did not have to mean any less gratitude. In 1930s Cheam, a middle-class family did this after breakfast and initial lunch preparations, but there were 'occasional pauses to admire something particularly exciting. Copious thanks and expressions of surprise and gratitude were expected. Kisses were exchanged for any particularly tremendous present.'[263] Not every family had these strict rituals but for those who did they were one of the most important ways a family defined how they 'did' Christmas.

All Christmas rituals were chosen and shaped by people's aspirations and tastes. Christmas gave people an opportunity to say something about themselves, whether that was through a virtuous wait for presents, stylish decorations, ironic kitsch, carefree extravagance or anything that showed one had a sense of humour or was able to put aside aesthetic concerns for the enjoyment of the children. The origins of family rituals may be rather unspecific and perhaps a little imaginary and they were not always re-enacted exactly each year, but they had a powerful attraction.[264] They were statements of commitment to family and heritage and an important part of intergenerational dynamics and bonds. Newspapers even told people that Christmas customs helped build bridges across misunderstandings between people.[265] Of course, there was some negotiation and evolution, especially when new children or spouses arrived. Families coming together had to reconcile their desires for relaxation or bustle, for structure or chaos, for refinement or going with the flow, for people or materials. Rituals were thus rarely imposed by just one family member.[266] But it was because they were implicitly or explicitly negotiated that they were so powerful.

Rituals could be especially important as symbols of identity when they were related to non-British ethnic origins. Thus, for Spaniards, for example, giving presents on Christmas Eve rather than the 25th could be a conscious way of keeping in touch with their roots.[267] Interwar Italian immigrants who ate pasta on Christmas Day were also showing a commitment to their roots.[268] Christmas rituals were also inevitably tied up with class. The rules of this were not obvious but it was widely accepted among those who followed them that not putting decorations up early, playing charades or waiting until late to open presents were markers of the middle class.[269] Yet, before 1939, this seems to have been less true and the diaries of Mass Observation offer no suggestion that more middle-class families generally opened presents later. Christmas was thus an example of how markers of class were increasingly subtle in a post-war world where occupational and even to some extent financial differences had blurred. As the workers earned more and the expanding middle classes lost some of their old signs of status such as servants and private education, consumption became a refuge where people could exert their status through their taste. Christmas thus illustrates the embourgeoisement of the working class and the limits of that process. Undoubtedly it was a very visible sign of how much of the working class was better off from the 1950s but it also marked how powerful taste remained as a marker of class status.

Quite how universal any specific Christmas ritual was is unknown. Some certainly spent completely different Christmas Days. For example, 1937 saw a group of men and women in their twenties at a holiday camp in Kent. They played cards for money, told smutty stories, discussed politics, went to a pub and for walks and searched for a stable where they could ride horses. Although they did not know each other, the day clearly encouraged them all to come together and socialize.[270] Three-quarters of a century later, one supermarket worker noted how some people to choose to have their Christmas dinner after the 25th in order to pick up bargains in the supermarket.[271] On 25 December 2012, 1,548 people filed their tax returns online and nearly 8,000 people logged in to tax or declare their vehicles off road.[272] Such people were not being as different as they would like to imagine. Much of Christmas Day, once present-opening was over with, was actually rather mundane, consisting of tasks that were not that different to an ordinary weekend: feeding pets, walking the dog, a trip to the pub and watching television. An unmarried 33-year-old speech therapist, spending Christmas 1937 with her mother and adult sister in Birmingham, noted that they had begun to give up keeping Christmas traditions in recent years and were happy for it. The only difference between her day and a normal Sunday was they ate turkey and her mother went to chapel.[273] Yet the mundane could still be perfectly pleasurable. Bernard Donoughue, head of the prime minister's policy unit, recorded in his diary in 1975: 'No telephone or television. Just the old radio, a log fire and the children. Lovely.'[274]

No matter how personal they were to someone, rituals were always a blend of personal preference and a wider cultural heritage. Rytting thus writes of a 'crafting of tradition' by families.[275] Like all forms of consumerism, Christmas may have given people the opportunity to define their own personality, to mark themselves out from the crowd, but they were doing so in a way that mirrored hundreds of thousands of other people. Those people using Christmas rituals to demonstrate their taste, even if this meant opting out altogether, were still operating within a broad culture of conformity. The variations were just that, variations within a theme and most people still adhered to the general rules and traditions of sending cards, playing along with Santa, erecting a tree or decorations and having a substantial meal.

This broad conformity might seem trivial but it says something very significant about Britain. It shows how strong the nation's cultural unity was, it shows how committed people were to tradition and established ways of doing things. Of course, this extended far beyond Christmas to things as varied as respect for the monarchy to people's commitment to queuing. But Christmas is different in that people regard Christmas rituals as traditional rather than functional in the way queuing is. Agatha Christie's Poirot was right when he claimed that the British fondness for Christmas traditions and goodwill was a sign of their sentimentality.[276] Indeed, some commentators argue that this sentimental nostalgia gathered pace in Britain after the Second World War, as people turned to the past for reassurance amid the dislocations and apparent national decline of the post-imperial world.[277]

But the adherence to Christmas tradition cannot just be seen as the product of an ultimately conservative society. Sociologists have pointed towards how the atmosphere and feel of Christmas is important to people.[278]

It was the rituals of decorations, presents and food that made the Christmas atmosphere and distinguished the day from others; they made the day fun, special and out of the ordinary. This also meant that the Christmas was a very material practice. As Marling points out, 'Christmas makes its connections to the past through *things*', some of which are real, some imagined.[279] This took different forms. There were some goods, such as special presents or decorations made by children and rescued each year, that were retained because of their sentimental meanings.[280] But there were also wrappings and decorations that were cast aside quickly, their function to brighten the day and show a commitment to a way of doing things fulfilled.

People also marked the specialness of Christmas in other material ways. Throughout the period, Britain was a very home-based society and that characteristic grew as the quality of housing improved.[281] Christmas itself was as much a celebration of the home as it was the family since the two concepts were inseparable. People were proud of how decorations made their home look. They also behaved in ways that demonstrated that material pride in home. Early and mid-century working-class families used the parlour, a room reserved for Sundays and special occasions. Some even made it the only night of the year when they lit bedroom fires.[282] Laundries enjoyed a pre-Christmas rush as people had their tablecloths and dress shirts cleaned. A wallpaper shop in Bolton noted in 1938 that the run-up to Christmas led to an upturn in sales as people decorated for the festival.[283] Adults and children often dressed up for the day, wearing their best dress or suit, something encouraged by women's magazines. A 1930s observer noted the poor retrieved their best clothes from the pawnbrokers for Christmas. New clothes might be bought for the day too, while women had their hair done.[284] In 1962 *Woman's Own* told readers that there was 'Nothing like a flattering new hairstyle to give that Christmas lift'. It also recommended that a ribbon bow would add a 'decorated-for-Christmas look'.[285] Such habits lessened as society became more casual in its attitudes towards dress in the late twentieth century but by then the material consumption of Christmas had increased so much that people did not need to dress up to ensure the day was special.

However much rituals mattered because they were traditional, there was actually some flux over the century. The coming of electricity was one cause, as it allowed more elaborate cooking and generated new entertainments that hurt the popularity of more traditional games and activities. The virtual disappearance of snap-dragon, a popular Victorian festive game where people rescued raisins from a bowl of burning brandy, showed that twentieth-century sensibilities could kill some traditions. It was the absence of large fireplaces that probably did for the burning of the Yule Log, a large piece of wood lit on Christmas Eve that was supposed to bring luck for as long as it remained alight, although there was some evidence of it in rural counties in the 1930s.[286]

The Yule log was a remnant of older Christmas traditions that were rooted in superstitions. These extended far beyond notions of what would bring good or bad luck to beliefs that girls could knock on the door of chicken houses on Christmas Eve to discover if they would marry or that livestock knelt down to pray on Christmas Eve. Education and greater scientific knowledge eradicated much popular superstition by the interwar period but there were still remnants of feelings that certain things were bad luck and this encouraged a degree of Christmas conformity. One working-class woman, who with her sons away and little money was not doing much celebrating in 1941, told Mass Observation that she would still have a special dinner because it would be bad luck if they did nothing to mark Christmas.[287] In the middle of the century, people were still making wishes over the turkey wishbone or with their first mince pie of the season. This was hardly surprising in a world where new superstitions developed around sports and gambling and luck gave hope to a working class that so often had to struggle against material shortages.[288] The genuine belief in whether rituals could bring good or bad luck probably disappeared by the late twentieth century but people still encouraged children to make Christmas wishes because it fitted in with the enduring idea that Christmas was a magical time.[289] Magic is not a concept much used in the modern world but it was an adjective often used to describe the season. This was not the kind of magic embodied in witchcraft or the occult but in Walt Disney and the movies. It was something that gave people a gasp of awe or wonder in a climate of modernity where so much of the everyday was safe and explainable. Indeed, this was in keeping with the festival's religious roots, which were a celebration of God coming to earth. This led a German professor to claim in 1927, 'Christmas can be understood as a *wonder*.'[290] The wonder or magic of Santa or glittering decorations might not be quite the same as the creator coming among his people but the terms were the same.

In the James Bond novel *On her Majesty's Secret Service* (1963), M called Christmas dinner 'Damned sentimental rubbish', but he nonetheless went along with the meal his housekeeper had prepared.[291] As a 1912 writer observed, 'the sense of obligation to keep the feast is very strong, and there are few English people, however unconventional, who escape altogether the spell of tradition in this matter.'[292] The American sociologist Theodore Caplow has pointed out of Christmas rituals: 'There are no enforcement agents and little indignation against violators. Nevertheless, the level of participation is very high.'[293] Ultimately, that was because the rituals were very flexible; they were personal rather than formal rites. There were a multitude of different ways of feasting, decorating and remembering friends and family which meant people could conform in ways that they felt comfortable with. The rituals also had social and cultural functions; they bonded families, they allowed people to confirm their place in traditional British culture but in a way that still declared their individuality, taste and status within it. Two 1947 writers even argued festive traditions were an emotional desire for 'something unchanging in a chaotic modern world'.[294] Conforming to these rituals was not always everyone's choice and those with children were particularly vulnerable to peer pressure. But that did not change the fact that there was a remarkable degree of conformity in people's festive behaviour. However fractured Britain was in terms of its social and economic structure, Christmas was at least an indicator that its cultural web was still intact.

CHAPTER FOUR

The spirit of Christmas

In the film *Miracle on 34th Street* (1947), Kris Kringle, an old man who thinks he's Santa Claus, remarks that 'Christmas isn't just a day, it's a frame of mind'. He was right. How people reacted to the festival was a measure of how they felt about their lives and about the nature of society. This was often a very conscious act because Christmas itself was widely felt to have essential qualities. It was a time of charity and togetherness and the festival presented an ideal of fellowship and goodwill to others. These qualities offered a comparison between past and present and were often called the 'spirit of Christmas'. They were held up against the material and spiritual poverty that people saw around them. There was often a religious dimension to such thinking because Christians saw the spirit of Christmas as being rooted in the tenets of their faith. However, it was not just among Christians that the festival encouraged contemplation and reflection. For many people the festival was, as one writer in the *Daily Mail* noted in 1936, a time to pause and to look both back and forward; it marked the end of one year and the approach of another.[1] Similarly, in 1923 a writer reflected: 'I suppose I am not peculiar in looking, from habit or inherited instinct, on the days between Christmas and the New Year as furnishing an opportunity for meditation, recollection, and moral reflection. If one does not dance, I don't see what else there is to do.'[2] Such meditations happened at a collective level too, as the media, deprived of conventional news, filled its pages and schedules with reflections and predictions, further encouraging individuals to indulge in their own ponderings.[3]

The very notion of Christmas was thus caught up with people's conceptions of time and history. Much of the imagery of Christmas was rooted in the past and cards often depicted Victorian carriages and street scenes. Like Scrooge facing the Ghost of Christmas Past, for adults, it was a time to look back, whether that was to their own childhood or to the very beginnings of Christmas and the birth of Christ. The festival could be a nostalgic source of comfort and continuity amid the uncertainty of modern developments, but it could also be a time of regret and sorrow, a reminder that happier times had passed by and finished. Christmases past and present were also directly compared, but rarely in a way that was favourable to the present. Indeed, lamenting the loss of a traditional Christmas dates back to the seventeenth century. By 1922, the *Saturday Review* was noting, 'It has become a truism to say that Christmas to-day is not as good as the Christmases of old. Like *Punch*, Christmas is never as good as it was and never will be; but like most truisms this one is only very partially true.'[4] The Victorian reinvention of Christmas itself had also been based on a sense of the past. It was an attempt to regain something that contemporaries felt was lost, a rural England, a time of goodwill, benevolence and social harmony, something in contrast with the poverty and tensions of the modern world. Thus the Victorian Christmas was a celebration of what used to be and might still be.[5] That never went away and it infused the spirit of Christmas.

Defining anything as loose as the Christmas spirit is no easy task: it was essentially just an abstract idea on which everyone had their own take.[6] Yet there were recurring and widely shared themes that were rooted in the festival's origins. Christmas's Christian dimension put religion and its values at the heart of the spirit. This also meant charity was important but the idea of goodwill resonated far further than religious practitioners, demonstrating how embedded Christian values were in British society even if organized Christianity was not. Indeed, Christmas helped ensure Christianity retained a relevance in a secularizing society, giving an outlet to the faith of the increasing numbers who believed in God but did not belong to a church, and reminding others of the existence of Christianity and the Christian message.[7] There were always, though, those who saw the Christmas spirit as lacking or complained that the festival embodied all that was wrong with society. Yet, the Christmas spirit actually embodied one of the most fundamental characteristics of British society: decency. For all the problems of society, most people respected others, were nice to those who they encountered and were generally reasonably content with their lives. That decency might not have often translated into selflessness, but it mattered all the same.

Christianity

It is probably not quite true to say that without Christianity there would not be a Christmas. The cultural and social significance of Christmas is powerful enough that we can suppose that if it did not exist, something very similar would; after all, all major religions have their grand feasts. But that does not get away from the fact that Christmas was and is a religious festival, a celebration of not just the birth of Christ but of the values that Christianity embodies: tolerance, charity and togetherness. Yet the fact that Christmas is also a commercial and secular celebration has meant that Christianity has actually had a rather uncomfortable relationship with its primary festival. It is supposed to be a time when Christianity occupies centre stage in public life, but what the festival often did was suggest to Christians how little influence their religion actually had on the lives of the majority of the British people.

It is important not to romanticize the dedication to religion before the Second World War, even at Christmas time. The memories of war, population movements within and between communities, and a lack of leadership all meant trying times for organized religion between the wars. This was evident in how drunks would sing ribald parodies of carols in the East End of London and in claims that some children there would not go carolling because they feared ridicule in a district with so few active Christians.[8] Although the majority of British people described themselves as Christian and were heavily influenced by Christian mores, regular churchgoing was as low as one in ten adults in some urban areas, although two to three times this number went irregularly.[9] Attending church was thus never as cemented in the routines of Christmas Day as might be imagined. In 1949 one Welsh vicar complained in his parish magazine that many people only regarded Sundays as sacred, to the neglect of Christmas Day and Good Friday. He summed up: 'Try as we may we cannot get many church members to regard them otherwise than as secular days, to spend as they do Bank holidays.'[10] In 1926, the parish magazine in Gosforth (near Newcastle) complained that the church would have gone undecorated had it not been for the efforts of local schoolgirls. It was Easter that people saw as the more important religious festival, both socially and spiritually. Church attendance for this festival could be double that at Christmas time,[11] although this sometimes owed something to rather prosaic reasons – for example, some mothers did not attend church on Christmas morning in order to prepare lunch.[12] The greater religiosity of Easter Sunday meant it was more vulnerable to secularization than Christmas and by the time national figures were first collected in 1960 communicant levels at the two festivals were very similar.[13]

Just because some people were not going to church does not mean the festival had no religious significance for absentees. Oral history has shown how non-church-attending parents still often encouraged their children to pray, and how they respected and valued religious institutions and beliefs.[14] Moreover, churches achieved much higher levels of attendance at Christmas than on ordinary Sundays and the festival is a reminder of how pervasive a Christian culture was in mid-twentieth-century Britain. In a large 1950s survey, a quarter of respondents only went to church once or twice a year, with Christmas and Easter presumably being those occasions.[15] In Akenfeld in rural Suffolk, an average Sunday congregation in 1967 had thirty-one people; however, that year's carol service attracted 110 people and the Christmas Eve service fifty-five.[16] In 1957, nearly a thousand people were actually locked out of Brompton Oratory after the doors were closed. There were 4,000 there for midnight Mass and the police had to be called to control

PLATE 15 *Christmas crib, St Vincent de Paul school, London, 1954. Keystone/Getty.*

the crowd.[17] It is important not to underestimate the joy and sustenance that people drew from such occasions. Attending a service or hearing the bells that marked Christmas morning were joyous occasions that gave people a sense of calm and belonging. Within the Christmas story and message, people throughout the century found hope, confidence and inspiration.[18] Politician Paddy Ashdown recorded of a midnight Mass in 1991:

> The little church was a joy to be in. All lit by candles, the light bouncing warmly off the whitewashed walls and reflected in the glistening humidity on the stone floors. To celebrate in the company of your fellows an event of 2,000 years ago, on such a bright, moonlit night and in such surroundings, says more about the existence of God than all the texts ever written.[19]

In contrast to Anglicans and Catholics, other Christian denominations were less enthusiastic in their Christmas celebrations. In the north of England, chapels could be found holding Christmas concerts, fairs and even pantomimes, but elsewhere Nonconformist attitudes were more solemn.[20] In Wales chapels celebrated its emphasis on charity and giving, but they took a rather dour approach to the festival. A Rhondda man remembered that in his interwar childhood, many who did not normally attend chapel would go to festive services, but that 'All the laughter and fun of Christmas would be stifled under a load of solemnity'.[21] Indeed, many chapels did not have services on the 25th and instead held their Christmas worship on the nearest Sunday. Presbyterians in Scotland, meanwhile, could reject celebrating Christmas at all (see Chapter 5).

Whatever form Christmas worship took in the middle century, it took place in a context of the beginnings of secularization. In 1960, the first year for which national statistics are available, 2,074,000 people took Christmas communion in the Church in England. Twenty years later, the figure had fallen to 1,807,000 and by 2010 it stood at 903,000. This meant that in fifty years the communicant rate per 1,000 adults had fallen from 62 to 21. It is thus no surprise that by 1986 polls were suggesting three-quarters of people felt Christmas was less religious than it had been when they were a child. Such statistics do not, however, represent the full extent of churchgoing at Christmas. In 2010, 2,298,400 adults were attending Christmas services in the Church of England, compared with 784,300 on an average Sunday.[22] Yet, as Brown notes, even the constituency of occasional and festive churchgoers was falling away.[23] Of those that remained, it is probable that not all had a strong or perhaps any faith. Some people attended out of obligation to relatives who did believe. Others went from a sense of tradition or because it offered them a momentary sense of being part of some sort of community.[24] In a twenty-first-century survey of occasional attendees at Worcester and Lichfield cathedrals, 94 per cent said the music was a motivation for going, whereas just 55 per cent said they wanted to worship God and only 42 per cent believed in the virgin birth.[25] The desire for a singsong led some to head to midnight Mass straight from the pub. Some vicars had to remind their congregations that it was inappropriate to attend a party straight before a religious service. On introducing midnight Mass to Pontnewydd in 1948, the vicar even told his parish that they should fast for two hours before attending.[26]

In a 1969 opinion poll, 36 per cent said they normally went to church at Christmas, but only 9 per cent regarded the festival as primarily a religious occasion. In contrast, 37 per cent said it was equally a family and a religious festival and 53 per cent that it was primarily a family occasion.[27] Such surveys illustrated how religion was not central to the majority's festival and that trend could only increase with the onwards march of secularization. Historian Callum Brown has argued that the 1960s was the crucial decade here; religion simply stopped mattering as much and lost its dominance on both the public realm of British culture and individual behaviour within it.[28] One small illustration of that was the fact that through the 1950s and previous decades, the *Radio Times* had published full-page religious tracts in its Christmas issues. These shrunk in size through the 1960s and then disappeared altogether in 1969. The programming itself also showed how religion was losing its place at the heart of public culture even before the 1960s. In 1955 and 1956, ITV's first two years of broadcasting, there were religious programmes in its 7.00 pm Christmas Day slot. However, in subsequent years religious programmes lost their primetime slots, and the *TV Times* was exaggerating when it described the channel's 1960 Christmas schedule as 'a blend of reverence and gaiety'.[29] That year there was nothing religious on television on 25 December between 1.00 pm and 10.20 pm on the BBC and between 12.15 pm and 11.35 pm on ITV.

Surveys, however, showed that secularization was far from universal. By 2011, polls suggested that a quarter to two-fifths of people intended to attend a Christmas service of some sort and that attendance was highest in London (due to higher levels of immigrants and ethnic minorities there) and among those over sixty-five. These statistics were far above normal Sunday attendance but whether everyone acted on their intention was a different matter. Some respondents may have been saying what they thought they should, which in itself highlights a latent religiosity. Others may have included school nativity plays in their definition of a religious service. Some analyses put the figure actually attending a religious service at Christmas at 11 per cent.[30]

Concerned about the place of worship in people's lives, churches in the middle of the century tried to simplify their approach to Christmas by concentrating on one or two services. Increasingly, the focus became a Christmas Eve midnight Mass and a family service on Christmas morning. Although long established, midnight Masses were unusual in Anglican churches before 1914 because of their association with Catholicism. However, the interwar years saw them gain rapidly in popularity, first in Anglo-Catholic places of worship and then in low churches.[31] A 1947 writer attributed their popularity to a new taste for the 'dramatic in worship' and the fact that most people no longer had servants, meaning there was no other time husbands and wives could worship together.[32] Influenced partly by the desire to incorporate schools into their worship, many churches also moved their carol services from the traditional twelve days of Christmas to the period before the 25th. This was advent, a time when the Christian focus was supposed to be on judgement, heaven and hell but shopping and preparations meant it was actually when people's minds were most focused on Christmas.[33] The shifts were not always straightforward. Midnight Mass caused falls in attendance on Christmas morning and attracted people unused to church. In 1949 a church near Wolverhampton announced it would not be holding a midnight Mass for the first time in thirty years. The vicar felt he needed to protect his parishioners from those who turned up drunk and did not last the service.[34] Similarly, in the early 1960s there were reports in south Wales of churches giving up on midnight Mass because of 'rowdyism and intemperance'.[35]

Anglicanism was nonetheless becoming more tolerant of innovations related to the secular Christmas, in the hope this might spread the Christian message. It utilized the radio throughout the interwar period to broaden its reach but it also tried to ensure that worship itself was more appealing.

A few churches had Christmas trees and cribs before the Great War but this became far more common in the 1930s, first at larger churches and cathedrals and then, more gradually, in small parishes. Cribs in particular proved popular and this practice quickly spread to people's homes too, helped by the sale of cheap sets in Woolworth's.[36] By the 1950s, churches were also giving gifts to children such as books or bibles, and even organizing their own pantomimes.[37] Liberal vicars began asking children to show off their presents to the congregations. In the hamlet of Dinnington, a tradition emerged of holding a carol service in the local pub on Christmas Eve. The bar was open but it was a proper service, officiated over by the vicar and with the local MP reading one of the lessons.[38] Nor was it just the Anglicans who were adapting. Nonconformists, with their own proud tradition of communal singing, increasingly embraced popular carols, cribs and secular ideas. Thus, for example, Tamworth Congregational Church held a Nursery Land Grotto in 1949 where Santa would emphasize 'the real meaning of Christmas' amid scenes from nursery rhymes.[39]

PLATE 16 *Christmas tree at St Paul's Cathedral, London, 15 December 1953. Warburton/Getty.*

The modernization of Christmas worship upset some traditionalists. Opposition to a tree in St Paul's Cathedral was only overcome by a senior official asking the King to donate it, a present which could not be turned down. The Catholic associations of cribs meant not everyone approved of that development either and in 1938 a member of the Protestant Truth Society even interrupted the blessing of the crib at Canterbury cathedral.[40] In contrast, midnight Mass became regarded as customary in itself and one woman complained to *The Times* in 1984 that she could not find a traditional midnight service. She wanted candlelight, traditional carols (rather than modern improvements sung from photocopied lyric sheets) and no request to shake the hands of other members of the congregation. She recounted that a year earlier, several people had walked out of a service at the university church in Oxford because it was a 'dreadful hybrid'.[41] Clergy and regular congregations, meanwhile, could get irritated by the people who only attended at Christmas, resenting their lack of commitment, reverence or familiarity with the service.[42] In 1973 the vicar of Abercarn was annoyed at the popularity of his midnight services. Apart from the fact that they had attracted drunks, he wondered whether they were diverting attention from Christmas Day itself. The much smaller attendances at the Christmas morning services led him to 'the suspicion that people are getting the religious bit of Christmas over and done with, so that the "day" itself can be free'.[43]

Ministers regularly felt that they needed to remind people that religion was supposed to be at the heart of the festival. In 1935, a Cheltenham curate, for example, gave a talk claiming that 'Christmas without Christ was like a summer's day without the sunshine'.[44] There was a fine line to tread here. The giving of gifts owed something to the legacy of the Three Wise Men. The emphasis on children and family owed much to the essential theme of the nativity story.[45] But the compliant was how the essence behind these practices was being overshadowed. In 1964, the Bishop of Blackburn announced he was 'increasingly perplexed' at the commercialization of Christmas. The festival's 'frippery' was conspiring to hide 'true meaning' he wrote.[46] Such despair could even lead some Christians to actually rather dislike Christmas. In the film *The Holly and the Ivy* (1952), a vicar remarks, 'Do you know I hate it … The brewers and the retail traders have got hold of it. It's all eating and drinking and giving each other nick-naks. No one remembers the birth of Christ.' He also hated giving a sermon on Christmas morning because no one wanted to listen, impatient to get home to dinner. Even if there was not despair, most Christians did seem to feel Christmas had lost something. By 2011, a survey of churchgoers found that 93 per cent of respondents thought that the true meaning of Christmas had been devalued and 88 per cent that the festival was now more about presents than Jesus.[47]

It was probably children who had the strongest encounters with Christianity at Christmas. Interwar Sunday school attendance far outstripped adult churchgoing, with working-class children often sent because of their parents' latent religiosity.[48] Encouraged by broadcasts on the wireless, nativity plays by schools, churches and youth groups became popular between the wars.[49] In the post-war period, they became rather ubiquitous in primary schools and rehearsals could dominate the last couple of weeks of term. Although they were infamous for pushy parents showing off about their offspring's talents or lamenting the fact that their child had been relegated to the role of a sheep, the plays played an important role in spreading knowledge of the Christian tradition and surveys show high levels of knowledge of the basic features of the nativity story.[50] Indeed, for many parents and children they could be rather magical occasions, filled with the 'beauty of simplicity – of children telling and taking part in the most powerful story in the world' as *Woman's Own* put it in 1962.[51] Yet, towards the end of the twentieth century, school nativity plays also gradually became more secular. Elves and fairies were sometimes added or the story of Christ's birth was put aside in favour of another tale of goodwill and charity, especially in more multicultural areas where schools might be keen to ensure parents of other religions were not excluded or annoyed (whereas few expected atheists to be offended or at least no one seemed afraid of offending them).

Like the trees inside churches and the vicars who asked children to show off their presents at family services, the evolution of nativity plays was an example of how Christianity came to accommodate rather than compete with the secular Christmas. Few Christians begrudged the feasting, as long as the religious message was remembered too. Thus, for example, in 1932, a Bristol vicar told his congregation that when Christmas fell on a Sunday, the festival should take precedence over the Sabbath. After morning worship, he felt that 'the remainder of the day should be spent in hilarity'.[52] In reconciling the Christian and secular festivals, Christmas supported and underpinned Christianity in British society, stemming the flow of secularism. By the mid-twentieth century, more people went to church on the 25th than at any other time of year. Most importantly, Christmas offered many people who otherwise had little contact with religion, a subconscious flagging of the Christian message. Christmas was a popular day for getting married because it allowed one day off for the ceremony and another for the honeymoon. That brought people into church who would not have gone otherwise. In one East End church alone there were fourteen marriages solemnized on Christmas Day 1932.[53] Outside churches, Christian imagery was more visible in December than in any other month. There were primetime religious plays and services on the radio between the wars. In 1965, the *Woman's Own Christmas Annual* contained carol lyrics and a cut-out crib. Religious Christmas cards became more common too (see Chapter 3). In 1966 the Royal Mail began issuing Christmas stamps and it alternated each year between religious and secular designs, meaning that at least biannually everyone who sent a card used religious imagery. In as late as 1999, the *Radio Times* had an angel on the cover of its Christmas edition.

Carols, even if just heard at the doorstep, on television or in a shopping centre, were another way that many people encountered religion. Their playing was a marker of the approaching festival and a popular part of the season's atmosphere, a component of the cultural mix that made Christmas Christmas. Of course, their popularity should not be thought of as an acceptance of the religious message; it was perfectly possible to listen or even sing along without thinking about what the words meant. A 32-year-old housewife, for example, recorded that the conventional religion of a talk on the wireless on Christmas morning 1937 irritated her but that she liked the carol that followed it.[54] As the century progressed, fewer people actually knew the words because fewer people learnt them at school or at church. In 1958 and 1962 the *Radio Times* felt the need to publish a four-page spread of lyrics to help readers enjoy the BBC's various carol programmes.[55] The popular knowledge of carols was not helped by the way the canon was diversifying and by the 1960s carol books were including non-traditional tunes and music from other countries.[56] As early as 1951 there had been a complaint in the *Daily Mirror* about modern and little-known carols on the

PLATE 17 *The Raiders rehearsing for a Christmas service, Liverpool cathedral, 1964. Keystone-France/Getty.*

radio that children could not join in with.[57] Yet what constituted a carol had never been defined and even for the Victorians not all carols were actually religious. In that sense, when Elvis Presley released his 1957 *Christmas Album*, which reached number 2 in the British charts and mixed carols, secular songs and rock 'n' roll, he was actually part of a longer tradition of varied festive music. That album, like other similar recordings, played a role in updating the religious message, taking it into a secular context and associating it with something fashionable.[58] Yet as carols moved into the secular context, they did lose some of their meaning, sometimes acting as not much more than a nice festive tune whose words were not thought of. On a 1989 tour, for example, the rock band Marillion used an excerpt from 'O come, O come, Emmanuel' to begin a song about global warming. By the end of the century, there were books of musical scores that made no distinction at all between carols and modern festive songs.[59] In a 2012 survey, 6 per cent of respondents listed 'Jingle Bells' as their favourite carol and 5 per cent 'Rudolph the Red-Nosed Reindeer'.[60] But that did not change the fact that there was no other time of year when Christian songs were so widely sung and heard.

Carols in popular culture, like busy, modern services and the general Christmas message, offered some hope to Christians, not just for their religion but the state of society too.[61] In 1959 one writer argued that

> Christmas love can cure the cancer of the human spirit which distorts our friendship and love and art and politics into loneliness and lust and pornography and apartheid. And having done that, it is bound to cure our sentimentality, so that eventually we may even contemplate the Holy Family without self-consciousness or fatigue.[62]

Most Christians were not so philosophical in their faith, but it is difficult not to conclude that for those who believed in God Christmas was a particularly special time. Historians need to be careful about misinterpreting the retreat of religion from the forefront of public culture as a collapse in religion *per se*. In many ways, Christmas reflected a wider characteristic of secularization, where faith increasingly became something private, personal and less formal. As late as the 1980s, polls were suggesting that nearly three-quarters of the population believed in God, a figure far in excess of those who actually went to church.[63] That figure fell quite rapidly in subsequent decades but belief in some form of higher entity was stronger and more widespread than atheism, especially in Northern Ireland, a place that challenges all simplistic notions of secularization. The 2008 British Social Attitudes Survey suggested that, although belief levels were much lower among the young, half the UK population as a whole were either sure or somewhat sure that they believed in God, while only a fifth were sure they did not believe.[64] In the 2011 census only a quarter of the population listed themselves as having no religion. This all explains why in a 2010 survey half of people disagreed with the statement that Jesus was irrelevant to their Christmas.[65] Moreover, more widespread than a belief in God was a commitment to the broad values of Christianity. Its restrictions on sexual matters lost most of their power but the commitment to doing to others as you would have done to yourself remained how most people lived their lives. Christmas both reflected and bolstered this general commitment to the traditions and, above all, the values of Christianity. Maybe half the population might not have thought Christmas had anything to do with God but the festival still helped those who did keep in touch with Christianity and it reminded everyone of the non-spiritual ideas of goodwill and charity that Christianity embodied.

Charity and goodwill

It was Christianity that had infused Christmas with a widespread belief that it was a time of year when people should help those less fortunate. Before the First World War, many working-class families were only able to experience Christmas celebrations through the philanthropy of others. Indeed, so engrained was this that by the Great War many poor children, inmates of workhouses and even prisoners had come to expect some sort of charitable Christmas treat.[66] The initial driving force of such charity may have been religious but it was also a response to the poverty people saw around them and that meant Christmas philanthropy extended beyond Christians. Thus, in the 1920s, it was reported that agnostics and Jews were joining with the religious and those of the right and left to raise money for festive treats for children in London institutions.[67] In an echo of Victorian attitudes, a writer in the *Spectator* argued in 1932 that such giving at Christmas was a matter of citizenship and obligation.[68]

Christmas charity between the wars was a relatively straightforward affair that focused on giving the poor a better Christmas. It did not even have to involve outsiders or raising money. Staff in hospitals, for example, put up decorations and gave carol concerts for the patients. Some cinemas offered children free showings, sometimes accompanied by a toy and even a medical examination. Seasonal charity could also mean buying goods where the money went to a good cause – such as toys made by disabled war veterans.[69] But most common was the distribution of practical goods among the poor. The unemployed might thus get a Christmas dinner and many of their children were given new shoes or a small gift.[70] These charitable acts often had a public profile, which both increased the sense that charity was the 'done thing' and broadened the rewards for the giver. In 1937, for example, a newsreel showed London policemen giving out new boots to poor children and feeding them a special tea.[71] Children got involved too. In 1924 children from across London responded to a wireless appeal to donate old toys that could be distributed to children in need or hospitals. It also became common for Boy Scouts to collect and repair old toys for those in need.[72] So widespread were such acts that the poor continued to expect charity at Christmas. In 1924, for example, an out of work father of eight wrote to the press to complain that Plymouth seemed to be the only town where something was not being done for the unemployed and their children. The National Unemployed Workers' Committee Movement campaigned for extra relief from the poor law guardians, declaring: 'Demand your share of the Christmas Feast. Make your demands high.'[73] Yet ideas that only the deserving poor should benefit were never too far beneath the service. In Hastings in 1933, people who wanted vouchers for meat, groceries and coal from the Mayoress' Christmas appeal had to fill out an application form which was 'sifted by vigilant eyes' to ensure the help went to the most 'desperate' cases.[74]

Such charity did not simply happen but rather was something that charities, rotary clubs and other voluntary organizations campaigned for, indicating how strong Victorian-style philanthropy was despite the growth of welfare provision by the local state and the suggestion of some historians that the interwar middle classes were retreating from such activities.[75] Pages of charitable causes were thus common in newspapers and their advertising explicitly appealed to the spirit of the season and people's consciences. Giving was also encouraged by frequent broadcasts, sermons and newspapers articles that spoke of the importance of fellowship and charity. Even

PLATE 18 *Distribution of charitable presents, Children's Aid and Adoption Society, Leytonstone, 20 November 1931. Fox Photos/Getty.*

the Prince of Wales used Christmas 1928 to appeal for help for unemployed miners and their families.[76] The Salvation Army's 1935 Christmas Appeal announced that 'It is the season when half the world of Christendom draws together in one common festive, family bond and the other half, friendless, forgotten, misses the treat'. It aimed to offer Christmas entertainment to at least 44,000 and asked people to donate 2s. If anyone donated 10s., it would buy 'a wonder parcel' that allowed people to celebrate in their own home. The advertisement concluded: 'You give a real meaning to Christmas when you give through the Salvation Army.'[77] Others were rather blunter in their approach. A 1936 appeal to raise money for dinners for 'Christmas in Slumland' asked people if they could sit down to their own meal without any twinge of conscience knowing they had done nothing to help.[78]

There was inspiration to be drawn from what was being done to help alleviate poverty at Christmas. In 1927, the Labour politician George Lansbury remarked that 'if only East London could have Christmas every day, even "slumdom" would eventually become bearable because slums would soon disappear, broken up by the spread of the Christmas spirit'. He continued, 'we did do our best in East London to give our neighbours and friends a good time, and we did it because we are resolved to organise and work harder for Socialism, which is the message and teaching of Christmas.'[79] In a world of unemployment, dictators and war, Christmas was a reminder that there was still goodness and humanity. Nor were such feelings just limited to those receiving and giving charity. The greetings of strangers and the anticipation of the day were simple joys but ones that people appreciated and seemed to make the world more human.[80] Thus, appeals to the Christmas spirit were not just to give but to be happy and nice to others. In 1938, the *Spectator*, noting the darkness of the world and how the rise of dictatorships threatened simple values of kindness, claimed people had a duty to be happy at Christmas.[81]

Upholding the charity and goodwill that Christmas could embody became an explicit concern during the war. Broadcaster Howard Marshall told his children in a 1939 public letter that it was their job to keep the spirit of Christmas alive. He claimed this was 'Just as important, in its way, as defending the coast or sweeping the seas. Important, because in this festival – or so it seems to me – are symbolised many of the things that must we build in the new world after the war.' To him celebrating Christmas was showing the world that Britain had something that made life worth living. He concluded, 'Don't let the war spoil your Christmas. Let Christmas remind you that peace will come again.'[82] He was far from alone in such sentiments. In 1943 General Montgomery told the Eighth Army that the Christmas message of peace on earth and goodwill to all men was what they were fighting for.[83] In 1939, *Picture Post* told readers to spend at Christmas, saying that the festival was more important than ever because it would help the economy and was an 'escape from the horrors of the war' and 'a remembrance of nobler ideals'. It concluded that 'if we are merry at Christmas, we shall be showing the Nazis that we are winning the war of nerves, and maintaining the gallant spirit which has overcome the adversities which are no novelty in this very windswept isle'.[84] Politicians also used such imagery. In 1941, the home secretary, Herbert Morrison, told the police 'Christmas stands for peace and good will among men, for neighbourliness and charity, for the home and family life. The Nazi spirit is the antithesis of the Christmas spirit.' By 1942, the government was allowing a two-day holiday and bells to be rung on Christmas morning. *The Times* remarked, 'If total war modifies the pattern of Christmas, the spirit of the festival continues unimpaired, and indeed exerts a powerful influence even amid the grim events and heavy tasks of these days.' It also noted that bereavement, anxiety and a fear of the telegraph messenger meant Christmas could be difficult to enjoy but still concluded that 'the supreme gift of a wartime Christmas is to illuminate a dark world with hope'.[85]

This was also true for those away from home during the war. One former British POW recalled how at Christmas 1940 he and fellow prisoners were given a small bottle of lager and invited to join the guards in songs around a Christmas tree. The prisoners and guards particularly enjoyed singing 'Silent Night' together.[86] American servicemen put on parties for local children, made toys and even forewent their own turkey supplies.[87] Charities abroad donated presents to Blitzed areas. In the aftermath of war, the festive season provided an opportunity to build bridges with defeated peoples. Cinema newsreels showing American troops dressed as Santa distributing sweets to German children were powerful symbols of reconciliation.[88] Although not everyone approved, there were British appeals for people to give up their chocolate and coffee rations for the women and children of Germany. In 1946 some offence was taken at the government's refusal to increase the festive ration of German POWs still held. A year later, one German POW was so touched by the kindness of the 'fairy-tale' Christmas that he received in a British family home that he publicly declared his determination to always be a man of goodwill to others.[89]

This ideal of Christmas goodwill continued long after the war but the establishment of the welfare state changed the dynamics of festive charity. Whatever its problems, the welfare state raised the living standards of the poor significantly. Hunger and dire housing may have disappeared but poverty is relative and even in the 1950s, when unemployment was at its lowest, there were still people who were poor, especially among the elderly. However, poverty was less visible on the streets than it had been before the war and that meant people did not always remember it existed. Christmas thus continued to have a role as a time when people's attention could be drawn to those less fortunate. In 1957, the year of Macmillan's 'never had it so good speech', the *Children's Newspaper* told readers:

It is hard for some of us to realise that there are still children in need. They do not clamour at our doors, or beg in the streets. Poverty is no longer as apparent in our own land as in bygone times. ... Yet for all that there are still many children needing care and attention. There are motherless boys and girls, and children who have lost both parents. There is still the tragedy of the unwanted child. And beyond our shores there are countless thousands of refugee children living in dismal camps where there can be little joy even at Christmas ... These are the hapless ones, unseen by most of us and unheard of for most of the year, who need all the help that can be given by those of us who are more fortunate.[90]

As the welfare state blunted the worst of material poverty, attending to emotional need emerged as a new source of festive concern. Christmas was a festival of the family so those alone were a natural target. In 1952 *Picture Post* used Christmas to draw attention to the plight of families with fathers who were prisoners of war in Korea.[91] As Chapter 2 explored, the elderly were a particular focal point for concern but loneliness was not the only social concern to gain new impetus from the post-war Christmas. The festival became an important time for homeless charities to raise the profile of people who suffered from both emotional and material exclusion. Indeed, an emphasis on homelessness in the media became something of a Christmas tradition in itself. The campaigns did not pull their punches. Shelter's 1970 appeal, for example, centred on a picture of an unhappy-looking young child and the headline 'Why I hate Christmas'.[92]

These charitable Christmas campaigns clearly transcended religion and instead drew on the wider notion of a Christmas spirit. So powerful was that spirit that some began to see it as something that defined all acts of giving. The *Children's Newspaper* claimed in 1944 that Christmas 'is really always present whenever anyone gives, and gives with all his heart, warming the world and melting the ice of selfishness and greed'.[93] Santa Claus became a synonym or byword for unselfish generosity, whether from charities or even chancellors of the exchequer. Notions of the Christmas spirit also extended beyond charity into more general ideas of peace and harmony. This was evident in the 1972 song 'Happy Xmas (War is Over)' by John and Oko Lennon. Originally a protest song against the Vietnam War, it merged the spirit of Christmas with political optimism in a way that had a more widespread appeal than conventional political protest songs. Basing it around Christmas also gave the message a less naive feel than would otherwise have been the case. The most successful musical use of the Christmas message for charitable purposes was the 1984 Band Aid single 'Do They Know It's Christmas?' Its contrasting of the Western world of plenty and the Ethiopian famine had a significant impact, even if some fashionable music magazines were rather scathing.[94] The call to let the world know it's Christmas time was not about spreading Christianity but the goodwill and charity that Christmas embodied. It sold 3 million copies in the UK and another 47 million worldwide. Even the government was forced by public pressure to donate the VAT to charity.[95]

Band Aid illustrated how popular culture was taking over from religion as the driving medium behind Christmas goodwill and encouraging people to see it as a unique time when they should behave in certain ways. There was nothing new in this. Stirring the consciences of the middle class had been Dickens' goal in writing *A Christmas Carol* and his story continued to be very influential. In 1934 an actor who claimed to have played Scrooge more than 2,000 times said he had received thousands of letters from people saying that the character had inspired them 'to some sort of act of charity which they would not otherwise have done'.[96] The story was, however, open to interpretation. In 1932, the *Daily Worker* thought Scrooge represented modern capitalism and Cratchit the whole working class, but some interwar commentators thought Dickens' vision had been realized with the disappearance of Victorian poverty and the existence of a new social conscience. Others, in contrast, preferred to dwell upon the story as a nostalgic link to the past, an escape from contemporary horrors such as the depression and memory of war.[97] A 1935 British film adaption sidestepped Dickens' social critique and added new scenes, such as the rich and poor both singing 'God Save the Queen', which stressed British social cohesion.[98] But whatever the nuances of emphasis, the idea of Christmas charity remained in the story's endless retellings. Indeed, inspired by Dickens, stories about grumpy men (and to a lesser extent women) who did not get into the spirit of Christmas resounded in popular culture and the character of Scrooge was adapted and updated again and again, each time hitting home the idea that Christmas could be a time of redemption which enabled individuals to realize the importance of family and charity over materialism or personal pride.[99] A legion of other films told similar messages with varying degrees of subtlety, sentimentality and schmuck but the best could tug the heartstrings of the even more cynical members of the audience. This was evident in the British animation *Arthur Christmas* (2011) where even Father Christmas's family come to see that who is actually Santa is not as important as ensuring children experienced the festival's magic. Guides to how to celebrate Christmas suggested watching such films to get into the spirit of Christmas but in offering this advice they were actually only reflecting what some families already did.[100]

Such products of popular culture did not construct the goodwill of Christmas; they reflected and reinforced Christmas messages rather than created them. But the fact that in the run-up to Christmas they filled the television schedules meant they were very influential. Similar messages were also common in the short stories inside mid-century women's magazines, which implicitly and explicitly encouraged readers to do everything from reuniting with old friends, to giving presents to the poor or not leaving elderly parents alone. Yet popular culture also played upon the ambiguities of the Christmas spirit. The darker side was highlighted in films such as *Black Christmas* (1974) which sees a killing spree at a festive party where

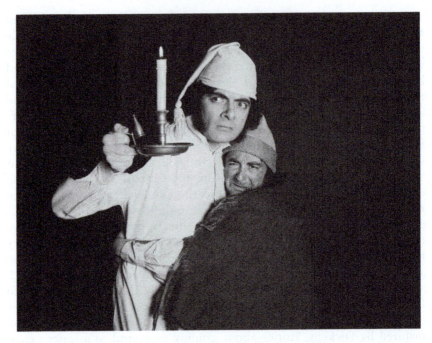

PLATE 19 Blackadder's Christmas Carol, *1988. Tim Roney/Getty.*

the screams of victims are drowned out by carol singers, or *Silent Night, Deadly Night* (1984), where the central character's parents are murdered by someone dressed as Santa and he in turn grows up to become a murder who kills similarly attired. Soap operas too got in on the act, with their own dark storylines and the power of such narratives was their setting at a time that was supposed to be about happiness and goodwill. Similarly, *The War Game* (1965), a film about the nuclear devastation of Britain, ends with a Christmas scene in a refugee camp; the music of 'Silent Night' plays while the camera shows the radiation-ravaged faces of children. Christmas was thus a trope that signified happiness and setting scenes of sadness at this time reinforced their tragedy.

However much church, charity or cinema might encourage giving, there were limits to what people were willing to do. Stepney Board of Guardians decided in 1922 not to give residents a ration of beer because it would make them quarrelsome and fight.[101] In 1953, a canon complained that among the gifts placed on the St Paul's Christmas tree were unwashed threadbare socks and an almost empty box of children's pants. He claimed that people thought they could give away their old junk because it was for the poor.[102] In the late twentieth and early twenty-first centuries, only around 30 per cent of Christmas cards sold were in aid of charity.[103] In the 2000s, research suggested that the number of people making charitable donations went up by just 5 per cent at Christmas time. Much of this seemed to be down to people putting money in collection boxes while shopping or attending Christmas events. Only just over half of households were giving and the typical household gave little compared to what it spent on food, drink and presents.[104]

Nonetheless, Christmas still meant more giving than normal. The charity that the festive spirit encouraged was strongest in small acts: a card to a lonely relative or forgotten friend, giving home-baked biscuits to neighbours, tips or chocolates to delivery boys or secretaries, or even just speaking more nicely to one's domestic servants.[105] Christmas thus reunited people with the world around them. Across the whole period there were observations of how strangers in public places were friendlier and happier than normal on Christmas Day.[106] Even in normally austere institutions, such as interwar schools or early post-war homes for unmarried mothers, Christmas could lead to a softer and kinder demeanour among staff.[107] In an echo of the parcels sent to soldiers in the trenches of the Great War, a reporter with British troops fighting in the Gulf noted in 1990 the letters sent by strangers to troops serving there: 'The fact that good-natured, generous and kind people took the time and trouble to sit down and write words of friendship to men and women quite unknown to them, struck the troops as evidence of an essential goodness in British life.'[108] Such acts of goodwill and charity may have been limited and temporal but they still mattered. Those in need benefited from the festival's spirit, while at least some others were reminded of their good fortune and the fact that not everyone was so lucky.

Hypocrisy and humbug

Charity is a complex behaviour, based on both altruism and a degree of self-gratification and even status-seeking. This meant charity at Christmas raised awkward philosophical questions. Was it only done out of conscience and self-interest? Why did it take a festival to prompt it? How much was enough? No matter how much charity was actually going on, there were those who felt there was something rather distasteful about the whole thing and thus despite all the celebrations of the Christmas spirit it could also seem wrong that it took a festival to stimulate charity, while some doubted that there was any genuine spirit behind the giving at all. As early as 1916, the *Saturday Review* was complaining of the 'usual mechanical "charity"', an impersonal giving of money that had replaced actual human relations between the classes.[109] Of course, some of the distaste was predictable – such as the anger of the right-wing tabloid press in the early twenty-first century that some prisoners were given temporary releases over Christmas – but it could also come from places that better might be expected of. The published 1933 Christmas message of one well-known priest claimed that the depression at its worst was people going without what their parents never had.[110]

For others, however, the Christmas talk of goodwill was shallow, misplaced or simply hypocrisy. Some struggled to enjoy the festival because they knew it was just a temporary reprieve from the pressures of the world.[111] An elderly novelist recorded in his 1920 diary: 'Another Xmas Day finds the world drowned in miseries and flaming with every sort of wickedness.'[112] In 1924, a left-wing publication claimed that the 'down and out' listened to Christmas chimes and messages and thought 'Lies. All lies. This world is a brute world.' In 1935 the *Daily Worker* declared that the 'ruling class probably wades deeper in the ocean of hypocrisy' at Christmas than any other time.[113] One 1931 writer asked 'Who can pretend Christmas is what it was when modern life breeds pessimism? Why pretend to be merry when everybody knows that everybody else is sad, worried, and anxious about the future?'[114] In the 1944 film *This Happy Breed*, the mood at a small Christmas gathering is upset by a Communist sympathizer telling the others that there are millions and millions of British homes 'where Christmas is naught but a mockery', with no warmth, food nor bare necessities. Accusations of hypocrisy continued throughout the post-war period and could be found on the right and left. In 1981, the right-wing journalist Auberon Waugh drew parallels between giving Christmas presents to children and the existence of a youth that felt so entitled to things it was prepared to violently rob the elderly and a society that expected government handouts. He even called Father Christmas a 'filthy foreign importation' and claimed that most men who dressed up as him were gay. There were plenty of other over-the-top laments about the absurdity of Christmas sentiments given the state of contemporary society. In 1996 the *Spectator* claimed: 'if you heard the sweet and dulcet sound of warmly clad and rosy-cheeked children outside your door singing "Once In Royal David's City" you would know that, if you opened the door, they would kick the shit out of you and rob you of every penny you had.'[115]

An antipathy towards Christmas was of course nothing new – it gave *A Christmas Carol* a central frame for its plot – but the reasons for that antipathy diversified as the century progressed and moved beyond the complications of the Christmas spirit and into a discomfort with nearly aspect of the festival as it had come to be celebrated. A typical complaint came from a middle-class writer in 1925 who bemoaned how commercialization had killed the magic, leaving 'a children's orgy', something to be endured and a pressure to pretend to enjoy oneself.[116] A 1922 writer demanded:

The rankest sentimentalist must surely acknowledge something on the debit side of the account: the boredom of ugly and futile presents; the often empty formality of giving; the surfeit of food and festivity; the weather, in murky contrast with the sparkling landscape of your Christmas cards. The robins are fed on Christmas Day, but there are wretched human beings left to starve.[117]

One 1915 commentator argued that the theory of Christmas was very pleasant but that its rituals, be that churchgoing, present-giving or anything more secular, were actually far less pleasurable in practice.[118] A letter from Liverpool to *The Guardian* in 1957 complained that Christmas was 'an archaic atavism of complete pointlessness, an unholy compound of commercial rapacity and Christian mythology, of drunkenness, gluttony, and bogus bonhomie, the whole overlaid with a thick blubber of slobbering sentiment'.[119] Others just thought what Christmas represented was out of place in the modern world. Some thus reflected on the fact that in post-war affluence, where there was always a surfeit of food and material goods, festive feasting and excess consumption was not right.[120] Much of the dislike came from how long it all lasted, with a prolonged build-up, sustained by advertisements, reminders, cards and work parties. One writer complained in 1980 that he had his first Christmas card on 4 November, heard his first carols in his local store on 24 November and saw his first Father Christmas on 29 November.[121]

It was not that most humbugs failed to recognize that Christmas did have some plus points but rather, as one self-confessed grumpy old man put it, 'the short list of good things about Christmas just doesn't compensate for all the bullshit'.[122] The strength of feeling this could induce should not be underestimated. Roy Strong, director of the National Portrait Gallery, writing in 1967, proclaimed that people were 'being mentally asphyxiated' by the 'ghastly' cards and 'gaudy' and 'nauseating' decorations. He argued that the British Christmas was the 'triumph of tastelessness, vulgarity and cheap sentiment'.[123] How widespread such feelings were is impossible to know. In 1935, the *Daily Mail* claimed that the effort of Christmas could bring out elements of Scrooge in most people.[124] Yet digging beyond such generalizations is a different matter. The historian is faced with a surfeit of published complaints about the festival. Those who are unhappy are always more likely to advertise the fact than those who are content. Such feelings were something of a Christmas tradition in themselves, thanks to the legacy of Mr Scrooge. Indeed, moaning about Christmas was a staple of newspaper and magazine features and hating Christmas was almost a badge of honour to some people.[125] In 1960 Gwyn Thomas speculated that there were about ten million people in Britain 'who deplore its gluttony, its glutinous sentimentality, its way of accelerating the transmission of viruses at the sight of mistletoe, its horrific puddings and the tigerish exploitation of business interests of some very charming impulses of love and tenderness'.[126] That would mean roughly a quarter of the adult population. Opinion polls suggest he was not that far out. In 2000, a British survey found that 38 per cent of female and 27 per cent of male respondents had negative feelings about Christmas. Overall, one in five went as far as saying they were stressed or anxious about Christmas.[127] Yet what such surveys also showed was that the majority of people still actually liked Christmas overall. Not untypical was the 1969 poll where 86 per cent of respondents said they enjoyed Christmas and 49 per cent did not want to cut down on their spending for it.[128]

After the Second World War, psychoanalysts began to note that Christmas was a source of stress, arguing it made people feel bad because of some childhood trauma or because they could not live up to Jesus' ideals.[129] By the 1970s there was some talk of 'Christmas depression syndrome', although mental health professionals were fairly dismissive of the idea.[130] More prosaically, some of the Christmas antipathy was sheer snobbery, especially the degradation of what was regarded as the tasteless kitsch of Christmas with its faux sentimentality, idealized imagery of goodwill and family, and gaudy decorations, particularly when they were on display outside rather than inside a house.[131] Such behaviour simply did not fit in with a middle-class ideal of decorum and taste. The published Christmas grumblings are undoubtedly concentrated in middle-class publications. But some of these grumblings were also rooted in the nature of masculinity and its emphasis on upholding a sort of grown-up dignity in the face of what it might be seen as a rather childish occasion, with its hats, games and magical stories. A 1930 writer argued that beneath many people's jovial Christmas demeanour was a sense of guilt and anxiety that they were making a fool of themselves and she saw this as symbolic of a generation that was too uptight and self-conscious.[132] One ethnographer even claimed that some thought there was something effeminate about men who openly enjoyed Christmas.[133] Undoubtedly, some of the male dislike of Christmas was also just a general grumpiness. One 1980 columnist summed up: 'I can't stand sitting about, pulling crackers, silly hats on, looking at the box and my mother-in-law falling asleep. The Christmas lunch is murder: sprouts, carrots, turkey, roast potatoes, brandy, indigestion, oblivion.'[134] The relationship between a dislike of Christmas and a grumpy personality was evident in Kenneth Williams, an unhappy and lonely man. He recorded in his diary in 1963: 'All my *loathing* of Christmas and Public Holidays poured over me during the walk home. All those groups of "merry people", windows open & awful noise of singing, and daft decorations everywhere & drunks and bad driving just beneath the surface.' In 1967 he even complained about the volume of telephone calls from friends over Christmas. He spent Christmas morning 1970 washing his Venetian blinds.[135]

Perhaps the dislike of Christmas was wider than it appears because throughout the period it was difficult to actually do much about it. Within families there was a sort of emotional blackmail and obligation to go along with the festivities but many did actually rather enjoy themselves when they let themselves be bullied into this. It was because some did not like admitting this that a 1935 writer had to encourage readers, 'Let us be truthful, and admit the quite juvenile delight that fills us because Christmas is here again.'[136] In contrast, in 1961 the Countess of Bandon wrote that even though she enjoyed Christmas, with her children now grown, the heart of it had gone and she longed for it and the associated 'ghastly exhaustion' to be over.[137] We should not thus imagine Christmas phobia was a constant or straightforward condition. People who claimed to dislike it could still enjoy Christmas, while others who went along with the festivities might dislike them deep down. It might spring up as part of teenage rebellion against the family and the angry idealism of youth but it could fade again with the coming of children, reappear as those children grew older, more demanding and cynical at Christmas time, and then fade again when young grandchildren came on the scene. Moreover, there was some inconsistency in people's feelings. One female writer recorded in private in 1937 her dislike of and boredom with Christmas but then proceeded to say how much she liked present-giving, Christmas radio and glitzy decorations.[138] Indeed, it could often be the thought of Christmas more than the reality that appalled. Noël Coward wrote in his diary on the morning of 25 December 1960:

> This is a day of goodwill to all men and the giving and receiving of presents which nobody particularly wants, a time for planned gaiety, determined sentiment and irrelevant expense; a religious festival without religion; a commercial orgy of love without heart. Ah me! I fear I am becoming cynical, but how lovely it would be if it were an ordinary day on which I could get on with my work and read and play patience and perhaps paint a picture; if there were not so many ecstatic 'thank yous' looming ahead and *not* an accumulating pile of thank you letters to be written.

If he had read back through his dairies, he might have remembered that he did sometimes have a very pleasant day and subsequent entries also showed that 'contrary to all expectations' he could enjoy 'every minute of it'.[139]

Nostalgia

Whether people liked Christmas or not, there was a widespread feeling that it was not what it once was. Some people argued this was simply because after all the build-up and preparations Christmas was over quickly and thus bound to disappoint.[140] But for others there were deeper sociological explanations. The *Saturday Review* argued in 1922 that for many life was now 'too smooth and simple and comfortable … for the simple joy of Christmas to have much meaning. Christmas means the most to those who have least, and for those who have the hardest work to make it merry.'[141] Others saw it as being attacked by the forces of the modern world, such as Russian Communists, American commercialism, urbanization, mechanization and speed according to one 1932 writer.[142] A 2001 survey found that for every one person who thought that society was more caring at Christmas time than thirty years ago, there were five who thought the opposite.[143] In making such judgements people were really commenting on their view of society as much as Christmas. As Mrs Garnett remarked in a 1972 edition of *Till Death Us Do Part*, 'Christmas ain't what it used to be; nothing is.'[144] As a significant event that happened every year, it offered an easy point of comparison with the past, a measure of how things had changed both at an individual and collective level. The festival led a few to reflect on the decline of extreme wealth and in 1932 one writer noted that city dwellers now had minimal domestic servants and a kitchen that 'cannot cope with any Christmas dinner worth talking of'.[145] For much of the century, Christmas, like society itself, seemed more wholesome and straightforward in the past. As a 1966 writer put it: 'The simple Christmas is dead ... we have killed Christmas with too much fancy work.'[146] Even the decorations could be a spring to lament for simpler times. Thus one 1925 writer bemoaned that modern children bought rather than made decorations. She went on:

> Alas for the Christmas heart that the shops have stolen away, and the legends they have commercialized and the innocence that they have exploited in their abominable Christmas bazaars! What with their wadding snow and pennysworth of frost, their ready filled Christmas stockings, their crimson flannel travesties of the midnight mystery of St. Nicholas and the rest of their gross beslavering of the Christmas tradition, they have outraged, they have all but killed the Christmas heart.[147]

Some went as far as wondering if presents gave as much delight as they had in the past. In 1931 one writer concluded, 'The body and bones of Christmas survive, the spirit of Christmas is dead. Is there any point in celebrating the ghost of the past any longer?'[148]

Yet more common than reflecting on how Christmas itself had changed was looking back at individuals' own childhood, a time when Christmas meant most. The fact that people might spend Christmas with their parents at their childhood home encouraged this. But even if they did not, Christmas was part of the story of people's lives and a vivid reminder of their childhoods. Such reflections were not always pleasant. Christmas could be a struggle because it reminded people of personal loss or a childhood blighted by a difficult family. It also encouraged people to think about relatives who had passed away and were no longer there to share in the festivities. But probably more common was, as a 1935 writer noted, for people to forget their adult cares and to remember their childhoods, enjoying 'the Christmas magic which has set Time rolling back upon itself and made us all children again'.[149] The pleasure of this was partly because memories of childhood are always fragmented and imprecise, often focusing on the moments of extreme emotion. The excitement of presents meant Christmas was undoubtedly that and that memory blanked out the more mundane moments of the festival. Indeed, the pleasures people remembered were actually assemblages of all the good times of several Christmases combined. Poet Cecil Day Lewis was right in noting: 'For memory there are no Christmases, there is only

Christmas – a composite day made up from the haunting impressions of many Christmas Days, a work of art painted by memory. We cannot dig down through the strata piled up by our successive Christmases and pick out any particular one.'[150] Yet remembering the enjoyment of childhood often led people to note that Christmas did not enchant oneself as much as it once did. This was a growing and amiable habit according to one 1935 *Daily Mail* observer, although he excused women this on the basis that they were ones who had to organize the festival.[151] Such feelings were evident in the reflections of a 22-year-old female civil servant from Croydon: 'It is not now the wonderful exciting time of childhood. It seems to consist mainly in getting meals, eating them, and clearing away, and being artificially chock full of goodwill and childishness.'[152] Those who assumed such feelings meant Christmas as a whole had declined were mistaking the change in their personal circumstances for a change in the festival as a whole. Thus, as Weightman and Humphries point out, the sense that Christmas had lost its meaning owed much to adults not always realizing that children still shared the magic they had known in their own childhoods.[153]

Implicit in the nostalgia for childhood was a dissatisfaction with getting older. On Christmas Eve 1954 Noël Coward wrote in his diary: 'Oh how nice it would be, just for today and tomorrow, to be a little boy of five instead of an ageing playwright of fifty-five and look forward to all the high jinks with passionate excitement and be given a clockwork train with a full set of rails and a tunnel.'[154] Indeed, because dispersed families spent time together, Christmas was an occasion that brought home to people how their parents or children were ageing.[155] In 1922 the novelist Sir H. Rider Haggard was recording in his diary that Christmas was

> no joyous festival to the old. It brings too many memories, of some of which one cannot write. Thus the mind goes back some fifty or sixty years and shows the throng of merry youngsters – brothers and sisters, nine of them, most of whom are dead ... Where are they now? A few remain, bent, scarred and weary from struggling with the world, while the rest are dust – like the holly wreaths they wove. And whither they have gone we follow apace.[156]

Such contemplations might be regarded as a little narcissistic by those of a more unkind character. Certainly, the reflection could be a touch vain. In 1981 politician Alan Clark recorded in his Boxing Day diary his depression at the weight gain in his face and the general decline in his looks. He noted that only one woman had looked at him, 'even out of curiosity' at the Christmas Eve service. A decade later, he recorded that he was depressed, not through drink, but through reflecting on his diminishing sexuality and his lack of importance in politics.[157]

Nostalgia is a dissatisfaction with the present and a belief that the past was somehow better. It is a common condition in post-industrial societies, especially as the traumas of the twentieth century destroyed the Victorian sense of progress, although that too had sat alongside a sense that much had been lost with democratization, urbanization and industrialization. What Christmas did was give a focus to a wider feeling. It was the voice rather than the cause of nostalgia. A 1928 writer thus argued that 'We feel we must keep Christmas, just because there are so many things that we have been unable to keep'.[158] Yet nostalgia should not be imagined to be a universal condition. *Woman's Own* felt it had to tell readers in 1936 that however modern they were, they should still be tolerant and appreciative of the festival and its rituals.[159] This was because Christmas could seem to be peculiarly old-fashioned, a symbol of a society rooted in history rather than modernity. Before the Second World War, it was the traditions of Christmas that made some dislike it. They wanted something more modern, a break from the past, not a celebration of it.[160] Indeed, in the late 1950s to the early 1970s there was, in the words of one historian, a widespread 'assumption that the new was almost always better than the old'.[161] It was such feelings that helped push the popularity of the updating of old traditions such as the mid-century popularity of silver plastic Christmas trees.

Yet Christmas did not just provide people with a fear that the past had been lost; it could also provide some hope that things were not in decline. In 1932, *Woman's Own*, contemplating the spirit of happiness and service in Christmas, thought this would eventually see the world well and told readers not to believe those who said England was not what it was. In 1936 the *Daily Mail* claimed that in rural southern England Christmas was unchangeable. There shepherds still watched their flocks on Christmas Eve and people knew what a bleak midwinter really was.[162] Christmas could thus be reassuring link to the past and the reminiscing an intensely pleasant experience. A Barrow housewife recorded in her diary for Christmas Eve 1942: 'I was lost in memories – memories that tonight did not cut and wound, but brought smiles.'[163] Hope and looking forward were also important to many people at Christmas and the festival could also be about optimism and new beginnings.[164] This was perhaps most evident in Christmas 1918, which saw an outpouring of relief and happiness that war was over. The *Daily Mirror* thought people were determined to celebrate in a way that would make up for the 'grey Christmases of the war'. *The Times* thought it the happiest Christmas ever, 'a feast of love, not custom'. It continued: 'There has never been a Christmas like it. There will never be a Christmas like it, until the world has had once more to go through as sharp and long as trial as that from which it has just emerged.'[165] Within a generation the world had faced another trial that was longer and sharper and Christmas was again leading people to look back and forward. Indeed, such reflections never stopped and they were as integral to the spirit of Christmas as church and charity.

Conclusion

In 1915, Lady Cynthia Asquith recorded in her diary: 'We got through Christmas somehow, although we all felt sufficiently dejected and the weather added the last touch. It simply poured.'[166] The weather often plays a direct role in people's sense of well-being. This is less true of Christmas because it is a day when most people are inside but it was a time when there were certain expectations of the weather and these were central to ideas of the Christmas spirit. As a 1931 writer exclaimed, 'No little of the charm lies in the fact that it belongs to the season of frost and snow.'[167] The festival's popular culture and iconography clearly illustrated that and even penguins sometimes appeared on British cards. The idea of snow at Christmas also reinforced the idea that this was an un-normal time, when things looked different and people behaved differently. These associations were not coincidental. The date of 25 December owes more to the early Christian church's utilization of the celebrations of the winter solstice and the Roman festival of Saturnalia than any certainty about when Christ was actually born. Winter festivals were common across different cultures, a respite from the dangers of a cold and fallow season. For the Victorians, Christmas offered a moment of warmth and cheer that broke up the winter months and distilled the cold harshness the season brought. That continued to be the case into the twentieth century but there was a subtle change in the significance of Christmas's winter location because humanity's relationship with winter was changing. Gopnik has argued that the last two centuries saw winter shift from 'something to survive to something to survey'.[168] That was especially true of the second half of the twentieth century, when central heating, refrigeration and cheaper food imports took away from the danger and deprivations that winter had presented. People could thus enjoy the chilliness and darkness of late afternoons, not just because they could see the Christmas lights that gave the festival a magical otherness but because darkness itself was not threatening and easily dissipated by flicking a switch, while the cold could be dispelled by affordable heating at home and warm clothes for the outside.

The safety of winter did not mean that the need for a moment of brightness disappeared completely. In 1962 one London woman told a reporter that she thought 'winter would be dreary' without Christmas.[169] Self-help books played this up: 'Planning the table for various festive meals is the perfect antidote to midwinter blues' declared one.[170] But more common was for Christmas to encourage appreciation and reflection on the relationship with nature and our shelter from it. Winter was thus something picturesque and romantic rather than dangerous.[171] In 1949 one diarist recorded after his Christmas Day walk: 'How snug England is in the winter, with the cottage windows lit up, warm fires blazing and Christmas decorations hanging from the beams. So pretty all the rooms were, while outside grim and dusky.'[172]

This was an archetypal festive image that both appealed to the idea that Englishness itself was a rural phenomenon and encouraged the notion that Christmas was a rural festival.[173] There were similar feelings in Wales and vicar and poet R. S. Davies claimed: 'If we cannot get to the country for Christmas, we import it into our homes' through greenery, trees, fruits and nuts. For him this was a sign that 'we are country folk at heart'.[174] But in towns too, with the shops shut, the streets quiet and little transport, there could be a sense that people were seeing the world 'as it was when our grandfathers knew it' to quote a 1937 writer.[175] For others such reflection centred upon a sense of climate change, long before anyone had heard of global warming. People claimed it snowed more in Victorian times. In the 1920s there were people saying that until recently the Thames had frozen over in midwinter. Such ideas were not entirely fallacy and there had been something of a mini ice age between 1550 and 1850.[176] But by 2012 the Met Office was reporting that just four times in the previous fifty-one years had there been a widespread covering of snow in the UK, although snowflakes were recorded in thirty-eight of those years.[177] The occurrences were uncommon enough for it to be a matter of betting and in 1996 the first white Christmas in London for twenty years meant bookmakers paid out a six-figure sum.[178] More common than a white Christmas was something resembling grey. As Michael Palin noted in his dairy for 23 December 1979: 'Deep in the murky depths of pre-Christmas. Flat skies. Chill, damp, grimy weather'.[179] Another writer recorded in 1935: 'All my pictures of Christmas are wet and dripping.'[180] In such memories, once again Christmas was not living up to the ideal of its spirit.

In response to a 1978 aside about the 'increasingly appalling English Christmas' one reader wrote to The Times saying he had walked miles over glorious countryside in crisp fine weather, gone carolling, attended a midnight service in an eleventh-century church, seen a Shakespeare play at Stratford-upon-Avon and a delectable opera on television, listened to the King's College, Cambridge choir on the radio, and enjoyed good food and the company and conversation of good friends.[181] No matter how much a vocal minority complained about the weather or the terribleness of Christmas, no matter how much a much larger group thought Christmas was not what it was once, most people do seem to have enjoyed Christmas. The festival made people happy and that matters. Indeed this was its primary social function and in that it has remained remarkably consistent. Happiness was a far more powerful component of the spirit of Christmas than snow, nostalgia, charity or religion, although all those things could contribute to festive happiness. Observers noted the good humour on public transport and in the streets at Christmas and how widespread goodwill and kindliness were, even among those with no sense of religion.[182] One woman wrote in her 1942 diary, 'This is a joyous time in peace, and even in catastrophic wartime such as this it cannot be anything but joyous.'[183] A 1941 Mass Observation survey found just 5 per cent of people questioned thought the festival should not be celebrated because of the war. Far more common was a determination to have some fun and enjoy the rest and break.[184] That never went away. Seventy years later, a forty-year-old woman summed up what she loved about Christmas: 'family get togetherness. Celebrating together. Buying nice things for people. Wrapping nicely. Most of all going to Mass to celebrate the birth of Jesus. A lovely family time.'[185]

Late on Christmas Day 1937, a kitchen tap in a Hove family home broke, spurting water everywhere. A student who lived there noted that whereas on any other day it would have been a nuisance, his family actually treated it as a joke.[186] Most people's adherence to the Christmas spirit was something done in the private of the home. It was captured by such incidents rather than through public declarations or acts. People enjoyed the anticipation, the rituals, the opportunity to spend time with family and forget everyday cares, and to be spiritual or just silly.[187] This was not contained by age. Moreover, the happiness of Christmas was not just limited to those who could afford luxuries. As Zweig's late 1940s study of London workers found, it was perfectly possible to be happy and poor, provided people had good relations with others.[188] Thus, even for those with little money, as long as they were not alone, Christmas was a celebration of family and home and a rare moment of distraction from having to worry about the bills of today or the future. For those without much, an extra treat at Christmas made it a happy time, whether that treat came from a relative, a neighbour, a charity or even a do-gooder assuaging his or her conscience. Of course, for a few Christmas reinforced the tragedy of what they did not have, materially or emotionally, but for more it was a moment to appreciate what they did have. Indeed, Christmas probably meant most for those for whom treats at other times of the year were least common.

It was the difficulty and unfairness of life that put happiness at the heart of the Christmas spirit. There seemed to be no rhyme or reason for the luck that made some healthy, happy and comfortable. For most, the frustrations and stresses of life could be considerable. Christmas was a brief escape from this, a moment to enjoy and relax. For poor and rich alike, the festival was a contrast to the realities of the world in which it existed and that lay at the heart of its appeal. At times, the contrast was very acute. In 1917, for example, after a proper Christmas lunch and presents, Bombardier Dudley Gyngell began thinking of home, of the fire, the presents and the singing. 'The boys here were singing Christmas hymns – all "peace on earth and goodwill towards men" – and tomorrow we shall go on killing each other.'[189] Contrasts lay inside many of Christmas's other meanings too. Charity mattered because of the extent of poverty in the world. Before the coming of post-war affluence, feasting mattered for a working class that could rarely afford indulgence. By the later twentieth century, it mattered as a family festival because families did not often spend extended time together. Across the century, for men in employment Christmas was a break from the rigours of work. Yet for women, it usually represented significant domestic toil, even in the supposedly liberated times of the early twenty-first century. Thus, one American investigation found that men reported greater levels of happiness at Christmas.[190]

Its end of year timing, its break from work and its unusualness all encouraged people to reflect on the contrasts between Christmas and reality. Indeed, as the moral certainties that Christianity offered fractured, reflecting in general about one's personality and place in the world became more common.[191] In 1946, an editorial in *The Times* was quite right to note that amid the anxieties of the modern world Christmas was a refuge, 'the time of withdrawal into family celebrations and to the fireside; of falling back on the ritual of benevolence and simple pleasures'. Similarly, without seeming too clichéd or hackneyed, the *Daily Mail* could declare in 1972 that the spirit of Christmas had descended on Britain, 'banishing the gloom of economic uncertainty and terrorist atrocities'.[192] Around that time, a Northern Irish man approached an army checkpoint at Christmas. It would have normally been a tense moment, but there was a Christmas tree on the checkpoint's roof and one of the soldiers was wearing a Santa hat and said 'Ho, Ho, Ho' as he approached.[193] The IRA itself called Christmas truces in 1972, 1974 and 1990. Those truces did not last, but they still mattered. In 1986 *The Times* remarked:

> Christmas has an 'as if' quality: it is as if we were all kinder and better than we are. And with the excuse of Christmas, we may pretend what we dream: of an end of want; of universal generosity; of peace on earth. An annual transformation of the world into a better one, partly in imagination and partly even in reality, is not bad yearly therapy for a race weary with its own cruelty and indifference.

This writer thought that Christmas might not make the world better but the festival did slow down its deterioration.[194] It was because Christmas was important in these ways that people got so upset that it was not what they thought it once was, although their complaints were often about the state of their own lives or about society itself rather than about Christmas.

In the face of growing economic problems in 2008, the *Spectator* reflected: 'Belt-tightening does not mean that Christmas cannot be jolly. Indeed, it is precisely when the chips are down that the most basic of Christian virtues – decency – is most important.'[195] For all its importance, in offering happiness and escape to individuals and families, Christmas also reflected and cemented the essential decency of society. It was a moment when there was more charity than at other times of the year and when families came together, even when they did not always get on. Of course, the goodwill also highlighted its absence for much of the rest of the year, but a day of charity was surely better than none at all, no matter what the festival's detractors said. It was also evidence of the legacy of a Christian culture in the UK. From Christianity had come a culture of decency where people generally treated others with respect and dignity and Christmas helped uphold that, long after its spiritual significance retreated from being central to the festival. Indeed, without Christmas, Christianity would have retreated even further from public culture than it did anyway. The festival encouraged churches to bring their practices into line with modern tastes and, in December at least, kept Jesus and all he represented in the public eye.

And yet, no matter how angry or delighted people could get because of Christmas, the reality was more complex. Much of Christmas was rather more mundane. There were pleasures and there were annoyances and the tendency to make big proclamations about the festival said as much about the personality of the espouser as about the reality of the day. If the history of Christmas does anything, it highlights how within the structures of society, people are still individuals with their own personalities. Even those who loved Christmas could get annoyed by aspects of it. Even those who hated it could still enjoy dinner, or a few moments away from work or with the kids. The spirit of Christmas was never all-conquering but nor was it simply another festive myth.

CHAPTER FIVE

The shared Christmas

In Jonathan Coe's novel *The Rotters' Club* (2001) a teenager watching *Morecambe and Wise* on Christmas Day 1977 has a 'fleeting vision':

> It came to him that he was only one person, and his family was only one family, out of millions of people and millions of families throughout the country, all sitting in front of their televisions, all watching these two comedians, in Birmingham and Manchester and Liverpool and Bristol and Durham and Portsmouth and Newcastle and Glasgow and Brighton and Sheffield and Cardiff and Stirling and Oxford and Carlisle and everywhere else, all of them laughing, all of them laughing at the same joke, and he felt an incredible sense of ... oneness, that was the only word he could think of, a sense that the entire nation was being briefly, fugitively drawn together in the divine act of laughter.[1]

The entire nation was an exaggeration, but there was nothing else that came remotely close to television's power to bind millions of people together. And it was on days like Christmas that this power was at its height, not just because people watched together but because they later talked about and reminisced over what they had seen.

The idea that Christmas integrated the nation was both a powerful and an old one that extended beyond the impacts of a mass media. For the Victorians and Edwardians, the festival was an expression of the antiquity of the nation and its civilized, good-natured and tight social bonds. There was a pride and interest in the history of traditions and upholding them was seen as a way of maintaining British heritage. Indeed, so strong was this feeling that the first two volumes of a suet manufacturer's interwar booklet of 'olde time Christmas customs, games and recipes' had a circulation of 1.25 million copies.[2] Such beliefs extended beyond Britain and colonials across the Empire consciously followed the traditions of home as a means of expressing their national identity. This has led historian Mark Connelly to argue that Christmas epitomized Englishness.[3] Even in the more cynical post-war days, such ideas continued to be expressed. In 1960 *The Times* claimed that at Christmas 'the whole nation becomes one kith and kin'.[4] Yet this rhetoric of social and cultural unity was often just that, rhetoric. The feeling of being at one with the nation that the teenager in *The Rotters' Club* experienced only lasted a moment. His joy quickly passed as the sketch is replaced by 'some boring singer' and he realized he is 'just an ordinary teenager in an ordinary family … and once again everything in his life seemed fraught, complex and uncertain'.[5]

Just because a feeling is temporary does not mean it is not significant. National identity is rarely based on explicit and prolonged feelings. It is more often banal and taken for granted, underpinned by and embedded in shared everyday practices that are experienced at a local level.[6] Christmas was one such practice and a Derby newspaper claimed in 1948 that a 'Christmas instinct' was 'part and parcel of our national life'.[7] As this chapter explores, it produced a widely known canon of customs, music, films and stories that were part of the cultural web that bound people together. One did not have to like these or even take part for them to produce a national community; it was enough to know that they existed. Thus, no matter how rooted Christmas was in the home, it was also something that united people across Britain, making them more than just a collection of individuals. Moreover, British culture actually had a series of national, regional, ethnic and local cultures within it, many of which people felt deep personal attachments to and all of which demonstrated how Britain was inherently multicultural. This, too, was evident at Christmas, with its kaleidoscope of overlapping but distinct local festive practices. Some of these faded over the course of the century, but large-scale immigration brought new diversities. Whatever their source, local variations were not alternatives to a national culture but an exemplar of it. British culture was simultaneously plural and monolithic and that was what defined it.[8]

Local communities

In 1932 the *Hull Daily Mail* argued that people in the city enjoyed Christmas because their Yorkshire spirit was to make the best of everything. This, like its use of local dialect in wishing people 'A Right Merry Christmas', exemplified how within the national Christmas culture there was still room for people to interpret it at a regional and local level.[9] Indeed, in the small Carmarthenshire village of Bethlehem, Christmas was one of the defining local characteristics. In the 1960s the local post office's festive stamp mark meant it became a popular place to post cards. The post office closed in the 1980s, but its name brought its resurrection in 2002. Although it only opened for a day a week, this expanded to seven days for the duration of December.[10]

This was an unusual case but in the interwar years 'all kinds of quaint, picturesque, and amusing' Christmas customs could be found across rural Britain.[11] They were occasionally held up as examples of the diversity of British culture, but they also helped define local communities, giving them a sense of their own past and identity.[12] This latter function was often unspoken and it was far from the primary purpose of the festival, but it happened nonetheless. The character of these local traditions varied significantly, but most shared the elements of carnival and community that characterized early modern Christmas celebrations and were supposed to simultaneously entertain and cement neighbourliness. In some places, the traditions were simply an annual Christmas play or pantomime. But other traditions were fading continuations of much older festive rituals. In remote parts of the West Country in the 1920s, for example, an ancient tradition of families burning the ashen faggot (a collection of ash sticks) for luck on Christmas Day was upheld.[13] This was just one of a whole series of rituals that may have even been pagan in their roots and were intended to bring good luck or deter ill fortune. Many were based on Christmas Eve or Christmas Day but others – notably wassailing, where people either visited homes with songs and a bowl of drink, or drank and sang around fruit trees to ensure a good crop – centred on Twelfth Night, the end of the Christmas season but also regarded as 'old Christmas Day' by those who kept up the popular memory of pre-reform calendars. Wassailing at orchards could still be found in the interwar West Country, but by then it had been reduced to something practised by groups of friends.[14] Many of these festive traditions were essentially visiting customs, where people went from house to house or pub to pub, often in some form of fancy dress, offering some form of performance in return for drink or money.[15] The most common and resilient of such practices was the mummers' play, variations of which could be found across the UK into the 1950s. Although there were loose scripts, they were more performances and recitals than stories.[16] The weakness of such rituals compared to wider Christmas culture was evident in how the costume of the Father Christmas character (who was to be found in most incarnations of the mummers) changed in the twentieth century from a traditional assemblage of long strips of paper to a hooded red gown. One 1957 writer explained the tradition's fading by arguing 'their humour is old fashioned and must suffer in comparison with the work of the slick comedians' on television.[17]

Where such rituals had faded away, the spirit of hospitality they represented might be kept up by different festive activities. In 1920s Yorkshire, for example, there were rural villages with traditions of a round of Christmas cake-tasting parties.[18] Elsewhere, the communal ideal had shifted away from the home to participative public spectacles. Some villages thus had married versus unmarried men Christmas Day football matches. Swimming competitions were common across the country, first on Christmas Day, and then, as the interwar period continued, on Boxing Day, no doubt to avoid clashing with the family day. The most famous was the race on the Serpentine lake in London, held every Christmas since 1864. That could actually be a rather serious affair, but others were little more than a mass plunge into the sea or a lake, the humour of which seemed more in keeping with the day.

While such events were fun, and often tests of one's bravery on a cold morning, the primary motive for mummers' plays seems to have been the significant financial rewards of taking part, although oral evidence suggests participants were proud of their performances too.[19] Financial considerations were also a key reason for the continuation of other customs, although that sometimes meant acknowledging a form of social hierarchy that seemed out of place in class-conscious interwar Britain. Christmas had long given the gentry an opportunity to reaffirm their traditional role as local altruists and to make up for the accumulated grievances and inequities that could easily develop. The remnants of the resulting early modern practices could still be found in some rural communities. For example, in some Cotswolds villages there were people who went 'a-Thomasing' in the 1930s, a ritual where poor families would call on the local big house on St Thomas Day (21 December) and receive 6d. and a little food.[20] In as late as 1953, Harold Macmillan was acting as the local squire by reading the lesson at Matins and, with his family, taking presents to the children of his Sussex estate.[21] In 1928, the writer Hilaire Belloc described an anonymous large farm where a pine tree was erected on Christmas Eve and decorated with candles. Adults and children from the village came up to see it and to be fed. The children also received a small present and a coin. Afterwards there were games, songs, carols, a prayer and the lighting of a Yule log. Belloc was aware that such scenes were then far from common, but argued that for those involved they were normal and even sacred. Indeed, he maintained that the house's celebration of 'Christmas binds it to its own past and promises its future'.[22] Belloc's concerns were rooted in how unusual the spiritual and cohesive experiences he described were. The aim of bonding communities through parties for local children remained elsewhere, but it was Santa rather than the squire who gave out the presents and his charity came from a religious group or community collection rather than the largesse of any one individual. In itself, this was a symbol of how the dynamics of local power were changing in an era when taxation and democracy were distancing the gentry from those whose labour they had once built their wealth on.

It was often children who were most important in taking the lead in the local visiting customs, including some mummers' plays, that did survive into the middle of the twentieth century. In 1920s Leeds children could be found going round with a wassailing box, decorated with Christmas ornaments, asking for coppers or sweets. After complaints and a conviction of two eight-year-olds for begging, the local authority sent a letter to all schools pointing out it was illegal.[23] In Scarborough in the 1950s children went 'ceshing', which involved knocking on doors on Christmas morning and shouting:

'Wish you Merry Christmas, mistress and master.'[24] Yet even these simple exchanges of a greeting for money were becoming less and less common by the 1950s. That decade's growing affluence benefited children too and the generosity of their parents meant they had less need to go out looking for money. Perhaps more importantly, the development of the welfare state had shifted popular notions of how the poor should be helped. The state and charities now took over the role of giving to those in need and people were thus less comfortable with handing out gifts of cash to those who knocked on their doors, whether they were known or not. Thus what in effect were forms of ritualized begging came to a near end.

By 1978 Pimlott claimed that most festive local traditions that had managed to survive would die out within another generation.[25] That overstated the case because there were a series of attempts to revive customs such as wassailing in order to conserve local heritage. The first such revivals dated back into the interwar years, a period when there was a growing interest in traditional rural culture and newspaper discussions of the origins of old traditions.[26] The local and national publicity given to such events fuelled the desire of others to follow suit and by the 1950s and 1960s some were even televised.[27] Of course, revivals rarely took the exact form of the original custom and they were not simply about keeping up traditions. Just as they were for earlier participants, prestige and profit were motives too.[28] This was all clear in Bampton (Oxfordshire) where the mummers' tradition had been performed up to 1939. It was revived in the late 1940s with the performers calling at houses on Christmas Eve and pubs on Boxing Day. The revivers were children, whereas it had formerly been an adult activity, but the same individuals carried on as adults and were very consciously maintaining an old tradition. Their family commitments, however, saw the tradition shift to just calling on pubs on Christmas Eve, the more profitable of the two dates.[29]

Another example of an evolving local tradition was plygain in Wales. These were forms of Welsh-language carol services that had traditionally taken place at chapels and churches very early on Christmas morning, so the congregation emerged at dawn or first light. Like all local rituals, it was much diminished by the end of the nineteenth century, but in the Tanad Valley in Powys (and probably elsewhere) it had extended into parties moving on to sing from door to door through the night of Christmas Eve. Occupants, even though they were probably in bed, were expected to throw money out of the window to the singers. This practice continued into the interwar years, but during the Great War came to be seen by some as begging. In the early 1960s the Welsh Folk Museum recorded evening plygain services in the Tanad Valley that could last up to two hours and feature as many as thirty carols, some seemingly unique to the valley, sung in turn by different parties of singers. After the motor car had become common, a system had emerged where services were held on different dates, to enable parties of singers to appear at all the local services. Divisions between church and chapel were forgotten, but some carols had local or family associations and parties avoided singing the tunes of their neighbours. The tradition appeared not to have been understood as unusual until the museum came enquiring, but after that it was more consciously upheld as a marker of community spirit and tradition.[30]

Such traditions were rural phenomenon. Even the oldest urban communities could not claim the stability that was required for them to survive from their premodern roots. Yet in interwar towns and cities too, there were communal activities that brought people together. Richard Burton remembered Welsh miners on Christmas Eve gathering round a bonfire to cook chestnuts and potatoes.[31] A Greenwich woman remembered that men would go from house to house for a Christmas morning drink, while the women were left to cook.[32] One adult Leicestershire woman remembered going to people's homes to taste the 'pudding' as it was being mixed.[33] In the Swansea area, people called on neighbours and family to taste as many puddings as possible after Christmas, believing that personal fortune accumulated with the number tried.[34] There were also more practical acts of urban neighbourliness, such as helping with plucking poultry, inviting in a widow to ensure she was not alone, cooking dinner for an unemployed family or even just giving a few sweets or coins to the children next door.[35] These acts of kindness helped uphold one of the survival mechanisms of working-class life, which was the practice of people to draw on the support of others.[36] This extended far beyond Christmas, but the festival offered people an opportunity to say thank you and affirm their neighbourly bonds.

In both towns and the countryside, the spirit of calling customs lived on late into the twentieth century through carol singing. Groups of adults, sometimes called the waits and often led by the church choir or a pre-existing social network, travelled around communities, singing outside houses in return for money, food or drink. This was being discussed in a 1947 book as a new innovation, but it dated back at least into the 1920s in some places.[37] This suggests it grew up at the time when other visiting customs were dying out, but like those customs it replaced there was a clear social function, especially in rural areas where both the performers and recipients would usually be known to each other. Newcomers could integrate themselves through taking part, while the receivers had an opportunity to demonstrate their commitment to the community, especially given how many groups gave the money they raised to charity. Indeed, generous giving was often expected of the richer members of a community.[38] Even receiving a call could be meaningful. In 1956, Sylvia Townsend Warner recorded in her diary that a group of elderly carol singers had called and 'were friendly in their merry Christmasses'. She thought this might be a sign that she and her gay partner were 'mellowing into popularity'.[39] But carolling could also cause, or at least play upon, pre-existing social tensions. In the Shropshire village of Clun in the 1920s, different groups of carol singers had their own territory. This was partly hereditary but it was open to dispute.[40] One man

PLATE 20 *Brass band called The Essex Strollers playing carols, c. 1925. Topical Press Agency/Getty.*

remembered of the same decade in Tyneside, how his working-class choir was determined to prove its talent to another more well-to-do group. He also noted that carol singing was 'a famous time for match making' among boys and girls sharing a hymn book under lantern light.[41] But carolling did not have just a social function and one 1966 story declared, 'As the country voices carolled the eternal story of joyous birth, Mary felt she had never been so happy.'[42] A Leicestershire woman recalled being woken on an inter-war Christmas Eve by the beautiful singing of the waits and thinking she was heaven.[43] Yet, the level of seriousness with which carolling was taken varied significantly. While some groups practised for weeks and had established routes, others, especially children, were more spontaneous.[44] Nor were carols above humour and one Oxfordshire woman recalled hearing in 1936: 'Hark the Herald Angels Sings, Mrs Simpson stole our king.'[45]

The writer Laurie Lee wrote that in his interwar Cotswold childhood the right to visit the big houses to sing for money was the reward for being in the church choir but that it required careful timing because an early visit would not be welcome, while a late one would see others having got there first. His group carried a book around so that people could record their donations. They visited the squire first to ensure that others felt they had to match his generosity.[46] Such ruses contributed to the view throughout the period of carolling as a nuisance. Indeed, many regarded it as little more than begging. In 1951 one man even referred to carollers as 'baby spivs' with their demands for sixpence.[47] The fact that it went on for so long and that many of the singers could not hold a tune did not help. Whereas in the country, carollers might wait until as late as Christmas Eve, in towns it could begin in late November.[48] Some people groaned when they turned up and paid as quickly as possible so they would stop.[49] The sense of nuisance was added to by the calls of charity collectors, which led one servant to make the following remark in a 1938 Agatha Christie novel: 'Nothing but begging this time of year.'[50] With so many children calling, and often every night and at late hours, people's anger could be quite considerable. Some would not give to singers who came before Christmas Eve and one man complained to the *Henley Standard* in 1924 that he had a stone thrown through his window when he would not give money. Some just tried to avoid it by not answering the door or keeping the lights off. In 1924, the chief constable in Hythe (Kent) actually banned children from carolling except from 6.00 pm to 8.00 pm.[51]

Some complaints seem to be based on the discomfort of coming into close proximity with working-class children. One commentator wrote in 1925:

> To-day in large towns, for a month or more before Christmas, dirty music-less boys yell 'Woil sheppids wortched' on your doorstep, in the hope of extracting coppers for desisting. Many presents that once gave pleasure have by iteration become a recognised tax. Aspirants put in their claims at the back-door with as much assurance as the gas company's collector when the meter has told its quarterly fairy-tale. You pay, as you would the collector, with a relief that it is over, and the payment is received with some satisfaction as it cannot yet be legally enforced.[52]

C. S. Lewis complained one year that all but one of the forty-six visits he got were from singers who had not even tried to learn the words or how to sing and he was sure 'some of them are the very same hooligans who trespass in my garden, rob my orchard, hack down my trees and scream outside my windows'.[53] Such people were letting their wider prejudices influence how they viewed carolling, but this was not unusual. In 1937 a Cotswold writer claimed that in towns singers were running a racket and ran off after being paid, whereas in the countryside they stayed to sing another carol or two and knew they were singing something religious.[54] Children demanding money before singing was the subject of humour in *Hancock's Half Hour* in 1959: 'money mad they are – it's a sign of the times.'[55] In 1993 Julian Barnes argued that over the course of the 1980s carol singers became more

PLATE 21 *Schoolgirls singing carols, c. 1932. Imagno/Getty.*

mercenary, illustrating the impact of Thatcherism on society.[56] Yet the fact that such complaints were present throughout the century shows that people were reading too much into what was happening. Researchers in the 1950s found people complaining that carol singers were becoming more commercial. They were told that in one district carol singers asked before performing so if permission was refused they had not wasted their efforts. Yet, children themselves told the same researchers that they liked singing carols because it was fun to go out on a winter night and because Jesus was born at Christmas.[57] If there was a significant change in carol singing it was its decline. Television sitcoms were still making jokes about being ripped off by carol singers in 1980 but fewer and fewer children were doing it.[58] By the end of the century, parents were simply less likely to let their young children wander the streets unaccompanied. But it was not just children who had virtually stopped. Adults groups rarely went from door to door either, perhaps another sign of the secularization of society. Whatever the cause, the result was the near disappearance of a ritual that connected people to their communities, even if some had never really appreciated that in the first place.

Music, broadcasting, film and pantomime

One cause of the decline of the carol was the volume of more modern festive songs that now existed and had become part of the canon of a shared national Christmas culture. Many of the first modern Christmas tunes were American novelty songs such as 'Santa Claus is Coming to Town' (1934), which were rooted in the rising culture of children as consumers. They quickly took hold across the Atlantic and by the 1940s were even making appearances at carol concerts. Similarly, 'I Saw Mommy Kissing Santa Claus' was released in 1952 and was being sung by carol singers just a year later.[59] The popularity of such songs was rooted in their light heartedness, but a conservative sentimentality was a more common characteristic of contemporary Christmas songs in the middle of the twentieth century. In 1955, the Christmas number one spot was held by Dickie Valentine with a sentimental tune 'Christmas Alphabet' that emphasized all the expected festive secular iconography, while 'Mary's Boy Child' by American Harry Belafonte was the bestselling single of the 1957 Christmas week. Its simple religious message and pretty tune hit a Christmas chord and it sold 1.18 million copies in the UK. But even in the 1950s there was a feeling in parts of the establishment – let alone among rock 'n' roll teenagers – that such tunes left something to be desired. A review in *The Times* concluded that only Belafonte could sing such a song without any risk of being 'schmaltzy'.[60]

The difficulty of producing Christmas music that was not schmaltzy meant most credible pop acts avoided the genre in the 1960s. Instead, new Christmas music tended to be novelty songs by novelty acts. This was clear in The Go Go's 'I'm Going to Spend my Christmas with a Dalek' (1964), where one of Doctor Who's enemies demanded more plum pudding and custard. The popularity of such songs was confirmed when the silly but comic 'Lilly the Pink' by The Scaffold was the Christmas number one in 1968. The following year's festive number one was Rolf Harris' 'Two Little Boys', an Edwardian music hall song about two brothers' love for each other during the hardships of war. 'Do you'd think I'd leave you to die when there's room on my horse for two?' had nothing to do with Christmas, but its sentiment was everything the festival meant to people. The song was the bestselling single of 1969 and completely at odds with the image of the late 1960s, but its power, like Christmas itself, was how it crossed the traditional boundaries and confines of popular culture.

Modern music was also maturing so it too could become part of the canon of contemporary nostalgia. As its first teenage listeners grew into adulthood, pop music itself became embedded in daily life, something that was popular across generations rather than being simply for the young.

It lost something of its radical overtones and became mainstream. This underpinned the way Christmas pop supplanted carols as the music of the festival. The process was gradual because there simply was not that much Christmas pop before the 1970s. Only in that decade did Christmas-themed songs become integral to December sales. It was in 1973 that the Christmas number one really became a matter of particular public interest. That year Slade and Wizzard competed for the top spot with two rocky and explicitly festive party tunes. Wizzard only made number four in the end, but Slade's 'Merry Xmas Everybody' grew into a tune as well known as any carol and into an integral part of the Christmas landscape, played every subsequent year at parties, in shops and other public venues, and on television. Indeed, by the 2000s there were reports of a hotel and airport removing it from their playlist because people found it irritating.[61] Yet, it was still widespread enough that it generated over £500,000 in various royalties and performing rights in 2013. The song was a conscious attempt to be an antidote to the conditions of the time. Noddy Holder, its singer, later recalled:

> We'd decided to write a Christmas song and I wanted to make it reflect a British family Christmas. Economically, the country was up the creek. The miners had been on strike, along with the grave-diggers, the bakers and almost everybody else. I think people wanted something to cheer them up – and so did I.[62]

Whether it was escapism or not, from that point forth the Christmas number one became something of an institution and even something to bet

PLATE 22 *Slade on* Top of the Pops, *25 December 1973. Michael Putland/Getty.*

on. Here, it was helped by the popularity of *Top of the Pops*. The show's first Christmas Day edition was in 1967, when it preceded the Queen's Speech. The late lunch slot meant whole families watched together after eating. Even if some only saw the end, through turning on early for the Queen, it established itself as another festive tradition. In 1986 one 51-year-old man recorded in his diary that he had 'a very boring day', but he had enjoyed *Top of the Pops* which 'proved that the top records of the year are, in general, quite appealing and not just a lot of modern rubbish'.[63]

In reviewing 'Rudolph the Reindeer is a Punk Rocker Now' by The Slay Belles in 1977, the *New Musical Express* declared: 'Can the devastated desolate decade take much more of this sanitised Santa schmaltz? ... This is pathetic.'[64] The charts themselves, however, continued to offer evidence that the appeal of tunes that met the secular frivolity or religious sanctity of the festival were more popular that anything the *NME* might think was cool. At Christmas 1976, for example, the Sex Pistols' seminal 'Anarchy in the UK' had only reached number 28, whereas the number one was 'When a Child is Born' by Johnny Mathias. Doing anything explicitly Christmassy and cool may have been difficult, but it was not impossible as evidenced by Boney M's disco cover of 'Mary's Boy Child', which reached number one in 1978 and sold 1.85 million copies by crossing markets. The cultural significance of the Christmas number one position was also evident in the success Cliff Richard had at the end of the 1980s and in the early 1990s with two sentimental tunes that had explicitly Christian messages. 'Mistletoe and Wine' (1988) and 'Saviour's Day' (1990) both reached number one thanks to sales from people who would never normally buy a record, and it seemed that some were partly motivated by the wish to see a Christian message occupy the number one slot. Richard's success caused a degree of resentment among younger people who had felt that the Christmas number one was something to care about and that feeling again resurfaced in the 2000s when the position came to be dominated by the winners of television talent shows. Such was the annoyance that in 2009 a grassroots internet campaign managed to make an old rock song by Rage Against the Machine the festive number one with half a million downloads. The campaign was about the sterility of modern music, but it was still significant that Christmas was its focus and many of those who took part were not teenagers but older music fans wanting to recapture a cultural highlight of their own younger years.

Christmas pop music was nostalgic in evocation, if not actually in lyrics; it often conjured up simpler times.[65] That was often down to the songs' whimsical or romantic feel, but it was also simply because of the frequency with which they were played. They were heard so often that they represented Christmas itself. Hearing them signified the coming of a pleasant time and was a reminder of happy times gone by. Even those songs which were rather grittier in their content still often had romantic content. This was evident in 'Fairytale of New York', released by the Pogues and Kirsty MacColl in 1987, a rare example of a mainstream Christmas song that was 'cool'. This owed much to its lyrics that dwelt on the misery and hypocrisy of Christmas. But it was also a romantic song, where love conquers personal failures, and that was at the root of its popularity. By 2011, British performing rights data showed it was the most played Christmas song of the twenty-first century.[66]

One way that people heard Christmas songs was, of course, on the radio. After the BBC's creation in 1922, radio's ascent was rapid. By 1934, more than 70 per cent of British households had licences.[67] Christmas Day proved to be a popular day for listening, at least partly simply because most people were at home. As early as 1927, the *Radio Times* was selling over 1 million copies of its Christmas edition, when its average weekly circulation was 850,000.[68] The interwar schedules conformed to rather than challenged festive preconceptions: there were religious plays and services, Christmas-themed variety performances, greetings from across Britain and the Empire and the day's football results. Those who wanted light music could tune to Radio Luxembourg. Programmes both emphasized a shared Christmas culture and local characteristics through items on how the festival was being celebrated in homes across the UK and the Empire, exemplifying the plurality that existed within British identity. Indeed, after one 1933 programme of Christmas greetings, the *Western Morning News* proudly declared: 'Empire hears Devon Dialect.'[69]

At 8.00 pm on Christmas night 1944, BBC research suggested that nearly half the nation were listening to the radio, and just 11 per cent of potential listeners had heard no programmes that day. Indeed, such was radio's interwar pull that some individuals worried that it was monopolizing entertainment.[70] By 1933 the *Radio Times* was ruminating on how listening had become a new habit on the most traditional of days, arguing, quite rightly, that it complemented rather than superseded established rituals. Research by the BBC found that people listened in many different ways. Some were following programmes very carefully, but others just wanted some cheerful background noise. Other less interested commentators realized the new role of radio too and claimed that it was overcoming both individual and collective isolation. It was certainly helping establish new traditions and listening to the Festival of Nine Lessons and Carols from King's College, Cambridge, became an annual rite for many middle-class listeners as it connected with their sense of the religiousness, Englishness and historicity of Christmas.[71] But, however much such programming appealed to some, it was not what dominated popular tastes. This was evident in replies to a 1931 *Daily Mirror* competition asking people to describe their ideal wireless entertainment for Christmas. While many did want 'a touch of seriousness' to remind them of the significance of the day, the entries were dominated by calls for 'jollity' in the form of dance tunes, comedy, light opera and musical plays. Similarly, the BBC was told in 1944 that people wanted programmes that marked the special nature of the day, whether that was through carols or programmes that encouraged audience participation on what was a family day.[72]

It was probably the Christmas Day royal broadcast that provided the most people with their touch of seriousness. The instigator was John Reith, the BBC's director general, who had been trying to persuade the King to make a broadcast since radio's beginnings. George V felt he lacked the flair and technique required for broadcasting, but with some persuasion from his private secretary and the prime minister Ramsey MacDonald, who appealed to the monarchy's importance in maintaining the Empire, he relented and the first royal Christmas message went out in 1932.[73] It was written by Rudyard Kipling, and spoke of the marvels of science bringing the Empire together and of a simple emotion:

> I speak now from my home and from my heart to you all. To men and women so cut off by the snows, the desert, or the sea, that only voices out of the air can reach them; to those cut off from fuller life by blindness, sickness, or infirmity; and to those who are celebrating this day with their children and grandchildren. To all – and to each – I wish a Happy Christmas. God Bless You![74]

Although the King maintained nerves had ruined his Christmas, the speech's emphasis on home, understanding and family touched people and made royalty seem human and not so remote. The *Daily Mail* called it 'stirring' and declared it one of the most memorable events of the year. *The Listener* recorded the BBC received a heavy postbag of admiration and appreciation.[75] Its popularity meant a repeat was inevitable and the same basic sentiments were retained. Thus, in 1934 the monarch told his audience, 'My words will be very simple but spoken from the heart on this family festival.' That year the speech was introduced by a 65-year-old shepherd from the Cotswolds, who spoke of his own memories of Christmas. It was reminder of a rural England and one that touched many at home and in the Empire, even if it was an image that had little to do with the actual England that the majority of listeners lived in. Research for the BBC suggested that 91 per cent of possible listeners had heard the broadcast.[76] A year later the *Spectator* was calling the broadcast 'a national institution' that touched those suffering from grief or loneliness and which should encourage among listeners the same sense of brotherhood and obligation towards the rest of the nation that the King felt.[77]

His son George VI was uncomfortable with public speaking and his struggle with a stammer was the subject of a 2010 film *The King's Speech*. Christmas 1936 was too close to his unexpected accession for a broadcast, but he went ahead in 1937 to say thank you for the support of people but making clear that he did not see himself carrying on the tradition of an annual broadcast. He did not enjoy the experience and declined in 1938, but he was persuaded to resume in 1939 by a sense of duty.[78] As with his father, advisers and the BBC had pushed him to broadcast because of the perceived role of the speech in uniting the Empire, making it seem both more intimate and together. This was something that the speeches repeatedly played upon, mixing up and conflating the ideas of the families of home, nation and empire. Historian David Cannadine has thus argued that they 'enhanced the image of the monarch as the father-figure of his people'.[79]

This is certainly what the BBC and Royal advisers hoped for, but they could not control who listened and how they listened and historians should never assume that media outputs were received in the ways intended. The response of press around the world clearly indicated that at least some people thought it bonded the Empire, but the private writings of listeners in Britain show a more complex picture.[80] There were certainly those who were touched by the words and solemnity of their monarch. Some looked forward to it, were impressed by the dignity and modesty of it all and as early as 1937 were noting that it had become part of the 'English Christmas'. That year a wireless was even taken into the afternoon service of a number of churches so people could hear the speech.[81] During the war it took on particular significance. The 1942 diary of one woman, whose son was a POW, showed its impact:

> The King broadcast a Christmas message very strongly and clearly, seeming much less nervous. He is, alas, now one with those who mourn someone near and dear in the loss of the Duke of Kent this year. We stood for 'God Save the King' and even tried to sing it. All the time we had Nevill and Alan in our minds and hearts, and the King spoke of the thoughts of the Queen and himself being with those 'who have lost their dear ones, those wounded and in hospital ... the prisoners of war who bear their long exile with dignity and fortitude'.[82]

Yet some people's reaction was rather different. In a Barrow canteen in 1943, a Welsh soldier stood up at the end of the national anthem and sang the 'Red Flag', before sitting back down and falling asleep.[83] Responses to a 1937 Mass Observation survey also show a variety of negative or indifferent reactions. While some were touched enough to cry, others forgot it was on, thought it said nothing, or worked on in the kitchen while listening. An eighteen-year-old student recorded that he was not interested enough in the speech to stop eating his dinner. What struck many listeners was the King's stammer. While some respected his efforts, when he clearly did not want to do it, others were embarrassed and one woman even wondered how a man with a stammer could be King. In Keswick (Cumbria) a 62-year-old housewife reported that while all her family listened to the speech, they all felt it was a 'rather painful affair'. Only her neighbour, who was invited for dinner because she was alone, was really 'loyal' and one man stood for the national anthem out of deference to her, while her son refused to do so. The others were 'sympathetic and tolerant, without being sentimental or adoring'. At another gathering in Bradford the men refused to listen and the women did so for entertainment, treating it as a joke and standing up in mockery for the anthem. But once it began the women were all rather moved by his ordeal and they stood in seriousness for the anthem's second playing.[84]

The question of whether to stand for the national anthem was one that clearly perplexed some people, especially since it was played both at the beginning and the end of the broadcast. It forced people to do more than simply listen because in other contexts one always stood for the anthem. Some families, especially those part of the middle class, stood for both playings, even if they were in the middle of dinner or listening in a hotel, and could even get annoyed with members who did not stand straight. Other families had mixed responses, sometimes standing for the first playing, but not the second. Yet it was not always easy to stand. One man noted that the solemnity of the national anthem, for which his whole family stood, was rather spoilt by the dog getting very excited because he thought everyone was going out.[85]

Elizabeth II continued the tradition and after her first broadcast *The Guardian* thought she had come through the 'ordeal', which placed a great strain on the speaker because of the need to avoid sounding artificial or

PLATE 23 *The Queen's first televised Christmas speech, 1957. Bentley Archive/ Popperfoto/Getty.*

condescending. The *Radio Times* had called the tradition her 'inheritance' and her speeches turned out to be dominated by the same slightly dull platitudes of her father.[86] The biggest change came in 1957 when, to celebrate its quarter century, the speech was televised for the first time before an audience of 16.5 million.[87] The *Daily Mail* gushed that it brought 'fresh and added meaning' to the broadcast, making the Queen less impersonal and concluding that she could 'now put herself into the minds and hearts of her people more intimately than ever before'. In contrast, a columnist in the *Daily Express* criticized the set, production, and her dress and make-up, but this drew a barrage of criticism from readers who had been touched by the broadcast.[88] In 1959 the speech was recorded because of the Queen's pregnancy, but the freedom that gave Commonwealth countries to broadcast at a suitable local time meant this practice continued. In the UK the popularity of the speech had owed much to its 3.00 pm timing, which allowed many people to watch or listen just after their lunch or while still together at the table, but the move away from a live broadcast allowed some experimenting. Thus, in 1959 the first broadcast was actually at 9.00 am on BBC television, before being repeated on the radio at 1.00 pm and on ITV at 3.00 pm. The following year, between the television and radio services of the BBC and ITV, it could be seen or heard at 1.00 pm, 3.00 pm, 5.00 pm and 6.00 pm.[89]

In 1968 the Queen and Prince Philip decided to write the speech themselves and their draft included a reference to Britain's 'serious economic difficulties'. The government was unimpressed and the sentence was deleted.[90] A year later, the Queen decided not to do a broadcast at all, apparently because the royal family had been on television a lot that year after making a documentary. A writer in *The Guardian* thought it the right decision because the speech had become routine and its sentiment was becoming phoney. *The Sun* noted that while many people's Christmas timetable had been organized around the speech, it had lost something of its homeliness and intimacy with the move to a recorded televised broadcast. Others, however, were less sure. The *Daily Telegraph*, for example, thought the speech gave people something constant and durable in an age of change. Mary Whitehouse organized a petition against the decision, announcing that Christmas would not be the same without it.[91] There was a feeling within the government that the Queen owed her position to tradition and that every break with it undermined her. It worried about how the replacement written statement would be distributed within the Commonwealth, but chose not to interfere, despite fearing that this might be seen an attempt by the prime minister to hog the limelight.[92] The following year the broadcast was back.

By the early 1960s, over 70 per cent of the population was thought to be watching the Queen's annual speech. That was probably an exaggeration, but the broadcast still demonstrated how central the monarchy was to British culture. Yet we should be wary of reading too much into these figures and the idea that the speech represented a unified nation. An opinion poll suggested just over half of people were not disappointed that there was no broadcast in 1969, although among women the figure fell to 42 per cent and nearly two-thirds of respondents had seen or heard it the year before. In 1962, the *TV Times* acknowledged there were people complaining that it was no longer live or Christian in focus, or that it was boring or had become just another annual institution.[93] Viewing figures owed much to the fact that there was usually nothing else on. The changes brought by recording the broadcast meant that while ITV had the Queen at 3.00 pm, the BBC had showed a circus in 1959 and a programme about Walt Disney's life in 1960. It tried another circus at 3.00 pm in 1963, but it was 1970 before television viewers had a choice again, when BBC2 broadcast a film called *Sammy Going South*. The following year BBC2 had a children's programme, but then went back to broadcasting the Queen, and it was not until 1977 that audiences had a choice once more when BBC2 scheduled a ballet against the monarch. From then onwards, BBC2's 3.00 pm programming grew more popular. By 1978, 25 million watched the Queen's Speech, less than half the population, and the competition was a choral concert on BBC2. By 1983 the Queen was competing against both BBC2 and Channel 4 and her combined audience for the various broadcasts of the speech was 18.5 million.[94] But there was no clear pattern and in 1987 the combined audience was back to 28 million, perhaps because the competition was a nativity play on Channel 4 and a programme about playing the cello on BBC2.[95]

Historian Joe Moran has argued that television's greatest significance is the way it has become embedded in the habits of daily life and this was true of both Christmas Day and the Queen's Speech.[96] It was a habit, something many people regarded as something that you did on Christmas Day. But, like radio listeners before them, that does not mean they took much notice. In a 1982 episode of *Terry and June*, the women all watched the Queen, while the men were fast asleep.[97] In 1986 one woman recorded that she and everyone she knew always watched the speech. 'It's never particularly interesting, but it's one of those traditional activities we openly scorn but secretly enjoy because of its familiarity.' Another woman recorded that year that the men in her family regarded watching the speech as a bind, but that she liked to hear what the Queen had to say, although she wished the monarch would relax more.[98]

People expected the Queen's stiff and unsmiling formality and the speech remained important to those of a particular kind of patriotism. This was despite the fact that, even late in the century, the content remained a little banal, with its optimistic, reassuring, comforting words, and nods to the Christmas spirit of goodwill and family amid acknowledgements of the anxieties of the day.[99] Whereas once the deference towards the monarchy meant a fairly wide acceptance of such sentiments at face value, in the less formal and more cynical era that gradually emerged in post-war Britain, they just seemed increasingly old-fashioned. In 1987 the *Sunday Times* remarked: 'Even by past standards, this year's message was brief and anodyne ... a bland appeal to loving and caring, "to treat others as you would like them to treat you". In cold print, it read like a curate's first stab at a sermon.' Yet it went on to note that few others in society could deliver such sentiments without having their sincerity questioned.[100] Indeed, for all the cynicism the speech attracted, most people probably agreed with the general sentiments it usually espoused.

Of course, not everyone even thought the UK should have a monarch, and by the 1980s some were explicitly making a point of not watching her speech in a way that they would not with any other programme. In some households, men even did the washing-up to avoid watching it.[101] Through such actions people were not necessarily rejecting the monarchy *per se*, but they were rejecting the traditional deference and values associated with it. Indifference to the Royal Family grew through that decade and in 1989 the speech was dropped by Radio 1 for the first time, although how popular it had been in the 9.00 am or 9.30 am slot it had had since the station's launch was a different matter. Indifference to the royal family then gathered speed and began turning into outright dissatisfaction. This culminated in the Queen's annus horribilis in 1992, when the marriages of Princes Charles and Andrew finally broke up in a very public and undignified fashion and a row broke out about the £60 million bill the public purse faced for repairing fire damage to Windsor Castle. Things did not get better in the coming years as details of royal infidelities were traded in public and then the Royal household completely misjudged the public grief that followed the death of the Princess of Wales.[102] The impact of this was very clear in the broadcast's audience figures, which by 1999 were down to 10 million. But just as important that year the Queen was up against *The Simpsons* on BBC2, a soap opera on Channel 5, and an alternative Christmas message from comedian Ali G on Channel 4, not to mention whatever people had videoed and any satellite channels they subscribed to. Both audiences and schedulers no longer felt any compunction about not putting Her Majesty at the heart of Christmas Day.

Like radio before it, television itself remained an important feature of Christmas. The percentage of households with sets had risen from 35 per cent in 1955 to 85 per cent in 1965 and 96 per cent in 1975.[103] Over the course of that period watching television became embedded in people's expectations of the day and it marked the biggest transformation in twentieth-century Christmas. People watched for entertainment, because there was little else to do and sometimes because it avoided arguments. As early as 1953, newspapers could joke that a television breakdown could put an end to a family's Christmas.[104] That decade saw regular jokes in the festive editions of the *TV Times* about television distracting people from parties or even Christmas dinner. By 1958, an advertisement for ITV was claiming that Christmas was not 'complete' without television. A year later, almost three-quarters of the UK population over the age of five watched television at some point on Christmas Day, with the average viewer watching two and a half hours on the BBC and one and a half hours on ITV.[105] Audiences peaked in the evening; 70 per cent of the population, for example, were watching television at 8.00 pm on Christmas Day 1984. Nearly 20 million were watching one film, *Raiders of the Lost Ark*.[106]

This was a long way removed from 1936, the first year of Christmas television. Then there were probably fewer than a thousand sets and programmes only went out at 3.00 pm to 4.00 pm and 9.00 pm to 10.00 pm. They opened with a demonstration of carving the turkey and were followed with carols, news and shows about unusual Christmases and the festival in the arctic and around the Empire. In subsequent years, schedules did diversify, particularly after the arrival of ITV created competition and raised audience expectations. Variations of light entertainment and celebrity-focused shows now dominated schedules. They were given a Christmassy theme, through studio decorations, and the odd carol or charitable visit, but they reflected an audience that generally thought Christmas was more about gentle humour and fun than anything intellectual or profound. Indeed, even humour that was dated could go down well. At Christmas 1963 the biggest BBC audience was 20.6 million for *The Gold Rush,* a 1925 Charlie Chaplin film, shown at 9.25 pm. Some even objected when there was more serious programming and in 1964 a letter to the *Daily Mail* complained that the BBC were showing a documentary about the Great War on Christmas Day, arguing that something less macabre was needed for Christmas. A year earlier a Leeds woman had written to the *TV Times* asking that festive programming be 'Christmassy'. She wanted carols and a snowy film.[107]

Christmas light entertainment was self-effacing and mildly irreverent without being offensive or threatening and at its best it was very funny. In 1953 a middle-aged woman from Morecambe recorded in her diary how much she had enjoyed *Christmas Party*: 'it was such fun and made us feel almost though we were there taking part.'[108] Nonetheless, it was not to everyone's taste and we should again not assume all viewers liked what they were watching. In a world of two or three channels, there was not exactly much choice and many people found themselves forced to watch something to compromise or to keep the peace. That did not stop them complaining. In 1962 *The Times* remarked that even the Queen's Speech was fitted in 'as if it were topping the bill at the royal variety performance'. It bemoaned the lack of serious programming or anything that showed how Christmas 'revealed the split in the community between the haves and have-nots'. It did, at least, approve of the *Z Cars* episode that focused on a mentally deranged child out on a dark Christmas night. A decade later, a letter to the same newspaper was asking, 'Must we subjected to yet another Christmas of Disney, Ken Dodd, and Billy Smart?'[109]

The fact that people chose to complain to newspapers shows how ingrained watching television at Christmas had become in national culture. Indeed, for far more people, festive programming was something of an event in itself. Broadcasters saw it as the year's highlight and their choice of content over the holidays was a matter for comment at work, home and in the press.[110] People scanned the listings to plan what to watch, focusing in particular on what films were on because, before video recorders became widespread in the 1980s, Christmas was a rare opportunity to see a recent blockbuster or a classic movie that was not on cinema release. Television's establishment as a Christmas tradition in itself was cemented in 1969 when the *Radio Times* and the *TV Times* published their first double-issue Christmas specials. There were then people who thought of themselves as ITV or BBC families and the different tastes (and by implication class) of the audiences were clear from the covers: an artistic montage with a reindeer at its centre for the BBC's *Radio Times* and Des O'Connor in a Santa hat for ITV's *TV Times*.[111] Such was the importance of festive television that some families only ever bought a listing magazine at Christmas. By 1990, the last year it had a monopoly in publishing the BBC schedules, the *Radio Times* sold 10.6 million copies of its Christmas special, compared with an average weekly sales that year of 2.83 million.[112] Moreover, the publication of these special issues, like trailers for Christmas broadcasting and on-screen decorations, became another popular marker of when the Christmas season started and ended.

In 1977 the television critic of *The Times* noted that the box would exert a 'tyranny' over Christmas, but beyond some good films there was nothing actually 'worth missing a party or a walk in the country for'.[113] Yet the 1970s marked the highpoint of Christmas viewing and there is now considerable

PLATE 24 *Morecambe and Wise, 1983. P. Shirley/Getty.*

nostalgia for its most popular programmes, particularly *Morecambe and Wise*. Their festive special rarely had much actual Christmas content, but Ernie Wise himself said it was as integral to Christmas as turkey and plum pudding. Morecambe, meanwhile, felt the stress of trying to live up to expectations and a belief that a poor show could spoil people's Christmas.[114] But a good show could do quite the opposite, as was evident from the delight caused by newsreader Angela Rippon dancing on the show in 1976. The *Daily Mirror* had devoted almost a whole page to a leak that she would appear and that her 'long and shapely' legs would be visible thanks to a 'saucy slit' in her dress.[115] As Joe Moran has argued, such moments are evidence that much of the population was not preoccupied by the serious crises of that decade. Yet there was and is a degree of myth around quite how integral the show was to the British Christmas of the 1970s. The BBC's estimates suggest that Morecambe and Wise's Christmas audience peaked at 28.8 million in 1977, six million more than the Queen's Speech that year, but the more accurate measuring of ITV suggested the actual audience was 21.3 million. Immediately before the Morecambe and Wise 1977 special was the *Mike Yarwood Christmas Show* and that actually attracted 100,000 more viewers.[116] Moreover, as with the Queen, many millions of people being in the same room as a switched-on television set does not mean they were actually watching or paying attention.[117]

Morecambe and Wise was not the only show that did not draw people together at Christmas quite as much as popular memory suggests. With the exception of the royal wedding, the highest television audience of the 1980s is usually listed as the 30.1 million figure for the 1986 Christmas Day episode of *EastEnders* that saw Dirty Den turn on his wife Angie, who had been pretending to be dying, and present her with a demand for a divorce. However, this figure also includes the audience for the Sunday repeat and the figure for 25 December was actually 19.5 million.[118] Similarly, a historian of *Coronation Street* has pointed out that in the show's first two decades the Christmas episode could often be the least seen of the year, an indication of how soap operas were still establishing themselves. In 1967, for example, the highest watched episode came in September when 9.45 million tuned in, whereas just 2.78 million watched the Christmas Day episode. It was broadcast at 7.00 pm, but when *Christmas with the Stars* was on the other channel. The result of such experiences was that in the 1970s there was just one 25 December broadcast of the show (in 1972), even though in 1974 and 1978 Christmas fell on a normal transmission day. It was *EastEnders'* success in 1986 that changed the stakes by demonstrating people would watch if there was a special storyline. *Coronation Street* followed it up in 1987 with Hilda Ogden's departure, which, together with its repeat, was watched by 26.63 million. Except for 1993, *Coronation Street* has been broadcast on 25 December every year since.[119] Although other soaps followed the lead of *EastEnders* and inflicted arguments, misery and sudden deaths on viewers, *Coronation Street* better reflected how people actually thought about Christmas. Before 1986 its Christmas storylines had been rather tame, mundane affairs that probably reflected most people's Christmas, although perhaps with more participation in pantos and pub sing-alongs. The emphasis was clearly on humorous and sentimental scenes and that continued even after *EastEnders* raised the stakes, freeing it from sharing in the ridicule that other soaps started to attract in their annual efforts to bring despair to people's Christmas living rooms with storylines where characters could declare that they just wanted to 'wallow in my own misery'.[120]

Soap operas needed dramatic seasonal storylines because the video recorder was changing television habits. The ability to record programmes and watch them later may not have made a significant impact on viewing figures on a normal day, but on Christmas Day it allowed people to fit watching the box around the demands of dinner and other rituals rather than vice versa. Moreover, with pre-recorded films being given as presents there were also new rivals to live television over the holiday. The result was some dramatic falls in viewing figures that extended far beyond the Royal broadcast. As early as 1982, the *Two Ronnies* got 11.1 million rather than the 15.1 million it attracted in 1981. *Last of the Summer Wine's* audience fell from 17 million in 1981 to 9.9 million a year later.[121] By 1991, Christmas Day was again *Coronation Street's* lowest audience of the year, when just 10.7 million watched compared with the 21.6 million highpoint for that year. When 13 million watched *Doctor Who* on Christmas Day 2007, it was one of the highest audiences for a Christmas show since the 1980s. These were still huge numbers compared to any activity outside the home, but they marked how specific television programmes were no longer the same kind of shared experience that they once were. Television itself remained a Christmas habit but what, when and how people watched had fragmented.

One mainstay of television listings was films about Christmas. By the late twentieth century they were a distinct genre of their own and regarded as a defining feature of the season. Yet they had not been common before the Second World War. This was mostly a matter of logistics. Filmmakers then tended to produce 40 to 120 physical copies of a film, which meant it took months for it to do the rounds of the country's cinemas. Thus, the maker of a festive film risked it showing in the summer.[122] The taste for reassuring images in the war-torn 1940s, however, led to a series of Hollywood Christmas movies that celebrated home and family.[123] One of them is now widely regarded in the UK as one of, if not the greatest Christmas film of all time. Not all contemporary reviewers of *It's a Wonderful Life* (1947) were so impressed. The *Sunday Post* said it was a 'mixture of comedy and humanity' but felt 'a vague feeling of dissatisfaction at the result'. Nor did contemporary British reviews even see it as a Christmas film, partly because in many parts of the UK it was released in June, but also because it was not marketed as such either.[124] The majority of the storyline had nothing to do with the festival, but its climax was set on Christmas Day and its emphasis on redemption and looking after others certainly fitted the Christmas spirit.

It was first shown on British television on Christmas Eve 1957 but, never became the mainstay on UK Christmas schedules that it was in North America.[125] Nor did *Miracle on 34th Street* (released in the UK in 1947 under the title *The Big Heart*), but this film also subsequently became a seasonal favourite thanks to its celebration of children's imagination and apparent attack on the commercialization of Christmas. The *Daily Mirror* said on its release: 'Don't miss this really brilliant comedy with its lacing of tears. It's a peach of a picture.'[126] *The Times,* however, was not impressed and thought it was designed to foster the Christmas trade that it was satirizing. Other now classic Christmas films also took time to attain that status. *The Times'* review of *White Christmas* (1954) was impressed by the clarity of the picture on a big screen but not much else, calling it 'resolutely sentimental and without inspiration of any kind, drags along for two hours and is very expert and smart and imposing in all things that do not matter'.[127] By the late twentieth century, Christmas films were satirizing their genre's own sentimentality. One such favourite was the action movie *Die Hard* (1988), which was set on Christmas Eve and full of seasonal imagery amid its guns and explosions. Indeed, some in the UK even regarded it as the greatest Christmas movie.[128]

The fact that people would argue about such things was further evidence that by the late twentieth century Christmas films were regarded as an integral part of a shared cultural inheritance. Whether they were made in Britain or not, the outputs of cinema and television provided memories and stories that people grew familiar with. They replaced the traditions of local communities and the street, both literally in terms of providing seasonal entertainments and in their social role in uniting people. They provided talking points within families and between friends and even strangers. They reinforced Christmas's position as a cornerstone of British culture and acted as a bridge that united the individualized experiences of celebrating at home. Christmas television and films may not have hit the standards of high culture, but you did not have to like a story to know it.

Another Christmas genre of dubious cultural merit was pantomime. Their comic mix of revenue, variety, dance, song and fairy tales had a long heritage, but its link with Christmas was one of timing rather than storylines. As with so much of festive culture, there was some discussion between the wars of whether pantomime was in artistic decline. Some even argued it represented a culture that had shifted away from making its own entertainment and humour to watching others.[129] Its defenders, however, argued that 'Pantomimes are often, for scenic splendour, genial humour, and lively displays of dancing, among the best shows of the year' and that they represented 'the greatest triumph of the Christmas spirit in modern life'.[130] They were certainly growing in number. In 1933, around 100 were produced, but that figure rose to nearly 200 by 1948. The 1933 production of *Queen of Hearts* at London's Lyceum Theatre was seen by 300,000 people. As with Christmas movies, the content was comforting rather than challenging. The humour was a little childish, irreverent and gently mocking of those in authority. Jokes about underwear and cross dressing remained staples long after such humour had gone out of fashion in the cinema. Indeed, Pimlott argued in 1978 that panto exemplified 'the conservatism of popular taste in Christmas art and entertainment'.[131] While productions were always adapted with local and topical references, that conservatism was evident in the reliance on a stock of basic stories. Throughout the period, *Cinderella* was generally the most popular of these, perhaps because its story of rags to riches suited both the Christmas season and working-class audiences. Other productions, however, were more subject to fashion. *Babes in the Woods*, the second most popular production in 1919, had virtually disappeared nearly a century later. This was partly because its storyline involved child murder, but also because other cultural forms had not reinforced knowledge of its plot and characters. In contrast, Disney movies helped cement the popularity of old stories such as *Snow White* and *Aladdin* and created new favourites such as *Beauty and the Beast*. Nonetheless, pantomime, by and large, remained rooted in its live setting. Although productions had been broadcast on radio and then television throughout the period, for the majority of people panto was something you went to see and indeed it was probably the majority of the audience's only annual trip to the theatre. Its popularity was evident in the fact that in 2013 more than 1.5 million tickets were sold to pantomimes run by Qdos, the UK's largest producer, making it central to the economic viability of many theatres. Theatrical purists probably resented that, but panto was as much part of Christmas culture as anything else. Indeed, it also represented one of the few instances of survival of the idea that Christmas could be silly and childish. The days of fathers donning costumes, charades, parlour games and clothes swapping had largely been overtaken by the more sophisticated entertainment on screen, but in pantomime their spirit lived on.

Scotland and ethnicity

In 1871 Christmas Day was made a bank holiday in Scotland. That did not mean, however, that it immediately became a day off for everyone. It was Hogmanay, the Scottish New Year, that was the main winter celebration and in some homes even the chosen occasion for Santa's visit. While many places of work stayed open on the 25th, the rituals of present-shopping and present-giving were embedding themselves north of the border and Christmas folk traditions, such as guising and burning the Yule log, were practised too.[132] In 1885 an Aberdeen newspaper remarked how even Presbyterians were being 'weaned over to the customs of our English brethren' and that Christmas was 'speedily overcoming our Scotch prejudice'. In 1902 the *Dundee Courier* suggested that 'Something of the same spirit of mirth and revelry is beginning to creep into the Scottish Christmas as in the English, and the customs in North and South Britain are practically the same'. By

1912 *The Scotsman* was claiming the festival had even reached the farthest Hebrides. Yet, in 1904, a Falkirk newspaper maintained that beyond the decorations in shop windows and the pressure at the Post Office, the 'event passed without too much to mark its approach'.[133]

Between the wars, Christmas in Scotland remained a mixed affair, varying from place to place according to local holiday customs and religious influences, but comments on its increased observance continued. Indeed, some claimed that Christmas in Scotland was more esteemed than in England because it was observed more as a religious event. In 1919 the *Dundee Courier* told readers that 'Scotland is gradually coming into line, but complete unity of the observance is still a long way off'.[134] Newspapers were not published on the day, but it remained a working day in much of Scotland, although sources are vague on how widespread this was. Churches certainly encouraged people to observe the festival. Christmas Day services were common in Catholic and Anglican places of worship, while religious bodies ran charitable events and vicars gave sermons about the Christmas spirit. In 1923, an Aberdeen newspaper noted how within a generation the fact that Christmas used to pass 'almost unnoticed' had gone and the festival was now acknowledged among 'all sections of the population'. It conceded that the 'more exuberant manifestations of joy' were confined to Hogmanay, but felt that was in keeping with the religious significance of Christmas. Two years later, the same paper was describing how shopkeepers decorated their windows and largely postponed half-day closing on 23 December to take advantage of festive trade. It expected working-class men and women to head out on Christmas Eve to buy presents for their children. There were numerous private parties and dinners and dances in the town's hotels. Unemployment was hitting the festivities, but wards and benevolent organizations were putting on entertainments and giving out treats. Those too old or feeble to attend had 'parcels of good things delivered to their homes'. It was not, however, thought the paper, an English Christmas and one difference was that few sent cards, although many did exchange calendars.[135]

Above all, the interwar Scottish Christmas was considered an event for the children. It was common for children across Scotland to hang stockings, and even those who grew up in homes that were not decorated could later remember vividly their excitement at the whole event.[136] Adults too might get a few presents in the morning before heading out to work.[137] Special meals were not as central to the Scottish Christmas as they were in England, but they were certainly not unknown. One Glasgow woman remembered getting a stocking, but having broth for dinner and a communal bonfire around which people roasted potatoes.[138] The relatively low-key celebrations typical across Scotland were captured in the 1937 Mass Observation notes of a steelworker in Kilbirnie. On Christmas Eve he worked the nightshift as usual and the only reference heard to Christmas was the 'usual' joke about 'going home to fill the wife's stocking', which caused much hilarity. He received chocolates from his wife and sister and a cardigan from his parents, which surprised him since his father was out of work. There was duck, a present from a sister-in-law, for dinner. While relaxing at home, he also heard the King's Speech, although he had not known it was on.[139]

Christmas, however, had Catholic undertones that Presbyterians disapproved of. They also complained that it was associated with debauchery, had no real scriptural basis and painted Christ as a child rather than a saviour. Thus, some families did not celebrate Christmas in any way. The son of a Glasgow shipyard worker remembered: 'My father was very strict Presbyterian and New Year was the only time you could hang your stocking, Christmas was a time to sing carols and go to church. No Christmas dinner, no Christmas pudding; it was like every other day of the week.' When one Edinburgh schoolboy asked his grandmother why they did not celebrate Christmas like his friends he was told: 'We're no heathens, laddie'.[140] There was some feeling that such attitudes were concentrated in the working class, although one interwar writer hotly denied this.[141] Yet, even at the beginning of the interwar period, observers were noting that this 'Calvinistic spirit' was less assertive than in the past and that Christmas as a social festival was increasingly popular in Scotland. Many Presbyterian churches did hold Christmas services on the nearest Sunday, sang carols and objected to the more traditional opponents of the festival in their sect.[142] In 1935 a Presbyterian minister from Dornoch was suspended for six months after his daughter held a Christmas Eve party where there was dancing. The Northern Presbytery of the church expressed its displeasure thus: 'We would prayerfully and lovingly warn the young against promiscuous dancing and giving countenance to such Romish practices as that of observing Christmas Eve.' Another minister in the church however thought this comment 'outrageous'.[143] Indeed, Presbyterianism's stance on Christmas was beginning to suggest that all its moral strictures were outdated and even a little pathetic. One 1931 letter writer to *The Scotsman* suggested to a public proponent of Christmas as a pagan custom that he re-read *A Christmas Carol* and ask himself if he was a disciple of Scrooge.[144]

Between the wars, Christmas observance became a tide that was impossible to turn back. The forces driving it were both public and private. One girl remembered that it was because she was upset that her friends got presents that her family allowed Father Christmas in future years.[145] The radio and cinema was another bringer of English customs into Scottish homes. As early as 1922, one newspaper claimed that the press was leading public opinion by giving so much attention to how Christmas was observed. But it also thought that Scotsmen's experience elsewhere in the world probably had an influence too. It argued that men who had served in the Great War had 'obtained a wider outlook than ever they had the opportunity of acquiring in the past: and it is since the war years that the Christmas spirit has seen its greatest manifestation in Scotland'. In the next war too, serving in the forces gave another generation of Scotsmen a taste of English Christmas festivities that they found to their liking.[146]

Christmas' Scottish growth continued to gather pace after the Second World War and again there was public encouragement of this through, for example, newspaper editorials about the value of Christmas goodwill. In 1949 alone, there was a rise of 20 per cent on the year before in the volume of Christmas mail posted in Aberdeen between 12 and 19 December.[147] By 1950, the dean of the Thistle and Chapel Royal was telling Edinburgh City Business Club that Christmas would soon replace Hogmanay as the main festival. That year, the appearance of Santa in Edinburgh department stores in November was also causing comment and concern.[148] Where some men had worked all day on the 25th, they might now come home at lunchtime or increasingly have the whole day off. Growing levels of festive trade in the 1950s showed that rising incomes were creating the same desires to spend and indulge that were found elsewhere in the UK. One Aberdeen paper noted in 1954 that while in some northern homes and communities Santa still came on New Year's Eve, this was becoming less and less common and thought one cause was his presence in shops. Yet even in those homes where his call was delayed, Christmas Day was still celebrated and children were rationalizing the situation through a belief that he could not call everywhere on a single night.[149] On Christmas Day itself, church services were now said to have become the rule rather than the exception. By 1958 *The Times* was claiming that Scotland had 'caught up with the rest of Christendom as celebrants of Christmas'. As evidence, it cited the 120,000 Clydeside shipyard and engineering workers who were having Christmas Day off for the first time after having forfeited two half-day holidays at New Year and in the summer.[150] The spread of the traditional Christmas to Scotland was also a marker of growing cultural integration within the UK. The experience of war and the role of the state in reconstruction were important underpinning factors, but the media again played its role in turning symbolic ideas into lived experiences. Depictions of Anglo-American feasts and celebrations on television sped up the process of creating festive expectations and aspirations that newsreels, films and radio had begun before the Second World War. As Pimlott points out, the change may have owed much to better relations with the Church of England and a move away from literal interpretations of the Bible, but it was also rooted in the simple appeal of the festival itself.[151] As anyone watching on screen realized, Christmas was fun.

Of course, there were still limitations to what was happening and, indeed, there was some pride in Scottish festive apathy as a sign of a distinct national identity within the UK. In 1948, the MP for Perth even claimed that Christmas was practically unobserved in Scotland.[152] That was plainly untrue but it was not until 1974 that Boxing Day was made a bank holiday in Scotland (the same year New Year's Day became one in the rest of the UK), thus expanding the time people had at home to celebrate. The year 1971 saw the last full set of Scottish league football fixtures on Christmas Day (in England it was 1957), and five years later the last league games were played that day. Even in the 1980s, there were urban Baptist churches choosing not to hold Christmas Day services, but it was in the Highlands and islands that old values died hardest. In the late 1970s, at Dingwall, north of Inverness, a headmaster removed a Christmas tree brought into his primary school. A year later, he fell out with parents and teachers who wanted carol singing practice to be held in school time and ended up being suspended from his job. A decade later, there were similar tensions on the Isle of Skye after a Canadian exchange teacher brought a tree into school, unaware of how Presbyterians disapproved and of how powerful their influence was. As late as the early 1990s, a minister on the Isle of Raasay was deploring Christmas as 'a heathen festival' that was superstitious and 'deeply offensive'. The island's primary school had a tree and a Christmas party, but the minister refused to attend it, despite being the school's chaplain.[153] To outsiders, such attitudes seemed silly and obstinate, and it is difficult not to conclude that such ministers were cutting the throats of their own religion.

A 2007 opinion poll suggested that 93 per cent of the UK population would celebrate Christmas.[154] Who the other 7 per cent were and what they were doing was unclear, but it is not unreasonable to suggest that the majority were from non-Christian ethnic minorities. The festival had always put those of other faiths in a difficult position, but this did not mean they could not celebrate what was far from simply a religious festival. Thus, throughout the century Jehovah's Witnesses often had Christmas dinner, trees and presents because they did not associate these things with faith. In 1937 in a Jewish refugee centre in London, there was no special dinner, but there was singing and dancing and some Christmas cards and chocolates.[155] This was probably then unusual, as older Jews especially seemed reluctant to acknowledge Christmas. One man even remembered his father eating scrambled eggs in the dark at Christmas to prove he was not celebrating. Yet there could still be a holiday atmosphere in non-celebrating families simply because schools, workplaces and transport shut down meaning the family was together at home. In the 1980s one rabbi told the story of how as a young man he visited a family who promptly hid all their decorations because they did not want him to know they were celebrating. He then learnt that one of the laws for rabbis in modern Britain was: 'Do not visit your congregants on Christmas Day.' Individual recollections suggest that Christmas dinner seemed to become more common in Jewish families at the end of the twentieth century.[156] Again, the increasing secular nature of the festival helped justify this, but in order to lessen any sense of betrayal of their own culture some families also merged Christmas with their own festival of Hanukkah, which lasts for eight days but shifts its date within a period from late November to late December. Jewish families might thus have a turkey dinner and give Hanukkah presents on the 25th, but without regarding themselves as celebrating Christmas.[157] Indeed, some historians have suggested that Hanukkah only became a major Jewish festival because people wanted an alternative to Christmas.[158]

PLATE 25 *A black Father Christmas, London, 1950s. Heritage Images/Getty.*

Christmas also created complications for the large numbers of immigrants that began to arrive from the Commonwealth from the 1950s onwards. Before the late 1960s, the majority were Christian, but that did not mean they found things easy. Part of this was because their daily experience of racism betrayed the goodwill that Christmas was supposed to embody. Indeed, in 1959 the BBC broadcast *Break in Festivities*, a television play that retold the nativity through two newly arrived black immigrants who, after failing to find accommodation because of their colour, end up in a squalid attic where their child is born. There were more prosaic reasons to find Christmas difficult too. In 1960 ITV news interviewed black immigrants who gave the impression that Christmas was duller in England. Another immigrant remembered the festival in the 1960s as a time of sadness, because it made her remember and miss Jamaica. She found it cold, with 'nothing happening'; there were no visits from friends, which would be expected in Caribbean culture.[159] The nostalgia Christmas could engender in immigrants was dramatized in another television drama, *Black Christmas* (1977). One character complains that the festival in Britain is 'Godless'. She misses 'our kind of Christmas with our kind of food' and complains, 'This country brings me pain.'[160]

Even if they might not like it, taking part in Christmas rituals could be a measure of integration. Research on Ghanaian immigrants in London at the end of the 1990s showed they cooked traditional Christmas dinners, even though they placed great emphasis on eating their own ethnic foods at other times.[161] A Hindu man from London interviewed in the 1990s noted:

This is part of integration. Christmas is the most important festival, occasion of this country, so how can we just ignore it? ... the feeling of Christmas is there, everywhere, you go out in the shops and they see the programmes on the TV, and it's all about Christmas. ... We have come from other land, we, we still have links with that land ... [but] we have a Christmas tree in our house every Christmas, with Christmas lights and everything, and on that day we, in our own way, not with the turkey, we have a cake, and we have a pudding. And then Christmas is very much part of our life now, because we live in this country, so we, in a way we benefit from both cultures ... we celebrate Diwali, and we celebrate Christmas.[162]

The offspring of immigrants were bombarded by Christmas through December, when it provided a focus for lessons and school play rehearsals dominated many days. This, together with the prevalence of the festival in the shops and in popular culture, made the festival exciting, whereas their own religious festivals did not seem as remotely as fun and might even seem odd without wider cultural reference points to reinforce their value. Within ethnically diverse schools, there could be hierarchies among the children over whose families celebrated Christmas. This led children to put pressure on their parents to adopt Christmas rituals, something which could cause significant tensions and anxieties within families. This could be especially true within families where partners were from different ethnic backgrounds.[163] The outcome was often compromise and a mix of cultural practices that embodied a multicultural society. This was clearest at mealtimes when samosas might be served alongside turkey or crackers were pulled with curries. In the 1980s one Asian woman, whose husband and mother-in-law disapproved of celebrating Christmas but whose children got upset when the family did nothing, started having a tree but covered it with a white sheet when her spouse was there.[164] At the start of the 1990s, an anthropologist noted that Punjabi families in Southall were giving Christmas gifts but not bringing Santa into the equation. Both children and adults assessed the extent of Christmas celebration as a way of measuring a family's integration into wider society. Some children would even exaggerate the celebrations at home in order to ensure their parents were not seen as backwards.[165] Other children of immigrants could reconcile their difference by playing up to their friends that being a Muslim, with its twice-yearly Eid, meant two Christmases a year and thus two lots of presents, even when that was not true.[166]

Again, non-Christian ethnic minorities often felt able to take such positions because they did not think Christmas's place in British culture was primarily religious. Nonetheless, the lack of religion in Christmas annoyed some from other faiths.[167] They could also feel the faith of their own family was undermined by the festival's ubiquity and resentful of the pressure to conform. In 1987 one reporter noted that parents at a London school that was 99 per cent Asian were angry about the emphasis it placed upon Christmas but were not willing to complain. A younger generation, however, were more assertive in their rejection of Christmas and the same reporter was told by a young Asian: 'They hate you and then ask you to celebrate their things.'[168] Such voices grew with notions of individual rights and the stronger self-assertiveness that developed within the British Muslim community in response to its occasional demonization after 11 September 2001. A very few Muslims would not even say 'merry Christmas' to others because they felt it inappropriate.[169] These, however, were extreme examples and on the whole there was far more tolerance. Even the fact that most people were not working meant that some non-celebrating families still had a party or get together, although others just spent the day watching television.[170]

While newspaper columnists could celebrate children from ethnic minority backgrounds taking part in nativity plays as a symbol of integration in the UK, others worried about the dynamics of it all.[171] Research found that some people fretted that decorations at work might offend non-Christian colleagues or customers. One survey reported in the *Daily Mail* claimed that two-thirds of employers were not allowing decorations for this reason.[172] That is very difficult to believe but this does not mean there were no such cases. In Peterborough there were reports in 2005 that staff at a jobcentre had been told they were not allowed to put up decorations for fear of offending minorities but by the time it was reported in the press, the decision had been reversed.[173] Rumour and supposition was in danger of replacing reality in some public rhetoric and it all fed the paranoia of some on the right that there were politically correct attempts afoot to ban Christmas in order to promote some kind of multicultural harmony. The *Daily Express* ran a frontpage headline in 2005 declaring 'Christmas is banned: it offends Muslims.'[174] The story was based on a claim that Lambeth Council had renamed its Christmas lights 'winter lights'. That was true, but the council still had decorations, a Christmas tree, carols and other celebrations. The change of title had simply come from one administrator erring on the side of caution.[175] Another example widely cited was a Birmingham City Council marketing campaign for Winterval in 1997, an attempt to join and promote together its various Christmas, New Year and Diwali celebrations and entertainments. Despite the fact that the promotional literature and advertisements clearly embraced Christmas, this was wrongly interpreted by the local and national press as a ban on the festival and the story was also used by American right-wing Christians to support their claims of a 'War on

Christmas'.[176] The fact that the story was repeated added to the perception that some minorities felt Christmas was offensive and that a liberal left was accommodating them and thus further sacrificing traditional British culture at the altar of politically correct multiculturalism. It was paranoid nonsense but at its roots was a real and deep-felt unease at the direction of British society, born out of the same reverence for the comfort of tradition that helped underpin Christmas itself.

Conclusion

The Victorian and Edwardian middle class may have predominantly celebrated at home but for the working class, whose residences were often uncomfortable, overcrowded and unappealing, a rare day free from work was reason to take to the streets, not relax at home. Between the wars too, there were sporting events, pantomimes, cinema showings, folk rituals and informal gatherings on Christmas Day. But these communal entertainments were clearly on the decline as the festival took greater root in the home. In 1923, the zoo and nearly every cinema and theatre in London were closed on Christmas Day. The trams shut down at 4.00 pm, the tube was running a Sunday service and the bus service was reduced to a skeleton.[177] In Tyneside, one observer noted how the interwar unemployed, who normally stood on the streets 'day after day', were not to be seen on the 25th.[178] In the countryside too, people noted how quiet it was on Christmas afternoon, with no one out but the odd couple and famers who had to feed and milk stock. In 1937, *The Economist*, pointing to how Christmas was slowly becoming more private than public, argued that there was 'no time of the year when the average citizen withdraws more completely and gratefully to his domestic hearth'.[179] First radio and then television added to that process, relieving people of some of the need to entertain themselves. Communal celebrations of course did not disappear but they were increasingly focused on the days before Christmas or a midnight church service rather than on the 25th itself.

The Christmas at home was an expression of people's appreciation of domesticity and simply being at home. It was the rising living standards that began between the wars and gathered pace in the 1950s that created and cemented what George Orwell called 'the *privateness* of English life'.[180] As homes got more comfortable and new estates were built, people were able to live more domestic lives, anchoring themselves in their wider family rather than in the neighbourhood. This raised fears about the loss of traditional community, but privateness was often what people liked about the new estates.[181] This did not mean that they did not appreciate neighbourliness and community; those concepts both existed and were valued on the new estates that were so often blamed for killing traditional working-class communities. Indeed, the importance of community was evident at Christmas time, and throughout the twentieth century the festival continued to play a role in bringing people together. There were conscious revivals of old local traditions that had defined communities and communal attempts at raising money for charity that were said to be bring the classes together.[182] People who put extravagant lighting displays on the outside of their homes had a strong sense that in doing so they were giving something to the community. Not all their neighbours and passers-by agreed, but organizations also tried to raise spirits with public decorations. Even before 1939, public places such as offices and pubs had their 'festoons of paper flowers and silver bells cut out of card'.[183] When the Norfolk village of Hunworth erected a 22-foot illuminated tree on its village green in 1935, it was unusual enough to be newsworthy, and the rector told the press that he hoped that every English village would soon do the same.[184] By the end of the decade, public trees could be found in a number of city centres and even rail stations.[185] This new custom was given a boost when, to much media coverage, a tree was erected in Trafalgar Square, an annual gift from the people of Oslo as thanks for the help rendered during the Second World War. By 1949 the *Western Gazette* was noting the profusion of public trees in the Southwest, arguing they were 'the centres of colour, life and laughter in the market places of many towns'.[186] Enjoying such trees was part of the simple unifying fact that Christmas was something everyone experienced. People may have shopped and celebrated as individuals but they did so at the same time and it was a topic of conversation and shared concern. As a 1936 novel put it, Christmas was 'the most active, persistent and inescapable' of the 'focal points' in the yearly cycle of local community life.[187]

Above all, it was the media in all its forms that created a new shared festive experience and one whose scale far outstripped anything that had happened on the streets. In 1952 the *Radio Times* argued that broadcasting was widening the 'great British family' and 'at the same time drawing it closer together'.[188] This process extended beyond people simply listening or watching to the same broadcast at the same time. During December, Christmas entered virtually every area of popular culture. It was even the setting for the odd erotic novel, and naked girls wearing Santa hats could be found in that month's pornographic magazines.[189] There were annual tropes of Christmas news reporting – such as rising prices, busy shops and the fate of the homeless or elderly – and a raft of well-known seasonal films, stories and songs. Even older stories such as *A Christmas Carol* found new, wider audiences that far surpassed anything they had reached in their original written form. These images that people saw on the small and big screens helped create a shared understanding of what the festival should look like and what people should do on the day. Christmas in the media, film and fiction began as resolutely romantic, sentimental or comical in tone, capturing and reinforcing people's perception of the season. Thus, as Miller argues, new technologies such as film and television appropriated rather than transformed Christmas.[190] Yet the genre did evolve to satirize and paint a more complex picture of Christmas that in its own way was just as much a cliché as what it was lampooning. Jokes about relatives, bad presents, overeating and drinking became staples of Christmas television that everyone recognized but were only part of the actual festive experience. Such outputs did not replace the more saccharine genre and there were thus now films, songs and stories that appealed to all tastes. This variety of Christmas popular culture lessened the chances of people being alienated by the festival and reinforced it as a shared experience and marker of British culture.

Seeing the decline of local traditions, one writer argued in 1951 that 'There is a standard Christmas on its way, as there is to be a standard speech and standard dress and a standard wage and a standard goodness-knows-what else.'[191] That was most evident in the growth of Christmas in Scotland but the ubiquity of the festival forced other groups to decide whether they wanted to celebrate or not. So prominent was Christmas that any decision not to celebrate had to be a conscious one. Thus ethnic groups, so often marginalized in mainstream society, signalled, intentionally or otherwise, their part in the national culture through celebrating Christmas. Of course, this did not mean there were not tensions; the resentment of the explicit and implicit pressure on immigrants and different faiths to integrate could come out at Christmastime. There were also times when Christmas allowed others to demonstrate their national and cultural allegiances. This was clear during the Great War when German-made toys, so common before 1914, became taboo.[192] Patriotism remained a strong interwar theme in Christmas shopping and customers were continually exhorted to buy British (a concept which then included the whole Empire). In 1931 the *Daily Mail* reported that shoppers were demanding British manufactured goods and making a real English Christmas.[193] Whether or not that was actually the case, it would have encouraged any readers not buying British to consider their position. After the war, there were advertisements that told consumers to 'Choose British Toys this Christmas'.[194] Such ideas were already starting to look dated by the 1950s. Although in other spheres buying British remained an important call well into the 1970s, it just seemed out of place at Christmas time. So too did any sense of imperial or Commonwealth loyalty. Whereas in the 1930s the BBC had tried to tighten imperial bonds through Christmas broadcasts from across the Empire, by the 1950s this programming was attracting less and less interest at home and abroad. Having lost its novelty and its emotional resonances, it was finally dropped in 1965.[195]

Instead of being used to celebrate England, Britain or the Empire, Christmas after the Second World War was increasingly seen as an international festival. It was, after all, celebrated in all Christian countries and its Christian message was about the fellowship of man not nations. Even Santa was an international figure rather than the benefactor of any one country. Thus, when Scotland fell into line it was not just integrating into a British culture but a global tradition. One anthropologist has even suggested that festive rituals repeated across the globe created 'a relationship between the celebrant and the world at large'.[196] Here, once again, the media was central. Images of Christmas in other parts of world were staples of newsreels, newspaper reports and television and radio broadcasts. The songs and films that made up so much of festive popular culture were often from the United States. Indeed, Christmas demonstrated how so much of what was taken as the globalization of popular culture was really about the Americanization of the world. This was not just a product of the post-1945 world. 'Jingle Bells' was an American song penned in 1856. The holly wreaths on front door and public trees that began to become popular in interwar Britain were imitations of American fashions. Santa Claus himself was a Victorian American import, even when he went, often self-consciously, by his more British name of Father Christmas. But the Americanization of Christmas was not a complete process and there were traditions such as civic parades that never found a home on this side of the Atlantic despite being depicted in American films.

Christmas was thus simultaneously a symbol of local, national and global cultures.[197] But beneath the facade of unity were diverse communities. Not everyone took part in local traditions or welcomed the calling of neighbours and children. Just because people were watching the same programme did not mean they were thinking the same thing or watching in the same conditions. Not everyone even felt themselves to be British. Unity may have been an illusionary concept but it was a powerful one nonetheless. Nations may have been divided by wealth, region, gender and ethnicity but history and culture gave the people within them a sense that they all belonged to the same country and Christmas was part of the shared culture that engendered the sense of togetherness. It may not have been celebrated as a sign of national culture any more but it was still part of the array of habits and routines that defined British society, an example of what Michael Billig called 'banal nationalism'.[198] There may not have been that much about it that was peculiarly British, but that did not make Christmas any less something that the British shared, and by sharing it, in whatever guise they wanted, they reaffirmed their place in British culture.

CHAPTER SIX

Officialdom and Christmas

On 5 December 1973, amid power and petrol shortages and growing numbers of strikes, the front page of the *Daily Mirror* asked, 'Is everybody going mad?' It noted that with just twenty days to Christmas, the country seemed to be drifting towards breakdown. To capture what it thought was the spirit of the times, the paper ran a humourous article about a Father Xmas Union that was demanding that the outdated white beard and sleigh be replaced with something more modern. There were more genuine seasonal problems to concern the authorities. In East Anglia, the police distributed 40,000 leaflets that warned of the dangers of drink-driving. In Wiltshire, the Forestry Commission put on special patrols to stop Christmas tree poachers. On 13 December, the prime minister described the national situation as 'a very grave emergency' and announced austerity measures that included a three-day week and an end to television broadcasting after 10.30 pm. Those watching his special broadcast were told that Britain faced 'a harder Christmas than we have known since the war'.[1] The energy restrictions even extended to public Christmas trees, which were only allowed to be lit for four days, including Christmas Day itself.[2]

There were limits to what the government was willing to put people through and the television curfew was lifted for four days over Christmas. The prime minister, meanwhile, advised the Queen against her idea of adding a section to her already-written Christmas speech about the deteriorating economic situation to show she was aware and concerned about the problems people faced.[3] Yet the public were not always quite as put out as might be imagined. On Christmas Eve, the *Daily Mirror* concluded that while it had been a 'lousy year', Christmas would still be a good day and there would be power to cook dinner and petrol to visit family.[4] Power shortages meant that places of work went on extended shutdowns, giving some people almost two weeks off. Comedian Michael Palin noted in his diary how there was 'a melancholy atmosphere', but one he rather liked. He thought people were more aware of each other and willing to smile, rather than preoccupied with the normal Christmas tasks.[5]

Historian Neil Armstrong has argued that in the nineteenth century, Christmas was 'an important site of contest for the complexities of modern life to be played out'.[6] That remained true a century later, and this chapter shows that, just as in 1973, Christmas became entangled with a number of wider ideological debates that illustrate something of the state's nature in twentieth-century Britain. The state may not have taken any sort of lead in influencing how people celebrated, but Christmas raised questions about public safety, crime levels and workers' entitlements that encouraged state intervention. In fact, the state was often rather late in responding to some of these concerns and it repeatedly found itself following rather than leading popular opinion. Nor was government people's only relationship with authority; much of life was defined by encounters with those in charge. This might range from the boss at work to the official at the post office or someone anonymous writing a health and safety order. In many ways, it was these lesser forms of authority that formed people's closest relationships with government and all of them had some influence over how people could celebrate.

Safety and crime

Some of the state's earliest festive concerns relate to threats to public and individual safety. In 1912 the British Fire Prevention Committee ran its first Christmas campaign. This was in response, the committee claimed, to reports of 'numerous fires' which 'frequently' involved the loss of life. The campaign was based on London and the Home Counties and focused on the danger of tree candles to curtains and evergreen, celluloid, paper and cotton-wool decorations. It also advised that matches should be kept out of the reach of children and that the game snap-dragon needed to be played carefully. That year there was just an 'exceptionally small' number of fires and no Christmas festivity fatalities anywhere in England. This led the campaign to be extended throughout the country and 23,000 posters were distributed in 1913 for display in hospitals, asylums, orphanages, places of worship and shops, an indication of how common decorations were in public places. The committee again claimed a 'remarkable diminution' in the usual number of Christmas fires.[7] Interwar families did become more cautious about lighting tree candles; electric fairy lights served as a replacement, despite the trip hazards they presented. Yet paper decorations continued to be a considerable fire risk. In 1939, for example, a baby in Birmingham received fatal burns after a draught blew paper festoons onto a naked gas mantle. At the resulting inquest, the coroner lamented: 'It happens nearly every Christmas somewhere or other in the country.'[8]

Avoiding fire was never going to be controversial, but safety concerns diversified between the wars. In 1933, the National 'Safety First' Association, formed in 1923 amid concerns about safety on the roads and in the workplace, drew up guidelines for Christmas, which included warning people about small articles in the pudding and not giving children toys that were heavily painted or had sharp edges.[9] At one level, this marked how the embryonic health and safety movement was moving beyond road and workplace safety and into the domestic space, although these warnings were later regarded by some as trivial and overprotective. But there were good reasons to think Christmas presented more than just a fire hazard. People often drank and travelled more at Christmas and they took part in activities they were not used to. In 1933, a fifteen-year-old in Rochdale even died after swallowing a pin when putting up decorations. That same year, a 42-year-old man from near Yeovil died from poisoning after pricking his thumb when decorating his home. Falling off chairs when putting up decorations could also be fatal.[10] Some women had always had doubts about the safety and hygiene of putting money in their Christmas puddings, but improvements in silver-coin manufacturing in the 1920s, which meant they were less likely to turn green or yellow, reassured housewives. From 1937 nickel 3d. coins came into circulation and the Royal Mint made clear they were not suitable for puddings. The power of tradition was such, however, that when 6d. coins began containing a metal that might react with fruit acids, *The Times* doubted housewives would be put off.[11] There were other new concerns too. In 1946 warnings were issued about decorations made from glass wool that might contaminate food stuffs or be put in children's mouths.[12] In 1961, the British Standards Institute introduced the first toy safety regulations, which included bans on sharp edges or pieces that might break off and choke. New cheap electric toys were another hazard because their wiring might electrocute.[13] A 1971 Home Office circular reported that most electric Christmas light sets were not designed to extinguish if one light failed, with the result that failures built up the voltage in the remaining lights, overheating the plastic holdings. There were regulated safety standards to avoid this, but not all imported sets complied with them.[14]

Such warnings were rooted in realities. In 2002, around 1,000 people went to hospital after being injured by accidents involving Christmas trees, and another 350 after accidents involving Christmas lights. Furthermore, the chances of being killed in a house fire were 50 per cent higher than normal at Christmas. At some insurers, claims for fire damage were more than double the average day.[15] When the period 21 December–19 January was compared for 2010 and 2011 to those years' daily averages in December and January, the number of deaths by assault was 25 per cent higher, by accidents in the home 15 per cent higher, by transport accidents 7 per cent higher, by alcohol or drugs 13 per cent higher and by respiratory diseases 15 per cent higher. The peak in death rates was around New Year's Eve, but on Christmas Eve too the death rate was typically 10 per cent higher than in early December.[16]

Despite the real dangers and the deaths, Christmas also illustrated the scepticism that grew around health and safety in the late twentieth century.

A series of festive public safety warnings in 1970 led one reporter to conclude thus: 'It sounded as if the way to be sure of surviving the next week intact is to stay in bed with the curtains drawn and the mouth shut.' The fire warnings made sense, but the Health Education Council's condemnation of coins in Christmas puddings (a threat to teeth and a possible cause of choking) was at least untraditional, while its list of things that should not be given as presents – cigarettes, sweets, chocolate and cakes – was bordering on the 'Scroogian'.[17] By the twenty-first century, rumours and half-truths that decorations were banned were being lambasted as part of a general attack on political correctness, a nanny state and multiculturalism.[18] Attacks on what people ate did not help the reputation of health and safety. In 1998 there were claims that a typical Christmas dinner was 7,500 calories, four times the normal load of a meal. One 1990s nutritional study found what it called 'Significant increases in weight' and even some evidence of increased blood pressure over Christmas.[19] There was a degree of scaremongering here however. Longitudinal studies showed weight gains of just 0.5 kg at Christmas time, and that tended to be lost in the following months.[20] Other newly identified threats were so minuscule they furthered popular cynicism. In 2012 medical researchers in Australia found that excessive consumption of brussel sprouts could cause problems for heart patients on anticoagulation drugs. This resulted in some jovial headlines, but the problem was real – one Scottish man was hospitalized after eating the vegetable several times over the Christmas period.[21]

It was not just humans who were unsafe. In 1968 one writer claimed Christmas could bring a 'holocaust of domestic animal disaster', with goldfish dying of resin poisoning caused by people decorating their bowls with Christmas tree sprigs, cats getting shocks from crackers and budgies left gasping because of cigar smoke.[22] Giving pets as gifts was a new trend after the Second World War, but the pets were sometimes promptly abandoned, a fate suffered by 300 dogs in Christmas 1964 according to one news report. Campaigns against pets as presents began that decade and reached a climax with the 1978 slogan 'a dog is for life, not just for Christmas'. They were not entirely successful and in 1986 Battersea Dogs' Home alone took in around 150 dogs after Christmas.[23] Nonetheless, giving animals to those who might not want them declined enough that by the end of the century pets were more commonly being mentioned in Christmas campaigns in terms of how festive food was not good for their health.[24]

A more widespread concern was the impact of Christmas on road safety. In 1934, a motoring writer claimed that drivers were more courteous and less reckless on Christmas Day.[25] However, as the number of vehicles on the road mushroomed in the 1950s, that perspective disappeared completely. Early that decade it was reported that road accidents normally trebled at Christmas time. The average daily number of deaths on the road was typically thirteen but on Christmas Eve 1952 it was forty-one. Such statistics were partly attributed to the distractions of Christmas excitement, people who rarely drove travelling, and to pedestrians stepping off pavements without looking.[26] But it was also down to people driving after drinking at seasonal parties. Drink-driving was then illegal, but there was no clear definition of it, which meant many people did not regard getting behind the wheel 'after a few' as a problem. However, scientific evidence on the influence of even small amounts of alcohol on driving skills was growing and drink-driving became the focal point of rising concerns about road safety. A particularly bad year was 1959 when problems were exacerbated by poor weather and 137 people were killed in traffic accidents in England and Wales between 24 and 26 December. There was another spike in 1963 when 104 people were killed in the same three-day period, and this time research clearly put the blame on drink.[27] With a temporary Christmas 50mph night-time speed limit having failed to make much impact that year, more substantive change became inevitable and the 1966 Road Safety Act introduced breathalyser tests. Some saw this as an intrusion into private behaviours, but it was effective and by 1967 fatal road accidents at Christmas had been halved.[28] But gradually people began to realize that the chances of being caught were low and in the 1980s and 1990s the government had to resort to increasingly graphic Christmas advertising campaigns. The 'shock ads' contributed to drink-driving becoming widely considered as socially unacceptable, but they were also another example of how the state sometimes tried to dictate public values. Not everyone approved of that, but state intervention undoubtedly made the roads safer. In 1987 there were around 1,000 drink-driving deaths in the UK; by 2008 this had fallen to 400.[29]

Drink-driving was not the only crime linked to Christmas. The season also created numerous opportunities and motives for theft. In 1921, detectives were thought to be unable to prevent pickpockets, purse snatchers and bag thieves in the festive shopping crowds. The problem was said to be exacerbated by 'over-bold' women who took out too much money and did not pay enough attention to their belongings.[30] The 1920s also saw a growing risk of thefts from cars, where people left their parcels before heading back to shop some more. In 1955, the police in London even left Christmas cards on motorists' windscreens, warning them not to leave parcels on display.[31] That decade also saw reports that women in Luton were using the busy crowds as cover to shoplift items such as toys, ties and hosiery.[32] Poultry and trees were also targets for thieves, especially just after the Second World War when both were scarce, leading the police to employ special patrols to guard farms. Forestry Commission plantations were another obvious target for thieves. By the mid-1950s, trees were even being stolen by the lorry load and in 1959 the Forestry Commission began twenty-four hour patrols in the New Forest in the run-up to Christmas.[33] Empty houses also meant burglaries rose over the festive season, leading police in Leeds to send Christmas cards to suspected burglars in 1997 to warn them that they were being watched. However, some thieves also took a holiday and in 2013 insurance companies reported that 25 December had over 50 per cent fewer burglaries than the average day.[34] Some festive thefts seemed to embody the greed that critics read into Christmas. In 1966, a Christmas charity party at a Doncaster bingo club was wrecked when mothers tried to grab as many gifts as possible. The organizer said they behaved liked animals and their action denied some thousand children presents. In Bridgend in 1987, a schoolboy sang carols on a 95-year-old's doorstep and then stole money from her handbag while she went to get him a lemonade. Her comment that she did not know how people could do such a thing 'especially at this time of year' illustrated the belief that somehow Christmas crime was worse. Yet, some of the crimes were rather tragic (assuming the stories told in court were true). In 1963, a fourteen-year-old from Lancashire was sentenced to three months after breaking into a toy warehouse to steal presents for his eleven brothers and sisters. He had overheard a conversation between his mother and unemployed father about whether they could afford to buy presents for their children.[35]

Far more common than theft was petty crime, much of which was very trivial and linked to drink. In 1953, for example, a Royal Navy officer was charged with being drunk and disorderly after climbing the thirty-foot tree in the centre of Bristol to take the star from its top.[36] Such incidents meant that festival was caught up with wider concerns about public drunkenness. The 1921 Licensing Act limited Christmas Day opening to five hours, but it was the days around the festival when there were greater problems. In 1949, for example, a magistrate told the people and publicans of Birmingham that they were all on trial after a 'wave of drunkenness and assaults' the previous Christmas. Pubs in the city were still, however, granted an hour extension for the 24th, 26th, 27th and 31st. Attitudes to opening-hour extensions and, indeed, to the festive opening of all venues, varied from town to town and often depended on the religiosity of magistrates. In Burnley in 1934, the authorities allowed the cinemas and theatres to open on Christmas Day, but a dance was refused a licence and the pubs were denied an extra hour on Boxing Day.[37] The 1961 Licensing Act retained the special status of Christmas Day and, as on Sundays and Good Friday, allowed pubs to open from 12.00 pm to 2.00 pm and then from 7.00 pm to 10.30 pm. Permitted opening times were extended in 1995, but the decline in religious ideals in government was evident in the fact that Christmas was now the only day of the year when pubs had to have a break, although this was reduced to four hours beginning at 3.00 pm. That arrangement remained until 2003 when a new system, under which opening hours were agreed between the licensee and local authority, was introduced. Neither these restricted hours, extensions before or after Christmas nor the eventual liberalization of licensing laws caused significant problems, whatever the odd magistrate might have said. Prosecution statistics across the century do not show that December was worse for drunken disorder than other months. It was thus perhaps no surprise that official concerns around drinking at Christmas began to focus more on the health implications than on public drunkenness. This was another sign of how the state's concern with what people did in private was shifting from being based on moral or religious values to being based on the impact that private behaviours have on public resources.[38]

The relative triviality of much festive crime perhaps contributed to the humanity that judges could show during the season. In 1933, it was reported that a Bow Street magistrate had arranged for several habitual offenders to be released from prison on Christmas Eve and that others got lighter than normal sentences. One was said to have pleaded: 'Don't send me away for Christmas, it is the only time when I am really happy.' Similarly, in 1927, London county courts were said to be being more lenient on debtors.[39] As late as 1959, Huddersfield magistrates decided to pay the electricity bill of a woman who had been cut off and resorted to altering the fuses to reconnect her supply. This was, they said, to help get her on an even keel in the season of goodwill and have a 'little Christmas enjoyment'. In 1961, a man awaiting a prison sentence for stealing a van got bail because his wife asked the judge if he could be at home with his children over Christmas. Criminals too could have their consciences stirred by the festival. On 21 December 1960, a gang of three gunmen barged into a London house, tied up a thirteen-year-old girl and then ransacked the bedrooms. A few days later, one of them sent the girl a Christmas card, saying how brave she was and that they had not meant to upset her.[40]

In 1955, a 73-year-old labourer asked to be sent to prison for Christmas after being found guilty of being drunk. He said he had nowhere to go, but knew he would be able to see a doctor and be looked after in prison. The chairman of the magistrates said she was reluctant to send anyone to prison at Christmas, but the man declined the alternative of a 10s. fine and was thus sentenced to seven days.[41] While this story says much about the lives of elderly habitual offenders, it also perhaps indicates the depth of people's desire not to be alone at Christmas. The state was not indifferent to people in its care either. Even in prison, Christmas could be a festive moment, a break from routines and monotony. Films were shown, although it was not until the late 1930s that they were not educational or cultural. From 1948, some prisoners in Northern Ireland were allowed parole over Christmas. A decade later, this policy had caused no problems.[42] Elsewhere in the UK, some prisoners also began to be given early or temporary releases to allow them to be with their families over Christmas, although the statistics do not exist to know how widespread this was. Moreover, it was not always strictly down to Christmas goodwill, and in 2009 one Scottish prison closed for the festival to save money, with 110 of its 175 inmates being allowed to spend it at home.[43] In 2001 Jeffrey Archer recorded in his diary: 'Christmas Day for those who are incarcerated can be summed up in one word: dreadful.' He noted inmates staring at photographs of their children or 'just lying on their beds willing the day to pass'. He did, however, watch television, telephone his family and eat an 'excellent' Christmas lunch.[44]

The workplace

In a romantic story in a 1977 women's magazine, a nurse decides to work Christmas Day because it would be preferable to the bedlam of the extended family at her parent's home.[45] It was in public utilities such as health that the highest numbers of people at work on Christmas Day could always be found. But into the 1960s public transport and postal services were also operating on the 25th, while many cinemas, theatres, pubs, restaurants and the like were always open or required staff to work in preparation for a busy day on the 26th. Even parts of industry opened in order to meet demand or because shutting production lines down cost money, although that became less common as the century progressed and holidays grew longer. How much choice people had about working varied. In large organizations there might be unspoken pressure on those without children to accept the Christmas shift, but in smaller outfits people might have little option not to work. Farmers, for example, had to milk the cows, while vicars had no choice but to take midnight Mass and then get up early for the morning service. There was never any legal protection against such requirements and few professions had the contractual clause that footballers enjoyed (although rarely exercised) that they could refuse to play on Christmas Day or Good Friday.[46] The nurse in the 1977 short story ends up kissing a handsome registrar and others too found that working did not have to be an unpleasant or unwelcome experience. In 1962, a milkman delivering on Christmas morning was invited into eight houses for a drink. Although the result was that he crashed his van and ended up in court for drink-driving, it is evidence of the public's goodwill towards those serving them on Christmas Day.[47] Even at sea there were attempts to minimize work, decorate ships, enjoy a traditional dinner and partake in some singing.[48] In a Lancashire mill that opened on Christmas Day 1967 in order to fulfil an order, some employees declined to work, but those who did got double pay and bonuses and saw it as a chance to secure their jobs. When such rewards were not forthcoming, some workers struck in protest, while others used the seasonal demand for their labour to press home wider demands. In 1948 the *Spectator* remarked: 'A strike, preferably in one of the transport services, threatens to become a permanent feature of the English Christmas.'[49]

In 1931, there were more than 1.4 million domestic servants in Britain. This made them the largest occupational group in the country, but they increasingly resented the drudgery, long hours and low pay and status of their profession.[50] Added to this, at Christmas they had to cope with missing their own family and with the strenuous work involved in serving someone else's gathering. Indeed, some servants felt more overworked and resentful at this time of the year than any other. In 1936, one wrote to a Hull newspaper to complain: 'During this holiday time, when everyone has been enjoying the spirit of Christmas time I have been hard at it as usual. I wonder if some mistresses ever realise the meaning of the word "humanity".[51] Most employers did, however, use Christmas to mark their gratitude, something which was becoming more and more important with women's reluctance to enter the profession or stay with an employer who was too demanding. Most servants could thus expect presents and a good dinner on the 25th.[52] The society hostess Lady Cunard even remarked in 1934 that Christmas was 'only for servants'. In 1919 *The Times* noted with satisfaction that shops had stopped displaying 'uninviting bales of goods marked "suitable presents for servants".' It claimed that 'Now only the best is good enough for them', although it noted that some people simply took their maids to the theatre.[53] There was sometimes a genuine concern for employees. A middle-class Keswick woman recorded that she thought her two maids had enjoyed Christmas 1937, and done splendidly in the catering. She thought they liked having guests and had entered into the zest of the day.[54] But others were more parsimonious in the treats or praise they offered. In 1927 Lady Astor asked her twenty-plus guests at Christmas lunch to use the same plate for all courses to reduce work in the kitchen. In the evening her servants were allowed to listen to the recitals.[55] Another woman described the tour of the Christmas quarters as a 'yearly nightmare'. One London lady even decided in 1937 to gift her parlour maid and cook tablecloths rather than the gloves they had asked for because she disliked these two employees.[56] Festive obligations could also leave a middle class, that was desperate to keep up appearances, rather badly off. On Christmas Eve 1947, writer James Lees-Milne recorded in his dairy that he had given thirty-seven presents, most of which had gone to servants, but received only one in return (a wireless from his parents). 'Financially, I am utterly broke,' he concluded.[57] Not every household actually retained servants for the entirety of or even part of Christmas Day. This could be a source of relief to both the servants, who got the day off, and the family who might then be able to relax and not worry about having others around. Some families even ate lunch earlier than normal in order to allow their maids to get back to their own families. Such arrangements do show that domestic servants were not simply victims of an oppressive class system. Indeed, some servants enjoyed the festive atmosphere and the excitement of children. They might give the family presents too, while their witnessing of middle-class Victorian celebrations was probably one of the ways the traditional family Christmas had spread down the social ladder in the first place.[58]

If there was one category of worker who was most associated with Christmas it was the postman. Before the Second World War, Post Office staff typically tripled in the weeks leading up to Christmas. By 1965 it was employing 150,000 temporary seasonal postal workers.[59] To cope with the volume of mail, people were asked to 'post early' and because the post was regarded as a public service some were willing to comply despite the preference for cards to arrive as close to Christmas as possible. More efficient delivery and sorting methods eased Post Office needs, but in 1991 it was still employing 25,000 additional Christmas staff.[60] The work tended to attract those without steady incomes, such as housewives, the retired, students and artists. Indeed, so common was the experience that the official history of the Royal Mail called a Christmas job there 'almost a rite of passage for two generations of young people'.[61] But it was also tiring and sometimes difficult work. In 1937, a Cheam woman noted that her postman on Christmas Day 'seemed thoroughly dazed and exhausted with overwork and anxiety as to whether he was delivering the right number of parcels for us'.[62] One postal worker recorded in his diary on 23 December 1960: 'I am living in a dream-like world with one's whole existence tied up with Christmas cards to be sorted, primarily and secondarily. Three of us have personally sorted 150,000.'[63] Twelve-hour shifts were not uncommon mid-century, sometimes starting in the middle of night and even involving delivering heavy turkeys along with the presents and cards.[64] Mistakes thus naturally happened and the unreliability of Christmas post was a reoccurring concern that was entangled with other prejudices. One rich woman remarks in a 1936 novel: 'These temporary postmen are often most dishonest; they'll steal whole bags of stuff to avoid the trouble of delivering it! The working class has no sense of responsibility nowadays.'[65] Yet permanent postmen also often felt appreciated at Christmas time because they were delivering presents and glad tidings rather than bills or bad news.[66] In 1919

PLATE 26 *Postman delivering Christmas parcels and bird, Chelsea, 1925. Topical Press Agency/Getty..*

the *Dundee Courier* declared: 'No caller is more welcome on Christmas morning than "postie". He is the living link which humanizes the senti-ment of goodwill which we seek to express in tangible form towards one another at Christmastide.'[67] Historian Neil Armstrong has also argued that the public saw postmen as essential intermediaries 'in the process of creat-ing and maintaining a merry Christmas'.[68] Nonetheless, although there was additional pay for those who made the Christmas morning deliveries, they were not popular with postmen and in 1960 workers demanded they cease. A spokesman said that the post early campaigns were so successful that 'The Christmas Day work is now nothing more than the delivery of belated replies to Christmas cards, and if people cannot be bothered to send out greetings until Christmas Eve they do not deserve to have them delivered'. Their campaign was successful and 1960 was the last year with a Christmas morning delivery.[69] On Sunday 27 December 1964, a Sheffield accountant complained in his diary: 'The third day without post. What a disgrace for a civilised country.'[70]

In other industries, the run-up to Christmas could see a slacking off. Christmas Eve in interwar offices might see little work done after some drinking at lunchtime, no smoking rules cast aside and generous whip rounds for the errand boys. Some industrial works in this period closed down altogether at midday on Christmas Eve.[71] By the late 1950s, even partners in firms could feel helpless to stop staff bringing food and alcohol on the last day before the holidays and having an unofficial party. One moaned in 1960: 'It is a good job that Christmas comes only once year, for an office is a wrong place for a party.'[72] The easing of the work rate could stretch back further into December. A hat factory assistant manager recorded on 1 December 1938 that an office girl had told him that people there were thinking more about Christmas than work.[73] Decorations in workplaces became fairly ubiquitous in the second half of the century, as employees looked for ways to celebrate with their colleagues rather than just family. Some supermarkets even encouraged their staff to dress up for Christmas.[74] New rituals such as 'secret Santa' emerged, where everyone bought one present which was then allocated anonymously. There could be a degree of coercion to join in such rituals. On Friday 23 December 1949, one young woman recorded in her diary: 'Work. Was kissed under the mistletoe every few minutes. Heaven, sometimes Hell.' Her office officially finished work at 3.15 pm, but staff stayed behind for drinks.[75] Other workers faced similar situations and in 1957 a barmaid wrote to the *Daily Mirror* to say how she dreaded the beery customers who expected a kiss under the mistletoe. She did not feel she could refuse because it would be bad for business.[76] Although such incidents were unwelcome, far more people seemed to enjoy some festivity at work. Indeed, Christmas antics in the workplace are evidence that the division between work and leisure is often rather overplayed. Leisure was not something that simply happened outside working hours. There was always leisure time to be had at work, something evident in the gossiping and fag breaks, but the run-up to Christmas undoubtedly saw people extend those moments of pleasure that normally punctuated the working day.

One reason for the ebbing of work was excitement over Christmas parties. These were not new phenomenon – some late nineteenth-century factories had held them for example – but they undoubtedly increased in number in the middle of the twentieth century and by 1978 one historian suggested that the office or works party was 'almost universal'.[77] Some were put on by the workers themselves without the support or sometimes blessing of the employers. For example, some post-war miners held their own underground parties when they were supposed to be working.[78] That would probably have been unthinkable before nationalization, when workers were more controlled through the enforcement of regulations and payment by performance. But, after 1918, there was gradually more emphasis on both workers' rights and rewarding their hard work and loyalty. This might be through a festive party or outing for employees or even their children. One of the members of the family of Farmiloes, a prosperous lead and glass merchant, remembered that the firm's interwar Christmas dinners in a hotel was 'something that was looked forward to very much … [because] for many people it was a fairly drab sort of life'.[79] Indeed, for shy people who did not socialize, such occasions could be rare opportunities to talk to people.[80] There was always, however, a danger that staff might not respond in the way intended. Attempts to get different grades and sections to mingle could lead to some awkward social situations.[81] In 1938 one young Yorkshire man told Mass Observation he was not attending his works' pantomime party because as a socialist he did not like his employer organizing his private life but more than that he objected to having pay for it, did not like panto, and did not want to use his own time up seeing people he could see any day, especially when he loathed some of his fellow workers.[82]

After the war, company celebrations grew more elaborate. The 1952 Christmas party of the Welsh Directorate of the Forestry Commission, for example, took place at an Aberystwyth hotel and featured a concert given by staff, dancing and games. There were prizes too, including a bottle of sherry, a duck and a pair of nylons.[83] By the late twentieth century, people were even wearing festive headgear, such as Santa hats, reindeer antlers and tinsel halos, for their Christmas dos.[84] But the more elaborate works and office parties became, the more they developed a reputation for excessive drinking. In 1970 the Health Education Council warned of the hazard of office parties for young females who might not be used to several quick rounds of free drinks and claimed it was the duty of senior staff to make sure they did not become hospital or police statistics. The reputation of office parties was not helped by the fact that some happened early in December, partly because venues could actually be difficult to book close to Christmas. In 1984 one writer claimed he had seen his first drunk secretary with tinsel in her hair on 12 November.[85] That was untypical but it did not help the office party's cause. Nor did what the drinking could lead to. In 1970 one magazine joked that office parties could be an 'unbridled riot'.[86] An anthropologist claimed 'misbehaviour is what office Christmas parties are all about' – it was expected and customary. In a survey for her research, 90 per cent of respondents confessed to some form of office-party misbehaviour. Eating and drinking too much was the most common misdemeanour, although kissing and flirtation (especially among those under forty), as well as telling rude jokes, saying things that would not normally be said and acting a little silly were common behaviours too. None of this was the debauchery that was often imagined. Indeed, there could be positive outcomes; feuds were made up and long-held attractions brought out into the open.[87] But those attractions were sometimes between people married to someone else and by the twenty-first century many companies had moved away from having an organized party because of concerns about excessive drinking, bad behaviour and sexual harassment. In 2004 a joint report by the Royal Society for the Prevention of Accidents and the Trades Union Congress (TUC) advised that mistletoe should not be provided at such parties. Some estimates put the number of firms not willing to have office parties as high as 80 per cent, but a 2005 survey in London found that 65 per cent of companies were having one.[88] Some of those were probably meals or receptions rather than parties and a 2004 survey suggested that over 80 per cent of businesses were doing something for their employees.[89] Indeed, the state sanctioned this and by 2013 companies were allowed to spend up to £150 a year on Christmas (or other) entertainment or presents for staff without it being regarded as a taxable benefit.

Business researchers have argued that Christmas parties helped create a sense that organizations were fun and caring places to work and that a temporary relaxation of rules and powers structures meant those same hierarchies could be maintained in the rest of the year without challenge.[90] In some organizations, the coming together of different grades was formalized through festive role reversals such as the officers serving the men in the armed forces or surgeons carving the turkey in hospital. Christmas thus perhaps played its part in maintaining workplace discipline and upholding the morale of staff often caught up in dull and repetitive jobs. Indeed, those firms that did nothing for their staff at Christmas risked demoralizing staff and encouraging a sense that they were not valued. So, too, could those who gave derisory festive benefits. A woman who worked for a chocolate manufacturer complained to the *Daily Worker* in 1938 that while she got an additional day off she received no overtime or bonus for all her hard work in the busy run-up. There were accusations in 2004 that one cleaning company had given its workers a £3 voucher for a local cafe as a Christmas bonus.[91]

A seasonal bonus was an alternative, and sometimes an addition, to Christmas parties. It is impossible to know how widespread this was and they were certainly not universally expected.[92] Where they were paid, their value varied between the wars from small gifts to sums that were quite

PLATE 27 *Packing Christmas chocolates at a confectionary factory, 1922. Hulton Collection/Getty.*

substantial for working-class artisans. In a Derby engineering firm, for example, the 1936 bonus was two weeks wages and there was also a party for employees' children and gifts of meat. In a Tiverton factory the bonus reached as much as 15 per cent of workers' annual wage in 1949. The use of bonuses to retain staff was also clear at that firm by its requirement that people had to have worked there for three years to qualify for the full payment.[93] Many workers relied on these bonuses to see them through the holidays, especially if they were losing pay for not working over Christmas. The timing of bonuses was crucial too if they were going to be used for Christmas shopping and preparations. In 1953, 600 female Lanarkshire millworkers went on strike when their employer decided to pay their bonus one week rather than the normal two weeks before Christmas.[94]

In the middle of the century, tradesmen could also expect a Christmas tip from their customers and might become friendlier in order to ensure they got their 'box' as they were known.[95] The sums involved could quickly add up both for those giving and receiving. In 1937, the wife of a London journalist gave a shilling each to the milkman, butcher boy, laundry boy, dustman and postman, 9d. to the window cleaner and 2s. 6d. to her charwoman.[96] The middle classes did not always feel they had much choice about the practice.[97] This was because there was the danger of offending or even retaliation if a box was not given. Newspapers published jokes about dustmen that spilled rubbish because they had not been given a Christmas tip and, despite the practice having given its name to 26 December, it was generally deemed not a good idea to wait until then to give a box.[98]

Both Christmas bonuses and boxes were practices that gradually fell away in the 1950s and 1960s. As early as 1946, one middle-class woman recorded being told by an aunt not to bother with boxes because most tradesmen were better off than 'we are now'.[99] The decline of boxes owed much to the depersonalization of the service sector, as people increasingly bought from companies rather than individuals, but it was also rooted in the middle classes' growing annoyance with what they saw as a culture of fiddles and scams and in workers themselves expecting more formalized better conditions rather than relying on the goodwill of customers or employers. As early as 1919, there were reports that postmen were not asking for Christmas boxes because it was degrading and that instead they wanted better wages. Yet, in 1924, there was uproar at a conference of the National Union of Post Office Workers when a motion was put forward outlawing the solicitation of Christmas boxes.[100] Although it took some of the responsibility of offering better pay away from them, some employers were not keen on boxes either because they could annoy customers. Some post-war delivery boys were thus explicitly told not to ask for a Christmas tip, although that did not always stop them.[101] Local authorities also frowned upon their employees getting them, which led the TV Times to remark in 1969 that it was difficult to know how widespread they were. A Yorkshire binman told the magazine that he had too much pride in his job to beg for tips but accepted drinks and whatever was offered.[102] There were still books in the 1980s that told people to tip the dustmen, paperboys and milkmen and which contained reports of bad service when tips were not forthcoming.[103] Boxes also probably fell away because seasonal bonuses became less common. In 1962, for example, falling revenue led Rolls Royce to announce that it was not paying its workers a Christmas bonus for the first time in forty years. Such examples did not lead to significant revolts because they took place in the context of falling working hours and rising living standards. In an affluent society, where basic and desired needs were increasingly met, time was becoming the most sought after commodity and many employees were more concerned with their festive holidays than bonuses.

Holidays

In 1919, with Christmas being on a Thursday and the support of manufacturers, the government approved making Saturday 27 December a holiday. This gave many people four days off work and caused debate about whether such a long holiday was good or bad for workers.[104] Such incidents are reminders both that long holidays were a rarity for most people and that there was still a puritan ethic that thought this a good thing. The

Christmas break was normally just two days. This was rooted in the 1871 Bank Holidays Acts which gave Boxing Day this designation in England and Wales. It had not done the same for Christmas Day or Good Friday because they were established days of rest and worship. The act did not give anyone the right to not work on 25 and 26 December, but it did introduce a period in England and Wales when those who were required to work either day could usually expect other days off in lieu. The designation of Boxing Day as a holiday owed something to the campaigns of the Early Closing Association, which since its establishment in 1842, had been fighting to limit opening hours to protect shopworkers. A Boxing Day at home was supposed to compensate shopworkers for longer opening hours and the fact that half-day closing was generally suspended in the week before Christmas, something formalized in the 1911 Shops Act. Problems, however, continued to arise when Christmas fell on a Saturday and thus workers were in effect losing a day of holiday because they would have had Sunday the 26th off anyway.[105] Moreover, as Boxing Day became a general holiday for everyone, the sense that shopworkers were not being compensated for their extra hours in the run-up to Christmas returned. In 1935 one union estimated that the average shopworker was doing twenty hours of enforced unpaid overtime at Christmas.[106] Moreover, some small shops actually opened on the morning of the 25th for people to collect Christmas orders and perhaps share a glass of wine.[107]

When Christmas fell on a Sunday in 1921, the Early Closing Association lobbied successfully for Tuesday 27 December to be made an additional bank holiday. Such an arrangement had begun in 1910 and continued with every interwar Sunday Christmas, although it was not guaranteed by legislation and did not happen during wartime. In 1921, however, some towns also kept their shops closed on Wednesday the 28th. That reflected a growing 1920s practice of local agreements between shops to stay shut beyond Boxing Day. In 1923, for example, it was reported that more than 180 towns were closing down from 25 to 27 December. Yet arriving at such arrangements was not always straightforward. Stores selling food were particularly reluctant to close for three days.[108] Commercial rivalries and patterns of ownership did not help either. For example, in Plymouth in 1930, local trade associations decided shops should shut on Saturday 27 December but multiples in the town were ordered to open by their head offices, which in turn forced some local shops to feel they had to follow suit.[109] Some more progressive retailers, however, compensated for lost holidays and long hours at Christmas through days off later in the year. In 1936, John Lewis, for example, gave their 10,000 workers three paid holidays in February and March to compensate for their hard work over Christmas and the January sales.[110]

In most interwar industries employees were not paid for the Christmas holiday. This meant that although Christmas was a rare break from work, millions of workers had to save not just to cover the cost of any celebrations but lost wages too and the result was that some dreaded the festival.[111] Paid holidays were thus a major campaigning issue for trade unions, not least because it seemed grossly unfair that they were very common among white-collar workers. In the wake of the Great War, a greater emphasis on negotiating with workforces did bring paid holidays to some industries and by 1920 they had been granted to around 1m manual workers.[112] The main focus was on the summer but these concessions could include a paid festive break too. In 1918, for example, it was announced that dock and naval workers employed by the state would get three paid holidays at Christmas. But this was not typical and the interwar downturn in trade actually saw the problem deepen in some areas because manufacturers gave workers an enforced extended break to save money. In 1937, for example, many mills in Lancashire decided to close for six rather than three days at Christmas because of the poor state of trade. Workers were able to claim unemployment benefit for the three additional days but this hardly made up for the loss of six days' wages.[113]

A paid summer break remained a prime concern for unions between the wars and their pressure allied with an improving economy led the government to establish of a committee of inquiry in 1937. It concluded that 'an annual holiday contributes in a considerable measure to workpeople's happiness, health and efficiency' and recommended that paid holidays be established as part of people's contract of employment.[114] This resulted in the 1938 Holidays with Pay Act which allowed the regulatory wage boards that oversaw some industries to include paid holidays in their decisions. The threat of legislation, union agitation and employers' eventual willingness to go further than required had actually led to rapid advances before the inquiry had even reported. By June 1939, the number of employees receiving paid holidays had risen to around 11 million (out of a workforce of 18.5 million).[115] Most of these agreements included paid breaks in the summer and at public holidays. For example, in 1938 Chichester Rural District Council gave Christmas Day, Good Friday and bank holidays as paid holidays to all its temporary employees in service for more than three months and to all its permanent workers. Bradford Corporation brought in a similar scheme but with double pay for those who worked Christmas Day. Such gains were not just limited to the public sector and could also be found in areas where there was collective bargaining and wage boards. Agricultural workers in Derbyshire, for example, got holidays with pay at Christmas and other bank holidays in 1939.[116]

Employers were actually finding that paid holidays could be used to instil discipline and loyalty among their workforce and were not as costly as feared.[117] Yet there remained workers who had gained a paid summer holiday but not a paid Christmas break and millions remained without any paid break. The war interrupted plans to make paid holidays compulsory but afterwards there was a new period of increased attention to workers' rights. In this climate many of the cases of unpaid Christmas holidays breaks came to an end. In 1947, for example, unions and employers in the building and civil engineering industries came to an arrangement for Christmas pay to be given. In 1948, 30,000 hosiery workers, already with paid summer holidays, won Christmas, Easter and Whitsun pay after a ruling by the National Arbitration Tribunal.[118]

As such battles were won and wages rose in general, attention turned to the length of the Christmas break. As the masses grew more affluent, holiday rights became as important as good pay. In 1950 there were even calls to ensure Christmas Day was always on a Monday to maximize the time off it gave people.[119] Some workers simply took matters into their hands and stayed away. Thus, in 1946 there were reports of mass absenteeism among miners after the two-day Christmas break. At some Derbyshire collieries, the absentee rate exceeded 50 per cent.[120] Such issues continued into the 1950s and forced many employers to concede a three-day break, even if the third day was not always paid. In 1957, for example, Wednesday the 25th and Thursday the 26th were holidays but many workers also took Friday the 27th off, some with and some without their employers' permission. A year later, a similar situation arose on Saturday the 27th. Many industrial works and offices saw no point opening for a morning and so the Central Council of Bank Staff Associations campaigned for the day to be made an official holiday, although the government refused on the grounds that it would mean shops would probably close inconveniencing the public. Some food shops were open, as were large department stores who started their January sales early, but the day marked how the Christmas break was extending because of popular demand rather than government intervention.[121] The process gathered momentum because the more firms who extended their festive break the less work there was for others to do, encouraging them to shut too. The fact that workers might simply absent themselves from any day that interceded between their weekend and Christmas holiday also marked the new confidence and power of the working class. Moreover, it was not just a process that helped the working class and thus managers and employers put up little resistance to extending a holiday that benefited them too. In 1968, Christmas again fell on a Wednesday and this time most industries saw little sense in opening for Friday the 27th and Saturday the 28th, thus giving millions of industrial workers five consecutive days off if the Sunday is included. In the coal industry many miners took their annual rest days in Christmas week too, giving them a total of nine days off.[122]

The rise of the five-day week, something enjoyed by around half the workforce in the early 1960s, did lead the government to consider in 1968 making the 27th or 28th an official holiday when Christmas fell on a Friday or Saturday thus ensuring people had at least two normal working days off.[123] Since the five-day week was not universal, it decided not to intervene, preferring to leave the issue to collective bargaining but the reality was it was already behind popular practice that was by then more commonly following a three-day official Christmas break. Nor did advances stop at three paid days off and unofficial absenteeism and official holidays both began to extend towards the New Year. In 1970, the government was criticized because many of its offices were shut on Monday 28 December, despite it not being an official holiday. The prime minister, who had inherited the situation, was angry that the government was not practising what it preached by giving civil servants an extra day off because Boxing Day was a Saturday.[124] But, again, the reality was that many employers were ahead of government and had also shut despite it not being a bank holiday. By 1972, a *Times* editorial noted how the period between Christmas and New Year was increasingly becoming as a 'fallow period for industry and commerce'. Skeleton staffs were used in many workplaces and among those who were working there was a trend to start later and finish earlier in the day. In a context of fear about British industrial decline, the editorial pointed out that this was not a 'British disease' but something happening across the Western world and which had social and psychological benefits.[125] Following pressure from the TUC, entry to the European Economic Community (which drew attention to the relatively few number of public holidays in the UK), and the fact that many simply took the day off anyway, the government then further encouraged longer holidays by making New Year's Day a bank holiday from 1974 onwards.[126] This, along with the uncertain economic climate that made companies sensitive to operating costs and anything that might endanger industrial relations, cemented the growing trend for the period between Christmas and New Year to become a holiday. In 1975 *The Times* estimated that half of Britain's workforce was having eight days off over Christmas. A year later, the press estimated that two-thirds of workers in the north

PLATE 28 *Paddington station, London, 20 December 1935. London Express/Getty.*

and Midlands were still on holiday on 30 December. Although there were complaints about the effect on output and some criticism from abroad, the trend was unstoppable and there was little point resisting if competitors and customers were also shutting down and workers might not turn up anyway.[127]

Longer holidays meant there was less demand for services on Christmas itself, a trend exacerbated by the fact that many workers did not want to work that day. In the 1950s the Post Office suspended cheap evening telephone calls over Christmas in order to reduce demand and thus the number of staff required to work.[128] The use of public transport on the 25th fell as, encouraged by rail companies, people travelled to their family ahead of the day and returned later. In 1961 British Railways began significant cuts to already curtailed Christmas Day services and by 1965 most of Britain was without trains on the 25th.[129] Such cuts had unintended impacts. In 1952 there were complaints in Leeds that the council was only running buses between 11.30 am and 6.00 pm on Christmas Day which would prevent many from attending church.[130] Transport problems for fans and players meant a full Football League Christmas Day fixture list was scheduled for the last time in 1957 and by 1960 there were no league games at all that day in England and Wales.

Retail again was a crucial sector in the changing pattern of service provision. In 1975 trade union pressure led many major chain stores and supermarkets to close from the 25th to the 28th, a four-day break that gave shopworkers a genuine holiday.[131] But this concession did not last. As more and more workers had the post-Christmas period off, shops began to bring forward their January sales to take advantage of the fact that people were now free to shop at the end of December. In the 1980s Boxing Day itself became an important shopping day. This did not seem to be the result of any overt consumer pressure but rather retailers sensing a commercial opportunity and prioritizing that over the holidays of their own staff. Yet it was a success and it normalized the idea that other services should be available over the Christmas holiday. Indeed, as the service sector both grew and placed more emphasis on meeting consumer demand, the longer holidays of the 1970s reached fewer people. By the end of the 1990s, even some banking telephone lines were open on Christmas Day.[132] In 2003, the number of people working on Christmas Day in the UK was calculated at 771,000.[133]

Another sign of placing consumers before employees was the growth of Sunday trading in the 1980s and 1990s, something which generated fears that it would spread to Christmas Day itself. In 1999 a few chain stores did begin opening on the 25th but the scale was small. In 2000, Woolworth's, for example, opened just three stores and only in areas of what it called 'high ethnicity'. The government estimated that 13,000 shop employees, 0.8 per cent of the total number in England and Wales, had worked on Christmas Day that year.[134] Nonetheless, to prevent any escalation or domino effect, the 2004 Christmas Day (Trading) Act prohibited large shops from opening.

There were MPs who opposed this measure on the grounds of cost, the possibility other religions might demand similar measures and the very principle of the state regulating when people worked.[135] Nonetheless, it was a parliamentary intervention to protect the uniqueness of Christmas and a recognition that in a secular society the festival still mattered as a family and public holiday in a way that Sundays no longer did. Yet there remained no statutory right not to work at Christmas and in 2003 the TUC calculated that 3.3 million workers did not get a specific paid Christmas holiday but instead had to take the day from their annual leave entitlement.[136]

State intervention

Regulating shopping hours was not the only state recognition or utilization of the importance of Christmas. In the wake of the ruptures of war, economic uncertainties and fears about food supplies, the interwar British state was keen to promote the Empire and imperial togetherness. This was explicit in both the motives for and the wordings of the royal broadcasts but the festival's commercial and family foundations also enabled the state to utilize Christmas for imperial means. In 1931, for example, a new Christmas air mail service was introduced and it came to be seen as having an important practical and symbolic role in bridging the nations of the Empire.[137] In 1927, a campaign began that called upon people across the Empire to follow the King's example and order a pudding made only from imperial ingredients. The pudding was part of the canon of traditions that led Christmas to be seen as an expression of Englishness and colonials often ate it in a conscious attempt to uphold and demonstrate their national identity, despite its heavy character being not particularly appetizing in hot climates. The campaign had been begun by the British Women's Patriotic League and was taken on by the Empire Marketing Board, a body set up by government as an alternative to the use of protectionist tariffs. It progressed to include the King stirring the pudding mix in front of newsreel cameras, although behind the scenes there were tensions over where the ingredients should come from.[138] The Empire pudding was just one of a number of official and unofficial campaigns to encourage the buying of imperial goods. With the bulk of cheaper Christmas presents being made outside the Empire, government ministers were calling in 1925 for a British Shopping Week in December when imperial goods could be promoted. It was taken up by different towns across Britain and by 1930 the press was remarking how common imperial shop displays at Christmas were and that shoppers responded to notices such as 'No foreign birds sold here'.[139] The level of propaganda aimed at women was rather emotional, telling them that the prosperity of their country and children depended on their shopping habits. In 1934 the *Saturday Review* summed up: 'With everyone "home for Christmas" it is essentially the housewife's hour ... It is up to her to see she has done her important part by "Shopping

Imperially"'.[140] Even the Christmas cracker became caught up in the issue. In 1933, the Board of Trade reported that it received annual complaints that boxes labelled as British made actually contained toys manufactured overseas. Although the board acknowledged it was a trivial issue, they still put pressure on manufacturers, most of who agreed to change their labelling.[141]

While some in interwar Britain were being hectored to Christmas shop in certain ways, others were pushing the authorities to show them some festive generosity. Through the 1920s the unemployed agitated for relief bonuses at Christmas and it was common for local public assistance committees to award an extra shilling or two and some coal.[142] However, tightening central regulations and growing financial pressures complicated what was allowed and possible. Indeed, in 1926 it was reported that boards of guardians in the north-east of England were paying higher than normal Christmas allowances as a mark of defiance.[143] In Glasgow tensions over the issue led to a serious riot in which fourteen policemen were injured after the council refused to hear a delegation of unemployed men. The following day the local authority did vote to raise the allowance for children by 2s. for two weeks but then recanted after the government advised this would be illegal.[144] In 1935 the government standardized unemployed benefits and refused to allow a general festive payment of extra relief. Local campaigning did win concessions in some areas thus continuing the uneven geographic pattern of giving the unemployed a little Christmas cheer.[145] When lobbying continued, Baron Rushcliffe, chairman of the Unemployment Assistance Board, told a deputation of Welsh MPs in 1937 that Christmas allowances had 'something of patronage and the Lady Bountiful' about them and he again refused a general payment.[146] Instead, the board decided to allow the unemployed to earn up to 10s. over Christmas without it affecting their relief.[147] That helped some but it is difficult not to think that those unemployed families who continued to get bonuses thanks to local officials sidestepping regulations appreciated such old-fashioned patronage.

The local state was more susceptible to pressure on Christmas bonuses than the government because it was neither an issue on which there was a national campaign nor one that affected the whole nation. In contrast, wartime rationing impacted on everyone. During the First World War, rationing did not begin until late 1917, but it was relaxed for Christmas 1918 when turkey, duck, goose, fowl, chicken and game restrictions were removed and the coupon for other meats was doubled. There were also additional sugar allowances for children under six and residents of hospitals and workhouses. In England and Wales, the new regulations operated for the week before Christmas, whereas in Scotland it was for the week after.[148] Like additional payments to the unemployed, this was a recognition that it was not unreasonable that people wanted the means to enjoy themselves at Christmas. During the Second World War, food supplies were not generally plentiful enough for additional Christmas rations but there was still demand for traditional fare. In 1940 Lord Woolton, minister of food, declared turkeys were 'not necessary, only pleasant' and decided not to fix their prices. But prices rose so they ended up being fixed after all. By then, many retailers had already agreed to higher prices for their supplies so started charging very high supplements for plucking and preparation to recoup what they had paid. The price and short supply of turkey actually led to a resurgence in roast beef for Christmas dinner. That year, only tea and sugar rations were increased, with the government proclaiming that the shipping space that could have been used to import additional meat, butter and fruit would instead be used for planes, guns and tanks.[149] Where prices were controlled, people seemed to accept the lack of additional rations. In 1942, the minister of food claimed that of the 557 letters he had received the week before Christmas, only one called for greater festive rations. Nor was there any resentment of the limits placed on Christmas holidays, with most people having just Christmas Day itself off in the early years of the war. By 1944, the conflict was going well enough for the government to incur the cost of giving extra sweet rations for those under the age of eighteen and extra meat, fat and sugar entitlements all round. The government hoped there would be a turkey for everyone who wanted one but to help ensure this, it prohibited serving the bird in restaurants between 22 and 30 December except on Christmas Day.[150]

After the war, people's patience grew shorter and some festive restrictions just seemed petty. There were restrictions on the use of electricity for shop lighting displays. Gifts of food on ration were prevented, even when it was just a few potatoes.[151] In 1948, when the Christmas extras were limited to 4oz of tea, 2oz of sweets and ½lb of sugar, as well as increased supplies for the manufacture of sausages, the minister of food told Cabinet: 'I realise that the proposed Christmas bonuses may seem to the housewife not too generous for the fourth Christmas of peace, but I think we should give something, however small.'[152] A cartoon in the *Daily Mail* joked, 'I hear that we'll be able to see our bacon ration with the naked eye for a couple of weeks at Christmas.'[153] Morale was the prime motive and in 1949 the minister of food told his colleagues 'a little extra tea at Christmas is most welcome, particularly to the elderly'.[154] Yet there were limits to how far the government would go. In 1952 rationing and supply problems were easing but conditions did not allow for any bonus and the Chancellor maintained that a rise in the sugar ration 'would be a pure luxury'.[155] The whole issue was one that could vex government somewhat. In 1950 the Cabinet discussed the possibility of importing turkeys from Hungary and Canada to satisfy demand. Buying from the former would break its trade embargo with that nation and be a sign of weakness that could handicap dealings with other countries in the Soviet orbit, while extra purchases from Canada might make it difficult to restrain the dollar expenditure of other Commonwealth countries. Cabinet was divided on what to do with some ministers fearing 'severe political criticism' if people 'were unable to obtain their traditional fare at Christmas time'. In the end, it put international concerns ahead of Christmas and refused to buy from either Hungary and Canada, although it did look for other means of securing turkey imports to bring prices down to within the reach of poorer families.[156]

Rising living standards after the Second World War lessened the need of government to intervene to help people celebrate. Yet poverty did not disappear, even if its consequences were not as dire or visible as before the war. Rising inflation in the early 1970s, however, drew attention back to the poorest of society. Pensioners, in particular, suffered as their incomes struggled to keep up with rising prices. After pressure from Labour backbenchers and the TUC, the Conservative government gave pensioners a £10 Christmas bonus in 1972. This was a significant boost to their incomes given that the weekly state pension was then £6.75 and many spent the bonus on small extras such as clothing. In Clevedon (Somerset), a postmaster even gave out the bonuses dressed up as Santa. But, while people did not

PLATE 29 *The Christmas tree gifted to London by Norway, Trafalgar Square, 1 December 1948. Keystone-France/Getty.*

want to be ungrateful, it also generated some resentment that pensions were not high enough.[157] The bonus was paid every subsequent year (apart from 1975 and 1976) but there were constant worries about the cost. This meant no government ever increased the bonus in line with inflation and what had been a significant gift became worth very little.[158] Given its minimal value, the fact that it still existed at all was perhaps rather bizarre but it seems no Chancellor wanted the inevitable Scrooge headlines that would come from its abolition.

There were other limitations in how far the state was willing to go in recognizing Christmas as both a moment to celebrate and a time when normal practices might be put aside. In the wake of civil war, the government refused in 1922 to lift a curfew in Northern Ireland to allow Catholics to hold their normal Christmas Eve midnight Mass. When the Cardinal of Armagh announced he would hold one anyway, he was told that the police would surround the cathedral and not let anyone out until morning. Protestant groups who wanted to go carol singing that night were also refused permission.[159] In 1954, a judge ruled that a 1921 bequest that seasonable food and drink be given out to twenty members of a church in Woodford Green (who were to be told where it had come from) was vanity not charity because there was nothing to indicate that the food was for the poor and that giving out plum pudding did not advance religion.[160] In 1958 and 1959, despite protests from the public and press, the police refused to approve the lighting of the Trafalgar Square Christmas tree after 11.00 pm for fear it would lead to drunks assembling there. The government did at least decide to overlook the fact that it broke a ban on the import of trees and special licences were subsequently granted to the twenty or so similar trees donated to British towns and cities for public display, despite the risk they presented of bringing disease into the country. In 1963 the Forestry Commission decided to stop these licences in all cases except the Trafalgar Square tree. However, the minister concerned overruled the commission and the imported public Christmas tree was saved.[161]

Conclusion

The state grew, both in size and reach, over the course of the twentieth century. The process may not have been even or continuous but government undoubtedly had more influence over the lives of British citizens at the end of the century than at its beginning. This was not welcomed by everyone but even those who decried the state's waste and reach in the last quarter of the century failed to roll back its frontiers as much as they claimed. The history of Christmas also shows that the state was not as all pervasive as its critics often made out. Before the Second World War, the local and national state had relatively little influence on the most important day in the British calendar beyond ensuring a short break from work for most people, a little financial help for the poorest of the working classes and the occasional encouragement to everyone to remain safe. A branch of the state did, however, influence how people got their seasonal post and that in itself was an indicator of how the state was coming to be seen as an important provider of services that mattered to people's lives. The Second World War saw the reach and size of the state grow beyond recognition but there were still limits to its interventions in everyday life. Only when it did not interfere with other priorities was the government willing to do something to help people enjoy Christmas. After the war and the subsequent austerity, the state's direct intervention in the festival lessened again as it concentrated on individual and collective economic security. It was public opinion and industry that led to the holiday growing rather than the guidance of central government. Nonetheless, in the twenty-first century, the state did step in when it worried that commercial forces might diminish Christmas as a family and religious break and legislated to ensure large shops remained shut. In these actions, we see something of the nature of the post-war British state: it often followed opinion rather than led it. Only in the issue of drink-driving could the state be said to be ahead of popular festive behaviour but that was more because deaths and accidents brought costs to other parts of the state rather than from any moralistic wish to tell people how to behave.

Christmas was actually most political for groups outside the state. In 1971 a Civil Rights Association in Newry campaigned against some Christmas celebrations as a symbolic gesture against British policy in Northern Ireland. It advised people not to buy British toys for their children and to display candles and black flags instead of Christmas trees. The press claimed that a high proportion of the population was following the instruction that there should be 'no external signs of joy'. To avoid trouble, the army declined invitations to soldiers to have Christmas lunch in local homes and the chamber of commerce decided not to erect its annual town centre tree.[162] That was an extreme example but it was certainly not the only time that Christmas became entwined with wider concerns. German toys were widely boycotted during and after the Great War and some families would not even use their German-made decorations anymore.[163] Amid a growing awareness of the importance of conserving the natural world, there was an appeal in *The Times* in 1934 for people not to cut holly bushes because of the impact on birds.[164] In the late twentieth century such environmental concerns became widespread. With the festival's unwanted presents, use of wrapping paper, and indulgent eating and drinking, one book concluded that Christmas had become 'a symbol of our throw-away society'.[165] People were even buying things they would never use and in 2012 the Waste and Resources Action Programme claimed that food and drink wastage increased by 80 per cent over Christmas and that 230,000 tonnes of food was being binned at the festival.[166] There were ethical concerns too. Decorations, for example, were often made in factories in the Far East that employed child labour, paid poorly and exposed workers to dangerous chemicals.[167] Animal rights

PLATE 30 *Father Christmas union protesting against the commercial exploitation of Christmas, 1969. Keystone-France/Getty.*

campaigners also worried about Christmas. In 1991 it was estimated that between 10 and 12 million turkeys were killed for British Christmas dinners. The conditions they were kept under could be quite horrendous, with the typical British turkey living in a windowless shed with 10,000 other birds. They could suffer breast blisters, eye diseases and feet ulcers. Some young birds died from starvation or thirst because they did not learn how to access food and water. The conditions made them stressed and aggressive, which meant 70–80 per cent were de-beaked without anaesthetic. Most were killed before they were twenty-four weeks old, whereas wild turkeys can live for up to ten years.[168] Concern about this was not merely a product of the late twentieth century. In 1952 one diarist noted that no one laughed at what was supposed to be a humorous cinema newsreel about turkeys awaiting their Christmas fate.[169] Of course, the mass consumption of animals and resources continued unabated throughout the century but that does not mean there were not moments of guilt from people about what they were doing.

In this sense, Christmas illustrates how hegemonic practices were able to continue despite people's awareness that they were somehow not right. But there have also been suggestions that the festival actually plays a direct role in maintaining the status quo. One religious writer claimed that those in authority used Christmas to consolidate their power. His examples ranged from the Queen's broadcast to the seasonal announcement of policy initiatives by politicians. Yet he argued that Christmas itself was almost anti-establishment since its story represented a questioning of the prevailing powers and the promise of a new order.[170] Some of the interventions discussed here by both the state and employers might be seen as political play. Employers gave parties to ensure their workers remained with them and subdued the rest of the year. The government sanctioned bonuses for pensioners and the unemployed because it was cheaper than raising the normal payments. Longer holidays made for more efficient work by rested employees afterwards. Even the government's 1940 decision not to bomb Germany or Italy on Christmas Day (unless there was a German attack the day before or an unanticipated strategic reason to do so) had ulterior motives. It did not announce the truce in advance for strategic reasons but it still hoped to get credit for the decision and had feared looking bad in American eyes should it carry out raids but the Germans did not.[171]

But actions rarely have singular motives and those in authority also genuinely saw Christmas as a special time. Early interventions along these lines were motivated by religion, such as the restrictions on pub opening or the 1934 Betting and Lotteries Act which outlawed gambling on Christmas Day, Easter and Sundays. By the twenty-first century, secularism had destroyed much of the legal protection given to the Sabbath but 25 December retained a unique status, something evident in the 2004 Christmas Day (Trading) Act which sought to 'preserve the special nature of that day'.[172] That special nature was rooted in the importance of the day for family and individual happiness. In its discussions of whether to pay a pension bonus in 1978, the cabinet heard that pensioners appreciated it because it allowed them to buy gifts for relatives and grandchildren.[173] This may have been a trivial motivation but the cost of paying the bonus was some £80 million. Indeed, Christmas also produced occasional moments when people showed some gratitude to the state, or at least its representatives. In 1961 members of the public sent Sir Winston Churchill Virginia ham, a 'huge' box of matches, three books, three case of fruit, a diary, some pate de foie, four calendars, smoked salmon, a cigar, a stud diary, three cases of alcoholic drinks, socks, a desk block and pen.[174] Until sometime in the middle of the century, postal and refuse workers could expect a tip. That disappeared as they became more anonymous figures but giving primary school teachers a present did become quite widespread in the twenty-first century, to the extent that, in an echo of early century dealings with tradesmen, some parents felt obliged to give one.

In 1945 the cabinet decided to encourage all senior civil service officials to take as much leave as possible at Christmas because of their high work load. An official week's holiday in the civil service was felt to be unpractical because of public needs and the possible embarrassing repercussions should similar demands then arise in industry. Yet the cabinet also decided not to publicize its decision.[175] In this one episode we see some of the dynamics of the British state. It was not always equally concerned with the welfare of all its citizens, it was unwilling to intervene too far or too directly in some matters that did concern it and it was always vulnerable to public pressure.

But the incident is also a reminder that Christmas was always regarded as an opportunity for people to have a break from the pressures of work. As both a major employer in itself and a regulator of other employers, the issue of holidays meant the state could not avoid the questions Christmas raised.

CONCLUSION

In 1937 volunteers for Mass Observation were asked to record how they spent Christmas Day. In Laindon (Essex), a 48-year-old housewife had not received a gift from her husband or her son and was glad when her husband went out to a football match in the morning. She later ate her beef dinner in a different room to him. Nor was she impressed with her mother's card, which was accompanied by a present but not a letter, or by the King's Speech, although her heart was tied in knots by his struggle with the words. Her festive treat was a cup full of chocolates that she bought herself. In Barnstaple, the weather was foggy and a 33-year-old teacher recorded that she did not feel Christmassy; she was depressed and gloomy, and unable to stop thinking of the wars in Spain and China. Her mood was not helped by the fact that the radio was on during dinner, annoying her with light music. Afterwards, she would have preferred to be dancing, singing carols and performing charades with her friends, but instead was playing darts with her family.

Elsewhere there were more mixed emotions. In London, a twenty-year-old student recorded that her father thought Christmas was 'jolly' but 'unimportant', but she was all for celebration of any kind. In Norbury, a 32-year-old housewife recorded her annoyance at the amount of washing-up she had to do, and the fact that people chattered during a family game of cards. But she was also excited thinking about how her niece and nephew would be enjoying themselves. There were mundane moments too. In Peterborough, a 27-year-old secretary discussed the state of the cotton trade with his brother-in-law, while their wives talked about children's education, gas cookers and sewing. Some just had a very pleasant day. In a Ramsgate boarding house, the inhabitants had lunch together and gave each other presents. The owner said it was very exciting, that everyone got what they wanted, and they were all 'very well pleased' and 'well satisfied'. In Farnborough, an unmarried 31-year-old electrician spent the day with friends, recording that 'There was much laughter for many reasons and that is what a Xmas party is for'. The family he was with were 'somewhat religious' and Christmas was one of the few times they allowed themselves 'to have a bit of fun'.[1]

The reality of Christmas was thus more complex than what was suggested by the *Saturday Review* in 1922 when it said that 'Opinions on Christmas may be conveniently, if unscientifically, divided into the cynical and the sentimental.'[2] Christmas was too varied an experience to be so neatly pigeonholed but, ultimately, how people spent and responded to Christmas was a matter of temperament and personality. The fact that society is made up of very different individuals is sometimes rather brushed aside by historians in their attempts to explain and describe, but if the history of Christmas does one thing it is to remind us how central personality was to people's outlooks on and reactions to the world they lived in. They did, however, respond within wider cultural and economic frameworks that confined their thought and behaviour and encouraged a degree of common experience. Christmas was part of those frameworks in which everyone lived their lives.

This book has argued that, regardless of how people spent and responded to the festival, over the century that followed the outbreak of the Great War, Christmas had a number of different functions in society. None of them touched every single member of the country but, combined, they meant that Christmas had a central role in British society.

The first function was economic. Christmas generated significant levels of spending. It provided a focus or climax for people's material aspirations and desires. It gave those who could not usually afford much an excuse to enjoy spending more than they would normally. The commercialism of the festival upset some, but without it Christmas would not have been as visible, intense or pleasurable an experience. Throughout the period, people also complained that the festival's commercialism was intensifying. That complaint not only overlooked its own recurrence, but also the facts that all aspects of society had become more obviously dominated by consumerism, and that consumerism grew, not just because of the ambitions of manufacturers and sellers, but because people enjoyed spending.

Many of the complaints about the commercialism of Christmas were rooted in the idea that this was marginalizing the festival's religious meanings. However, this book has suggested that the festival's second function was stemming the secularization of society, not through upholding organized religion but by ensuring Christianity still had an inescapable public profile and by creating a moment when people thought about and often acted on the goodwill and charity that was at the heart of the Christian faith. That might not have brought people closer to God, but it did bring them closer to what He was said to represent. Christmas was thus evidence that the increasingly multicultural, secular UK was still profoundly influenced by a Christian legacy.

That influence was part of Christmas's third function: it was an integrative experience. It brought people closer to their family, friends, neighbours, community, compatriots and, occasionally, the poor and suffering. It crossed any notional boundaries between the private and public spheres and helped maintain a common way of life in a society divided by class, ethnicity and taste. Sometimes this integration was literal and physical. Sometimes it was through the medium of a shared media or even just because of the fact that it was something everyone encountered. The vast majority of people did celebrate Christmas and partook in its key rituals of feasting, gift-giving and the shopping required for both. Even those who did not celebrate or tried to keep their adherence as minimal as possible could not escape Christmas unless they literally shut themselves away for the whole of December, never leaving the house, or turning on a television or reading a newspaper. While all this made Christmas an integral part of British culture, individuals still had freedom to celebrate in their own way, to manipulate and recast its rituals, to put their own stamp of personality and status on it. Without that flexibility, Christmas could never have had the powerful integrative role it did; a shared culture is rarely a monolithic one. Yet for a few, Christmas was actually an exclusionary experience. So powerful was Christmas as a cultural norm that when people, through choice or circumstance, did not celebrate, it could leave them feeling outside or removed from the mainstream.

Most were content to adhere to Christmas because of the festival's fourth function in twentieth-century Britain: it made people happy. The roots of this were varied. It was a chance to be with those who you loved and loved you. For some, it was just the break or pause from normal life and activities, although for those cooking and clearing up, work could actually intensify. It might be the excuse to drink and eat too much and act a little silly, without having to worry about normal concerns such as calories, cost or dignity. In later life, the festival could provide a focus for nostalgic reminiscing, particularly based around one's childhood or the childhood of one's grown children.

The season's happiness also drew on the uniqueness of the day. There is a long history of holidays inverting social norms and behaviours, but in modern society this only remains evident at Christmas. It seemed to have a special quality, a time apart when the norms of behaviour and even aesthetics were turned upside down. 'There is magic in the word Christmas,' as the *Cornishman* said in 1922.[3] Children in particular felt this and it gave them immense pleasure and even a sense of wonder. In 1974, a Welsh actor, in recalling the Christmases of his childhood concluded, 'The rest of the year might be a dull bread-and-butter existence, but this was the day of delights.'[4] But for adults too, Christmas was a chance to smile and, in difficult times, a rare chance. Historians do not often consider happiness. Nor do intellectuals and the sentimentality and kitschness of Christmas does not encourage the festival to be taken seriously. But, as the novelist William Sansom noted in 1968, while it is easy to laugh at the 'bourgeois fuss', it is 'far more profound to recognise the need for the sanctification of sentiment and the dramatic pleasures of social effort'.[5]

Those who did take this seriously saw deep anthropological meanings in it. Aldous Huxley argued that holidays and festivals existed to fulfil the love of excitement that was rooted in human nature.[6] In 1917 a religious writer extolled that Christmas 'is the protest of the human race against gloom'.[7] Thirty years later, the *Derby Daily Telegraph* argued that the festival would never disappear because 'There is a kind of "Christmas instinct" which gets into the very bones and marrow of us and will not let us be'.[8] But perhaps the less hyperbolic 1986 analysis of a 39-year-old woman is better: 'I like Xmas because it's a time of complete relaxation for me. ... I can switch off completely and I feel great afterwards. None of us is very religious so we don't go to church, but Xmas is a nice time for everyone to get together, to eat and talk and just relax. It was a normal, nice Xmas.'[9]

Such feelings should not be underestimated since scientists have demonstrated how those who are happier tend to be healthier and live longer.[10] Of course, not everyone was happy at Christmas and people's relationship with the festival was also affected by their personal, social and economic circumstances. But that was true of every pastime and phenomenon and does not distract from what Christmas did do. Indeed, the levels of happiness at Christmas should not be underestimated. In a 1975 poll, 88 per cent of respondents said they expected to have a happy Christmas.[11]

Yet Christmas was not a static phenomenon. Beneath the surface of the essential ingredients of family and feasting were subtle changes such as a greater role for fathers in domestic chores, a falling off in the prominence of religion, a decline in entertainments outside the home, and a lengthening in the time off work. Some rituals disappeared. Nurses no longer, for example, walk the wards holding candles and singing carols. Where people still burn the Yule log or take part in mummers' play, they are doing so as a conscious attempt to keep alive an old tradition. New technologies evolved the season's aesthetics and entertainments. Electric lights gave public places a wondrous feel, adding to the otherness of the season. Television gave many people's day a new ending, while the internet and social media allowed people to share their photographs and sentiments, communicating with friends and family scattered across the globe or even just down the road. It was because Christmas evolved that its grip was so tight and that it avoided being cast aside as old-fashioned. Yet evolution did not simply happen; it was something that people ensured and that was because Christmas's four functions appealed to them, at both an individual and collective level. Perhaps another reason why they adapted Christmas was that it gave them an anchor and link to their individual and collective pasts. Historian Mark Connelly has gone as far as suggesting that 'Christmas helped the English through the swirling currents of the emerging modern world'.[12]

In contrast, one anthropologist has suggested that Christmas flourishes because it creates an alternative reality. It constitutes 'an *imaginary*, family centred-society, which ignores time and breaches secular boundaries, which centres on children and reaches out to the dead and to outcasts'.[13] Another academic regards Christmas as the 'season of lies', where people lie to themselves that they are happy and love their families, but she also states that 'we can sometimes makes ourselves genuinely experience the emotions we are faking'.[14] Even with the authors' caveats, such perspectives seem to suggest that somehow society is broken and that Christmas matters because it represents things we care about but that do not actually exist. Christmas may have presented a contrast to the everyday, but that does not mean what it represented was imaginary or a lie. Instead, it was an ideal and intensification of what people believed in and sought.

Two other historians of the festival have written that on the surface,

> it is a very strange season for an industrial, and supposedly rational society – for it engenders a kind of collective will to fantasize; to pretend it is snowing when clearly it is not; to embrace family ties when relations are strained; to be nice to people who at other times you cannot stand; to make believe that Santa Claus is coming, and go to great lengths to convince young children that he has been and gone, leaving presents behind him.[15]

Yet, once the collective and individual functions of Christmas are considered, then the festival is perfectly rational. Indeed, spending a little time, relaxing and having fun with those closest to you is perhaps one of the most rational things in the world. In *A Christmas Carol*, Scrooge's nephew remarks: 'I believe that it *has* done me good, and *will* do me good.' That might not have always been very obvious to those trying to cope with the shopping, cooking and personal relationships, but it was nevertheless true throughout the twentieth century. Of course, Christmas, may rarely have met the perfection of aspirations and sentimental films; it may rarely have snowed too, but that does not mean Christmas did not do people, and thus society as a whole, good. And if people did not have a great time, there was always next year. Indeed, living amid all the imperfections and problems of society, people needed a little escape and distraction, a little fantasy and hope. Perhaps if people were prepared to dream and fantasize a little more the rest of the year, to remember the Christmas spirit of goodwill to all, then society might not have had so many problems in the first place.

NOTES

Introduction

1 *Birmingham Gazette*, 31 December 1914. For a full account see Malcolm Brown and Shirley Seaton, *Christmas Truce* (1984; London: Pan, 2001).

2 *Western Daily Post*, 1 January 1915.

3 Gary Sheffield and John Bourne, eds, *Douglas Haig: War Diaries and Letters, 1914-1918* (London: Weidenfeld and Nicolson, 2006), 87.

4 *Evening Telegraph*, 24 December 1914. *Western Mail*, 21–22 December 1914.

5 *The Times*, 22 December 1914. *Manchester Courier and Lancashire General Advertiser*, 29, 31 December 1914.

6 'Some Christmas thoughts', *Nash's and Pall Mall Magazine*, December 1914.

7 The most comprehensive account of the Victorian Christmas is Neil Armstrong, *Christmas in Nineteenth-Century England* (Manchester: Manchester University Press, 2010). For a discussion of the festival's historiography see Neil Armstrong, 'Christmas in nineteenth-century Britain and America: A historiographical overview', *Cultural and Social History*, 1, no. 1 (2004): 118–25.

8 Mark Connelly, *Christmas: A Social History* (London: I. B. Tauris, 1999). For similar beliefs in Germany, see Joe Perry, *Christmas in Germany: A Cultural History* (Chapel Hill: University of North Carolina Press, 2010).

9 For an account of the history of Christmas centred on this idea, see Gavin Weightman and Steve Humphries, *Christmas Past* (London: Sidgwick and Jackson, 1987).

10 'Is Christmas what it was?', *Saturday Review*, 5 December 1931.

11 J. A. R. Pimlott, *The Englishman's Christmas* (Hassocks: Harvester, 1978), 154.

12 Lynn Abrams and Callum G. Brown, 'Conceiving the everyday in the twentieth century', in *A History of Everyday Life: Twentieth Century Scotland*, eds Lynn Abrams and Callum G. Brown (Edinburgh: Edinburgh University Press, 2010): 1–18.

13 C. S. Lewis, 'What Christmas means to me'. Reproduced in his *God in the Dock: Essays on Theology and Ethics* (Grand Rapids: Eerdmans, 1970), 304–5.

14 Pimlott, *Englishman's Christmas*, 182.

15 Armstrong, *Christmas in Nineteenth-Century England*, 46.

16 *The Likely Lads*, BBC1, 24 December 1974.

Chapter 1

1 *Daily Worker*, 23 December 1931.

2 Neil Armstrong, *Christmas in Nineteenth-century England* (Manchester: Manchester University Press, 2010), ch. 7.

3 Mark Connelly, *Christmas: A Social History* (London: I. B. Tauris, 1999), 190.

4 *The Times*, 28 November 1921. Bill Lancaster, *The Department Store: A Social History* (Leicester: Leicester University Press, 1995), 97.

5 *Daily Mail*, 20 December 1933.

6 Vernon Scannell, *Drums of Morning: Growing Up in the Thirties* (London: Robson, 1992), 28.

7 *Daily Mail*, 30 November 1921. *Daily Mirror*, 19 November 1928.

8 *Daily Mail*, 12 December 1938.

9 J. J. Bell, 'The smile of Father Christmas', *Quiver*, December 1920.

10 'Woolworths Christmas display, 19 November 1938', Mass Observation (hereafter MO) Worktown collection box 31.

11 John Benson, *The Rise of Consumer Society in Britain, 1880-1980* (London: Longman, 1994), 75.

12 *The Times*, 17 December 1920.

13 'What I enjoy most about my Christmas shopping', MO Worktown collection box 31.

14 In 1939 department stores represented around 5 per cent of total British retail sales. Lancaster, *Department Store*, 104.

15 Gavin Weightman and Steve Humphries, *Christmas Past* (London: Sidgwick and Jackson, 1987), 165, 169.

16 'West of Woolworths', 12 December 1938, MO Worktown collection box 31.

17 *The Times*, 16 December 1941. 'Christmas and New Year's Eve, 1941', MO file report 1030, 25–37.

18 *The Times*, 11, 24 December 1942, 14 October 1942. Norman Longmate, *How We Lived Then: A History of Everyday Life during the Second World War* (London: Arrow, 1973), ch. 16.

19 *The Listener*, 19 December 1946. *The Spectator*, 19 December 1947.

20 *The Times*, 13 December 1952, 20 December 1954. *Picture Post*, 24 December 1956.

21 Miss Read, *Winter in Thrush Green* (1961; London: Orion, 2007), 95.

22 For memories of people dressing up and the reserved nature of Christmas shopping see Paul Feeney, *A 1950s Childhood: From Tin Baths to Bread and Dripping* (Stroud: History Press, 2009), 194.

23 *ITV Early Evening News*, 12 December 1961.

24 Karal Ann Marling, *Merry Christmas! Celebrating America's Greatest Holiday* (Cambridge, MA: Harvard University Press, 2001), 112.

25 *The Scotsman*, 13 December 1934.

26 *Gaumont British News*, 16 December 1954.

27 *The Times*, 23 August 1978.

28 *Christmas Summary*, Manchester City Council Report for Information, 18 January 2012.

29 Ipsos MORI, 'Britain gears up for first cyber Christmas: one in three internet users are looking to buy presents online', 29 October 1999: https://www.ipsos-mori.com/researchpublications/researcharchive/1753/Britain-Gears-Up-For-First-Cyber-Christmas-One-In-Three-Internet-Users-Are-Looking-To-Buy-Presents-Online.aspx.

30 BBC News, 'Record online sales over Christmas, says BRC', 10 January 2014: http://www.bbc.co.uk/news/business-25671561.

31 Family Action, *Breaking the Bank: A Cut Price Christmas for Low-Income Families* (2011), 14.

32 *The Times*, 11 December 1968.

33 Michael Laroche, Gad Saad, Mark Cleveland and Elizabeth Browne, 'Gender differences in information search strategies for a Christmas gift', *Journal of Consumer Marketing* 17, no. 6 (2000): 500–22, 505.

34 Esther Swilley and Ronald E. Goldsmith, 'Black Friday and Cyber Monday: Understanding consumer intentions on two major shopping days', *Journal of Retailing and Consumer Services* 20, no. 1 (2013): 43–50.

35 Letter from Early Closing Association to Winston Churchill, 30 July 1934, Churchill Archive: CHAR 2/232/13-14.

36 Michael J. Winstanley, *The Shopkeeper's World, 1830-1914* (Manchester: Manchester University Press, 1983), 127.

37 *The Times*, 24 December 1956.

38 *The Story of Smedley's Fresh Frozen Foods*, John Johnson collection: Food 14 (30).

39 Brian Harrison, *Finding a Role? The United Kingdom, 1970-1990* (Oxford: Oxford University Press, 2010), 364.

40 Brian Harrison, *Seeking a Role: The United Kingdom 1951-1970* (Oxford: Oxford University Press, 2009), 335–6.

41 *ITV Late Evening News*, 28 February 1997. *ITV Early Evening News*, 20 December 1996.

42 *Daily Mail*, 17 December 1926.

43 Erika Diane Rappaport, *Shopping for Pleasure: Women in the Making of London's West End* (Princeton: Princeton University Press, 2000), ch. 5.

44 C. P. Hosgood, 'Doing the shops' at Christmas: Women, men and the department store in England, c.1880-1914', in *Cathedrals of Consumption: The European Department Store, 1850-193*, eds Geoffrey Crossick and Serge Jaumain (Aldershot: Ashgate, 1999): 97–108.

45 *Daily Mirror*, 14 December 1932.

46 *Daily Mirror*, 19 December 1919.

47 Ipsos MORI, 'Mrs Santa Lives Up North!', 21 December 2007: http://www.ipsos-mori.com/researchpublications/researcharchive/poll.aspx?oItemId=253.

48 *Daily Mirror*, 14 December 2004, 7 December 2000. *New Society*, 23 December 1971.

49 Lydia D. Morris, 'Redundancy and patterns of household finance', *Sociological Review* 32, no. 3 (1984): 492–523.

50 Laura Ugolini, 'Men, masculinities, and menswear advertising, c. 1890-1914', in *A Nation of Shopkeepers: Five Centuries of British Retailing*, eds John Benson and Laura Ugolini (London: I. B. Tauris, 2003), 82–104, 85.

51 *The Times*, 10 December 1919, 22 December 1922, 20 December 1935.

52 John Benson, *Affluence and Authority: A Social History of Twentieth-Century Britain* (London: Hodder Arnold, 2005), 40.

53 Lancaster, *Department Store*, 202.

54 Katherine Whitehorn, *Roundabout* (London: Methuen, 1962), 120.

55 *The Times*, 8 December 1973, 24 November 1970.

56 Laroche, Saad, Cleveland and Browne, 'Gender differences in information search strategies'. Eileen Fischer and Stephen J. Arnold, 'More than a labor of love: Gender roles and Christmas gift shopping', *Journal of Consumer Research* 17 (December 1990): 333–45.

57 Stuart Prebble, *Grumpy Old Men* (London: BBC, 2004), 190–1.

58 MO day survey 25 December 1937, respondent 147.

59 Ipsos MORI, 'The Stress Of Christmas Shopping', 13 December 2004: https://www.ipsos-mori.com/researchpublications/researcharchive/586/The-Stress-Of-Christmas-Shopping.aspx.

60 *The Times*, 28 November 1923. *Daily Mail*, 17 December 1926.

61 *Portsmouth Evening News*, 5 December 1938. *Daily Mirror*, 8 December 1964. *The Times*, 22 November 1930.

62 *Daily Mirror*, 7 December 1923.

63 'Christmas shopping and clubs', MO Worktown collection, box 31.

64 *The Times*, 29 November 1980.

65 *Christmas Summary*, Manchester City Council Report for Information, 18 January 2012.

66 For plans for London see *The Times*, 27 November 1959.

67 *Daily Mail*, 17 December 1926.

68 *The Times*, 23 December 1918.

69 *The Times*, 6 December 1919.

70 Theodore Caplow, 'Rule enforcement without visible means: Christmas gift giving in Middletown', *American Journal of Sociology* 89, no. 6 (1984): 1306–23, 1314.

71 For example, *Spectator*, 12 December 1925; *The Listener*, 9 December 1936.

72 Whitehorn, *Roundabout*, 120–1.

73 Gyles Brandreth, *Brandreth's Christmas Book* (Wokingham: Van Nostrand Reinhold, 1975), 46.

74 For example, *New Statesman*, 17 December 2007.

75 *The Times*, 15 November 1923. Joanna Brewis and Samantha Warren, 'Have yourself a merry little Christmas? Organizing Christmas in women's magazines past and present', *Organization* 18, no. 6 (2011): 747–62.

76 'Barbara Back's shopping gossip for Christmas', *Nash's Pall Mall Magazine,* December 1933.

77 India Knight, *Comfort and Joy* (London: Penguin, 2010), 6.

78 'Dear Christine', *Nash's Pall Mall Magazine*, December 1934.

79 Celia Lury, *Consumer Culture* (Cambridge: Polity, 1996).

80 *Picture Post*, 3 December 1956. *The Economist*, 19 November 1960.

81 *No More War*, December 1928.

82 *The Times*, 31 December 1971.

83 C. S. Lewis, 'What Christmas means to me'. Reproduced in *God in the Dock: Essays on Theology and Ethics* (Grand Rapids: Eerdmans, 1970), 304–5.

84 *The Times*, 3 December 1937.

85 *Scottish Sunday Express*, 26 December 1948.

86 *The Times*, 28 November 1921, 20 December 1924, 24 December 1980.

87 Celia Otnes, Tina M. Lowrey and Young Chan Kim, 'Gift selection for easy and difficult recipients: A social roles interpretation', *Journal of Consumer Research* 20, no. 2 (1993): 229–44.

88 *ITN*, 11 January 2000.

89 Brewis and Warren, 'Have yourself a merry little Christmas?'.

90 *Daily Mirror*, 24 December 1918.

91 'Barbara Back's shopping gossip For Christmas', *Nash's Pall Mall Magazine,* December 1933.

92 *New Society*, 23 December 1971.

93 Norman Collins, *London Belongs to Me* (London: Collins, 1945), 25–6.

94 Whitehorn, *Roundabout*, 120. 'Hoover help make happy Christmases' from *Readers Digest*, December 1972, History of Advertising Trust archive: HAT32. For a housewife's appeal against household goods being given as presents see *Daily Mirror*, 6 December 1958.

95 For example see the Craven Plain advertisement in *Daily Mail*, 14 December 1938.

96 *Daily Mirror*, 22 December 1964.

97 *Coronation Street*, ITV, 26 December 1967.

98 *New Society*, 23 December 1971.

99 James Obelkevich, 'Consumption', in *Understanding Post-War British Society*, eds James Obelkevich and Peter Catterall (London: Routledge, 1994), 148.

100 *ITN*, 11 January 2000.

101 Russell W. Belk, 'Materialism and the making of the modern American Christmas', in *Unwrapping Christmas*, ed. Daniel Miller (Oxford: Oxford University Press, 1993): 75–104, 93–4.

102 *Daily Mirror*, 24 November 1919.

103 'Interviews with Radio Shops', 9 December 1938, MO Worktown collection box 31.

104 Joe Moran, *Armchair Nation: An Intimate History of Britain in Front of the TV* (London: Profile, 2013), 81. *ITV Early Evening News*, 19 December 1959.

105 *The Times*, 24 December 1970, 22 January 1985. *News at Ten*, ITV, 23 December 1985. *ITN*, 11 January 2000.

106 *The Times*, 8 December 1973. *Western Mail*, 22 December 1914.

107 Kenneth D. Brown, *The British Toy Business: A History since 1700* (London: Hambledon, 1996), 58.

108 *The Children's Newspaper*, 27 December 1958.

109 See the interviews with shoppers on *ITV Late Evening News*, 18 December 1963. Andrew Collins, *Where Did It All Go Right? Growing Up Normal in the 70s* (London: Ebury, 2003).

110 Weightman and Humphries, *Christmas Past*, 168.

111 *The Times*, 23 August 1937, 24 December 1947.

112 Michael Palin, *Diaries 1969-1979: The Python Years* (London: Weidenfeld and Nicolson, 2006), 518.

113 J. A. R. Pimlott, *The Englishman's Christmas: A Social History* (Hassocks: Harvester, 1978), 160.

114 John G. Richardson and Carl H. Simpson, 'Children, gender and social structure: An analysis of the contents of letters to Santa Claus', *Child Development* 53, no. 2 (1982): 429–36. Cele Otnes, Young Chan Kim and Kyungseung Kim, 'All I want for Christmas: An analysis of children's brand requests to Santa Claus', *Journal of Popular Culture* 27, no. 4 (1994): 183–94.

115 Weightman and Humphries, *Christmas Past*, 172–3.

116 *ITV Lunchtime News*, 23 December 1997, 21 November 1997.

117 Scannell, *Drums of Morning*, 28.

118 *The Times*, 20 December 1941, 20 December 1937, 19 December 1958.

119 *The Listener*, 8 November 1933. UK Gift Card and Voucher Association, 'History of vouchers and gift cards': http://www.ukgcva.co.uk/ historyofvouchers.html *The Times*, 16 December 1941.

120 Lady Clanmore, 'It's the thought that counts', *South Wales Spectator* (December 1964).

121 Harrison, *Seeking a Role*, 263.

122 Pam Schweitzer, ed., *All Our Christmases: A Book of Christmas Memories by Greenwich Pensioners* (London: Age Exchange Theatre Company, 1983).

Gilda O'Neill, *My East End: Memories of Life in Cockney London* (London: Penguin, 2000), 218–20.

123 *Daily Herald*, 10 December 1929. *Daily Worker*, 22 December 1936.

124 A. J. Cronin, *The Citadel* (1937; London: NEL, 1968), 155–6.

125 'Christmas is coming in Worktown', MO Worktown collection box 27.

126 MO day survey, 25 December 1937, respondent 368.

127 'Sweet Shop, 192 Old Chorley Road' and 'Whitakers Shop', 9 December 1938, MO Worktown collection box 31.

128 John Brierley, *In the Shadow of the Means Test Man: Memories of a Derbyshire Childhood* (Highedge: Highedge Historical Society, 1995), 63, 65.

129 Richard Hoggart, *The Uses of Literacy* (1957; New Brunswick: Transaction, 1992), 97–8.

130 'Christmas is coming in Worktown', MO Worktown collection box 27.

131 *Daily Mail*, 14 December 1927.

132 Ferdynand Zweig, *Labour, Life and Poverty* (1949; Wakefield: EP Publishing, 1975), 80.

133 *The Walthamstow Democrat*, September 1922.

134 'Interviews with Christmas traders', 1938, MO Worktown collection box 31. For a discussion of saving clubs see 'Mutual Aid and the Pub', MO file report 2505 (August 1947).

135 Madeline Kerr, *People of Ship Street* (London: Routledge, 1958), 93–4.

136 Lyn Briggs, *A Shropshire Christmas* (Stroud: History Press, 1993), 136–7.

137 *Swindon Advertiser and North Wilts Chronicle*, 18 December 1936.

138 'Interview with Sweetshop', 2 December 1938, MO Worktown collection box 31.

139 Sean O'Connell, *Credit and Community: Working-class Debt in the UK since 1880* (Oxford: Oxford University Press, 2009), 225. For a contemporary report of such a suicide, where the coroner noted how common they were, see *The Star*, 7 December 1938.

140 Margaret Ashby, *A Hertfordshire Christmas* (Stroud: Sutton, 1998), 138–43. David Green, *A Berkshire Christmas* (Stroud: Sutton, 1994), 1.

141 MO day survey, 25 December 1937, respondent 345.

142 Gary Cross, *Time and Money: The Making of Consumer Culture* (London: Routledge, 1993), 148–9.

143 Cronin, *The Citadel*, 157–8.

144 Interview with Cedric Battye (b. 1922), British Library C1345/12. Jerry White, *The Worst Street in North London: Campbell Bunk between the Wars* (London: Routledge, 1986), 72. Schweitzer, *All Our Christmases*, 15.

145 *Daily Mail*, 27 December 1928.

146 Helen Forrester, *Twopence to Cross the Mersey* (1974; London: Harper Collins, 2010), 188.

147 Phyllis Willmott, *Growing up in a London Village: Family Life Between the Wars* (London: Peter Owen, 1979), 115–6. Louis Heren, *Growing up Poor in London* (London: Hamilton, 1973), 25.

148 George Orwell, *The Road to Wigan Pier* (1937; Harmondsworth: Penguin, 1962), 79–81.

149 Christmas questionnaire 1938, MO Worktown collection box 31.

150 Florence Bone, *Santa Claus's Treasury: A Book for a Christmas Stocking* (London: RTS, 1914), 31.

151 Weightman and Humphries, *Christmas Past*, 165. Callum Brown, *Religion and Society in Twentieth-Century Britain* (Harlow: Pearson, 2006), 147.

152 Richard Burton, *A Christmas Story* (1964; London: Hodder & Stoughton 1989), 32.

153 Christmas questionnaire 1938, MO Worktown collection box 31.

154 Jack Jones, *Me and Mine: Further Chapters in the Autobiography of Jack Jones* (London: Hamish Hamilton, 1946), 94.

155 Jack Lawson, HC Deb 22 December 1938, vol. 342 c3145.

156 *Welwyn Garden City and Hertfordshire Pilot*, 15 December 1922.

157 Alfred Peedle interview, London Transport Museum: http://www.20thcenturylondon.org.uk/audio/extract-2-interview-alfred-peedle.

158 *The Times*, 30 December 1946.

159 *Hancock's Half Hour*, Light Programme, 22 December 1959.

160 *ITV Late Evening News*, 24 December 1956. Kerr, *People of Ship Street*, 90.

161 *The Times*, 22 December 1966.

162 Eileen Evason, *On the Edge: A Study of Poverty and Long-term Unemployment in Northern Ireland* (London: Child Poverty Action Group, 1985), 45.

163 *The Times*, 2 December 1970.

164 *New Society*, 18 December 1987.

165 *The Times*, 17 December 1975.

166 Family Action, *Breaking the Bank*, 1, 4, 8, 12–3.

167 London Chamber of Commerce, *London's Christmas Economy: A Business Perspective on the Retail and Hospitality Sectors* (2005), 10.

168 See the memories in Jeff Pearce, *A Pocketful of Holes and Dreams* (Rearsby: W. F. Howe, 2011), 58.

169 Richard Coopey, Sean O'Connell and Dilwyn Porter, *Mail Order Retailing in Britain: A Business and Social* History (Oxford: Oxford University Press, 2005).

170 *Daily Mirror*, 23 October 1972. London Chamber of Commerce, *London's Christmas Economy*, 10.

171 Evason, *On the Edge*, 45.

172 Catherine Paton Black, *At the Coalface: My Life as a Miner's Wife* (London: Headline, 2012), 82–3.

173   For example, *The Times*, 28 December 1970.

174   Sally McKechnie and Caroline Tynan, 'Social meanings in Christmas consumption: An exploratory study of UK celebrants' consumption rituals', *Journal of Consumer Behaviour* 5, no. 2 (2006): 130–44.

175   Peter Townsend, *Poverty in the United Kingdom* (Harmondsworth: Penguin, 1979), 307.

176   Sheila Hunt, *Poverty, Pregnancy and the Healthcare Professional* (Edinburgh: Books for Midwives, 2004).

177   Winifred Holtby, *South Riding* (1936; London: BBC, 2011), 387–8. Lady Clanmore, 'It's the thought that counts', *South Wales Spectator*, December 1964.

178   British Retail Consortium, 'Christmas Facts and Figures' (2006): http://www.brc.org.uk/brc_news_detail.asp?id=1047. Department for Social Development, *Jobseeker's Allowance Summary of Statistics* (November 2006).

179   For a long-term view of working-class affluence see Jon Lawrence, 'Class, "affluence", and the study of everyday life in Britain, c.1930-64', *Cultural and Social History* 10, no. 2 (2013): 273–99.

180   Paul Addison, *No Turning Back: The Peacetime Revolutions of Post-War Britain* (Oxford: Oxford University Press, 2010), 168, 315–6.

181   Ferdynand Zweig, *The Worker in an Affluent Society: Family Life and Industry* (London: Heinemann, 1961), 209.

182   *The Economist*, 21 November 1959.

183   Elizabeth Roberts, *Women and Families: An Oral History, 1940-1970* (Oxford: Blackwell, 1995), 156.

184   Quoted in Weightman and Humphries, *Christmas Past*, 172.

185   See the interviews with shoppers on *ITV Late Evening News*, 18 December 1963.

186   Kate Fox, *Watching the English: The Hidden Rules of English Behaviour* (London: Hodder, 2005), 386–7, 394–7.

187   Ipsos MORI, 'Mrs Santa Lives Up North!', 21 December 2007: http://www.ipsos-mori.com/researchpublications/researcharchive/poll.aspx?oItemId=253.

188   Ipsos MORI, 'Half The Population Likely To Overspend At Christmas', 8 December 1998. http://www.ipsos-mori.com/researchpublications/researcharchive/poll.aspx?oItemId=1977.

189   Family Action, *Breaking the Bank*, 7.

190   Jim Pooler, *Why We Shop: Emotional Rewards and Retail Strategies* (Westport: Praeger, 2003), 78–81.

191   UK Data Service: SN: 69038 National Opinion Polls National Political Surveys; December 1969.

192   *The Spectator*, 25 December 1959.

193   *The Economist*, 26 December 1953.

194   Benson, *Rise of Consumer Society in Britain*, 60.

195 For an example of how thinking about New Year bills depressed someone see MO day survey 25 December 1937, respondent 147.

196 George McKay, 'Consumption, "coca-colonisation," cultural resistance – and Santa Claus', in *Christmas Ideology and Popular Culture*, ed. Sheila Whiteley (Edinburgh: Edinburgh University Press, 2008): 50–70.

197 Weightman and Humphries, *Christmas Past*, 73.

198 Clemence Dane, 'The Christmas heart', *Quiver*, December 1925.

199 *New Society*, 7 December 1978.

200 For such thoughts see *Daily Mail*, 24 December 1935.

201 MO day surveys, 25 December 1937 and 1938, respondents 231, 473 and 573.

202 *Daily Mirror*, 23 December 1925.

203 *Daily Mail*, 27 December 2013. *Daily Telegraph*, 28 December 2010.

204 *Daily Mail*, 22 November 1922. *ITV Lunchtime News*, 6 December 1972.

205 Aldous Huxley, *The Olive Tree and Other Essays* (London: Chatto and Windus, 1936), 125–8.

206 *Picture Post*, 23 November 1946.

207 'What is Christmas without Crawfords?', History of Advertising Trust archive: 12_11_1955 HAT_20_01.

208 William Sansom, *Christmas* (London: Weidenfeld and Nicolson, 1968), 199.

209 *The Times*, 22 December 1958.

210 Armstrong, *Christmas in Nineteenth-century England*, 164.

211 *The Times*, 17 November 1921.

212 *The Times*, 30 October 1933, 27 December 1952, 30 October 1959. *Yorkshire Post and Leeds Intelligencer*, 2 November 1953.

213 *ITV Early Evening News*, 18 October 1959.

214 *Daily Mirror*, 15 October 2008. *The Times*, 29 November 1926.

215 MO day survey December 1938, respondent 707.

216 *The Times*, 8 December 1973. *Daily Mirror*, 21 October 2002.

217 For example, Peter Clarke, 'A measure for Christmas spirit', *Journal of Consumer Marketing* 24, no. 1 (2007): 8–17.

218 William B. Waits, *The Modern Christmas in America: A Cultural History of Gift Giving* (New York: New York University Press, 1993), 25, 27.

219 Fox, *Watching the English*, 386. Jilly Cooper, *How to Survive Christmas* (London: Methuen, 1986), 91.

220 MO day survey 25 December 1937, respondent 20.

221 On Christmas commerce as 'sacred' see Jean M. Bartunek and Boram Do, 'The sacralization of Christmas commerce', *Organization* 18, no. 6 (2011): 795–806.

222 See James G. Carrier, 'The rituals of Christmas giving', in *Unwrapping Christmas*, ed. Daniel Miller (Oxford: Oxford University Press, 1993), 55–74, 63.

223   Advertisement for Pyramid Handkerchiefs in *Woman's Own Christmas Annual* (1964), 65. 'Things happen after a Badedas Christmas' adverts from *Readers Digest* in History of Advertising Trust archive: HAT32.

224   Julie A. Ruth, Cele C. Otnes and Frédéric F. Brunel, 'Gift receipt and the reformulation of interpersonal relationships', *Journal of Consumer Research* 25, no. 4 (1999): 385–402.

225   *Daily Mirror*, 9 November 1923.

226   G. H. Bennett, '"Part of the Puzzle": Northampton and other Midlands by-election defeats for the Conservatives, 1927-1929', *Midland History* 20, no. 1 (1995): 151–73.

227   For a humorous depiction see *Evening Standard*, 17 December 1931. For more serious discussion see *The Economist*, 20 December 1930.

228   *The Times*, 19 November 1932. Lewis, 'What Christmas means to me', 305.

229   *Daily Mirror*, 9 December 1978, 3 November 1938. *The Times*, 22 December 1956.

230   *The Times*, 20 December 1937. *Lichfield Mercury*, 18 December 1936. The *Economist*, 1 January 1938.

231   Cathy Pharoah and Tom McKenzie, *Charitable Giving by UK households at Christmas*, CGAP Briefing Note 2, December 2009. Grace Anyaegbu and Louise Barnes, 'Expenditure', *Social Trends* 41 (2010): 13.

232   Office for National Statistics, *Retail Sales*, December 2013, 8.

233   Money Advice Service, 'UK to spend "29bn on Christmas 2012', 5 November 2012: www.moneyadviceservice.org.uk/en/static/uk-to-spend-29bn-on-christmas-2012.

234   Mary Searle-Chatterjee, 'Christmas cards and the construction of social relations in Britain today', in *Christmas Unwrapped*, ed. Daniel Miller (Oxford: Oxford University Press, 1993), 176–92, 176.

235   *The Economist*, 26 December 1953, 21 November 1959.

236   *The Spectator*, 3 January 1998. *Director*, December 2011.

237   London Chamber of Commerce, *London's Christmas Economy*, 9.

238   British Retail Consortium, 'BRC Christmas facts and figures', 20 November 2006: http://www.brc.org.uk/brc_news_detail.asp?id=1047.

239   *Southampton's Christmas Economy: The impact of Festive Shopping* (TSE Leisure, Culture and Tourism Research and Consultancy 2008).

240   Colin Howard, *Cotswold Days* (London: Blackie, 1937), 274.

241   'Shops', 12 December 1938, MO Worktown collection box 31.

242   Interview with Tim Farmilo, Museum of London: MoL_2004.115/EX12.

243   For memories of this see Vera Hall interview, East Midlands Oral History Archive.

244   Philip Hancock and Alf Rehn, 'Organizing Christmas', *Organization* 18, no. 6 (2011): 737–45.

245   *The Times*, 31 December 1935.

246 Special report on unemployment, January 1924, The National Archives (hereafter TNA): CAB 24/164/24.

247 *Daily Mirror*, 11 October 2012.

248 *Gaumont Graphic*, 17 December 1931. *The Economist*, 16 December 1950, 2 January 1954.

249 *The Times*, 22 December 1984.

250 See the interviews with shoppers on *ITV Late Evening News*, 18 December 1963.

251 Ben Curtis, *The South Wales Miners, 1964-1985* (Cardiff: University of Wales Press, 2012), 235–6. For a contemporary media report see *News at 5.45*, ITV, 21 December 1984.

252 *ITV Late Evening News*, 14 December 1957.

253 *ITN News*, 16 December 1988.*The Times*, 24 December 1931.

254 *News at Ten*, ITV, 13 December 1973, 18 December 1974.

255 Ipsos MORI, 'The dentist's chair or Christmas shopping – you decide!', 16 November 2000: https://www.ipsos-mori.com/researchpublications/ researcharchive/1504/The-Dentists-Chair-Or-Christmas-Shopping-You-Decide.aspx.

256 *The Times*, 8 December 1973.

257 Benson, *Rise of Consumer Society*, 233–4.

258 Hugh Cunningham, *Children and Childhood in Western Society since 1500* (Harlow: Longman, 1995), 176–7.

259 Benson, *Affluence and Authority*, 27–8.

260 Selina Todd, 'Affluence, class and Crown Street: Reinvestigating the post-war working class', *Contemporary British History* 22, no. 4 (2008): 501–18, 513.

261 Lawrence, 'Class, "affluence"'.

262 Peter Kandela, 'Post-Christmas traumatic syndrome', *Lancet* 353, no. 9149 (23 January 1999).

263 *Coronation Street*, ITV, 25 December 1987.

264 For reports of families in this situation see *The Times*, 22–24 December 1976.

265 Zweig, *Labour, Life and Poverty*, ch. 14.

266 Collins, *London Belongs to Me*, 11.

267 *Sussex Agricultural Express*, 24 December 1954.

268 MO day survey 25 December 1937, respondent 368.

269 *Terry and June*, BBC1, 23 December 1980.

270 Lady Cynthia Asquith, *Diaries, 1915-1918* (London: Hutchison, 1968), 384.

271 Ipsos MORI, 'Homeless at Christmas', 20 December 2002: https://www. ipsos-mori.com/researchpublications/researcharchive/985/Homeless-At-Christmas.aspx.

272 Edwina Currie, *Diaries 1987-1992* (London: Little Brown, 2002), 26.

273 *Guardian*, 21 December 2013. *Sky News*, 25 December 2012.

Chapter 2

1 'When the generations meet', *Quiver*, December 1922.

2 *The Times*, 24 December 1960.

3 Ernest Jones, *Essays in Applied Psycho Analysis vol. II* (London: Hogarth Press, 1951), 223.

4 *The Guardian*, 9 December 1957.

5 Do You Remember? Christmas When You Were Growing Up: http://forums.doyouremember.co.uk/threads/7865-Christmas-When-You-Were-Growing-Up/.

6 Mass Observation (hereafter MO) day survey 25 December 1937, respondents 20, 225 and 231.

7 Gavin Weightman and Steve Humphries, *Christmas Past* (London: Sidgwick & Jackson, 1987), 85.

8 MO day survey 25 December 1937, respondents 345 and 368.

9 Weightman and Humphries, *Christmas Past*, 91, 95.

10 'Christmas and New Year's Eve, 1941', MO file report 1030, 11.

11 Interview with Don Thompson (b. 1933), British Library: C790/38.

12 MO day survey 25 December 1937, respondent 573.

13 Weightman and Humphries, *Christmas Past*, 97. MO diarist 5076, 26 December 1946.

14 Madeline Kerr, *People of Ship Street* (London: Routledge, 1958), 108.

15 Jeremy Seabrook, *Working-class Childhood* (London: Victor Gollancz, 1982), 121.

16 Jack Jones, *Me and Mine: Further Chapters in the Autobiography of Jack Jones* (London: Hamish Hamilton, 1946), 97.

17 Michael Young and Peter Willmott, *Family and Kinship in East London* (1957; London: Routledge, 1962).

18 Raymond Firth, Jane Hubert and Anthony Forge, *Families and their Relatives: Kinship in a Middle-Class Sector of London* (London: Routledge, 1969), ch. 8.

19 Ferdynand Zweig, *The Worker in an Affluent Society: Family Life and Industry* (London: Heinemann, 1961), 115.

20 A. H. Halsey, *Trends in British Society since 1900* (London: Macmillan, 1972), 55. Office for National Statistics, *Family Size in 2012* (2012).

21 *New Statesman*, 5 December 1986. For an earlier story of a family row over the issue see *Daily Mirror*, 23 November 1957. For the issue reaching the problems page see *Woman's Weekly*, 6 December 1930.

22 Firth et al., *Families and their Relatives*, 260–1.

23 Hugh Cunningham, *The Invention of Childhood* (London: BBC, 2006), 213.

24 Robert J. Wybrow, *Britain Speaks Out, 1937-87: A Social History as Seen Through the Gallup Data* (London: Macmillan, 1989), 32. UK Data Service: SN: 69038 National Opinion Polls National Political Surveys; December 1969.

25 *New Society*, 25 December 1975.

26 MO day survey 25 December 1937, respondent 20.

27 MO Autumn directive 1986, respondent B1106.

28 Barabara Pym, *No Fond Return of Love* (London: Granada, 1961), 119.

29 John O'Farrell, *The Man Who Forgot His Wife* (London: Transworld, 2012), 177.

30 Michael Bloch, *James Lees-Milne Diaries, 1942-54* (London: John Murray, 2006), 375.

31 MO day survey 25 December 1937, respondent 21.

32 John Benson, *Prime Time: A History of the Middle Aged in Twentieth-Century Britain* (London: Routledge, 1997), 101–5, 140.

33 Roy Strong, *The Roy Strong Diaries, 1967-1987* (London: Weidenfeld and Nicolson, 1997), 50.

34 See, for example, the entries in Michael Bloch, *James Lees-Milne, Diaries, 1984-1997* (London: John Murray, 2008).

35 Peter Kandela, 'Post-Christmas traumatic syndrome', *Lancet* 353, no. 9149, (23 January 1999): 336.

36 J. A. R. Pimlott, *The Englishman's Christmas* (Hassocks: Harvester, 1978), 171. *The Times*, 8 December 1975.

37 *Keep Safe This Christmas* (NHS, 2012), 6.

38 *The Guardian*, 21 December 2013.

39 Mrs Raymond Lee, 'Letter or spirit?', *Quiver*, December 1915.

40 For example, 'Yule log frolics', *Quiver*, December 1925.

41 Sally McKechnie and Caroline Tynan, 'Social meanings in Christmas consumption: An exploratory study of UK celebrants' consumption rituals', *Journal of Consumer Behaviour* 5, no. 2 (2006): 130–44.

42 Agatha Christie, *Hercule Poirot's Christmas* (1938; London: Harper 2013), 75.

43 On family tension see Elizabeth Roberts, *Women and Families: An Oral History, 1940-1970* (Oxford: Blackwell, 1995), ch. 10.

44 Jennifer Mason and Stewart Muir, 'Conjuring up traditions: Atmospheres, eras and family Christmases', *The Sociological Review* 61, no. 3 (2013): 607–29, 619.

45 *Daily Mirror*, 21 December 2007.

46 MO day survey 25 December 1937, respondent 171.

47 Ipsos MORI, 'Christmas procrastination', November 1997: https://www.ipsos-mori.com/researchpublications/researcharchive/2121/Christmas-Procrastination.aspx.

48 Tim Kasser and Kennon M. Sheldon, 'What makes for a merry Christmas?', *Journal of Happiness Studies* 3 (2002): 313–29.

49 On memories of the dead providing family identity see John R. Gillis, *A World of their Own Making: Myth, Ritual, and the Quest for Family Values* (Cambridge, MA: Harvard University Press, 1996), ch 10.

50 *Picture Post*, 25 December 1948.

51   Neil Armstrong, *Christmas in Nineteenth-Century England* (Manchester: Manchester University Press, 2010), 177, ch. 3.

52   Neil Armstrong, 'The Christmas season and the Protestant churches in England, c. 1870-1914', *Journal of Ecclesiastical History* 62, no. 4 (2011): 744–62.

53   Cunningham, *Invention of Childhood*, 203–4.

54   Muriel Wrinch, 'Christmas and the child mind', *Quiver*, December 1925.

55   *Evening Standard*, 9 December 1933.

56   'Happiness in Wartime', MO file report 1870. 'Christmas and New Year's Eve, 1941', MO file report 1030.

57   For example, MO day survey 25 December 1937, respondent 368.

58   *Church Times*, 22 December 1933, 30 December 1932.

59   For example, Zweig, *Affluent Worker*, 23–3. For oral evidence see Roberts, *Women and Families*, 142.

60   Selina Todd, 'Affluence, class and Crown Street: Reinvestigating the post-war working class', *Contemporary British History* 22, no. 4 (2008): 501–18, 509. Cunningham, *Invention of Childhood*, 213–15. Young and Willmott, *Family and Kinship*, 27–30.

61   On changing attitudes to child psychology and well-being see Roberts, *Women and Families*, ch. 8.

62   Quoted in Weightman and Humphries, *Christmas Past*, 172.

63   *The Times*, 17 September, 5, 7, 10 October 1966.

64   Cunningham, *Invention of Childhood*, 224–6, 229.

65   M. S. Burnett and D. A. Lunsford, 'Conceptualizing guilt in the consumer decision-making process', *Journal of Consumer Marketing* 11, no. 3 (1994): 33–43. David Hamlin, 'The structures of toy consumption: Bourgeois domesticity and the demand for toys in nineteenth-century Germany', *Journal of Social History* 36, no. 4 (2003): 857–9, 858–9. For a similar point in a contemporary context see Michael Laroche, Gad Saad, Mark Cleveland and Elizabeth Browne, 'Gender differences in information search strategies for a Christmas gift', *Journal of Consumer Marketing* 17, no. 6 (2000), 500–22, 514.

66   John Morgans, *Journey of a Lifetime: From the Diaries of John Morgans* (Llanidloes: John Morgans, 2008), 14.

67   Elizabeth Roberts, *A Woman's Place: An Oral History of Working-Class Women 1890-1940* (Oxford: Blackwell, 1984), 24–5.

68   William Woodruff, *The Road to Nab End: An Extraordinary Northern Childhood* (1993; London: Abacus, 2002), 18, 129.

69   Weightman and Humphries, *Christmas Past*, 168.

70   Daisy Meadows, *Holly the Christmas Fairy* (London: Orchard Books, 2004), 26.

71   Lady Cynthia Asquith, *Diaries, 1915-1918* (London: Hutchison, 1968), 115.

72   'Christmas and the hump', *Saturday Review*, 25 December 1915.

73 William Sansom, *Christmas* (London: Weidenfeld & Nicholson, 1968), 248.

74 *Evening Standard*, 9 December 1933. *Daily Mail*, 24 December 1921.

75 *Picture Post*, 22 December 1951. *Daily Mirror*, 24 December 1951.

76 Sir Osbert Sitwell, 'A bunch of snowdrops', *South Wales Spectator*, December 1964.

77 Sydney Frankenburg, *Common Sense in the Nursery* (London: Jonathan Cape, 1934 edn.), 144–5.

78 For memories see *New Society*, 18 December 1987.

79 Thomas Blaikie, *Blaikie's Guide to Modern Manners* (London: Fourth Estate, 2005), 217.

80 *Daily Mirror*, 24 December 1951.

81 Chris Mullin, *A View from the Foothills: The Diaries of Chris Mullin* (London: Profile, 2010), 340.

82 *The Times,* 24 December 1969.

83 For example see *Daily Mirror*, 20 December 1916.

84 Michael Davie, ed., *The Diaries of Evelyn Waugh* (London: Weidenfeld and Nicolson, 1976), 640.

85 Norman Longmate, *How We Lived Then: A History of Everyday Life During the Second World War* (London, 1973), 186.

86 *Yorkshire Post and Leeds Intelligencer*, 23 December 1953.

87 David Fowler, *The First Teenagers: The Lifestyle of Young Wage-earners in Interwar Britain* (London: Woburn, 1995).

88 MO day survey 25 December 1937, respondent 116.

89 For example see the 1970s item on 'worst Christmas presents' in Lorna Russell, ed., *The Best of Jackie Annual* (London: Prion, 2006), 130.

90 Davie, *Diaries of Evelyn Waugh*, 46. On young unmarried people disliking Christmas because they are bored with their families see *Yorkshire Post*, 24 December 1937.

91 William E. Thompson and Joseph V. Hickey, 'Myth, identity, and social interaction: Encountering Santa Claus at the mall', *Qualitative Sociology* 12, no. 4 (1989): 371–89.

92 Boy Calendar 1980. Reproduced in Lara Maiklem and Lorna Russell, eds, *More of the Best of Jackie Annual* (London: Prion, 2007), 13.

93 *Christmas Night With the Stars*, BBC1, 25 December 1964.

94 *Daily Mail*, 24 December 1935. *Tamworth Herald*, 22 December 1934.

95 *Coronation Street*, ITV, 25 December 1987.

96 Eileen Fischer and Stephen J. Arnold, 'More than a labor of love: Gender roles and Christmas gift shopping', *Journal of Consumer Research* 17, no. 3 (1990): 333–45.

97 Karal Ann Marling, *Merry Christmas! Celebrating America's Greatest Holiday* (Cambridge: Harvard University Press, 2001), 354–5.

98 Advertisement for Defiant kitchen table, *Nash's and Pall Mall Magazine*, December 1925.

99 *Woman's Weekly*, 6 December 1930.

100 Pam Schweitzer, ed., *All Our Christmases: A Book of Christmas Memories by Greenwich Pensioners* (London: Age Exchange Theatre Company, 1983), 23.

101 *Woman's Magazine*, December 1930.

102 *Woman's Own*, 5 December 1936, 10 December 1958.

103 *Woman's Own Christmas Annual*, 1965, 15.

104 *Daily Mirror*, 20 December 1949. *The Times*, 14 December 1966.

105 Pamela Westland, *The Best Christmas Ever* (London: Southwater, 2010), 54. Anthea Turner, *The Perfect Christmas* (London: Virgin, 2008), 16.

106 Joanna Brewis and Samantha Warren, 'Have yourself a merry little Christmas? Organizing Christmas in women's magazines past and present', *Organization* 18, no. 6 (2011): 747–62.

107 Jane Asher, *Good Living at Christmas* (London: BBC, 1998), 6.

108 *Woman's Own Christmas Annual*, 1964, 24.

109 Alan D. Gear and Barry L. Freestone, *Christmas Crafts* (London: Collins and Brown, 2005), 6. Polly Piner, *Making Christmas Table Decorations* (Tunbridge Wells: Search Press, 2006), 4. Westland, *Best Christmas Ever*, 7.

110 *Daily Mirror*, 17 December 1999.

111 Richard Eyre (b. 1943) in *New Statesman*, 25 December to 1 January 2000.

112 Barbara Castle, *The Castle Diaries, 1974-76* (London: Weidenfeld and Nicolson, 1980), 261.

113 Valerie Wright-St Clair, Clare Hocking, Wannipa Bunrayong, Soisuda Vittayakorn and Phuonjai Rattakorn, 'Older New Zealand women doing the work of Christmas: A recipe for identity formation', *Sociological Review* 53, no. 2 (2005): 332–50.

114 Leslie Bella, *The Christmas Imperative: Leisure Family and Women's Work* (Halifax: Fernwood, 1992).

115 McKechnie and Tynan, 'Social meanings in Christmas consumption', 137.

116 Turner, *Perfect Christmas*, 5.

117 *The Christmas Book for the New World Cook* (1934), John Johnson collection: Gas and Gas Appliances 3 (38).

118 *Woman's Own Christmas Annual*, 1964, 27.

119 MO autumn directive 1986, respondent C108.

120 Paul Addison, *No Turning Back: The Peacetime Revolutions of Post-War Britain* (Oxford: Oxford University Press, 2010), 318.

121 *Daily Mirror*, 14 December 2004.

122 Claire Langhamer, *Women's Leisure in England, 1920-60* (Manchester: Manchester University Press, 2000), 149–50.

123 Roberts, *Women and Families*, 36–40.

124 Joanna Bourke, *Working-Class Cultures in Britain, 1890-1960* (London: Routledge, 1994), 69–70. Kate Elliott and Wendy Cope, eds, *The Swansea Wartime Diary of Laurie Latchford, 1940-41* (Newport: South Wales Record Society, 2010), 205.

125 MO day survey, 25 December 1937, respondent 126.

126 Jeremy Hardy in *New Statesman*, 25 December to 1 January 2000.

127 Morrissey, *Autobiography* (London: Penguin, 2013), 14.

128 MO winter directive 1986, respondent B1215.

129 For this argument with regard to late twentieth-century shopping see Daniel Miller, *A Theory of Shopping* (London: Polity, 1998).

130 Ian Gazeley and Claire Langhamer, 'The meanings of happiness in Mass Observation's Bolton', *History Workshop Journal* 75 (2012): 159–89.

131 Quoted in Brewis and Warren, 'Have yourself a merry little Christmas'.

132 Norman Collins, *London Belongs to Me* (London: Collins, 1945), 35.

133 Jilly Cooper, *How to Survive Christmas* (London: Methuen, 1986), 25.

134 India Knight, *Comfort and Joy* (London: Penguin, 2010), 10.

135 *Daily Mirror*, 10 December 2005.

136 Caroline Tynan and Sally McKechnie, 'Sacralising the profane: Creating meaning with Christmas consumption in the UK', *European Advances in Consumer Research* 7 (2006): 182–8, 187.

137 On the criticism see *Independent*, 16 November 2012. For responses see netmums.com, 'Has anyone seen the Asda Christmas ad? Do you think it is sexist?': http://www.netmums.com/coffeehouse/general-coffeehouse-chat-514/news-current-affairs-topical-discussion-12/846508-has-anyone-seen-asda-christmas-ad-do-you-think-sexist.html.

138 For Christmas making women feel unappreciated see Hazel Wheeler, *Crackers at Christmas: The Festive Trials of a Yorkshire Housewife* (Stroud: Amberley, 2010), 88–9.

139 Tony Benn, *Against the Tide: Diaries, 1973-76* (London: Arrow, 1989), 484.

140 John Tosh, *A Man's Place: Masculinity and the Middle-Class Home in Victorian England* (New Haven: Yale University Press, 1999).

141 For example *Daily Mirror*, 30 November 1922, 27 December 1919.

142 'This goodwill business', *Saturday Review*, 25 December 1937. The author refused to sign his name.

143 MO day survey, 25 December 1937, respondent 490.

144 *New Statesman*, 25 December 1926.

145 John Tosh, *A Man's Place: Masculinity and the Middle-Class Home in Victorian England* (New Haven: Yale University Press, 1999). Julie-Marie Strange, 'Fatherhood, furniture and the inter-personal dynamics of working-class homes, c. 1870–1914', *Urban History* 40, no. 2 (2013): 271–86.

146 Roberts, *Women and Families*, 154.

147   For an overview see Laura King, 'Hidden fathers? The significance of fatherhood in mid-twentieth-century Britain', *Contemporary British History* 26, no. 1 (2012): 25–46.

148   Geoffrey Gorer, *Exploring English Character* (London: Criterion, 1955), 138–9.

149   Gary Cross, ed., *Worktowners at Blackpool: Mass Observation and Popular Leisure in the 1930s* (London: Routledge, 1990), 37–70. Gillis, *World of their Own Making*, 104.

150   J. R. R. Tolkien, *Letters from Father Christmas* (London: HarperCollins, 2004).

151   Pam Schweitzer, ed., *All Our Christmases: A Book of Christmas Memories by Greenwich Pensioners* (London: Age Exchange Theatre Company, 1983), 22.

152   For a description of men taking over a model railway from children see MO day survey 25 December 1937, respondent 170.

153   Laura King, '"Now you see a great many men pushing their pram proudly': Family-orientated masculinity represented and experienced in mid-twentieth-century Britain', *Cultural and Social History* 10, no. 4 (2013): 599–617, 609.

154   Roberts, *Women and families*, 40–1.

155   Lyn Briggs, *A Shropshire Christmas* (Stroud: The History Press, 1993), 111.

156   Martin Francis, 'The domestication of the male? Recent research on nineteenth- and twentieth-century British masculinity', *Historical Journal* 45, no. 3 (2002), 637–52, 640.

157   *Belfast Telegraph*, 21 December 1922, 27 December 1926.

158   Michael Palin, *Diaries 1969-1979: The Python Years* (London: Weidenfeld & Nicolson, 2006), 358.

159   See the entries in Alistair Campbell, *The Alistair Campbell Diaries* (London: Hutchison, 2010–12), 3 vols.

160   Ruth Winstone, ed., *Tony Benn: Free at Last! Diaries 1991-2001* (London: Hutchison, 2002), 575.

161   Wheeler, *Crackers at Christmas*, 40.

162   Richard Broad and Suzie Fleming, eds, *Nella's Last War: The Second World War Diaries of Housewife, 49* (London: Profile, 2006), 262.

163   King, 'Now you see a great many men'.

164   *Woman's Own*, 19 December 1936. Armstrong, *Christmas in Nineteenth-century England*, 173–5. *Daily Mail*, 26 December 1934. 'Is Christmas what it was?', *Saturday Review*, 5 December 1931.

165   Ralph Harold Bretheron, 'Christmas changes', *Saturday Review*, 22 December 1934.

166   *The Times*, 17 December 1934. *Chelmsford Chronicle*, 29 December 1950. *Daily Mirror*, 22 December 1927.

167   *The Times*, 28 December 1955, 24 December 1971. *ITV News*, 20 December 1996.

168   *The Times*, 22 December 1958.

169 Pimlott, *Englishman's Christmas*, 169.

170 Lynne Reid Banks, *The L-Shaped Room* (1960; London: Vintage, 2004), 186.

171 Barbara Pym, *Quartet in Autumn* (1977; London: Bello, 2013), 71–3.

172 *New Society*, 20/27 December 1979.

173 Ipsos MORI, 'Three calls a minute expected by the Samaritans at Xmas', 11 December 2000: https://www.ipsos-mori.com/researchpublications/ researcharchive/1654/Three-Calls-A-Minute-Expected-By-The-Samaritans-At-Xmas.aspx.

174 MO day survey 25 December 1937, respondent 182. Heath cemetery, 25 December 1937, MO Worktown collection box 27.

175 D. S. Higgins, ed., *The Private Diaries of Sir H. Rider Haggard, 1914-1925* (London: Cassell, 1980), 88.

176 James Bowen, *Bob: No Ordinary Cat* (London: Hodder, 2013), 150.

177 Russell Davies, ed., *The Kenneth Williams Diaries* (London: HarperCollins, 1994), 138.

178 *The Times*, 28 December 1981.

179 Benson, *Prime Time*, 105–6.

180 Sansom, *Christmas*, 234.

181 MO Autumn 1986 directive, respondent R1321.

182 *Woman's Own Christmas*, 1962, 43.

183 *The Times*, 24 December 1974, 22 December 1966.

184 *The Sun*, 19 December 2011.

185 Neel Burton, 'Is suicide more common at Christmas time?', *Psychology Today*, 23 December 2012.

186 Connelly, *Christmas*, 135.

187 MO day survey 25 December 1937, respondent 578.

188 *Daily Mirror*, 24 December 1951.

189 Friends of the Elderly, 'What does Christmas mean to you?': http://www.fote.org.uk/xmas/.

190 *ITV Lunchtime News*, 26 December 1955.

191 *Woman's Own Christmas*, 1962, 69.

192 *New Society*, 25 December 1975.

193 Hamlin, 'Structures of toy consumption', 857.

194 Theodore Caplow, 'Christmas gifts and kin networks', *American Sociological Review* 47, no. 3 (1982): 383–92.

195 MO day surveys, 25 December 1937 and 15 December 1938, respondents 473 and 573.

196 ONS, 'How popular is your birthday?' http://visual.ons.gov.uk/how-popular-is-your-birthday/.

197 For example, 'Shops', 12 December 1938, MO Worktown collection box 31. *Daily Mirror*, 14 December 1963.

198 'On present giving to friends', *Nash's Pall Mall Magazine*, December 1934.

199 Lady Clanmore, 'It's the thought that counts', *South Wales Spectator*, December 1964.

200 MO day survey 25 December 1937, respondent 170.

201 MO winter directive 1986, respondent R470. Mary Searle-Chatterjee, 'Christmas cards and the construction of social relations in Britain today', in *Christmas Unwrapped*, ed. Daniel Miller (Oxford: Oxford University Press, 1993): 176–92, 185.

202 Gillis, *World of their Own Making*, xvii.

203 'A Cosy Christmas', *The Fourth Girl Annual* (London: Hulton Press, 1955), 146.

204 *Picture Post*, 28 December 1946.

205 'Christmas and New Year's Eve, 1941', MO file report 1030. 'Happiness in Wartime', MO file report 1870.

206 Adam Kuper, 'The English Christmas and the family: Time out and alternative realities' and Searle-Chatterjee, 'Christmas and the construction of social relations', both in *Unwrapping Christmas*, ed. Daniel Miller (Oxford: Oxford University Press, 1993).

207 Roberts, *Women and Families*, 41–3. On families' worries about the lack of time they spent together see Gillis, *World of their Own Making*, ch. 11.

Chapter 3

1 H. Warner Allen, 'A War-time Christmas', *Saturday Review*, 22 December 1934.

2 P. G. Woodhouse, *Plum Pie* (London: Hodder and Stroughton, 1966), 13.

3 For example, see Nancy Mitford, *Christmas Pudding* (1932; London: Capuchin, 2012), 110.

4 Claire Langhamer, 'The meanings of home in postwar Britain', *Journal of Contemporary History* 40, no. 2 (2005): 341–62, 347.

5 J. M. Golby and A. W. Purdue, *The Making of the Modern Christmas* (Stroud: Sutton, 2nd edn., 2000), 90–4. On the interaction between advertising and ritual see Cele Otnes and Linda M. Scott, 'Something old, something new: Exploring the interaction between ritual and advertising', *The Journal of Advertising* 25, no. 1 (1996): 33–50.

6 For an introduction to the issues see Paul Addison, *No Turning Back: The Peacetime Revolutions of Post-War Britain* (Oxford: Oxford University Press, 2010), 176–88.

7 For this argument on holidays see Richard Hoggart, *The Uses of Literacy* (1957; New Brunswick: Transaction, 1992), 109.

8 Gerd Baumann, 'Ritual implicates "others": Rereading Durkheim in a plural society', in *Understanding Rituals*, ed. Daniel de Coppet (London: Routledge, 1992), 97–116, 98.

9 *The Times*, 3 November 1971.

10   For memories of this from the early part of the century see Lyn Briggs, *A Shropshire Christmas* (Stroud: History Press, 1993), 109.

11   George Buday, *The History of the Christmas Card* (London: Spring Books, [1954] 1964).

12   For example, Oak Tree Christmas Card Manufacturing Company (Accrington), The National Archives: BT34/2412/127498.

13   *The Times*, 21 December 1923, 20 December 1924.

14   For observations on cost see Miss Read, 'Village Christmas [1966]', in *A Country Christmas* (London: Orion, 2006), 4.

15   Margaret Ashby, *A Hertfordshire Christmas* (Stroud: Sutton, 1998), 139.

16   *Picture Post*, 21 November 1942.

17   J. A. R. Pimlott, *The Englishman's Christmas: A Social History* (Hassocks: Harvester, 1978), 161. *Sunday Times*, 19 December 1993.

18   *The Times*, 16 December 1952, 3 December 1956.

19   Robert J. Wybrow, *Britain Speaks Out, 1937-87: A Social History as Seen Through the Gallup Data* (London: Macmillan, 1989), 147. *The Times*, 12 December 1985.

20   Mass Observation (hereafter MO) winter directive December 1983, respondent R470.

21   Peter Kandela, 'Confused about Christmas', *Lancet*, 20–27 December 2003. *Daily Mail*, 24 December 1935.

22   Hoggart, *Uses of Literacy*, 98. MO day survey, 25 December 1937, respondent 82. MO winter directive December 1983, respondents G226 and W663.

23   Peter Donnelly, ed., *Mrs Milburn's Diaries: An Englishwoman's Day-to-Day Reflections 1939-45* (London: Fontana, 1980), 199.

24   Norman Collins, *London Belongs to Me* (London: Collins, 1945), 12.

25   On sentimental songs see Hoggart, *Uses of Literacy*, 109–23.

26   Family Action, *Breaking the Bank: A Cut Price Christmas for Low-Income Families* (London: Family Action, 2011), 9.

27   Pimlott, *Englishman's Christmas*, 106, 120.

28   MO winter directive December 1983, respondent G226.

29   Buday, *History of the Christmas Card*, 87–99.

30   'Christmas in war time', *Quiver*, December 1914.

31   *The Times*, 24 December 1954.

32   Llew and Pam Smith, *Glad Tidings of Struggle and Strife: A History of Protest Christmas Cards* (Stroud: Fonthill, 2012).

33   *The Times*, 28 November 1977. *Daily Mirror*, 27 November 1962.

34   *Daily Mail*, 11 December 2010.

35   *The British Stationer* 13, no. 12 (May 1933). *The Times*, 16 December 1952.

36   Buday, *History of the Christmas Card*, 188–9. The last 19 were miscellaneous.

37   *Daily Mirror*, 27 November 1962. *The Times*, 18 November 1966.

38   Pimlott, *Englishman's Christmas*, 161. *The Times*, 18 November 1966.

39   Mary Searle-Chatterjee, 'Christmas cards and the construction of social relations in Britain today', in *Christmas Unwrapped*, ed. Daniel Miller (Oxford: Oxford University Press, 1993), 176–92, 181.

40   *The Times*, 28 December 1971.

41   'Christmas cards', *The Athenaeum*, 2 January 1920.

42   MO day survey 25 December 1937, respondent 408. *The Times*, 5 December 1950.

43   Kathryn Ann Lindskoog, *Surprised by C.S. Lewis, George MacDonald and Dante: An Array of Original Discoveries* (Georgia: Mercer University Press, 2001), 24.

44   *The Spectator*, 22 December 1967.

45   Hoggart, *Uses of Literacy*, 109.

46   *The Spectator*, 31 December 1948.

47   Colin Howard, *Cotswold Days* (London: Blackie, 1937), 274. MO day survey, December 1938, respondent 707.

48   E. Vaughan-Smith, 'A Christmas dilemma', *Quiver*, December 1924.

49   *The Times*, 26 November 1962.

50   E. F. Benson, *Mapp and Lucia* (1935; London: Penguin, 2004), 228–9.

51   MO winter directive December 1983, respondent G226.

52   *Coronation Street*, ITV, 26 December 1967.

53   *Bath Chronicle and Weekly Gazette*, 8 December 1934.

54   *The Times*, 9 November 1959. William Sansom, *Christmas* (London: Weidenfeld and Nicolson, 1968), 136–7.

55   *The Times*, 27 November 1975. *Western Daily Press*, 28 December 1936.

56   *The Times*, 5, 7, 9 January 1961.

57   Searle-Chatterjee, 'Christmas cards', 178.

58   *Woman's Weekly*, 16 December 1950, 3 December 1960. *Sunday Times*, 19 December 1993.

59   Sally McKechnie and Caroline Tynan, 'Social meanings in Christmas consumption: An exploratory study of UK celebrants' consumption rituals', *Journal of Consumer Behaviour* 5, no. 2 (2006): 130–44, 139.

60   Thomas Blaikie, *Balikie's Guide to Modern Manners* (London: Fourth Estate, 2005), 219–21.

61   *The Economist*, 24 December 2013.

62   Steve Roud, *The Penguin Guide to Superstitions of Britain and Ireland* (London: Penguin, 2003), 83, 85. Susan Drury, 'Customs and beliefs associated with Christmas evergreens: A preliminary survey', *Folklore* 98, no. 2 (1987): 194–9.

63   G. Clarke Nuttall, 'Christmas decorations', *Quiver*, December 1921.

64   Cledwyn Hughes, *The Different Drummer and the Inn Closes for Christmas* (London: Pilot, 1947), 225.

65 *Portsmouth Evening News*, 16 December 1938.

66 Pimlott, *Englishman's Christmas*, 140.

67 Laurence Whistler, *The English Festivals* (London: William Heinemann, 1947), 46.

68 Iona and Peter Opie, *The Lore and Language of Schoolchildren* (Oxford: Clarendon, 1959), 287, 335.

69 *Picture Post*, 17 December 1938.

70 Barry Pain, 'Christmas as usual', *Nash's and Pall Mall Magazine*, December 1925.

71 *Evening Telegraph*, 20 December 1927.

72 Whistler, *English Festivals*, 19.

73 Kate Elliott and Wendy Cope, eds, *The Swansea Wartime Diary of Laurie Latchford, 1940-41* (Newport: South Wales Record Society, 2010), 203–4.

74 Arthur Barton, *The Penny World: A Boyhood Recalled* (London: Hutchison, 1969), 26.

75 Lilian Beckworth, *About My Father's Business* (London: Arrow, 1973).

76 Anne Eyles, *In the Shadow of the Steelworks: Reminiscences of a Splott Childhood in the 1930s* (Cardiff: O'Sullivan Trust, 1997), 49. Katheleen Dayus, *Her People* (London: Virago, 1982), 46.

77 Hoggart, *Uses of Literacy*, 105, 109.

78 *Woman's Weekly*, 17 December 1960. Sansom, *Christmas*, 139.

79 *Daily Express*, 12 December 1956.

80 Daniel Miller, 'A theory of Christmas', in *Unwrapping Christmas*, ed. Daniel Miller (Oxford: Oxford University Press, 1993), 32.

81 Quoted in BBC News, 'Mass observing the season', 26 December 2012: http://news.bbc.co.uk/today/hi/today/newsid_9780000/9780826.stm.

82 Christmas Questionnaire 1938, MO Worktown collection box 31.

83 For an American consideration of DIY and Christmas in the 1950s see Karal Ann Marling, *Merry Christmas! Celebrating America's Greatest Holiday* (Cambridge, MA: Harvard University Press, 2001), 36.

84 Countess of Bandon, 'Christmas – Then and now', *South Wales Spectator*, December 1961.

85 *Daily Mail*, 22 December 1924, 22 December 1934.

86 *Gloucestershire Echo*, 29 November 1950. *Do it Yourself*, ITV, 3 December 1955.

87 Mary Norden, *Christmas Details* (London: HarperCollins, 2000).

88 Emma Hardy, *Tree Top Decorations: 25 Dazzling Ideas for Angels, Stars, Ribbons and More* (London: Cico, 2008), 9.

89 The Christmas Decorators: http://www.thechristmasdecorators.com/faqs.html.

90 *Tamworth Herald*, 22 December 1934.

91 McKechnie and Tynan, 'Social meanings in Christmas consumption', 137.

92 See replies to Christmas questionnaire 1938, MO Worktown collection box 31.

93 *The Spectator*, 22 December 1967.

94 Pimlott, *Englishman's Christmas*, 165.

95 Richard Broad and Suzie Fleming, eds, *Nella's Last War: The Second World War Diaries of Housewife, 49* (London: Profile, 2006), 258.

96 Gyles Brandreth, *Brandreth's Christmas Book* (Wokingham: Van Nostrand Reinhold, 1975), 12.

97 *The Times*, 19 December 1984.

98 McKechnie and Tynan, 'Social meanings in Christmas consumption'.

99 Ashby, *Hertfordshire Christmas*, 63.

100 Whistler, *English Festivals*, 43.

101 Lynne Reid Banks, *The L-Shaped Room* (1960; London: Vinatge, 2004), 187.

102 *ITV Late Evening News*, 20 December 1964.

103 BBC News, 'Are Christmas decorations too tacky?', 30 December 2004: http://news.bbc.co.uk/1/hi/talking_point/4104297.stm. *King of Christmas Lights*, Channel 4, 19 December 2011.

104 Tim Edensor and Steve Millington, 'Illuminations, class identities and the contested landscapes of Christmas', *Sociology* 43, no. 1 (2003): 103–21.

105 Neil Armstrong, *Christmas in Nineteenth-century England* (Manchester: Manchester University Press, 2010), 52. On the history of the tree see Bernd Brunner, *Inventing the Christmas Tree* (New Haven: Yale University Press, 2012).

106 Hardy, *Tree Top Decorations*, 7.

107 *The Times*, 27 December 1918, 17 December 1926.

108 *The Spectator*, 17 December 1937. *The Times*, 28 December 1949.

109 MO day survey 25 December 1937, respondent 385.

110 See replies to Christmas questionnaire 1938, MO Worktown collection box 31.

111 *Evening Telegraph*, 8 December 1930, 12 December 1946.

112 Pam Schweitzer, ed., *All Our Christmases: A Book of Christmas Memories by Greenwich Pensioners* (London: Age Exchange Theatre Company, 1983), 5. *Daily Mail*, 20 November 1933. *The Times*, 24 December 1952.

113 *Daily Mirror*, 25 November 1924.

114 *Picture Post*, 14 December 1946. *Daily Mirror*, 5 December 1951.

115 MO diarist 5076, 22 December 1951. Wybrow, *Britain Speaks Out*, 32, 147.

116 Theodore Caplow, 'Rule enforcement without visible means: Christmas gift giving in Middletown', *American Journal of Sociology* 89, no. 6 (1984), 1306–23.

117 *The Times*, 2 December 1970.

118 *News at Ten*, ITV, 2 December 1971. *The Times*, 24 February 1932. *Portsmouth Evening News*, 5 December 1938.

119   See the memories in *New Statesman*, 13 December 2004. James Hewitt, *The Christmas Tree* (Lulu.com, 2007), 34.

120   *The Times*, 15 December 1984. British Christmas Tree Growers Association: www.bctga.co.uk/about-bctga.html.

121   McKechnie and Tynan, 'Social meanings in Christmas consumption'.

122   *Daily Telegraph*, 24 November 2009.

123   *Exeter and Plymouth Gazette*, 29 November 1927.

124   For memories of this see Briggs, *Shropshire Christmas*, 114.

125   Robert T. Iwamasa, Robert Iwamasa and Patrick J. Fay, *The History of the Christmas Figural Light Bulb* (Morrisville: Lulu, 2006). *Portsmouth Evening News*, 5 December 1938.

126   Rowland Grey, 'The charm of the Christmas tree', *Quiver*, December 1925.

127   Family Action, *Breaking the Bank*, 10.

128   Marling, *Merry Christmas*, 190.

129   *Daily Mirror*, 14 December 2004.

130   McKechnie and Tynan, 'Social meanings in Christmas consumption'.

131   Family Action, *Breaking the Bank*, 9–10.

132   Marling, *Merry Christmas*, 42.

133   *Derby Daily Telegraph*, 22 December 1949.

134   MO autumn directive 1986, respondent B1106.

135   *John O'Groat Journal*, 9 January 1852.

136   Armstrong, *Christmas in Nineteenth-century England*, 66.

137   *Dinesydd Cymreig*, 23 December 1914. *Y Cymro*, 24 December 1919.

138   *Llan*, 26 December 1919.

139   William Muir Auld, *Christmas Traditions* (New York: Macmillan, 1931), 159.

140   Schweitzer, *All Our Christmases*, 4. Ashby, *Hertfordshire Christmas*, 63. Gavin Weightman and Steve Humphries, *Christmas Past* (London: Sidgwick & Jackson, 1987), 149. Opie and Opie, *Lore and Language of Schoolchildren*, 286.

141   *Gloucester Citizen*, 20 December 1929. *Aberdeen Journal*, 23 December 1948. *Lancashire Evening Post*, 25 December 1946.

142   *Yorkshire Post and Leeds Intelligencer*, 27 December 1952. *The Times*, 8 December 1966.

143   Briggs, *Shropshire Christmas*, 110.

144   *Gaumont Graphic*, 20 December 1923.

145   MO day survey, 25 December 1937, respondent 47.

146   *The Times*, 24 December 1970.

147   Opie and Opie, *Lore and Language of Schoolchildren*, 285.

148   Mavis Doriel Hay, *The Santa Klaus Murder* (1936; London: British Library, 2013), 63–4. A. Lowndes Moir, *Christmas Customs* (Chester: Phillipson & Goldner, 1939), 19.

149 *Picture Post*, 25 December 1948.

150 Armstrong, *Christmas in Nineteenth-century England*, 41.

151 Margaret I. Cole, *A Story of Santa Claus for Little People* (London: G. Bell, 1920), 38.

152 *Santa Claus Story Book* (London: Thomas and Nelson, 1915), 7.

153 For an exploration of the role of Coca-Cola see Cara Okleshen, Stacey Menzel Baker and Robert Mittelstaedt, 'Santa Claus does more than deliver toys: Advertising's commercialization of the collective memories of Americans', *Consumption, Markets and Culture* 4, no. 3 (2000): 207–40.

154 *Daily Mirror*, 10 December 1924. For an interview with a man who played a store Santa see *Yorkshire Post and Leeds Intelligencer*, 23 December 1953.

155 Reginald Nettel, *Santa Claus* (Bedford: Gordon Gallery, 1957), 52.

156 David Hamlin, 'The structures of toy consumption: Bourgeois domesticity and the demand for toys in nineteenth-century Germany', *Journal of Social History* 36, no. 4 (2003): 857–69, 862.

157 Golby and Purdue, *Making of the Modern Christmas*, 88.

158 On adult satisfaction see *Belfast Telegraph*, 24 December 1926. On Santa as a 'secular version of Christ' see Russell Belk, 'Materialism and the American Christmas', in *Unwrapping Christmas*, ed. Daniel Miller (Oxford: Oxford University Press, 1993), 83.

159 James H. Barnett, *The American Christmas: A Study of National Culture* (New York: Macmillan, 1954), 47. Winifred Foley, *Full Hearts And Empty Bellies: A 1920s Childhood from the Forest of Dean to the Streets of London* (London: Abacus, 2009), 83–4.

160 For a discussion of the literature see Robert Cluley, 'The organization of Santa: Fetishism, ambivalence and narcissism', *Organization* 18, no. 6 (2011): 779–94.

161 See the complaints of 'bedraggled red-cloaked gentleman who frequent the gutters' in *Gloucester Citizen*, 15 December 1950. *Picture Post*, 2 December 1944.

162 *The Times*, 26 November 1962. For a philosophical argument on why it is wrong to teach children that Santa is true (rather than engage in the paraphernalia) see David Kyle Johnson, 'Against the Santa Claus lie: The truth we should tell our children', in *Christmas: Philosophy for Everyone, Better than a Lump of Coal*, ed. Scot C. Lowe (Chichester: Wiley-Blackwell, 2007), 139–50.

163 UK Data Service: SN: 69038 National Opinion Polls National Political Surveys; December 1969.

164 Renzo Sereno, 'Some observations on the Santa Claus custom', *Psychiatry* 145, no. 4 (1951): 387–96.

165 *Daily Mirror*, 14 December 1928. Advertising Standards Agency, 'The advertising Santa clause?', 1 December 2010: http://www.asa.org.uk/ News-resources/Media-Centre/2010/the-advertising-santa-clause.aspx#. VDJ8HPldXYg.

166 Opie and Opie, *Lore and Language of Schoolchildren*, 286.

167 For example, see the testimony in Weightman and Humphries, *Christmas Past*, 147.

168 *The Times*, 12 November 1955.

169 For contemporary observations on this *Belfast Telegraph*, 24 December 1926.

170 See John McVicar's memory of doing this in *New Statesman*, 25 December to 1 January 2000.

171 Opie and Opie, *Lore and Language of Schoolchildren*, 285.

172 Carl J. Anderson and Norman M. Prentice, 'Encounter with reality: Children's reactions on discovering the Santa Claus myth', *Child Psychiatry and Human Development* 25, no. 2 (1994): 67–84. Claude Cyr, 'Do reindeer and children know something that we don't? Paediatric inpatients' belief in Santa Claus', *Canadian Medical Association Journal* 167, no. 12 (2002): 1325–27.

173 Hay, *Santa Klaus Murder*, 40–1.

174 *The Times*, 15 December 1971.

175 On its quick establishment see Opie and Opie, *Lore and Language of Schoolchildren*, 287.

176 Jack Jones, *Me and Mine: Further Chapters in the Autobiography of Jack Jones* (London: Hamish Hamilton, 1946), 97.

177 *The Times*, 21 December 1921.

178 *Yorkshire Post and Leeds Intelligencer*, 13 December 1923.

179 For example, *Woman's Weekly*, 6 December 1930.

180 *The Times*, 22 December 1928. *Lichfield Mercury*, 18 December 1936. *Sunderland Echo and Shipping Gazette*, 17 December 1936.

181 *Woman's Own*, 3 December 1932.

182 *The Times*, 12, 21 December 1923. *Saturday Review*, 19 December 1936.

183 *Western Morning News*, 25 September 1937. *Dundee Courier*, 21 December 1928. *Daily Mail*, 20 December 1933. Weightman and Humphries, *Christmas Past*, 126.

184 *The Economist*, 23 December 1939.

185 On the uncertainties of poultry prices see *Yorkshire Evening Post*, 2 December 1932.

186 Ronald Blythe, *Akenfeld* (1969; London: Penguin, 2005), 112.

187 Schweitzer, *All Our Christmases*, 4. *Daily Worker*, 24 December 1935.

188 'Interview with a butcher', 6 December 1938, MO Worktown collection box 31.

189 Wybrow, *Britain Speaks Out*, 32. Pimlott, *Englishman's Christmas*, 169.

190 John Martin, 'The commercialisation of British turkey production', *Rural History* 20, no. 2 (2009): 209–28.

191 *ITV Early Evening News*, 25 December 1958. *Gaumont British News*, 25 December 1958.

192 *Till Death Us Do Part*, BBC1, 26 December 1972. Pimlott, *Englishman's Christmas*, 169.

193 Ipsos MORI, 'Christmas: a time for giving', December 1997: https://www.ipsos-mori.com/researchpublications/researcharchive/2172/Christmas-A-time-for-giving.aspx. YouGov surveys, 5–6 December 2010.

194 Kenneth Young, ed., *The Diaries of Sir Robert Bruce Lockhart, vol. 1, 1915-1938* (London: Macmillan, 1973), 280.

195 *The Independent*, 23 December 2010.

196 Sansom, *Christmas*, 247.

197 Rhydwen Williams, 'Christmas in the valley', reproduced in translation in Meic Stephens, ed., *Illuminations: An Anthology of Welsh Short Prose* (Cardiff: Welsh Academic Press, 1998), 166–9.

198 Brian Jackson, *Working Class Community* (London: Routledge, 1968), 52.

199 'Christmas Trade Interviews', 29 November 1938, MO: Worktown collection box 31.

200 Broad and Fleming, *Nella's Last War*, 88.

201 Alan Sillitoe, *Saturday Night and Sunday Morning* (London: W. H. Allen, 1958), 191–2.

202 Madeline Kerr, *The People of Ship Street* (London: Routledge, 1958), 99.

203 MO day survey 25 December 1937, respondents 21 and 82.

204 *Sunderland Echo and Shipping Gazette*, 17 December 1936.

205 *Daily Telegraph*, 3 December 2010. YouGov survey, 5–6 December 2010. Food and Drink Innovation Network, 'Pea sales rise by 100 per cent as Brits ditch Brussels Sprouts': http://www.fdin.org.uk/2013/12/pea-sales-rise-by-100-percent-as-brits-ditch-brussels-sprouts/.

206 Ibid.

207 Martin Pitts, Charles Pattie and Danny Dorling, 'Christmas feasting and social class', *Food, Culture and Society* 10, no. 3 (2007): 407–24.

208 Brian Harrison, *Seeking a Role: The United Kingdom, 1951-1970* (Oxford: Oxford University Press, 2009), 334–5, 337.

209 Joe Moran, *Armchair Nation: An Intimate History of Britain in Front of the TV* (London: Profile, 2013), 313. *Woman's Own*, 26 December 1936.

210 Nigella Lawson, *Feast* (London: Chatto and Wilson, 2004), 2–3.

211 *Director*, December 2011.

212 *The Times*, 12 December 1985.

213 Family Action, *Breaking the Bank*, 18.

214 On older generations disliking such food see Elizabeth Roberts, *Women and Families: An Oral History, 1940-1970* (Oxford: Blackwell, 1995), 42

215 *Engineering and Technology*, January 2012.

216 Interview with Alice Hannah (b. 1902), East Midlands Oral History Archive.

217 For example, *Gloucestershire Echo*, 21 December 1932. *Hull Daily Mail*, 28 December 1932.

218 *The Christmas book for the New World cook* (1934), John Johnson collection: Gas and Gas Appliances 3 (38).

219 MO day survey, 25 December 1937, respondent 32.

220 *Delia Smith's Complete Cookery Course* (1978; London: BBC, 1992), 200. Nigella Lawson, *How to Eat: The Pleasures and Principles of Good Food* (London: Chatto & Windus, 1999), 55.

221 *Christmas Cheer, or, Everyday Cookery for Families of Moderate Income* (London, 1870). *The Christmas Cookery Book* (London: J. Leng, 1928).

222 *The Royle Family*, BBC1, 25 December 2008.

223 *Bon Viveur's TV Christmas*, ITV, 18 October 1956.

224 Pitts et al., 'Christmas feasting'.

225 *The Times*, 9 December 1980.

226 MO winter directive 1986, respondent N403.

227 *New Statesman*, 13 December 2004.

228 For example, Elliott and Cope, *Swansea Wartime Diary*, 205.

229 'Christmas and New Year's Eve, 1941', MO file report 1030, 41.

230 Dylan Thomas, 'Memories of Christmas [1945]', in *Dylan Thomas Omnibus* (London: Orion, 2014), 291.

231 *Daily Mirror*, 25 November 1924. MO day survey 25 December 1937, respondent 284.

232 John Brierley, *In the Shadow of the Means Test Man* (Highedge: Highedge Historical Society, 1995), 66.

233 MO day survey, 25 December 1937, respondent 231.

234 For complaints and analysis see *The Times*, 6 November 1982.

235 MO day survey, 25 December 1937, respondents 20 and 250.Countess of Bandon, 'Christmas – Then and now', *South Wales Spectator*, December 1961.

236 Vera Hall interview, East Midlands Oral History Archive. Roud, *Penguin Guide to Superstitions*, 87.

237 *London Opinion and the Humourist*, Christmas 1949.

238 Elspeth, *Santa Claus and How He Came Again* ... (London: Sherratt & Hughes, 1912), 26.

239 YouGov survey, 5–6 December 2010.

240 *Daily Mirror*, 15 December 1923.

241 Armstrong, *Christmas in Nineteenth-century England*, 112.

242 *The Times*, 24 December 1985.

243 Robert Roberts, *The Classic Slum: Salford Life in the First Quarter of the Century* (Manchester: Manchester University Press, 1971), 9.

244 *Hull Daily Mail*, 27 December 1945.

245 Dylan Thomas, 'Conversation about Christmas', *Picture Post*, 27 December 1947. Jackson, *Working Class Community*, 48.

246 'Juvenile Drinking', MO file report 1837-7A.

247 *The Art of Drinking* (1932), John Johnson collection: Wines and Spirits 3 (30). *The Times*, 23 December 1963.

248 *Keep Safe This Christmas* (NHS, 2012), 2. Pitts et al., 'Christmas feasting'.

249 MO diarist 5318, 25 December 1948.

250 *Daily Mirror*, 24 December 1951.

251 *The Times*, 15 December 1962.

252 W. M. Williams, *The Sociology of an English Village: Gosforth* (London: Routledge, 1964), 135. Isabel Emmett, *A North Wales Village: A Social Anthropological Study* (London: Routledge, 1964), 126.

253 *Coronation Street*, ITV, 25 December 1972.

254 'Christmas drinking 1947', MO topic collection 85.

255 MO day survey, 25 December 1937, respondent 20.

256 Opie and Opie, *Lore and Language of Schoolchildren*, 287. Interview with Norma Winstone, British Library: C122/206. Interview with Alice Hannah (b. 1902), East Midlands Oral History Archive.

257 For example, 'A Cosy Christmas', *The Fourth Girl Annual* (London, 1955), 144–8.

258 'A Yuletide Mass Observation report on party games old and new', Mass Observation topic collection 41-1-A.

259 William Francis Dawson, *Christmas: Its Origin and Associations* (London: Elliot Stock, 1902), 274.

260 The spirit of Christmas', *Saturday Review*, 23 December 1922.

261 MO diarist 5076, 25 December 1954.

262 MO day survey, 25 December 1937, respondent 250. Elliott and Cope, *Swansea Wartime Diary*, 205.

263 MO day survey, 25 December 1937, respondent 20.

264 For an exploration of this in a contemporary context see Jennifer Mason and Stewart Muir, 'Conjuring up traditions: Atmospheres, eras and family Christmases', *Sociological Review* 61, no. 3 (2013): 607–29.

265 *Tamworth Herald*, 22 December 1934.

266 Mason and Muir, 'Conjuring up traditions', 616.

267 For this point in a US context see Elizabeth Rytting, 'Christmas as a reflexive commemoration', *Folklore Forum* 36, no. 1 (2005): 12–28.

268 Interview with Elena and Aldo Salvoni, Museum of London, MoL_99.23/EX5.

269 For reflections on this see *New Statesman*, 13 December 2004.

270 MO day survey, 25 December 1937, respondent 387.

271 Tazeen Ahmad, *The Checkout Girl: My Life on the Supermarket Conveyor Belt* (London: Friday Project, 2009), 50.

272 *Guardian*, 21 December 2013.

273 MO day survey, 25 December 1937, respondent 150.

274 Bernard Donoughue, *Downing Street Diary: With Harold Wilson in No. 10* (London: Jonathan Cape, 2005), 615.

275 Rytting, 'Christmas as a reflexive commemoration', 20.

276 Agatha Christie, *Hercule Poirot's Christmas* (London: HarperCollins, [1938] 2013), 74.

277 Robert Hewison, *The Heritage Industry: Britain in a Climate of Decline* (London: Methuen, 1987).

278 Mason and Muir, 'Conjuring up traditions', 614.

279 Marling, *Merry Christmas*, 356.

280 On objects as repositories of memory see Annemarie Money, 'Material culture and the living room: The appropriation and use of goods in everyday life', *Journal of Consumer Culture* 7, no. 3 (2007): 355–77.

281 Langhammer, 'The meaning of home'.

282 On the front room see Ben Jones, *The Working Class in Mid-Twentieth-Century England: Community, Identity and Social Memory* (Manchester: Manchester University Press, 2012), 158–60. William Woodruff, *The Road to Nab End: An Extraordinary Northern Childhood* (1993; London: Abacus, 2002), 18, 128.

283 *Derby Daily Telegraph*, 29 December 1950. 'Shops', 12 December 1938, MO: Worktown collection box 31.

284 *Woman's Weekly*, 13 December 1930. Opie and Opie, *Lore and Language of Schoolchildren*, 286. *Church Times*, 22 December 1933. Broad and Fleming, *Nella's Last War*, 81. MO winter directive 1986 respondent B1215. Alan Smith, 'Notes on the folk-life of the east London child', *Folklore* 69, no.1 (1958): 39–43, 40.

285 *Woman's Own Christmas* (1962), 34, 73.

286 Ashby, *Hertfordshire Christmas*, 138.

287 'Christmas and New Year's Eve, 1941', MO file report 1030, 40.

288 On the continuation of superstition see E. O. James, 'Superstitions and Survivals', *Folklore* 72, no. 1 (1961): 289–99.

289 A point made in Emma G. Duyre, *Xmas Customs and Legends* (London, 1935), 3.

290 Karl Barth, *Christmas* (Edinburgh: Oliver and Boyd, 1959), 18.

291 Ian Fleming, *On Her Majesty's Secret Service* (1963; London: Vintage, 2012), 255.

292 Clement A. Miles, *Christmas Customs and Traditions: Their History and Significance* (1912; New York: Dover, 1976), 18.

293 Caplow, 'Rule enforcement without visible means'.

294 L. D. Ettinlinger and R. G. Holloway, *Compliments of the Season* (London: Penguin, 1947), 37.

Chapter 4

1 *Daily Mail*, 23 December 1936.

2 Filson Young, 'A pilgrim's progress', *Saturday Review*, 29 December 1923.

3 For example, *Financial Times*, 24 December 1954.

4   'The spirit of Christmas', *Saturday Review*, 23 December 1922.

5   Neil Armstrong, *Christmas in Nineteenth-century England* (Manchester: Manchester University Press, 2010).

6   Australian consumer research found that people had a strong sense of Christmas spirit, but varied in what they meant by the term. It argued that the spirit was an attitude rather than behaviour. Peter Clarke, 'A measure for Christmas spirit', *Journal of Consumer Marketing* 24, no. 1 (2007): 8–17.

7   Grace Davie, *Religion in Britain Since 1945: Believing Without Belonging* (Oxford: Wiley-Blackwell, 1994).

8   *Church Times*, 22 December 1933, 30 December 1932.

9   Juliet Gardiner, *The Thirties: An Intimate History* (London: HarperCollins, 2010), 487.

10 Llanelly parish magazine, January 1949, Gwent Archives: D/Pa.22.37.

11 W. M. Williams, *The Sociology of an English Village: Gosforth* (London: Routledge, 1964), 181, 187, 190. This was not unusual and had its roots in the Victorian period. Neil Armstrong, 'The Christmas season and the Protestant churches in England, c. 1870-1914', *Journal of Ecclesiastical History* 62, no. 4 (2011): 744–62, 755.

12 For example, Miss Read, 'The white robin' [1979]', in *A Country Christmas* (London: Orion, 2006), 74.

13 *Church Statistics 2010/11* (Archbishop's Council, 2012), 26.

14 S. C. Williams, *Religious Belief and Popular Culture in Southwark, c. 1880-1939* (Oxford: Oxford University Press, 1999), ch. 6.

15 Geoffrey Gorer, *Exploring English Character* (New York: Criterion, 1955), 242.

16 Ronald Blythe, *Akenfeld* (1969; London: Penguin, 2005), 62.

17 *The Times*, 27 December 1957.

18 For example see editorial of *The Listener*, 21 December 1950.

19 Paddy Ashdown, *The Ashdown Diaries: Volume One, 1988-1997* (London: Allen Lane, 2000), 126.

20 Doreen Rosman, *The Evolution of the English Churches, 1500-2000* (Cambridge: Cambridge University Press, 2003), 300.

21 *The Treasury*, December 1946. Rhydwen Williams, 'Christmas in the valley', reproduced in translation in Meic Stephens, eds, *Illuminations: An Anthology of Welsh Short Prose* (Cardiff: Welsh Academic Press, 1998), 166–9.

22 *Church Statistics 2010/11* (Archbishop's Council, 2012), 16, 26. Adults defined as people aged 16+. Robert J. Wybrow, *Britain Speaks Out, 1937-87: A Social History as Seen Through the Gallup Data* (London: Macmillan, 1989), 147.

23 Callum Brown, *Religion and Society in Twentieth-Century Britain* (Harlow: Pearson, 2006), 4.

24 Stephen Law, *The Xmas Files: The Philosophy of Christmas* (London: Orion, 2003), 146–7.

25　David Walker, 'How far is Bethlehem? Exploring the ordinary theology of occasional churchgoers', in *Exploring Ordinary Theology: Everyday Christian Believing and the Church*, ed. Jeff Astley and Leslie J. Francis (Farnham: Ashgate, 2013): 137–46.

26　St Luke's, Abercarn, parish magazine December 1965, Parish Magazine of St Luke, Pontnewydd, December 1948, Gwent Archives: D/Pa.18.38 and D/Pa.39.1.

27　UK Data Service: SN: 69038 National Opinion Polls National Political Surveys; December 1969.

28　Callum Brown, *The Death of Christian Britain: Understanding Secularization* (London: Routledge, 2009).

29　*TV Times*, 18–24 December 1960.

30　*Church Statistics 2010/11* (Archbishop's Council, 2012), 2. British Religion in Numbers, 'Seasonal good intentions', 2 December 2011: http://www.brin. ac.uk/news/2011/seasonal-good-intentions/ and 'Christmas and other themes', 17 December 2012: http://www.brin.ac.uk/news/2012/christmas-and-other-themes/. The Children's Society, 'Brits prefer pews to panto at Christmas', 1 December 2011: http://www.childrenssociety.org.uk/news-and-blogs/press-release/brits-prefer-pews-panto-christmas.

31　Armstrong, 'Christmas season', 757–8. *Church Times*, 1 January 1937, 30 December 1938.

32　Laurence Whistler, *The English Festivals* (London: William Heinemann, 1947), 57.

33　Barry Cooper, 'Christmas carols', in *Christmas, Ideology and Popular Culture*, ed. Sheila Whiteley (Edinburgh: Edinburgh University Press, 2008): 88–97, 96–7. *Church Times*, 25 September 1987.

34　*Daily Mirror*, 7 December 1949.

35　St Luke's, Abercarn, parish magazine January 1963, Gwent Archives: D/Pa.18.38.

36　*Church Times*, 30 December 1938. J. A. R. Pimlott, *The Englishman's Christmas* (Hassocks: Harvester, 1978), 152. A. R. Wright and T. E. Lones, *British Calendar Customs, England vol. III: Fixed Festivals* (London: Folk-lore Society, 1940), 226-7. Whistler, *English Festivals*, 54-5. MO day survey, 25 December 1937, respondents 66 and 28.

37　See the memories in Maria Hubert, *The Great British Christmas* (Stroud: Sutton, 1999), 152.

38　Ashdown, *Ashdown Diaries*, 125.

39　*Tamworth Herald*, 10 December 1949.

40　R. W. Matthews and W. M. Atkins, *A History of St Paul's Cathedral and the Men Associated with it* (London: John Baker, 1964), 309. *Church Times*, 30 December 1938.

41　*The Times*, 22 December 1984.

42　*Church Times*, 22 December 1972.

43　Abercarn parish magazine, December 1973, Gwent Archives: D/Pa.18.41.

44 *Cheltenham Chronicle*, 21 December 1935.

45 On the festive emphasis on goodwill, childhood and home being rooted in Christianity see Archibald Alexander, *Everyman's Christmas* (London: James Clarke, 1931), 6.

46 *The Times*, 24 November 1964.

47 British Religion in Numbers, 'December 2011 Cpanel', 28 December 2011: http://www.brin.ac.uk/news/2011/december-2011-cpanel/.

48 Williams, *Religious Belief and Popular Culture*, ch. 6.

49 Pimlott, *Englishman's Christmas*, 151. *Western Morning News*, 19 December 1928.

50 Bible Society, 'Children and parents 6 out of 10 score on nativity knowledge', 17 December 2012: http://www.biblesociety.org.uk/news/children-and-parents-6-out-of-10-score-on-nativity-knowledge/.

51 *Woman's Own Christmas* (1962), 15.

52 *Western Daily Press*, 22 December 1932.

53 *Church Times*, 22 December 1933, 30 December 1932.

54 Mass Observation (hereafter MO) day survey, 25 December 1937, respondent 64.

55 *Radio Times*, 20 December 1962.

56 For example, W. L. Reed, ed., *The Second Treasury of Christmas Music* (London: Blandford, 1967), 7.

57 *Daily Mirror*, 24 December 1951.

58 Sheila Whiteley, 'Christmas songs – sentiments and subjectivities', in *Christmas, Ideology and Popular Culture*, ed. Sheila Whiteley (Edinburgh: Edinburgh University Press, 2008), 101.

59 For example, *The Best Christmas Song Book Ever* (London: Music Sales, 1999).

60 British Religion in Numbers, 'Carols + websites + prisoners', 10 December 2012: http://www.brin.ac.uk/news/2012/carols-websites-prisoners/.

61 *The Guardian*, 28 December 1987.

62 *The Spectator*, 25 December 1959.

63 John Wolffe, 'Religion and secularization', in *20th Century Britain: Economic, Social and Cultural Change*, ed. Paul Johnson (London: Longman, 1994): 427–41, 430.

64 Also see David Voas, 'Hard evidence: Is Christianity dying in Britain?', 27 November 2013: https://theconversation.com/hard-evidence-is-christianity-dying-in-britain-20734.

65 Theos, 'What Christmas mean to people in Britain?' 8 December 2010: http://www.theosthinktank.co.uk/comment/2011/12/08/what-does-christmas-mean-to-people-in-britain.

66 Armstrong, *Christmas in Nineteenth-century England*, 61–6, 99–123.

67 *Lansbury's Labour Weekly*, 1 January 1927.

68 *Spectator*, 16 December 1932.

69 *The Worker*, 15 January 1925. J. M. Golby and A. W. Purdue, *The Making of the Modern Christmas* (Stroud: Sutton, 2nd edn., 2000), 95–6. *The English Review*, December 1915.

70 For examples of such activities see *Gloucester Citizen*, 20 December 1923, 21 December 1921.

71 *Gaumont British News*, 20 December 1937. For memories of receiving boots from a charity see Arthur Barton, *The Penny World: A Boyhood Recalled* (London: Hutchison, 1969), 26.

72 *The Children's Newspaper*, 27 December 1924, 4 December 1937.

73 *Western Daily News*, 24 December 1924. *The Unemployed News*, 17 December 1928.

74 *Hastings and St Leonards Observer*, 16 December 1933.

75 On the continuation of such charitable work see Nick Hayes and Barry M. Doyle, 'Eggs, rags and whist drives: Popular munificence and the development of provincial medical voluntarism between the wars', *Historical Research* 86, no. 234 (2013): 712–40.

76 *Daily Mail*, 27 December 1928.

77 'You give a real meaning to Christmas …', Bishopsgate Institute: http://www.20thcenturylondon.org.uk/bgate-misc-2.

78 *Daily Mirror*, 9 December 1936.

79 *Lansbury's Labour Weekly*, 1 January 1927.

80 *Daily Mail*, 24 December 1937.

81 *The Spectator*, 16 December 1938.

82 *Daily Mail*, 23 December 1939.

83 Jeremy Archer, ed., *Home for Christmas* (London: Century, 2007), 157.

84 *Picture Post*, 9 December 1939. *Cheltenham Chronicle*, 21 December 1940.

85 *The Times*, 23 December 1941, 24 December 1942.

86 Sydney Pritchard, *Life in the Welsh Guards, 1939-46* (Talybont: Lolfa, 2007).

87 *The Times*, 28 December 1942.

88 For example, *Gaumont British News*, 15 December 1952.

89 *The Times*, 22 November 1946, 20 December 1946, 30 December 1947. For criticism of such sentiments see the angry letter in *Western Morning News*, 17 December 1946, which advocates that if food has to be sent to Germany it should be dull and unsavoury.

90 *The Children's Newspaper*, 7 December 1957.

91 *Picture Post*, 27 December 1952.

92 *The Times*, 10 December 1970.

93 *Children's Newspaper*, 30 December 1944.

94 See the critical review in *New Musical Express*, 8 December 1984.

95 On charity singles see Lucy Robinson, 'Putting the charity back into charity singles: Charity singles in Britain, 1984-1995', *Contemporary British History* 26, no. 3 (2012): 405–25.

96 *Bath Chronicle and Weekly Gazette*, 8 December 1934.

97 Paul Davis, *The Lives and Times of Ebenezer Scrooge* (New Haven: Yale University Press, 1990), 136–50.

98 Jeffrey Richards, *Film and British National Identity: From Dickens to Dad's Army* (Manchester: Manchester University Press, 1997), 336–7. For a discussion of other film versions of the story see James Chapman, 'God Bless Us, Every One: Movie adaptations of *A Christmas Carol*', in *Christmas at the Movies: Images of Christmas in American, British and European Cinema*, ed. Mark Connelly (London: I. B. Tauris, 2000): 9–37.

99 Karal Ann Marling, *Merry Christmas! Celebrating America's Greatest Holiday* (Cambridge, MA: Harvard University Press, 2001), ch. 4. Paul Davis, 'Retelling a Christmas Carol: Text and culture-text', *The American Scholar* 59 (Winter, 1990): 109–15.

100 For example, Guy and Steve Hobbs, *The Christmas Pocket Bible: Every Christmas Rule of Thumb at Your Fingertips* (Richmond: Crimson, 2009), 149.

101 'The spirit of Christmas', *Saturday Review*, 23 December 1922.

102 *The Times*, 5 January 1953.

103 Mary Searle-Chatterjee, 'Christmas cards and the construction of social relations in Britain today', in *Christmas Unwrapped*, ed. Daniel Miller (Oxford: Oxford University Press, 1993): 176–92, 181. Institute of Fundraising, 'Top tips for buying Christmas charity cards', http://www.institute-of-fundraising.org.uk/library/charity-christmas-cards/charity-christmas-cards.pdf.

104 Centre for Charitable Giving and Philanthropy, 'Charitable Giving by UK Households at Christmas', December 2009: http://www.cgap.org.uk/uploads/Briefing%20Notes/CGAP%20BN2%20Christmas%20giving.pdf.

105 For examples of such acts see *Bath Chronicle and Weekly Gazette*, 14 December 1935.

106 Josie Long, 'Things to make and do at Christmas', in *The Atheist's Guide to Christmas*, ed. Ariane Sherine (London: Friday Project, 2009), 110–11. MO day survey, 25 December 1937, respondent 282.

107 Angela Patrick, *The Baby Laundry for Unmarried Mothers* (London: Simon and Schuster, 2012), 101. For memories of the pleasures of Christmas in an otherwise harsh pre-war orphanage see *The Spectator*, 18 December 1982.

108 Quoted in Archer, *Home for Christmas*, 215.

109 'Christmas and the war', *Saturday Review*, 1 January 1916.

110 Ian O'Donnell and Yvonne Jewkes, 'Going home for Christmas: Prisoners, a taste of freedom and the press', *The Howard Journal* 50, no. 1 (2011): 75–90. H. R. L. Sheppard, 'Nash's Commentary for Christmas', *Nash's Pall Mall Magazine*, December 1933.

111 For example, James Boulton and Andrew Robertson, eds, *The Letters of D. H. Lawrence: vol. III part 1 1916-21* (Cambridge: Cambridge University Press, 207), 313.

112 D. S. Higgins, ed, *The Private Diaries of Sir H. Rider Haggard, 1914-1925* (London: Cassell, 1980), 211.

113 *The Clear Light*, 18 December 1924. *Daily Worker,* 24 December 1935.

114 'Is Christmas what it was?', *Saturday Review*, 5 December 1931.

115 *The Spectator*, 12 December 1981, 7 December 1996.

116 Clemence Dane, 'The Christmas heart', *Quiver*, December 1925.

117 'The spirit of Christmas', *Saturday Review*, 23 December 1922.

118 Mrs Raymond Lee, 'Letter or spirit?', *Quiver*, December 1915.

119 *The Guardian*, 13 December 1957.

120 *New Society*, 7 December 1978. *The Spectator*, 18 December 1999.

121 *Picture Post*, 22 December 1951. Jilly Cooper, *How to Survive Christmas* (London: Methuen, 1986), 11. *Bath Chronicle and Weekly Gazette*, 8 December 1934. *New Society*, 11 December 1980.

122 Stuart Prebble, *Grumpy Old Men* (London: BBC, 2004), 188.

123 *The Spectator*, 22 December 1967.

124 *Daily Mail*, 24 December 1935.

125 Kate Fox, *Watching the English: The Hidden Rules of English Behaviour* (London: Hodder, 2005), 385.

126 Gwyn Thomas, 'Father's Christmas', *Ingot*, 1 December 1960.

127 Ipsos MORI, 'Three calls a minute expected by the Samaritans at Xmas', 11 December 2000: http://www.ipsos-mori.com/researchpublications/ researcharchive/poll.aspx?oItemId=1654.

128 SN: 69038 National Opinion Polls National Political Surveys, December 1969.

129 Elizabeth H. Pleck, *Celebrating the Family: Ethnicity, Consumer Culture and Family Rituals* (Cambridge, MA: Harvard University Press, 2000), 60–1. Pimlott, *Englishman's Christmas*, 175–6.

130 *New Scientist*, 24/31 December 1988.

131 For a discussion of Christmas as kitsch see Law, *The Xmas Files*, ch. 4.

132 Lorna Rea, 'Modern angles on the great festival', *Nash's Pall Mall Magazine*, December 1930.

133 Fox, *Watching the English*, 385.

134 *New Society*, 11 December 1980.

135 Russell Davies, ed., *The Kenneth Williams Diaries* (London: HarperCollins, 1994), 224, 316, 390.

136 *Daily Mail*, 24 December 1935.

137 Countess of Bandon, 'Christmas – Then and now', *South Wales Spectator*, December 1961.

138 MO day survey 25 December 1937, respondent 99.

139   Graham Payn and Sheridan Morley, eds, *The Noel Coward Diaries* (London: Weidenfeld and Nicolson, 1982), 456, 489, 585.

140   Phillip Collins, ed., *English Christmas: An Anthology* (Bedford: Gordon Fraser, 1956), 7.

141   'The spirit of Christmas', *Saturday Review*, 23 December 1922.

142   *The Spectator*, 16 December 1932.

143   Ipsos MORI, 'Scrooge makes a comeback as crisis opens its Christmas shelters for the 30th Year', 21 December 2001: https://www.ipsos-mori.com/researchpublications/researcharchive/1182/Scrooge-Makes-A-Comeback-As-Crisis-Opens-its-Christmas-Shelters-For-The-30th-Year.aspx.

144   *Till Death Us Do Part*, BBC1, 26 December 1972.

145   *The Spectator*, 16 December 1932.

146   *The Times*, 22 December 1966

147   Clemence Dane, 'The Christmas heart', *Quiver*, December 1925.

148   'Is Christmas what it was?', *Saturday Review*, 5 December 1931.

149   *Daily Mail*, 24 December 1935.

150   C. Day Lewis, 'Remembering Christmas', *Picture Post*, 25 December 1948.

151   *Daily Mail*, 24 December 1935.

152   MO day survey, 25 December 1937, respondent 126.

153   Gavin Weightman and Steve Humphries, *Christmas Past* (London: Sidgwick and Jackson, 1987), 174.

154   Payn and Morley, *Noel Coward Diaries*, 249.

155   Sally McKechnie and Caroline Tynan, 'Social meanings in Christmas consumption: An exploratory study of UK celebrants' consumption rituals', *Journal of Consumer Behaviour* 5, no. 2 (2006): 130–44, 186.

156   Higgins, *Private Diaries of Sir H. Rider Haggard*, 249.

157   Ion Trewin, ed., *Alan Clark Diaries: Into Politics* (London: Weidenfeld and Nicolson, 2000), 287. Alan Clark, *The Last Diaries* (London: Phoenix, 2003), 40.

158   Hubert L. Simpson, *The Meaning of Christmas* (London: James Clark, 1928), 5.

159   *Woman's Own*, 5 December 1936.

160   For a criticism of such a perspective see 'Christmas and the hump', *Saturday Review*, 25 December 1915.

161   Paul Addison, *No Turning Back: The Peacetime Revolutions of Post-War Britain* (Oxford: Oxford University Press, 2010), 170.

162   *Woman's Own*, 10 December 1932. *Daily Mail*, 23 December 1936.

163   Richard Broad and Suzie Fleming, eds, *Nella's Last War: The Second World War Diaries of Housewife, 49* (London: Profile, 2006), 224.

164   C. Day Lewis, 'Remembering Christmas', *Picture Post*, 25 December 1948. India Knight, *Comfort and Joy* (London: Penguin, 2010), 10–1.

165   *Daily Mirror*, 24 December 1918. *The Times*, 24 December 1918.

166 Lady Cynthia Asquith, *Diaries, 1915-1918* (London: Hutchison, 1968), 115.

167 William Muir Auld, *Christmas Traditions* (New York: Macmillan, 1931), 120.

168 Adam Gopnik, *Winter: Five Windows on the Season* (London: Quercus, 2012), 5.

169 *ITV Late Evening News*, 22 December 1962.

170 Polly Piner, *Making Christmas Table Decorations* (Tunbridge Wells: Search, 2006), 4.

171 Gopnik, *Winter*, ch. 1.

172 Michael Bloch, ed., *James Lees-Milne Diaries, 1942-54* (London: John Murray, 2006), 428.

173 Clement A. Miles, *Christmas Customs and Traditions: Their History and Significance* (1912; New York: Dover, 1976), 155-6.

174 R. S. Thomas, 'Qualities of Christmas', *Wales*, 46 (1959): 17–20.

175 *Yorkshire Post*, 24 December 1937.

176 'The spirit of Christmas', *Saturday Review*, 23 December 1922. Gopnik, *Winter*, 8–9.

177 Met Office, 'Will there be a white Christmas?' http://www.metoffice.gov.uk/learning/snow/white-christmas.

178 *ITV Early Evening News*, 25 December 1996.

179 Michael Palin, *Diaries 1969-1979: The Python Years* (London: Weidenfeld and Nicolson, 2006), 608.

180 *The Spectator*, 20 December 1935.

181 *The Times*, 7 January 1978.

182 *Church Times*, 22 December 1933.

183 Peter Donnelly, ed., *Mrs Milburn's Diaries: An Englishwoman's Day-to-Day Reflections 1939-45* (London: Fontana, 1980), 199.

184 'Happiness in Wartime', MO file report 1870. 'Christmas and New Year's Eve, 1941', MO File Report 1030, 44.

185 Online Christmas survey by author (2013) respondent #25.

186 MO day survey, 25 December 1937, respondent 225.

187 See the different accounts of 'What Christmas means to me' in *Essex Newsman*, 5 December 1950.

188 Ferdynand Zweig, *Labour, Life and Poverty* (1949; Wakefield: EP Publishing, 1975), ch. 14.

189 Unpublished diary quoted in *New Society*, 18 December 1987.

190 Tim Kasser and Kennon M. Sheldon, 'What makes for a merry Christmas?', *Journal of Happiness Studies*, 3 (2002): 313–29.

191 Richard Sennett, *The Fall of Public Man* (Cambridge: Cambridge University Press, 1977).

192 *The Times*, 24 December 1946. *Daily Mail*, 24 December 1972.

193 *Newsletter* [Belfast], 4 December 2013.

194 *The Times*, 24 December 1986.

195 *The Spectator*, 20 December 2008.

Chapter 5

1   Jonathan Coe, *The Rotters' Club* (London: Penguin, 2002 edn.), 274.

2   *Atora Book of Olde Time Christmas Customs, Games and Recipes* (Manchester: Hugon, 1933–4), 1.

3   Mark Connelly, *Christmas: A Social History* (London: I. B. Tauris, 1999), ch. 4.

4   *The Times*, 24 December 1960.

5   Coe, *Rotters' Club*, 275.

6   Tim Edensor, *National Identity, Popular Culture and Everyday Life* (Oxford: Berg, 2002).

7   *Derby Daily Telegraph*, 24 December 1948.

8   Richard Weight, *Patriots: National Identity in Britain 1940-2000* (London: Macmillan, 2002), 595–6.

9   *Hull Daily Mail*, 24 December 1932, 24 December 1938.

10 *Western Mail*, 3 December 2010.

11 W. H. Owens, 'Christmas customs around Britain', *Chamber's Journal* (December 1938): 979–81.

12 For a celebration of the diversity of the British Christmas see *Sunderland Echo and Shipping Gazette*, 23 December 1933.

13 *The Spectator*, 25 December 1926.

14 On its scarcity see *Exeter and Plymouth Gazette*, 27 December 1924.

15 For 1930s memories of receiving a visit from guisers in Derbyshire see John Brierley, *In the Shadow of the Means Test Man* (Highedge: Highedge Historical Society, 1995), 64.

16 For the text of one of these plays from Gloucestershire see H. H. Albino, 'The Snowshill Mummers', *Folklore* 50, no. 1 (1939): 83–8.

17 Reginald Nettel, *Santa Claus* (Bedford: Gordon Gallery, 1957), 48–9.

18 *Spectator*, 17 December 1921.

19 Jacqueline Simpson and Steve Roud, *A Dictionary of English Folklore* (Oxford: Oxford University Press, 2003).

20 John Hudson, *A Cotswold Christmas* (Stroud: Alan Sutton, 1988), 33–4.

21 Peter Catterall, ed., *The Macmillan Diaries: The Cabinet Years, 1950-1957* (London: Macmillan, 2003), 281.

22 Hilaire Belloc, 'A remaining Christmas', in *A Conversation with an Angel and Other Essays* (London: Jonathan Cape, 1928), 274–85.

23 *Yorkshire Post and Leeds Intelligencer*, 19 December 1925.

24 Iona and Peter Opie, *The Lore and Language of Schoolchildren* (Oxford: Clarendon, 1959), 286.

25 J. A. R. Pimlott, *The Englishman's Christmas: A Social History* (Hassocks: Harvester, 1978), 135. For a lament on the loss of such customs see *The Spectator*, 30 December 1978.

26 For a contemporary report of a revival: *Western Times*, 21 January 1927. For a discussion of roots see *Taunton Courier, and Western Advertiser*, 11 January 1933.

27 For national coverage see *The Times*, 6 January 1954.

28 J. D. A. Widdowstone, 'Trends in the commercialization of English calendar customs: A preliminary survey', in *Aspects of British Calendar Customs*, ed. Theresa Buckland and Juliette Wood (Sheffield: Sheffield Academic Press, 1993), 23–35.

29 David Green, *An Oxfordshire Christmas* (Stroud: Alan Sutton, 1992), 8–11. For evidence of wassailing being kept because it is an old custom see *Nottingham Evening Post*, 6 January 1950.

30 D. Roy Saer, 'The Christmas carol singing tradition in the Tanad valley', *Folk Life* 7, no. 1 (1969): 15–42. Trefor M. Owen, *Welsh Folk Customs* (Cardiff: Welsh Folk Museum, 1959), 28–34.

31 Richard Burton, *A Christmas Story* (1964; London: Hodder & Stoughton, 1989), 35.

32 Pam Schweitzer, ed., *All Our Christmases: A Book of Christmas Memories by Greenwich Pensioners* (London: Age Exchange Theatre Company, 1983), 2.

33 Interview with Alice Hannah (b. 1902), East Midlands Oral History Archive.

34 *Western Mail*, 28 December 1939.

35 Interviews with Vera Hall and Alice Hannah, East Midlands Oral History Archive. Schweitzer, *All Our Christmases*, 6, 15.

36 Elizabeth Roberts, 'Women's strategies, 1890–1940', in *Labour and Love: Women's Experiences of Home and Family, 1850-1940*, ed. Jane Lewis (Oxford: Blackwell, 1986), 223–47.

37 Laurence Whistler, *The English Festivals* (London: William Heinemann, 1947), 53.

38 Miss Read, 'Village Christmas [1966]', in *A Country Christmas* (London: Orion, 2006), 14.

39 Claire Harman, ed., *The Diaries of Sylvia Townsend Warner* (London: Chatto and Windus, 1994), 233.

40 Lyn Briggs, *A Shropshire Christmas* (Stroud: History Press, 1993), 116.

41 Arthur Barton, *The Penny World: A Boyhood Recalled* (London: Hutchison, 1969), 18–22.

42 Read, 'Village Christmas', 14.

43 Interview with Mrs Stretton, East Midlands Oral History Archive.

44 See the contrasting memories in Briggs, *Shropshire Christmas*, 116 and 121.

45 Green, *Oxfordshire Christmas*, 110.

46 Laurie Lee, *Cider with Rosie* (1959; London: Hogarth, 1971), 172–9.

47 *Picture Post*, 22 December 1951. *Saturday Review*, 5 December 1931.

48 *Daily Mail*, 23 December 1936. Mass Observation (hereafter MO) day survey, 22 December 1938, respondent 722. *The Times*, 17 December 1965.

49 Eleanor Garland, *Welcome Christmas! Legends, Carols, Stories, Riddles etc* (London: Ernest Benn, 1931), 47.

50 Agatha Christie, *Hercule Poirot's Christmas* (1938; London: HarperCollins, 2013), 64.

51 MO day surveys, 13 and 25 December 1937, respondents 32, 99, 186. Green, *Oxfordshire Christmas*, 27. *Daily Express*, 8 December 1924.

52 Barry Pain, 'Christmas as usual', *Nash's and Pall Mall Magazine*, December 1925.

53 C. S. Lewis, 'Delinquents in the snow'. Reproduced in *God in the Dock: Essays on Theology and Ethics* (Grand Rapids: Eerdmans, 1970), 306–10.

54 Colin Howard, *Cotswold Days* (London: Blackie, 1937), 269.

55 *Hancock's Half Hour*, Light Programme, 22 December 1959.

56 *New Yorker*, 15 November 1993.

57 Opie and Opie, *Lore and Language of Schoolchildren*, 284.

58 *Terry and June*, BBC1, 23 December 1980.

59 *Hastings and St Leonards Observer*, 17 October 1936. *Tamworth Herald*, 20 December 1947. *Burnley Express*, 25 December 1953.

60 *The Times*, 18 August 1958.

61 *Daily Telegraph*, 9 December 2008. BBC News, 'Slade slashed from airport playlist', 26 November 2003: http://news.bbc.co.uk/1/hi/england/manchester/3240564.stm.

62 *Daily Telegraph*, 11 December 2013. *Daily Mail*, 16 November 2007.

63 MO Autumn directive 1986, respondent B1426.

64 *NME*, 24 December 1977.

65 For a discussion of Christmas music see Sheila Whiteley, 'Christmas songs – sentiments and subjectivities', in *Christmas, Ideology and Popular Culture*, ed. Sheila Whiteley (Edinburgh: Edinburgh University Press, 2008), 98–112.

66 *Daily Telegraph*, 15 December 2011.

67 Mark Pegg, *Broadcasting and Society, 1918-1939* (London: Croom Helm, 1983), 7.

68 J. M. Golby and A. W. Purdue, *The Making of the Modern Christmas* (Stroud: Sutton, 2nd edn., 2000), 102. Tony Currie, *The Radio Times Story* (Tiverton: Kelly, 2001), 242.

69 *Western Morning News*, 27 December 1933.

70 BBC Listener Research Department: Listener's Research Report LR/3166 Christmas Programmes 1944. MO day survey, 25 December 1937, respondent 126.

71 Connelly, *Christmas*, 134–5, 140–4. BBC Listener Research Department: Listener's Research Report LR/3166.

72 *Daily Mirror*, 9 December 1931. BBC Listener Research Department: Listener's Research Report LR/3166.

73 Matthew Glencross, 'The first Christmas speech', 24 April 2013: https://history.blog.gov.uk/2013/04/24/the-first-christmas-speech/. Asa Briggs, *The Golden Age of Wireless* (Oxford: Oxford University Press, 1965), 112.

74 Jeremy Archer, *A Royal Christmas* (London: Elliott & Thompson, 2012), 273.

75 *Daily Mail*, 20 December 1933. *The Listener*, 4 January 1933.

76 Briggs, *Golden Age of Wireless*, 272.

77 *The Spectator*, 20 December 1935.

78 John W. Wheeler-Bennett, *King George VI: His Life and Reign* (London: Macmillan, 1958), 361.

79 David Cannadine, 'The context, performance and meaning of ritual: The British monarchy, and the "invention of tradition," c.1820-1977', in *The Invention of Tradition*, ed. Eric Hobsbawm and Terence Ranger (Cambridge: Cambridge University Press, 1983), 101–64, quote from 142.

80 On imperial responses see Connelly, *Christmas*, 145–53.

81 MO day survey, 25 December 1937, respondents 89 and 255. *Western Times*, 30 December 1949.

82 Peter Donnelly, ed., *Mrs Milburn's Diaries: An Englishwoman's Day-to-Day Reflections 1939-45* (London: Fontana, 1980), 201.

83 Richard Broad and Suzie Fleming, eds, *Nella's Last War: The Second World War Diaries of Housewife, 49* (London: Profile, 2006), 225–6.

84 MO day survey, 25 December 1937, respondents 20, 28, 116, 150, 170, 182, 225, 290, 411 and 526.

85 MO day survey 25 December 1937, respondents 35, 150, 176, 184 and 269. Elizabeth Wallace, *Christmas Past in Essex* (Stroud: History Press, 2007), 88. *New Statesman*, 25 December to 1 January 2000.

86 *The Guardian*, 27 December 1952. *Radio Times*, 19 December 1952.

87 Archer, *Royal Christmas*, 293.

88 *Daily Mail*, 27 December 1957. *Daily Express*, 27, 30 December 1957.

89 *The Times*, 17 December 1960.

90 The National Archives (hereafter TNA): PREM 13/2899.

91 *The Guardian*, 18 December 1969. *The Sun*, 21 October 1969. *Daily Telegraph*, 21 October 1969. *Sunday Telegraph*, 26 October 1969.

92 TNA: PREM 13/2899, FCO 68/27.

93 *Sunday Telegraph*, 2 November 1969. *TV Times*, 23–29 December 1962.

94 *The Times*, 21 December 1979, 6 January 1984.

95 BBC News, 'The tradition of the Queen's speech', 30 December 1997: http://news.bbc.co.uk/1/hi/special_report/for_christmas/_new_year/message_to_the_commonwealth/36774.stm.

96 Joe Moran, *Armchair Nation: An Intimate History of Britain in Front of the TV* (London: Profile, 2013), 11.

97 *Terry and June*, BBC1, 24 December 1982.

98 MO winter directive 1986, respondents B1215 and L1002.

99 For the speeches' text see Tom Fleming, *Voices Out of the Air: The Royal Christmas Broadcasts, 1932-1981* (London: Heinemann, 1981).

100 *Sunday Times*, 28 December 1986.

101 MO winter directive 1986, respondent W729.

102 Alwyn Turner, *A Classless Society: Britain in the 1990s* (London: Aurum, 2013), ch. 11.

103 Paul Addison, *No Turning Back: The Peacetime Revolutions of Post-War Britain* (Oxford: Oxford University Press, 2010), 177.

104 *Evening News*, 24 December 1953.

105 *Daily Mirror*, 24 December 1958. *The Times*, 14 January 1960.

106 Golby and Purdue, *Making of the Modern Christmas*, 105.

107 *The Times*, 1 January 1964. *Daily Mail*, 18 December 1964. *TV Times*, 13 December 1963.

108 MO diarist 5338, 25 December 1953.

109 *The Times*, 29 December 1962, 15 November 1972.

110 For example, *Daily Mirror*, 23 December 1972.

111 Moran, *Armchair Nation*, 187.

112 Currie, *Radio Times Story*, 242.

113 *The Times*, 24 December 1977.

114 William Cook, ed., *Eric Morecambe Unseen: The Lost Diaries, Jokes and Photographs* (London: HarperCollins, 2005), 141.

115 *Daily Mirror*, 21 December 1976.

116 Joe Moran, '"Stand up and be counted": Hughie Green, the 1970s and popular memory', *History Workshop Journal* 70 (2010): 172–98. Cook, *Eric Morecambe Unseen*, 141, 157. Moran, *Armchair Nation*, 222–3.

117 For a discussion of this see Moran, *Armchair Nation*, 273.

118 Tim Roll-Pickering, '30.15m did not watch EastEnders on Christmas Day 1986', 22 July 2012: http://timrollpickering.blogspot.co.uk/2012/07/3015-million-did-not-watch-eastenders.html.

119 Corriepedia, 'Viewing figures', http://coronationstreet.wikia.com/wiki/Viewing_Figures.

120 Quote from Charity Dingle in *Emmerdale*, 25 December 2013. For a review of that year's soap miseries see *Daily Mirror*, 26 December 2013.

121 *The Times*, 11 January 1983.

122 *Daily Mail*, 16 December 1938.

123 H. Mark Glancy, 'Dreaming of Christmas: Hollywood and the Second World War', in *Christmas at the Movies: Images of Christmas in American, British and European Cinema*, ed. Mark Connelly (London: I. B. Tauris, 2000): 59–76.

124 *Sunday Post*, 15 June 1947, *Taunton Courier and Western Advertiser*, 28 June 1947. For claims of its greatness see *The Guardian*, 23 December 2013.

125 For an analysis of the film's appeal see Mark Cohen, 'Why return to Bedford Falls? A contribution to understanding the enduring appeal of the film It's a Wonderful Life', *Psychoanalysis, Culture and Society* 14, no. 4, (2009):

393–405 and Jonathan Murray, 'A Hollywood carol's wonderful life', in *Christmas at the Movies: Images of Christmas in American, British and European Cinema*, ed. Mark Connelly (London: I. B. Tauris, 2000): 39–57.

126 *Daily Mirror*, 26 September 1947.

127 *The Times*, 29 September 1947, 3 November 1954.

128 For such a case see Tom Ward, 'Why Die Hard is the best Christmas movie of all time', 24 December 2012: http://www.huffingtonpost.co.uk/tom-ward/why-die-hard-is-the-best-christmas-movie-of-all-time_b_2339117.html.

129 *Belfast Telegraph*, 22 December 1922. A. E. Wilson, *Christmas Pantomime: The Story of an English Institution* (London: George Allen & Unwin, 1934). On the history of panto see http://www.its-behind-you.com/.

130 M. Willson Disher, 'Pantomime's Mad Rout', *Nash's Pall Mall Magazine*, December 1932.

131 Pimlott, *Englishman's Christmas*, 155. Wilson, *Christmas Pantomime*, 247. *The Academy*, 9 January 1915.

132 F. Marian McNeill, *The Silver Bough: vol. III, A Calendar of Scottish National Festivals* (Glasgow: MacLellan, 1961), chs. 7 and 8.

133 Connelly, *Christmas*, 196–7. *Aberdeen Evening Express*, 25 December 1885. *Dundee Courier*, 24 December 1902. *The Scotsman*, 25 December 1912. *Falkirk Herald*, 31 December 1904.

134 *Daily Mail*, 26 December 1934. *Dundee Courier*, 24 December 1919.

135 *Aberdeen Journal*, 24 December 1924, 24 December 1923, 24 December 1925.

136 *Southern Reporter*, 21 December 1922. Molly Weir, *Shoes Were for Sunday* (1970; London: Penguin, 2012), ch. 10.

137 For memories of this *The Times*, 5 December 1981.

138 Gavin Weightman and Steve Humphries, *Christmas Past* (London: Sidgwick and Jackson, 1987), 31.

139 MO day survey, 25 December 1937, respondent 411.

140 Quotes from Weightman and Humphries, *Christmas Past*, 27, 29.

141 *Aberdeen Journal*, 24 December 1938.

142 *Southern Reporter*, 21 December 1922. *The Scotsman*, 2 January 1931.

143 *Daily Mirror*, 8 August 1935, 9 December 1935.

144 *The Scotsman*, 1 January 1931, 20 December 1950.

145 Weightman and Humphries, *Christmas Past*, 29.

146 *Southern Reporter*, 21 December 1922. Weightman and Humphries, *Christmas Past*, 35.

147 *Aberdeen Journal*, 24, 21 December 1949.

148 *The Times*, 20 December 1950. *Dundee Courier*, 28 November 1950.

149 *Aberdeen Evening Express*, 23 December 1954.

150 *The Scotsman*, 26 December 1950. *The Times*, 24 December 1958.

151 Pimlott, *Englishman's Christmas*, 149.

152 *HC Deb* 25 March 1948, vol 448 c3442.

153 *Independent Magazine*, 21 December 1991.

154 *Daily Mirror*, 21 December 2007.

155 Pimlott, *Englishman's Christmas*, 150. MO day survey 25 December 1937, respondent 117.

156 *The Times*, 22 December 1966. *New Society*, 19/26 December 1986. Gerry Bloustein, 'Reflections of a Jewish childhood during Christmas', in *Christmas, Ideology and Popular Culture*, ed. Sheila Whiteley (Edinburgh: Edinburgh University Press, 2008): 188–95. Raymond Firth, Jane Hubert and Anthony Forge, *Families and their Relatives: Kinship in a Middle-Class Sector of London* (London: Routledge, 1969), 258–9. *The Guardian*, 20 December 2013.

157 Jennifer Mason and Stewart Muir, 'Conjuring up traditions: atmospheres, eras and family Christmases', *Sociological Review* 61, no. 3 (2013): 607–29, 618.

158 Elizabeth H. Pleck, *Celebrating the Family: Ethnicity, Consumer Culture and Family Rituals* (Cambridge, MA: Harvard University Press, 2000), 68–70.

159 *ITV Late Evening News*, 26 December 1960. Interview with Connie Mark, Museum of London: MoL_99.40/EX3.

160 *Black Christmas*, BBC2, 20 December 1977.

161 Helana Margaret Tuomainen, 'Ethnic identity: (post)colonialism and foodways', *Food, Culture and Society* 12, no. 4 (2009): 525–54.

162 Interview with Brij Mohan Sood and Krishna Sood, Museum of London: MoL_2002.175/EX10.

163 Candace Hoffman-Hussain, 'Interfaith home decorating: An exploration of religiosity and home artefacts within British interfaith hybrid coupledom', in *Material Religion in Modern Britain: The Spirit of Things*, ed. Timothy Willem Jones and Lucinda Matthews-Jones (Basingstoke: Palgrave, 2015): 147–63.

164 Sheena J. Vachhani and Alison Pullen, 'Home is where the heart is? Organizing women's work and domesticity at Christmas', *Organization* 18, no. 6 (2011): 807–21. *New Society*, 18 December 1987.

165 Gerd Baumann, 'Ritual implicates "others": Rereading Durkheim in a plural society', in *Understanding Rituals*, ed. Daniel de Coppet (London: Routledge, 1992): 97–116, 105.

166 Zaiba Malik, *We Are a Muslim Please* (London: William Heinemann, 2010), 75–6.

167 See the explanations in BBC, 'A British Christmas', 8 December 2005: http://www.bbc.co.uk/religion/religions/christianity/christmas/nonchristian.shtml; and *New Society*, 19/26 December 1986.

168 *New Society*, 18 December 1987.

169 For interviews with London Muslims on how they felt about Christmas see JewishNewsOne, 'Multicultural London Christmas: Muslims in multi-ethnic English capital reflect on the holiday': https://www.youtube.com/watch?v=j9OyF_riKG8.

170 Baumann, 'Ritual implicates "others"', 102–5.

171 *Daily Mirror*, 11 December 2006.

172 Sally McKechnie and Caroline Tynan, 'Social meanings in Christmas consumption: An exploratory study of UK celebrants' consumption rituals', *Journal of Consumer Behaviour* 5, no. 2 (2006), 130–44. *Daily Mail*, 5 December 2005.

173 *Daily Mail*, 26 November 2005.

174 *Daily Express*, 2 November 2005.

175 Peter Oborne and James Jones, *Muslims Under Siege: Alienating Vulnerable Communities* (Colchester: University of Essex, 2008), 20. 'Christmas was not banned after all', 3 November 2005: http://www.ekklesia.co.uk/content/news_syndication/article_05113christmasban.shtml.

176 John Gibson, *The War on Christmas on Christmas: How the Liberal Plot to Ban the Sacred Christian Holiday is Worse than You Thought* (New York: Sentinel, 2005), xviii. For examples of the myth being repeated in Britain see Chris Allen, 'Winterval is coming: Busting the myths about banning Christmas', 19 December 2013: http://www.huffingtonpost.co.uk/dr-chris-allen/muslim-christmas-ban_b_4464410.html.

177 *The Times*, 24 December 1923.

178 Barton, *The Penny World*, 26.

179 *Daily Mail*, 24 December 1932. *The Economist*, 25 December 1937.

180 George Orwell, 'England, Your England [1941]', in *Selected Essays* (London: Penguin, 1957), 66.

181 See Juliet Gardiner, *The Thirties: An Intimate History* (London: Harper, 2010), ch. 11. Elizabeth Roberts, *Women and Families: An Oral History, 1940-1970* (Oxford: Blackwell, 1995), 238. For a comparison of new and old estates see Joanna Bourke, *Working-Class Cultures in Britain, 1890-1960* (London: Routledge, 1994), 155–9.

182 *Cambridge Independent Press*, 24 December 1920.

183 Description of a pub in Norman Collins, *London Belongs to Me* (London: Collins, 1945), 12.

184 *Daily Mail*, 17 December 1935.

185 For example, *Hull Daily Mail*, 7 December 1935.

186 *Western Gazette*, 30 December 1949.

187 Winifred Holtby, *South Riding* (1936; London: BBC, 2011), 387.

188 *Radio Times*, 19 December 1952.

189 Dennis Hall, 'The venereal confronts the venerable: "Playboy" on Christmas', *American Journal of Culture* 7, no. 4 (1984): 63–8.

190 Daniel Miller, 'A theory of Christmas', in *Unwrapping Christmas*, ed. Daniel Miller (Oxford: Oxford University Press, 1993), 4.

191 Michael Harrison, *The Story of Christmas: Its Growth and Development from the Earliest Times* (London: Odhams, 1951), 226.

192 'Christmas in war time', *Quiver*, December 1914.

193 Connelly, *Christmas*, 200. *Daily Mail*, 23 December 1931.

194 For example, *Picture Post*, 21 November 1953.

195 Paddy Scannell and David Cardiff, *A Social History of British Broadcasting, vol. I, 1922-1939: Serving the Nation* (Oxford: Blackwell, 1991), 286–7. Simon J. Potter, *Broadcasting Empire: The BBC and the British World, 1922-1970* (Oxford: Oxford University Press, 2012), 229–30.

196 Miller, 'A theory of Christmas', 31. For a global examination see Tara Moore, *Christmas: The Sacred to Santa* (London: Reaktion, 2014).

197 This was also true of other countries see Miller, 'A theory of Christmas', 22–6.

198 Michael Billig, *Banal Nationalism* (London: Sage, 1995).

Chapter 6

1 *Daily Mirror*, 5 December 1973. *The Times*, 14 December 1973.

2 *HC Deb* 12 December 1973, vol 866 c169W.

3 Note for the record, 19 December 1973, The National Archives (hereafter TNA): PREM 15/1880.

4 *Daily Mirror*, 24 December 1973.

5 Michael Palin, *Diaries 1969-1979: The Python Years* (London: Weidenfeld and Nicolson, 2006), 149.

6 Neil Armstrong, *Christmas in Nineteenth-century England* (Manchester: Manchester University Press, 2010), 89.

7 British Fire Prevention Committee, 14th and 15th Annual Reports, 1912 and 1913.

8 *Evening Telegraph*, 18 December 1939.

9 *The Times*, 23 December 1933.

10 *Exeter and Plymouth Gazette*, 5 January 1934. *Western Daily Post*, 6 January 1934. *Evening Telegraph*, 10 January 1939.

11 *The Times*, 20 December 1937, 24 December 1954. Mike Brown, *Christmas on the Home Front* (2004; Stroud: History Press, 2013), 41

12 *Taunton Courier and Western Advertiser*, 14 December 1946.

13 Kenneth D. Brown, *The British Toy Business: A History since 1700* (London: Hambledon, 1996), 188. *ITV Lunchtime News*, 18 December 1997.

14 Fire Service College: Home Office letter (no. 28) to all Chief Fire Officers, 24 November 1971.

15 Royal Society for the Prevention of Accidents, 'Christmas safety tips': http://www.rospa.com/home-safety/advice/christmas-safety/christmas-safety-tips/ *The Guardian*, 21 December 2013.

16 *Keep Safe This Christmas* (NHS, 2012), 10, 1–2.

17 *The Times*, 19 December 1970.

18 For example, see the reports collated at http://www.derbygripe.co.uk/santa.htm. For a reaction from the Health and Safety Executive: 'The twelve myths of Christmas': http://www.hse.gov.uk/myth/xmasmyths.htm.

19 *Channel 5 Late Evening News*, 28 December 1998. R. Reid and A. F. Hackett, 'Changes in nutritional status in adults over Christmas 1998', *Journal of Human Nutrition and Dietetics* 12, no. 6 (1999): 513–16.

20 John Garrow, 'Christmas factor and snacking', *The Lancet*, 1 January 2000, 8.

21 Stephen J. Pettit, Alan G. Japp and Roy S. Gardner, 'The hazards of Brussels sprouts consumption at Christmas', *Medical Journal of Australia* 197, no. 11 (2012): 661–2.

22 William Sansom, *Christmas* (London: Weidenfeld and Nicolson, 1968), 224.

23 *ITV Early Evening News*, 29 December 1964. *News at 5.45*, ITV, 29 December 1986.

24 *Channel 5 Early Evening News*, 25 December 1997.

25 Sefton Cummings, 'The Christmas motor drive', *Saturday Review*, 22 December 1934.

26 *The Times*, 24 December 1953. *ITV Late Evening News*, 26 December 1961.

27 Road Research Laboratory, *Fatal Road Accidents at Christmas 1963* (London, 1964). Bill Luckin, 'A kind of consensus on the roads? Drink driving policy in Britain, 1945-1970', *Twentieth Century British History* 21, no. 3 (2010): 350–74. 'Road Research Laboratory investigation into casualties during 1959 Christmas holiday', TNA: MT 92/99.

28 *ITV Late Evening News*, 26 December 1967. 'Road safety and the law', *British Medical Journal* 281 (1980): 1514.

29 *Social Trends* 40 (2010), 181.

30 *The Times*, 7 December 1921.

31 *Daily Mail*, 17 December 1926. *ITV Late Evening News*, 20 December 1955.

32 *Luton News and Bedfordshire Chronicle*, 14 December 1950.

33 *Evening News*, 17 December 1947. *Daily Mail*, 18 December 1964. *The Times*, 8 December 1955, 30 November 1959. *Financial Times*, 2 January 1954.

34 *Channel 5 Early Evening News*, 17 December 1997. *The Guardian*, 21 December 2013.

35 *Daily Mail*, 20 December 1966. *Daily Mirror*, 23 December 1987. *The Times*, 4 January 1963.

36 *The Times*, 28 December 1953.

37 *Daily Mirror*, 7 December 1949. *Burnley Express*, 15 December 1934.

38 *5 News*, Channel 5, 25 November 1997.

39 *Daily Mail*, 18 December 1933, 14 December 1927.

40 *The Times*, 22 December 1959, 21 December 1961, 3 March 1961.

41 *The Times*, 24 December 1955.

42 Sansom, *Christmas*, 221. J. M. Golby and A. W. Purdue, *The Making of the Modern Christmas* (Stroud: Sutton, 2nd edn., 2000), 96. *ITV Late Evening News*, 23 December 1959.

43 Ian O'Donnell and Yvonne Jewkes, 'Going home for Christmas: Prisoners, a taste of freedom and the press', *Howard Journal* 50, no. 1 (2011): 75–90.

44 Jeffrey Archer, *A Prison Diary: From Hell to Heaven* (London: Macmillan, 2005), 816–18.

45 *My Weekly*, 1 January 1977.

46 *Church Times*, 20 December 1968. *Picture Post*, 24 December 1956.

47 *Daily Mail*, 28 December 1962.

48 *Saturday Review*, 22 December 1934. *Hull Daily Mail*, 19 December 1936.

49 *ITV Early Evening News*, 17 December 1967. *The Times*, 23 December 1948. *The Spectator*, 17 December 1948.

50 Frank Dawes, *Not in Front of the Servants: Domestic Service in England, 1850-1939* (Newton Abbot: Readers Union, 1975), 151.

51 *Hull Daily Mail*, 28 December 1936.

52 Gavin Weightman and Steve Humphries, *Christmas Past* (London: Sidgwick and Jackson, 1987), 76, 80–1. Agatha Christie, *Hercule Poirot's Christmas* (1938; London: Harper, 2013), 27.

53 Robert Rhodes James, ed., *Chips: The Diaries of Sir Henry Channon* (London: Penguin, 1967), 19. *The Times*, 6 December 1919.

54 MO day survey, 25 December 1937, respondent 28.

55 Keith Middlemas, ed., *Whitehall Diary, vol. II, 1926-1930* (London: Oxford University Press, 1969), 126.

56 MO day survey, 25 December 1937, respondents 21 and 22.

57 Michael Bloch, ed., *James Lees-Milne Diaries, 1942-54* (London: John Murray, 2006), 318.

58 MO day survey, 25 December 1937, respondents 184 and 318.

59 *The Times*, 24 December 1965.

60 Mary Searle-Chatterjee, 'Christmas cards and the construction of social relations in Britain today', in *Christmas Unwrapped*, ed. Daniel Miller (Oxford: Oxford University Press, 1993), 176–92, 176.

61 Duncan Campbell-Smith, *Masters of the Post: The Authorized History of the Royal Mail* (London: Allen Lane, 2011), 363. Roy Dommett (b. 1933), British Library Oral History Collection: C1379/14. For a description of the conditions see *The Times*, 15 December 1956.

62 MO day survey, 25 December 1937, respondent 20.

63 John Morgans, *Journey of a Lifetime: From the Diaries of John Morgans* (Llanidloes, 2008), 91.

64 Work duty rota, Museum of London: MoL_83.812/9. Elizabeth Wallace, *Christmas Past in Essex* (Stroud: Tempus, 2007), 15–17.

65 Mavis Doriel Hay, *The Santa Klaus Murder* (1936; London: British Library, 2013), 37.

66 For a postman's memories of Christmas see Simon Evans, *Shropshire Days and Shropshire Ways* (London: Heath Cranton, 1938), 169–74.

67 *Dundee Courier*, 24 December 1919.

68 Armstrong, *Christmas in Nineteenth-century England*, 94.

69 *The Times*, 20 May 1960, 12 January 1961, 29 September 1961.

70 MO diarist 5076, 27 December 1964.

71 *Evening News*, 22 December 1952, 24 December 1954. *Belfast Telegraph*, 24 December 1936. For memories of Christmas Eve in a 1920s office see *The Times*, 20 December 1956.

72 MO Diarist, 5076, 23 December 1960.

73 MO day survey, 1 December 1938, respondent 547.

74 Tazeen Ahmad, *The Checkout Girl: My Life on the Supermarket Conveyor Belt* (London: Friday Project, 2009), 44–5.

75 Hazel Wheeler, *Crackers at Christmas: The Festive Trails of a Yorkshire Housewife* (Stroud: Amberley, 2010), 11.

76 *Daily Mirror*, 29 November 1957.

77 Armstrong, *Christmas in Nineteenth-century England*, 77. J. A. R. Pimlott, *The Englishman's Christmas: A Social History* (Hassocks: Harvester, 1978), 166.

78 *Hull Daily Mail*, 19 December 1936. Welsh Coal Mines, 'Christmas party': http://www.welshcoalmines.co.uk/forum/read.php?10,9316.

79 Interview with Tim Farmiloe, Museum of London: MoL_2004.115/EX13.

80 B. Seebohm Rowntree and G. R. Lavers, *English Life and Leisure: A Social Study* (London: Longmans, 1951), 118.

81 MO diarist 5076, 24 December 1953.

82 MO day survey, December 1938, respondent 473.

83 Barbara Spence, *The Forestry Commission in Wales 1919-2013* (Aberystwyth: Forestry Commission, 2013), 22.

84 Ann Rippin, 'Ritualized Christmas headgear or "Pass me the tinsel, mother: It's the office party tonight"', *Organization* 18, no. 6 (2011): 823–32.

85 *The Times*, 19 December 1970, 19 December 1984.

86 *South Wales Spectator*, December 1970.

87 Kate Fox, *Watching the English: The Hidden Rules of English Behaviour* (London: Hodder, 2005), 203–4.

88 London Chamber of Commerce, *London's Christmas Economy: A Business Perspective on the Retail and Hospitality Sectors* (2005), 17.

89 'Do you know it's Christmas?', 17 December 2004: http://www.smallbusiness.co.uk/news/outlook/19491/do-you-know-its-christmas-time.thtml.

90 Michael Rosen, 'You asked for it: Christmas at the bosses' expense', *Journal of Management Studies* 25, no. 5 (1988): 463–80. Rippin, 'Ritualized Christmas headgear'.

91 *Daily Worker*, 22 December 1938. *Morning Star*, 24 December 2004.

92 For example, see the report of an unexpected bonus in the Cornish clay industry: *Cornishman*, 30 December 1937.

93 *Derby Daily Telegraph*, 16 December 1936. *Exeter and Plymouth Gazette*, 2 December 1949.

94 *Dundee Courier,* 17 December 1953. On relying on the bonus for Christmas luxuries see MO day survey, December 1938, respondent 783.

95 *Picture Post,* 22 December 1951.

96 MO day survey, 25 December 1937, respondent 116.

97 For humour about this see *Daily Express,* 16 December 1947.

98 *Evening News,* 29 December 1952. *The Listener,* 23 December 1931.

99 Simon Garfield, ed., *Our Hidden Lives: The Remarkable Diaries of Post-War Britain* (London: Ebury, 2005), 325.

100 *Llais Llafur,* 27 December 1919. *Western Morning News,* 9 May 1924.

101 Sansom, *Christmas,* 208.

102 *TV Times,* 20 December 1969 to 2 January 1970.

103 Jilly Cooper, *How to Survive Christmas* (London: Methuen, 1986), 33. Gerald Mars, *Cheats at Work: An Anthology of Workplace Crime* (London: George Allen, 1982), 89–100.

104 TNA: CO 323/817. *Cambrian Daily Leader,* 27 December 1919.

105 For these tensions before 1914 see Armstrong, *Christmas in Nineteenth-century England,* 85–9.

106 *Daily Worker,* 14 December 1935.

107 For memories of this see Mary Parnell Davies, *Block Salt and Candles: A Rhondda Childhood* (Bridgend: Seren, 1991).

108 *The Times,* 13 December 1921, 1, 18 December 1923.

109 *Western Morning News,* 27 December 1930.

110 *Tamworth Herald,* 26 December 1936.

111 *Report of the Committee on Holidays With Pay,* Cmd 5724 (London: HMSO, 1938), 55. Sandra Dawson, 'Working-class consumers and the campaign for holidays with pay', *Twentieth Century British History* 18, no. 3 (2007): 277–305. For calls for paid Christmas holidays see *Cambrian Daily Leader,* 29 December 1919.

112 Stephen Jones, 'Trade union policy between the wars: The case of holidays with pay in Britain', *International Review of Social History* 31 (1986): 40–55.

113 *Dover Express,* 20 December 1918. *Burnley Express,* 29 December 1937.

114 *Holidays with Pay,* 54.

115 Jones, 'Trade union policy', 45.

116 *Portsmouth Evening News,* 22 September 1938. *Yorkshire Post and Leeds Intelligencer,* 30 May 1938. *Derbyshire Times and Chesterfield Herald,* 3 February 1939.

117 Gary Cross, *Time and Money: The Making of Consumer Culture* (London: Routledge, 1993), 96–7.

118 *Gloucester Citizen,* 3 July 1947. *Nottingham Evening Post,* 7 January 1948.

119 *The Times,* 27 December 1950.

120 *Derby Daily Telegraph,* 28 December 1946.

121 *The Economist*, 4 December 1958. *The Times*, 20 October 1958, 8 December 1958. *HC Deb* 20 November 1958, vol 595 c1320.

122 *The Times*, 24 December 1968.

123 TNA: T326/900.

124 TNA: PREM 15/434.

125 *The Times*, 27 December 1972.

126 *HL Deb* 27 April 1971, vol 317 cc1051-2. *HC Deb* 23 January 1973, vol 849 cc69-71W.

127 *The Times*, 30 December 1975, 30 December 1976, 31 December 1976, 19 December 1980, 3 December 1985. *The Spectator*, 17 December 1994. *The Economist*, 8 January 1977.

128 *The Times*, 22 December 1956.

129 *Picture Post*, 13 December 1947. *The Times*, 1 December 1961, 10 November 1965.

130 *Yorkshire Post and Leeds Intelligencer*, 1 December 1952.

131 *The Times*, 30 October 1975.

132 *ITN Early Evening News*, 25 December 1998.

133 TUC, 'Three million get no Christmas holiday from "Scrooge bosses"', 17 December 2003: http://www.tuc.org.uk/economic-issues/three-million-get-no-christmas-holiday-pay-%E2%80%98scrooge-bosses.

134 *HC Deb* 16 March 2001, vol 364 cc1294-334. *HC Deb* 1 February 2002, vol 379 c611W.

135 *HC Deb* 3 April 2001, vol 366 cc295-306.

136 TUC, 'Three million get no Christmas holiday from "Scrooge bosses"', 17 December 2003: http://www.tuc.org.uk/economic-issues/three-million-get-no-christmas-holiday-pay-%E2%80%98scrooge-bosses.

137 Mark Connelly, *Christmas: A Social History* (London: I. B. Tauris, 1999), 122–4.

138 Kaori O'Connor, 'The King's Christmas pudding: Globalization, recipes, and the commodities of empire', *Journal of Global History* 4, no. 1 (2009): 127–55. Rhiannon Donaldson, 'Revisiting a "well-worn theme": The duality of the Australian Christmas Pudding 1850-1950', *Eras Journal* 6 (2004).

139 *The Times*, 29, 30 October, 1 December 1925, 27 December 1930.

140 Connelly, *Christmas*, 126. Blanche, '"Shop imperially" for Christmas', *Saturday Review*, 22 December 1934.

141 TNA: BT 63/14/13.

142 For example, 'Report on Revolutionary Organisations in the United Kingdom, 22 December 1921', TNA: CAB 24/131/80.

143 *The Times*, 23 December 1926.

144 *Edinburgh Evening News*, 23, 28 December 1932.

145 *Daily Worker,* 10, 24 December 1935. *Sunderland Daily Echo and Shipping Gazette,* 3 December 1935. *HC Deb*, 9 December 1935, vol 307 cc550-2 and 19 November 1936, vol 317 cc1894-5.

146 Tony Lynes, *Reinventing the Dole: A History of the Unemployment Assistance Board 1934-40,* 25/7: http://tonylynes.wordpress.com/ reinventingthedole/chapter-25-discretionary-additions/.

147 *The Times,* 21 December 1937.

148 'Ministry of Food, Report for Week ending Wednesday, November 20, 1918', TNA: CAB 24/70/66.

149 *The Economist,* 28 December 1940. *The Times,* 25 September 1940, 6 November 1940, 4 December 1940.

150 *The Times,* 23 December 1942, 19 October 1944. *Western Morning News,* 22 November 1944.

151 *HC Deb* 4 November 1949, vol 469 cc83-4W. *The Times,* 24 December 1947, 22 December 1950.

152 'Christmas food bonus memorandum by the Minister of Food', 11 November 1948, TNA: CAB 129/30/36.

153 *Daily Mail,* 9 December 1948.

154 'Christmas food bonus memorandum by the Minister of Food', 11 October 1949, TNA: CAB 129/37/1.

155 'Christmas food bonuses, memorandum by the Chancellor of the Exchequer', 7 November 1952, TNA: CAB 129/56/48.

156 Cabinet minutes, 16 November 1950, TNA: CAB 128/18/34.

157 *The Times,* 1 December 1971, 5 December 1972.

158 For complaints see *Daily Mirror,* 22 December 2006.

159 *Belfast Telegraph,* 22, 23, 26 December 1922.

160 *The Times,* 20 March 1954.

161 TNA: WORK 20/321 and F 18/579.

162 *The Times,* 22 December 1971.

163 Brown, *British Toy Business,* ch. 4. 'Christmas in war time', *Quiver,* December 1914.

164 *The Times,* 4 December 1934.

165 Sheherazade Goldsmith, *The Christmas Book* (London: Dorling Kindersley, 2008), 10, 12.

166 *Engineering and Technology,* January 2012.

167 National Labor Committee, *A Wal-Mart Christmas Brought to You From a Sweatshop in China* (Pittsburgh: National Labor Committee, 2007).

168 *New Statesman and Society,* 20 and 27 December 1991. Vegetarian Society, *The True Cost of Christmas* (Altrincham: Vegetarian Society, 2012), 3–4.

169 J. R. Ackerley, *The Faber Book of Diaries,* ed. Simon Brett (London: Faber and Faber, 1987), 456.

170　Martyn Percy, 'The Powers at Christmas', in *Darkness Yielding: Angles on Christmas, Holy Week, and Easter*, ed. Rowan Williams, W. H. Vanstone, Sylvia Sands, Martyn Percy and Jim Cotter (Sheffield: Cairns, 2001), 65–8.

171　Cabinet conclusions, confidential annex, 23 December 1940, TNA: CAB 65/16/14. David Dilks, ed., *The Diaries of Sir Alexander Cadogan, 1938-1945* (London: Cassell, 1971), 344.

172　HC Deb 26 March 2004, vol 419 c1156.

173　Cabinet minutes, 12 October 1978, TNA: CAB 128/64/14.

174　Public and Political: General: Gifts: Birthday and Christmas gifts, Churchill Archive: CHUR 2/446.

175　Cabinet minutes, 13 December 1945, TNA: CAB/128/2.

Conclusion

1　Mass Observation (hereafter MO) day survey, 25 December 1937, respondents 38, 8, 116, 64, 536, 66 and 345.

2　'The spirit of Christmas', *Saturday Review*, 23 December 1922.

3　*Cornishman*, 20 December 1922. On festivals inverting norms see Peter Borsay, *A History of Leisure* (Basingstoke: Palgrave, 2006), 226.

4　Ray Milland, *Wide-Eyed in Babylon: An Autobiography* (New York: Morrow, 1974).

5　William Sansom, *Christmas* (London: Weidenfeld and Nicolson, 1968), 251.

6　Aldous Huxley, *The Olive Tree and Other Essays* (London: Chatto and Windus, 1936), 127.

7　Frank Crane, *Christmas the Year Round* (1917; London: John Lane, 1923), 13.

8　*Derby Daily Telegraph*, 23 December 1950.

9　MO Winter directive 1986, respondent W729.

10　Richard Layard, *Happiness: Lessons from a New Science* (London: Penguin, 2005), 23–4.

11　Adam Kuper, 'The English Christmas and the family: Time out and alternative realities', in *Unwrapping Christmas*, ed. Daniel Miller (Oxford: Oxford University Press, 1993), 157–75, 174.

12　Mark Connelly, *Christmas: A Social History* (London: I. B. Tauris, 2nd edn., 2012), xvi.

13　Kuper, 'English Christmas and the family', 169. My emphasis.

14　Wendy Doniger, Review of Miller, *Unwrapping Christmas*, in *London Review of Books*, 16 December 1993.

15　Gavin Wightman and Steve Humphries, *Christmas Past* (London: Sidgwick and Jackson, 1987), 10.

ANNOTATED BIBLIOGRAPHY OF ACADEMIC WRITING ABOUT THE MODERN CHRISTMAS

Historiography

Armstrong, Neil, 'Christmas in nineteenth-century Britain and America: A historiographical overview'. *Cultural and Social History* 1, no. 1 (2004): 118–25.

Limited to work on the US and the UK but an essential literature review and the starting point for any research into the historical Christmas.

Overview books

Armstrong, Neil, *Christmas in Nineteenth Century England*. Manchester: Manchester University Press, 2010.

The most comprehensive account of the emergence of the modern festival in the Victorian and Edwardian periods. It examines family, shopping and philanthropy but also less known themes such as print culture and public entertainments. Armstrong argues that the festival was shaped by wider cultural and economic forces and was gradually modernized, despite its strong associations with tradition. He is keen not to exaggerate the uniformity in Christmas celebration but maintains it was still a highly visible culture.

Connelly, Mark, *Christmas: A Social History*. London: I. B. Tauris, 1999.

Slightly selective in its themes but thoroughly researched and especially incisive on broadcasting, Empire and carols. Makes a convincing and important case that Christmas was an expression of Englishness.

Forbes, Bruce David, *Christmas: A Candid History.* Berkeley: University of California Press, 2007.

Straightforward and entertaining account of Christmas' evolution.

Golby, J. M. and Purdue, A. W., *The Making of Modern Christmas.* London: B. T. Batsford, 1986.

Not referenced but a contextualized and analytical account that focuses on the nineteenth and twentieth centuries. Argues that Victorian Christmas was 'so extensively refurbished and reinterpreted that it amounts to an invented tradition'.

Highfield, Roger, *Can Reindeer Fly? The Science of Christmas.* London: Weidenfeld and Nicolson, 2001.

Entertaining and well-researched consideration of the science of everything festive from snow and shopping to eating and drinking.

Hutton, Ronald, *Stations of the Sun: A History of the Ritual Year in Britain.* Oxford: Oxford University Press, 1996.

A wide-ranging, very readable and intelligent book that examines festivals over a broad time span. Notable more for its breadth rather than its particular observations on Christmas but especially useful for the premodern period.

Miller, Daniel, ed., *Unwrapping Christmas.* Oxford: Oxford University Press, 1993.

Employing a social–anthropological approach, this series of ten essays looks at the meanings and functions of Christmas and stresses both its unifying role in social networks and its amalgamation of local and globalized customs. It is the most 'academic' and heavyweight of all studies of Christmas and explores the festival more for what it tells us about wider ideas than for its own sake. The essays are all theoretically informed and strongly rooted in social science literature. Miller's introduction is a particularly useful introduction to theoretical considerations in studying Christmas. Belk explores the American festival's commercialization, focusing in particular on the Santa myth and Scrooge, while Carrier looks at the rituals of gifts giving. Kuper's essay on the English family and Searle-Chatterjee's on Christmas cards in Britain are also rich in argument and ideas. There are also essays on Japan, Trinidad, Sweden and Alaska.

Pimlott, J. A. R., *The Englishman's Christmas, A Social History.* Hassocks: Harvester, 1978.

A pioneering study of the emergence and development of the festival that places it clearly in its wider social and cultural context and highlights Christmas' functions without being sentimental or uncritical. An invaluable piece of research.

Weightman, Gavin and Steve Humphries, *Christmas Past.* London: Sidgwick and Jackson, 1987.

A lively study that focuses on the late nineteenth and twentieth centuries. Written to accompany a television series, it makes excellent use of oral sources and places much more emphasis on inequalities and the poor than other studies. Not referenced but well researched.

Whiteley, Sheila, ed., *Christmas, Ideology and Popular Culture*. Edinburgh: University of Edinburgh Press, 2008.

A diverse collection of essays that are mostly rooted in cultural studies and which use Christmas to explore wider society. There is a strong and profitable emphasis on Christmas in popular culture, especially music, but the book also includes essays on war, Americanization and religion, as well as some autobiographical writings.

Christmas in other countries

Anderson, David J., 'Nostalgia for Christmas in postbellum plantation reminiscences'. *Southern Studies: An Interdisciplinary Journal of the South* 21, no. 2 (2014): 39–73.

Shows how nostalgia for Christmas on slave plantations embodied a (white) sense that both Christmas itself and the South in general were better before the civil war.

Barnett, James, *American Christmas: A Study in National Culture*. New York: McMillan, 1954.

The first serious history of Christmas. Demonstrates how Christmas 'shows the impress of our national culture and draws vigor from this identification'.

Clarke, Alison, *Holiday Seasons: Christmas, New Year and Easter in Nineteenth-Century New Zealand*. Auckland: Auckland University Press, 2007.

Looks at the Christmases of colonial settlers in New Zealand, and the tensions that existed over how to celebrate.

Davies, Susan, '"Making night hideous": Christmas revelry and public order in Philadelphia'. *American Quarterly* 34, no. 2 (1982): 185–99.

Sees the festival as a site for conflict between working-class street culture and middle-class respectability.

Di Giovine, Michael A., 'La Vigilia Italo-Americana: Revitalizing the Italian-American family through the Christmas Eve Feast of the Seven Fishes'. *Food and Foodways* 18, no. 4 (2010): 181–208.

An ethnographic study of how a Christmas feast is used to uphold an ethnic identity.

Donaldson, Rhiannon, 'Revisiting a "well-worn theme": The duality of the Australian Christmas Pudding 1850-1950'. *Eras Journal* 6 (2004). Online at http://www.arts.monash.edu.au/publications/eras/edition-6/donaldson article.php.

An examination of colonists taking the English Christmas to Australia.

Franc, Martin, 'Merry and abundant: Celebrating Christmas in the Czech lands in the 1950s and 1960s'. *Food & History* 4, no. 2 (2006): 237–52.

An examination of the use and transformation of Christmas in Czechoslovakia by the USSR for political purposes.

Kimura, Junko and Russell W. Belk, 'Christmas in Japan: Globalization versus localization'. *Consumption Markets & Culture* 8, no. 3 (2005): 325–38.

Examines the extent to which Christmas in Japan should be regarded as cultural imperialism and global homogenization or an appropriation or hybridization of a Western tradition.

Knor, Sarah, 'Christmas in the diaspora: Dislocating symbols in Kipling, Cary and Dabydeen'. In *Symbolism: Special Focus – Symbols of Diaspora*, edited by Rüdiger Ahrens and Klaus Stierstorfer, 111–30. Berlin: Walter de Gruyter GmbH, 2014.

A literary study of celebrations of Christmas by English diasporas.

Konagaya, Hideyo, 'The Christmas cake: A Japanese tradition of American prosperity'. *Journal of Popular Culture* 34, no. 4 (2001): 121–36.

A historical study of Japanese adoptions and modifications of American festive traditions.

Marling, Karal Ann, *Merry Christmas! Celebrating America's Greatest Holiday*. Cambridge, MA: Harvard University Press, 2000.

A long but illuminating study of the visual and material culture of Christmas, in all its varieties. Emphasizes the importance of feelings and emotions for understanding the festival. One of the most original studies of Christmas and benefits from the author's lively and personal writing style.

Moore, Tara, *Christmas: The Sacred to Santa*. London: Reaktion Books, 2014.

An illustrated and wide-ranging study of the secular and sacred Christmas, and the tensions between the two, across the globe and a long chronology. A good starting point for further research.

Mortelmans, Dimitri and Sofie Damen, 'Attitudes on commercialisation and anti-commercial reactions on gift-giving occasions in Belgium'. *Journal of Consumer Behaviour* 1, no. 2 (2001): 156–73.

A Belgian study into attitudes towards the commercialization of present-giving at Christmas, Mothers' Day, Valentine's Day and other occasions.

Ngwane, Zolani, 'Christmas time and the struggles for the household in the countryside: Rethinking the cultural geography of migrant labour in South Africa'. *Journal of Southern African Studies* 29, no. 3 (2003): 681–99.

Examines 1990s celebrations in rural areas experiencing a population upsurge over Christmas as labour migrants return home.

Nissenbaum, Stephen, '"A visit from St Nicholas": The battle for Christmas in early nineteenth-century America'. In *The Mythmaking Frame of Mind: Social Imagination and American Culture*, edited by Amy Gilman, Donald M. Scott, Joan W. Scott and James B. Gilbert, 25–70. Belmont: Watson Publishing, 1992.

Nissenbaum, Stephen, *The Battle for Christmas: A Cultural History of America's Most Cherished Holiday*. New York: Vintage, 1996.

Nissenbaum's work argues that Christmas rituals 'reveal something of what we would like to be, what we once were, or what we are becoming despite ourselves'. Sees the festival as a site for conflict between working-class street culture and middle-class respectability.

Perry, Joe, *Christmas in Germany: A Cultural History*. Chapel Hill: University of North Carolina Press, 2010.

An examination of Christmas in Germany in the nineteenth and twentieth centuries. German festive traditions had a significant influence on Britain and Perry uses the German Christmas to 'explore the history of the modern self'. But he also shows how the festival was a site of political conflict and Germany's unstable history means the examples of this are far more vivid than in the UK or USA.

Perry, Joseph B., 'The Madonna of Stalingrad: Mastering the (Christmas) past and West German national identity after World War II'. *Radical History* 83 (2002): 7–27.

A study of memories of the 1942 'war Christmas' in West Germany. Memories of this event focused on community, comradeship and fellowship and were divorced from National Socialism, demonstrating how popular memory and national identity were being re-defined in the late 1940s and 1950s.

Restad, Penne, *Christmas in America: A History*. New York: Oxford University Press, 1995.

An overview of the evolution of Christmas, in all its varieties from the seventeenth century to the present day. Emphasizes the plurality and shifting nature of Christmas.

Salnikova, Alla, 'Not Yuletide? Fir tree ornaments as an integral part of Soviet socialization practices (1920s-1960s)'. *History of Education and Children's Literature* 5, no. 1 (2010): 355–74.

An examination of the Sovietization of the Christmas tree.

Santino, Jack, *All Year Round: Holidays and Celebrations in American Life*. Urbana: University of Illinois Press, 1994.

An excellent multidisciplinary study of holidays and associated rituals in people's lives.

Stokker, Kathleen, 'Anti-Nazi card tricks: Underground Christmas greetings in occupied Norway', *Journal of Popular Culture* 31, no. 1 (1997): 189–97.

An study of Christmas cards to analyse occupied Norway in 1941.

Shopping and gifts

Bartunek, Jean M. and Boram Do, 'The sacralization of Christmas commerce', *Organization* 18, no. 6 (2011): 795–806.

Argues that Christmas commerce has become 'sacred', subsuming to a large extent the religious festival.

Belk, Russell W. and Wendy Bryce, 'Christmas shopping scenes: From modern miracle to postmodern mall'. *International Journal of Research in Marketing* 10, no. 3 (1993): 277–96.

Examines movies to reveal the changing role of shopping in the celebration of Christmas. Suggests that shopping is now a postmodern spectacle and less reflective of a celebration of home and family.

Clarke, Peter, 'Christmas gift giving'. *Journal of Consumer Marketing* 23, no. 5 (2006): 283–91.

Argues that for parents the type of gift given to children is far more important than the brand.

Fischer, Eileen and Stephen J. Arnold, 'More than a labor of love: Gender roles and Christmas gift shopping'. *Journal of Consumer Research* 17, no. 3 (1990): 333–45.

Examines gender variations in festive shopping patterns and how it is widely regarded as women's work.

Gurau, Calin and Julie Tinson, 'Early evangelist or reluctant Rudolf? Attitudes towards the Christmas commercial campaign'. *Journal of Consumer Behaviour* 3, no. 1 (2003): 48–62.

Study of consumer responses to Christmas shopping commercial campaigns.

Halkoaho, Jenniina and Pirjo Laaksonen, 'Understanding what Christmas gifts mean to children'. *Young Consumers* 10, no. 3 (2009): 248–55.

Finnish research on letters to Santa that shows a strong brand awareness among children and the greater levels of politeness employed by girls.

Hamlin, David, 'The structures of toy consumption: Bourgeois domesticity and the demand for toys in nineteenth-century Germany'. *Journal of Social History* 36, no. 4 (2003): 857–69.

An important study of how giving toys as gifts allowed families to express love, while simultaneously encouraging individuality and shared middle-class ideals.

Hosgood, C. P., '"Doing the shops' at Christmas": Women, men and the department store in England, c. 1880-1914'. In *Cathedrals of Consumption: The European Department Store, 1850-1939*, edited by Geoffrey Crossick and Serge Jaumain, 97–108. Aldershot: Ashgate, 1999.

An invaluable study of how selfless Christmas shopping could empower women, although their 'irrationality' during the January sales reasserted their normal subordinate status.

Laroche, Michael, Gad Saad, Mark Cleveland and Elizabeth Browne, 'Gender differences in information search strategies for a Christmas gift'. *Journal of Consumer Marketing* 17, no. 6 (2000): 500–22.

Canadian research that shows women are more organized and informed Christmas shoppers.

O'Barr, William M., 'Advertising and Christmas'. *Advertising and Society Review* 7, no. 3 (2006). Online at https://muse.jhu.edu/journals/advertising_and_society_review/v007/7.3unit08.html.

An overview of the role of advertising in 'shaping' Christmas myths and rituals.

O'Cass, Aron and Peter Clarke, 'Dear Santa, do you have my brand? A study of the brand requests, awareness and request styles at Christmas time'. *Journal of Consumer Behaviour* 2, no. 1 (2002): 37–53.

An Australian study of how children make Christmas gift requests and their significant brand awareness.

Otnes, Cele, Tina M. Lowrey and Young Chan Kim, 'Gift Selection for easy and difficult recipients: A social roles interpretation'. *Journal of Consumer Research* 20, no. 2 (1993): 229–44.

Examines how gift buyers can categorize recipients as easy or difficult to select for.

Otnes, Cele, Young Chan Kin and Kyungseung Kim, 'All I want for Christmas: An analysis of children's brand request to Santa Claus'. *Journal of Popular Culture* 27, no. 4 (1994): 183–94.

Shows how children employ brand names in their Christmas requests.

Pollay, Richard W., 'It's the thought that counts: A case study in Xmas excesses'. *Advances in Consumer Research* 14 (1987): 140–3.

An American casestudy of 'excessive' festive celebration and spending.

Richardson, John G. and Carl H. Simpson, 'Children, gender and social structure: An analysis of the contents of letters to Santa Claus'. *Child Development* 53, no. 2 (1982): 429–36.

Found requests for similar numbers of presents from boys and girls but very gendered ideas of what toys they wanted.

Tynan, Caroline and Sally McKechnie, 'Sacralising the profane: Creating meaning with Christmas consumption in the UK'. *European Advances in Consumer Research* 7 (2006): 182–8.

An examination of Christmas consumption that argues it is varied in form but often 'sacred' in a non-religious sense.

Wachelder, Joseph, 'Toys, Christmas gifts and consumption culture in London's *Morning Chronicle*, 1800–1827'. *ICON: Journal of the International Committee for the History of Technology* 19 (2013): 13–32.

Looks at the establishment of the connection between toys and Christmas, showing how there was an increasing emphasis on their value for instruction and amusement.

Waits, William B., *The Modern Christmas in America: A Cultural History of Gift Giving*. New York: New York University Press, 1993.

A study of the buying and selling of presents since 1880 that makes extensive and profitable use of advertising as source material.

Customs and traditions

Barnes, Alison, 'The first Christmas tree'. *History Today* 56, no. 12 (2006). Online at http://www.historytoday.com/alison-barnes/first-christmas-tree.

Looks at Christmas trees in England before Prince Albert.

Belk, Russell W., 'A child's Christmas in America: Santa Claus as deity, consumption as religion'. *Journal of American Culture* 10, no. 1 (1987): 87–100.

An overview of the American Santa that sees him as having a religious-like function.

BCN, 'Santa Claus: Good or Bad for Children'. *Journal of Paediatric Care* 10 (1996): 243–4.

Brief survey of psychiatric and psychological literature on the Santa myth.

Bowler, Gerry, *Santa Claus: A Biography*. Toronto: McCelland & Stewart, 2005.

Wide-ranging account of Santa in history, film, music, literature, advertising and art.

Brunner, Bernd and Benjamin A. Smith, *Inventing the Christmas Tree*. New Haven: Yale University Press, 2012.

A short and global overview of the history of the Christmas tree.

Culley, Robert, 'The organization of Santa: Fetishism, ambivalence and narcissism'. *Organization* 18, no. 6 (2011): 779–94.

Argues that the Santa ritual can be understood through psychoanalytic concepts of fetishism, ambivalence and narcissism. Also offers an excellent summary of the literature on Santa in different disciplines.

Cyr, Claude, 'Do reindeer and children know something that we don't? Paediatric inpatients' belief in Santa Claus'. *Canadian Medical Association* 167, no. 12 (2002): 1325–27.

Evidence of a link between the age parents stopped believing in Santa and the age their children do.

Edensor, Tim and Steve Millington, 'Illuminations, class identities and the contested landscapes of Christmas'. *Sociology* 43, no. 1 (2003): 103–21.

Examines how extravagant exterior displays of Christmas lights have become a source of class conflict.

McKechnie, Sally and Caroline Tynan, 'Social meanings in Christmas consumption: An exploratory study of UK celebrants' consumption rituals'. *Journal of Consumer Behaviour* 5, no. 2 (2006): 130–44.

An important study of the variety of 'consumption' behaviours in the British Christmas.

Pitts, Martin, Charles Pattie and Danny Dorling, 'Christmas feasting and social class'. *Food, Culture and Society* 10, no. 3 (2007): 407–24.

An examination of class variations in expenditure on food and drink in December over the period 1975 to 2000. Uncovers a general decline in expenditure in some traditional Christmas foods.

Papatheodorou, Theodora and Janet Gill, 'Father Christmas: Just a story?' *International Journal of Children's Spirituality* 7, no. 3 (2002): 329–44.

Looks at how Santa can be used to transmit cultural values and help children make sense of the world.

Prentice, Norman M., Linda K. Schmechel and Martin Manosevitz, 'Children's belief in Santa Claus: A developmental study of fantasy and causality'. *Journal of the American Academy of Child Psychiatry* 18, no. 4 (1979): 658–67.

Relates belief in Santa to theories of development and cognitive maturity.

Rippin, Ann, 'Ritualized Christmas headgear or "Pass me the tinsel, mother": It's the office party tonight'. *Organization* 18, no. 6 (2011): 823–32.

A study of wearing tinsel halos, Santa hats and the like at Christmas work parties and nights out.

Rytting, Elizabeth, 'Christmas as a reflexive commemoration'. *Folklore Forum* 36, no. 1 (2005): 12–28.

An American study of how people commemorate Christmas.

Stronach, Ian and Alan Hodkinson, 'Toward a theory of Santa: Or, the Ghost of Christmas Present'. *Anthropology Today* 27, no. 6 (2011): 15–19.

Examines young children's interaction with Santa, suggesting there is a religious element to the myth but that he is in danger from an audit culture.

Reid, R. and A. F. Hackett, 'Changes in nutritional status in adults over Christmas 1998'. *Journal of Human Nutrition and Dietetics* 12, no. 6 (1999): 513–16.

Evidence of festive weight gain.

Thompson, William E. and Joseph V. Hickey, 'Myth, identity, and social interaction: Encountering Santa Claus at the mall'. *Qualitative Sociology* 12, no. 4 (1989): 371–89.

Examines how people react to Santa at the shopping mall, demonstrating variations by age and gender.

Christmas in popular culture

Cohen, Mark, 'Why return to Bedford Falls? A contribution to understanding the enduring appeal of the film It's a Wonderful Life'. *Psychoanalysis, Culture and Society* 14, no. 4 (2009): 393–405.

A study of the enduring popularity of perhaps the seminal Christmas film.

Connelly, Mark, ed., *Christmas at the Movies: Images of Christmas in American, British and European Cinema*. London: I. B. Tauris, 2000.

Brilliant study of both well-known and obscure Christmas films.

Cusack, Tricia, 'The Christmas snowman: Carnival and patriarchy'. *New Formations* 30 (1996–7): 135–51.

A reading of the meanings of the snowman as a British Christmas icon, that argues it helps sustain dominant ideas about family and gender.

Davis, Paul, 'Retelling A Christmas Carol: Text and culture-text'. *The American Scholar* 59 (1990): 109–15.

Davis, Paul, *The Lives and Times of Ebenezer Scrooge*. New Haven: Yale University Press, 1990.

Davis examines how Dickens' *A Christmas Carol* has been told, retold and re-interpretated since its publication, reflecting the changing identities and concerns of successive generations.

Hall, Dennis, 'The venereal confronts the venerable: "Playboy" on Christmas'. *American Journal of Culture* 7, no. 4 (1984): 63–8.

A study of Christmas in a pornographic magazine.

Lalumia, Christine, 'Scrooge and Albert', *History Today* 51, no. 12 (2001): 23–30.

More on the Victorian roots of Christmas.

MacDonald, Ruth K., 'Santa Claus in America: The influence of "The Night Before Christmas"'. *Children's Literature Association Quarterly* 8, no. 3 (1983): 4–6.

A look at the story that helped create the modern Santa.

Moore, Tara, *Victorian Christmas in Print*. New York: Palgrave, 2009.

An examination of the integral role of nineteenth-century publishing and reading in the reinvigoration and creation of the modern Christmas.

Moore, Tara, 'Starvation in Christmas fiction'. *Victorian Literature and Culture* 36, no. 2 (2008): 489–505.

Looks at how Christmas was used to encourage middle-class charity towards the poor.

Nathanson, Paul, '"You can't go home again ... or can you?" Reflections on the symbolism of TV families at Christmastime'. *Journal of Popular Culture* 27, no. 2 (1993): 149–62.

TV families going home for the festival.

Okleshen, Cara, Stacey Menzel Baker and Robert Mittelstaedt, 'Santa Claus does more than deliver toys: Advertising's commercialization of the collective memories of Americans'. *Consumption, Markets and Culture* 4, no. 3 (2000): 207–40.

Examines the role of advertising, particularly Coca-Cola, in defining the image of Santa Claus.

Rhodes, John David, 'White Christmas, or modernism'. *Modernism/Modernity* 13, no. 2 (2006): 291–308.

A study of the technologically-groundbreaking 1954 musical film *White Christmas*.

Rowell, Geoffrey, 'Dickens and the construction of Christmas'. *History Today* 43, no. 12 (1993): 17–24.

The influence of Dickens on the Victorian Christmas.

Saltmarsh, Susan, 'Spirits, miracles and clauses: Economy, patriarchy, and childhood in popular Christmas texts'. *Papers: Explorations into Children's Literature* 17, no. 1, 12 (2007): 5–18.

An examination of childhood in *A Christmas Carol, Miracle on 34th Street* and *The Santa Clause.*

Shouse, Eric and Bernard Timberg, 'A festivus for the restivus: Jewish-American comedians respond to Christmas as the national American holiday'. *Humor* 25, no. 2 (2012): 133–53.

A study of how American Jewish comedians respond to Christmas, illustrating Jewish culture's contribution to America but also its separation.

Thompson, Robert J., 'Consecrating consumer culture: Christmas television specials'. In *Religion and Popular Culture in America*, edited by Bruce David Forbes and Jeffrey H. Mahan, 44–55. Berkeley, CA: University of California Press, 2005.

Argues that television specials have helped uphold Christmas as a religious festival.

Christmas and the family

Armstrong, Neil, 'Father(ing) Christmas: Fatherhood, gender and modernity in Victorian and Edwardian England'. In *Gender and Fatherhood in the Nineteenth Century*, edited by Trev Lynn Broughton and Helen Rogers, 96–112. Basingstoke: Palgrave Macmillan, 2007.

Draws upon his book and shows the importance of fathers in family Christmases.

Bella, Leslie, *Christmas Imperative: Leisure, Family and Women's Work*. Halifax: Fernwood, 1992.

Argues that Christmas was feminized in the Victorian period and that there was a cultural imperative on women to recreate the rituals of their youth.

Brewis, Joanna and Samantha Warren, 'Have yourself a merry little Christmas? Organizing Christmas in women's magazines past and present'. *Organization* 18, no. 6 (2011): 747–62.

Exploration of evolving feminine identities through a study of Christmas in British women's magazines since the 1930s. Suggests that the pressure on women to create a perfect Christmas has intensified.

Caplow, Theodore, 'Rule enforcement without visible means: Christmas gift giving in Middletown'. *American Journal of Sociology* 89, no. 6 (1984): 1306–23.
Caplow, Theodore, 'Christmas gifts and kin networks'. *American Sociological Review* 47, no. 3 (1982): 383–92.

Caplow's pioneering work on Christmas studies the nature of family relationships and how the festival played a role in articulating and bonding these relationships. He revealed how despite the lack of any means of enforcement, there were elaborate unwritten rules on gift-giving and other rituals that were widely conformed to.

Gillis, John, *A World of their Own Making: Myth, Ritual, and the Quest for Family Values*. New York: Basic, 1996.

An important and wide-ranging examination of the history of family life and the role rituals play in creating and upholding nostalgic ideas of family values.

Mason, Jennifer and Stewart Muir, 'Conjuring up traditions: Atmospheres, eras and family Christmases'. *Sociological Review* 61, no. 3 (2013): 607–29.

An excellent British ethnographic study of how families use Christmas traditions to build atmospheres and intergenerational family identities.

Muir, Stewart and Jennifer Mason, 'Capturing Christmas: The sensory potential of data from participant produced video'. *Sociological Research Online* 1, 5, 17. Available online at http://www.socresonline.org.uk/17/1/5.html.

An examination of the benefits and challenges of using home-produced films to study family and traditions.

Vachhani, Sheena J. and Alison Pullen, 'Home is where the heart is? Organizing women's work and domesticity at Christmas'. *Organization* 18, no. 6 (2011): 807–21.

Argues that home is a feminist space and that Christmas offers an opportunity for women to challenge traditional ideas of domestic femininity.

Wright-St Clair, Valerie, Clare Hocking, Wannipa Bunrayong, Soisuda Vittayakorn and Phuonjai Rattakorn, 'Older New Zealand women doing the work of Christmas: A recipe for identity formation'. *Sociological Review* 53, no. 2 (2005): 332–50.

Looks at how food and other Christmas rituals are used to maintain and update female and family identities across generations.

Christmas and religion

Armstrong, Neil, 'The Christmas season and the Protestant churches in England, c. 1870-1914'. *The Journal of Ecclesiastical History* 62, no. 4 (2011): 744–62.

Demonstrates the importance of churches in the expansion and promotion of Christmas in public culture in an era often thought to be responsible for the secularization of the festival.

Bradley, Ian, 'Sing Choirs of Angels'. *History Today* 48, no. 12 (1998): 42–7.

The origins of Christmas carols.

Saer, D. Roy, 'The Christmas carol singing tradition in the Tanad valley'. *Folk Life* 7, no. 1 (1969): 15–42.

Examination of a Welsh localized carol tradition.

Schervish, Paul G., Raymond J. Halnon and Karen Bettez Halnon, 'Culture and emotion in Christmas: The elementary forms of the spiritual life'. *International Journal of Sociology and Social Policy* 16, no. 9/10 (1996): 144–70.

A theoretical consideration of spirituality and emotions at Christmas.

Schmidt, Leigh Eric, 'Joy to [some of] the world. Christianity in the marketplace: Christmas and the consumer culture'. *Cross Currents* 42, no. 3 (Fall, 1992): 350–1.

Schmidt, Leigh Eric, *Consumer Rites: The Buying and Selling of American Holidays*. Princeton, NJ: Princeton University Press, 1995.

Important history of the commercialization of American holidays and the reactions of religion to this. Argues that despite Christmas's place as America's 'peak consumer fête', the festival's religious status meant it was often contested and paradoxical.

Walker, David, 'How far is Bethlehem? Exploring the ordinary theology of occasional churchgoers'. In *Exploring Ordinary Theology: Everyday Christian Believing and the Church*, edited by Jeff Astley and Leslie J. Francis, 137–46. Farnham: Ashgate, 2013.

British study of people who attend church only on special occasions such as Christmas.

Miscellaneous

Armstrong, Neil, 'England and German Christmas Festlichkeit c.1800-1914'. *German History* 26, no. 4 (2008): 486–503.

Examines the influence of Germany on English festive customs and the parallel emphases within the two countries on family, children and pastoralism.

Brown, Mike, *Christmas on the Home Front*. Stroud: History Press, 2004.

Chronological and factual description of wartime Christmases. Richly illustrated.

Clarke, Peter, 'A measure for Christmas spirit'. *Journal of Consumer Marketing* 24, no. 1 (2007): 8–17.

Attempt to define and measure Christmas spirit, demonstrating how multidimensional the concept is.

Hancock, Philip and Alf Rehn, 'Organizing Christmas'. *Organization* 18, no. 6 (2011): 737–45.

An introductory article on the importance of studying Christmas.

Holmes, Stephen R., *The Politics of Christmas*. London: Theos, 2011.

Examines intersections between politics (broadly defined) and Christmas, especially in biblical stories.

Hudson, John, *Christmas 1914: The First World War at Home and Abroad*. Stroud: History Press, 2014.

Plenty of factual detail about a momentous Christmas.

Huelin, Gordon, 'Christmas in the city'. *Guildhall Studies in London History* 3, no. 3 (1978): 164–74.

A long local history dating back into the fifteenth century.

Kasser, Tim and Kennon M. Sheldon, 'What makes for a merry Christmas?' *Journal of Happiness Studies* 3 (2002): 313–29.

An American investigation that found people reported greater levels of happiness at Christmas when family or religion were more to the fore in their celebrations than spending and gifts.

O'Connor, Kaori, 'The King's Christmas pudding: Globalization, recipes, and the commodities of empire'. *Journal of Global History* 4, no. 1 (2009): 127–55.

A study of food globalization and imperialism through the interwar Christmas pudding.

O'Donnell, Ian and Yvonne Jewkes, 'Going home for Christmas: Prisoners, a taste of freedom and the press'. *The Howard Journal* 50, no. 1 (2011): 75–90.

A study of the home release of some UK and Irish prisoners for Christmas.

Prideaux, Bruce and Petra Glover, '"Santa Claus is coming to town": Christmas holidays in a tropical destination'. *Asia Pacific Journal of Tourism Research* 20, no. 9 (2015): 955–70.

Examines Christmas-themed holidays in tropical places.

Rosen, Michael, 'You asked for it: Christmas at the bosses' expense'. *Journal of Management Studies* 25, no. 5 (1988): 463–80.

An examination of how Christmas parties contribute to organizational social order.

Waldfogel, Joel, 'The deadweight loss of Christmas'. *American Economic Review* 83, no. 5 (1993): 1328–36.

Suggests that Christmas represents an overall economic loss because presents are not as valuable to recipients as their original cash value.

INDEX